The A⎯⎯⎯⎯⎯⎯⎯⎯⎯⎯⎯⎯⎯⎯⎯⎯⎯⎯⎯⎯⎯⎯iction

The American Quest

Whitman's Legacy in the Personal Epic

JAMES E. MILLER, JR.

for a Supreme Fiction

The University of Chicago Press · Chicago and London

The University of Chicago Press, Chicago 60637
The University of Chicago Press, Ltd., London

©1979 by The University of Chicago
All rights reserved. Published 1979
Phoenix edition 1981

Printed in the United States of America

88 87 86 85 84 83 82 81   2 3 4 5 6

Library of Congress Cataloging in Publication Data
Miller, James Edwin, 1920–
   The American quest for a supreme fiction.

   Includes bibliographical references and index.
   1. Whitman, Walt, 1819–1892—Influence.   2. American poetry—20th century—History and criticism.
3. Epic poetry—History and criticism.   I. Title.
PS3236.M5   821'.03   78-15176
ISBN: 0-226-52611-9 (cloth)   ISBN: 0-226-52612-7 (paper)

to Walt Whitman
and My Students at the University of Chicago
and Poets to Come

I Roots and Trunk

Contents

I have press'd through in my own right,
I have sung the body and the soul, war and peace have I sung, and
    the songs of life and death,
And the songs of birth, and shown that there are many births.

I have offer'd my style to every one, I have journey'd with confident
    step;
While my pleasure is yet at the full I whisper *So long!*
And take the young woman's hand and the young man's hand for
    the last time.

"So Long!"
Walt Whitman

Preface

The American Quest for a Supreme Fiction: Whitman's Legacy in the Personal Epic grew out of my curiosity about the interrelationships among America's "classic" long poems. The more deeply I read them, the more convinced I became that they would yield more of their meaning, provide richer experiences, when examined in the tradition of which they were all a part—the American epic tradition. It seemed to me significant that every time a segment of one of the modern long poems appeared—whether Ezra Pound's *Cantos* or John Berryman's *Dream Songs*—a critical debate over form raised the same questions that had been raised time and again and apparently never resolved: how can a poem have a form if it embodies or engages events unforeseeable when it was launched? how can a long poem be called an epic when it has no hero or narrative? how can a long poem be properly impersonal (with the obligatory "objective correlative") if it baldly embodies so much of the author's own life and experience? Often these questions were raised in such a way as to suggest that each time this form appeared, it was an original creation for which there was no apparent tradition.

In *The American Quest for a Supreme Fiction* I have traced out such a tradition. I have not attempted to provide an exhaustive history of the epic form in America, choosing instead to concentrate on those aspects of the tradition which will provide the most illumination for the reading of the classic modern examples. It was clear to me from the beginning of my study, and became even clearer as I went along, that Walt Whitman was the pivotal figure for the American epic form, looming large in the long path coming out of the past and leading into the future. With bare hands and boldness of imagination, he created the new forms out of the unlikely materials of his own naked self and his own chaotic, war-torn times.

And yet, Whitman had never been given his due. Modern American poetry was said to have shallow roots in its own country, deeper roots (the taproot even) in foreign lands and movements—the French Symbolists or the British Metaphysicals, for example. Pound and Eliot had nourished this myth, and their followers had been eager to confirm it. My book as it grew took on the mission of setting this record straight. But I must confess that, even with my long interest in Whitman, I was surprised by my discovery, *along the way*, of the depth of Whitman's lodgement in the American poetic psyche. It struck me as uncanny, for example, how John Berryman's essay on Whitman, posthumously published in 1976 (though written in 1957),[1] substantiated what I had already worked out and written about his *Dream Songs* before seeing his comments on "Song of Myself."

Indeed, everywhere I turned I found poets appealing to Whitman as some kind of mythic figure, holy man, prophet, or saint. I have dealt extensively with the Whitman connection in my treatment of individual modern poets and poems. Here I present only a sampling of comments gleaned by the way, gathered almost by accident, which suggest the complicated nature of the role Whitman has played and is playing in modern poetry:

> I reach toward the song of kindred men
> and strike again the naked string
> old Whitman sang from.[2]

> Where are you, Walt?
> The Open Road goes to the used-car lot.[3]

> Be with me, Whitman, maker of catalogues:
> For the world invades me again.[4]

Over and over again, references to Whitman call him into a kind of physical presence with the poet, as a kind of Wound-Dresser of the spirit. Listen to one eerie comment by John Berryman shortly before his suicide:

Walt! We're downstairs,
even you don't comfort me
but I join your risk my dear friend & and go with you.[5]

It is as though Whitman were there in the flesh, his words come alive:
"Camerado, this is no book, / Who touches this touches a man."[6]

American poets could by and large agree with their Spanish-Ameri-
can fellow poet Pablo Neruda when he wrote: "I do not remember / at
what age / nor where; in the great damp South / or on the fearsome /
coast, beneath the brief / cry of the seagulls, / I touched a hand and it
was / the hand of Walt Whitman. / I trod the ground / with bare feet,/
I walked on the grass, / on the firm dew / of Walt Whitman."[7] As in
these lines, so in the references to Whitman by many American poets,
the personal involvement with "Walt" appears intense, the relationship deep and life-sustaining, the currents of feeling almost beyond
words. When this emotion is turned upside down, and emerges as
hostility, it still betrays its profound connections.

But I should hasten to emphasize that those connections, although
deep, seldom or never manifest themselves in the poems I examine in
this book as simple imitations. The poets of these poems have found
their own languages, their own voices, their own *beings* in their
poems. Whatever models they found for their work, in Whitman or
any other poet, dead or alive, domestic or foreign, they all came to
realize that they and their work were on their own and must stand
independently, must somehow create anew. William Carlos Williams
put the matter this way: "The only way to be like Whitman is to write
unlike Whitman. Do I expect to be a companion to Whitman by
mimicking his manners?"[8]

The American Quest for a Supreme Fiction is not, then, a study of
surface influences. It is, rather, an exploration of the strong currents
that flow in the depths below. All the poets presented here as connecting with Whitman do in fact (with some rare exceptions, on some
rare occasions) "write *unlike* Whitman." They would probably not be
worth studying, or reading, if they did not. Whitman considered
himself a personal poet, and the *personal* of Whitman could not be the
genuinely *personal* of any other poet. It was in some such awareness
as this that Robert Creeley wrote, "If Whitman has taught me anything, and he has taught me a great deal, often against my will, it is
that the common *is* personal, intensely so, in that having no one thus
to invent it, the sea becomes a curious mixture of water and table salt
and the sky the chemical formula for air."[9]

After writing this book, I discovered that I had quoted two passages
from Whitman over and over again, two passages on the same theme:

the intensely personal (as well as cultural) nature of his poetry. My first impulse was to eliminate the repetition, but I found that the passages were so important that I would distort my meaning or dilute the emphasis I wanted by eliminating them. I therefore decided to convert a potential defect into a virtue by introducing the quotations here as representing a central theme of my book, quotations which the reader should carry with him into the book and which may without apology be brought back periodically because of the meaning they will gather as the book progresses. It was, again, uncanny how I found one or the other of these quotations turning up in unexpected places, as, for example, in John Berryman's essay on Whitman mentioned above, and as the opening sentence in an 1889 piece on Whitman by Oscar Wilde.[10] Both quotations come from "A Backward Glance o'er Travel'd Roads":

> I found myself . . .with a special desire and conviction. . . . This was a feeling or ambition to articulate and faithfully express in literary or poetic form, and uncompromisingly, my own physical, emotional, moral, intellectual, and aesthetic Personality, in the midst of, and tallying, the momentous spirit and facts of its immediate days, and of current America—and to exploit that Personality, identified with place and date, in a far more candid and comprehensive sense than any hitherto poem or book.[11]

> "Leaves of Grass" indeed (I cannot too often reiterate) has mainly been the outcropping of my own emotional and other personal nature—an attempt, from first to last, to put *a Person,* a human being (myself, in the latter half of the Nineteenth Century, in America,) freely, fully and truly on record.[12]

I shall resist the temptation to explicate these passages here and shall instead request the reader to keep them in mind as he reads, remembering especially the two activities *expressing* and *tallying* and the two subjects *self* and *society*.

In addition to the purposes suggested in the foregoing, *The American Quest for a Supreme Fiction* was written with the aim of coming to terms with the major long poems of American literature. I have, therefore, constructed the chapters on individual works to stand alone, comprehensible in their own right as commentaries on independent works of art. Thus I have not concentrated on the historical connections and the Whitmanian undercurrents in the poetry to the exclusion of those unique elements which give each of the works treated here a life separate, detached, and independent. However much they come into the world trailing the past, poems have a way of forging their own forms, living their own lives. In the American epic

tradition, in the continuing quest for a Supreme Fiction, there are
both continuity and variety. This book was written in the belief that
understanding of the one would enhance and enrich the other.

Acknowledgments

I have learned much from a number of seminars devoted to the American long poem given over the years at the University of Chicago. I gathered ideas at the earlier seminars, and I presented them for examination at a seminar during the autumn quarter, 1976; students patient enough to hear me out were John Allison, Lelon Bohne, William Cook, Robert Inchausti, Stanley Lourdeaux, Richard Meade, Noel Meriam, David Ringer, Henry Schipper, and David Shields. Other students have written dissertations with me and I have learned from what they have said in person and on the page: Hubert Cloke, David Kuebrich, and Louise Kawada on Whitman; John Simon and Augustus Kolich on Williams; Jack Barbera on Berryman. Still other students (among them Donald Pease on Hart Crane and Christine Foula on Pound) have fired my interest by studies they have written. I regret only that I cannot name them all.

The National Endowment for the Humanities awarded me a Senior Fellowship enabling me to spend the entire year of 1975 writing this book. The University of Chicago generously granted me leave to go to Antigua, Guatemala, where I could write in peace.

In August–September 1976 I tried out some parts of this book in lectures at various universities in Australia, beginning with an address at the meeting in Melbourne of the Australian–New Zealand American Studies Association; I am grateful to Elaine Barry, Monash University, for her invitation, and to other Australian colleagues who made my visit both pleasant and productive, including (among many): Kenneth Goodwin and Jane Novak, University of Queensland; Eugene LeMire, Flinders University; Ian Donaldson, Fred Langman, and Robert Brissenden, Australian National University.

In my work I made extensive use of the University of Chicago's Regenstein Library, and whenever I needed something I could not find, I turned to Robert Rosenthal, Curator of Special Collections. He was most helpful because he understands that books are for reading.

I am especially grateful to Albert Gelpi and John Gerber for reviewing the manuscript with care and making valuable suggestions. My wife Barbara was of great assistance in a reading of the manuscript.

All the poets with whom I deal have attracted scholars and critics who have produced a large amount of valuable work. I have tried to benefit from all of it as much as possible—without losing my way or my voice. And I have made clear in my text and my notes my indebtedness on particular points. I know that in attempting to write judiciously about so many major figures, I stand exposed in ways that incur great risks. But I have chosen deliberately not to cling to the shore but to venture into the deep. I have not attempted to encompass a limited subject definitively but to launch out on a large subject with vistas. I hope the book will be read in this spirit of openness.

Part One   Roots and Trunk

I match my spirit against yours you orbs, growths, mountains, brutes,
Copious as you are I absorb you all in myself, and become the
    master myself,
America isolated yet embodying all, what is it finally except myself?
These States, what are they except myself?

"By Blue Ontario's Shore"
Walt Whitman

One

It cannot be denied that at some point in mid-career Berryman momentously shifted his stance toward his art and the
experience his art fed upon, just as Lowell did with his
"Life Studies" (1959). And the shift seems to have to do, not
surprisingly, with that inescapable figure in every American
poet's heritage, Walt Whitman.

Donald Davie, 1976

Poetic Metamorphoses:

Lowell and Berryman (a Prologue)

Although this book is not devoted directly to literary history, it is best to begin with a neglected event in the history of American poetry. The event is not an event in the ordinary sense (as, indeed, events in literary history seldom are) but rather a sequence of barely perceptible changes that have come into focus only in retrospect. The time, the late 1950s and early 1960s; the principal characters, Robert Lowell and John Berryman.

The event of splashiest outward show is the publication—and trial—of Allen Ginsberg's *Howl!* in 1956. This event and the consequences that flowed from it, the rise to prominence in the mass media of the Beat Generation, have been sufficiently recorded in various histories, and have lingered sufficiently in the modern memory, as to need little elaboration here. Indeed, Ginsberg and his book should be placed at the beginning, but not at the center, of the literary incident I wish to explore briefly.

That Ginsberg's book was introduced by William Carlos Williams is as of much importance as that his model throughout was Walt Whitman (the title *Howl!* apparently evolved from Whitman's "barbaric yawp"). In short, the publishing event evoked a literary tradition that

3

had been long out of favor with establishment, or academic, poets. Ginsberg's poem was wild, long, vulgar, readable, and it violated most of the tenets of the New Critical well-made poem. It electrified or angered its audience, made up of readers used to consulting dictionaries or solving puzzles when reading modern poetry.

I do not suggest that *Howl!* was superior poetry: its publication is still too painfully near to be seen objectively. But both those who blamed and those who praised it might now agree that its date marks a turning point in poetic history. It was not the sole cause of change; rather, it was testimony to the obscure forces, cultural and sociological as well as literary, at work during those years to bring one poetic era—which might be termed with slight distortion the New Critical or Eliot era—to an end and to launch another in its place.

In contrast with Ginsberg, Robert Lowell was promoted beyond all other poets of his generation as the heir of received modernist truths about poetry, truths expounded by those who had won the poetic battles of the 1920s—such as T. S. Eliot, Allen Tate, John Crowe Ransom. Lowell sought out Tate in his home (pitching his tent on his lawn) to study with him, and he went to Kenyon College to study with Ransom. He sought their guidance, won their approval, carried their banner. For fifteen years Lowell modeled himself on the foremost of the "traditionalist" modern poets, and then in 1959, with the publication of *Life Studies,* he seemed suddenly to change, to shift allegiances and directions, to remake himself as a poet. It is this change that has an importance for contemporary poetic history, a change that still remains, I believe, inadequately assessed.

Given Lowell's stature on the poetic scene, we may take his shift as a profound symptom of deep changes then in motion. Lowell himself is the best observer of the change that came over him. In a 1964 essay written on one of the poems of *Life Studies* ("Skunk Hour"), he dated the beginning of his metamorphosis from March 1957:

> I had been giving readings on the West Coast, often reading six days a week and sometimes twice on a single day. I was in San Francisco, the era and setting of Allen Ginsberg, and all about very modest poets were waking up prophets. I became sorely aware of how few poems I had written, and that these few had been finished at the latest three or four years earlier. Their style seemed distant, symbol-ridden and willfully difficult. I began to paraphrase my Latin quotations, and to add extra syllables to a line to make it clearer and more colloquial. I felt my old poems hid what they were really about, and many times offered a stiff, humorless and even impenetrable surface. I am no convert to the "beats." I know well

too that the best poems are not necessarily poems that read aloud. Many of the greatest poems can only be read to one's self, for inspiration is no substitute for humor, shock, narrative and a hypnotic voice, the four musts of oral performance. Still, my own poems seemed like prehistoric monsters dragged down into the bog and death by their ponderous armor. I was reciting what I no longer felt.... When I returned to my home, I began writing lines in a new style.... When I began writing "Skunk Hour," I felt that most of what I knew about writing was a hindrance. [1]

In a 1961 interview with Frederick Seidel, Lowell first outlined the changes in himself as he had perceived them, giving much the same outline he was to set forth in detail later in the "Skunk Hour" essay. Some of the language and references of the interview help clarify his meaning. He saw himself and his generation as living in a "sort of Alexandrian age," able to write a "very musical, difficult poem with tremendous skill." But something was missing: "Yet the writing seems divorced from culture somehow. It's become too much something specialized that can't handle much experience. It's become a craft, purely a craft, and there must be some breakthrough back into life." Asked if he was going to continue writing poetry in the new style of Life Studies, Lowell remarked, "I don't think that a personal history can go on forever, unless you're Walt Whitman and have a way with you." [2] In 1961 Lowell could not, of course, foresee his writing of Notebook and other personal volumes during the late 1960s and 1970s. What he was to discover was that "personal history" does indeed go on, if not forever, at least for one's own life—especially when that life is lived through the turbulent decade of the sixties.

That Lowell clearly saw his own metamorphosis as part of a larger literary revolution then in progress is borne out by his brief 1961 essay on William Carlos Williams. To Lowell the change was deeply rooted: "A seemingly unending war has been going on for as long as I can remember between Williams and his disciples and the principals and disciples of another school of modern poetry. The 'beats' are on one side, the university poets are on the other. Lately the gunfire has been hot. With such unlikely Williams recruits as Karl Shapiro blasting away, it has become unpleasant to stand in the middle in a position of impartiality." Lowell then recalled the poetic battles of the "late Thirties" when he was a student under John Crowe Ransom: "My own group, that of Tate and Ransom, was all for the high discipline, for putting on the full armor of the past, for making poetry something that would take a man's full weight and that would bear his complete intelligence, passion and subtlety. Almost anything, the Greek

and Roman classics, Elizabethan dramatic poetry, 17th century metaphysical verse, old and modern critics, aestheticians and philosophers, could be suppled up and again made necessary." But, Lowell concluded, "that time is gone, and now young poets are perhaps more conscious of the burden and the hardening of this old formalism. Too many poems have been written to rule. They show off their author's efforts and mind, but little more. Often the culture seems to have passed them by." And Lowell made his final tribute to the enduring Williams: "Williams is part of the great breath of our literature. *Paterson* is our *Leaves of Grass*."[3]

M. L. Rosenthal was perhaps the first critic to see the major importance of Lowell's metamorphosis. In his 1960 *Modern Poets*, in a chapter entitled "Robert Lowell and the Poetry of Confession," he hailed *Life Studies* as a "revolutionary breakthrough": "*Life Studies* brings to culmination one line of development in our poetry of the utmost importance. Technically, it is an experiment in the form of the poetic sequence looser than but comparable to *Mauberly* and *The Bridge*." But its significance was even greater, Rosenthal added: "It is important, I think, to remember one implication of what writers like Robert Lowell are doing: that their individual lives have profound meaning and worth, and that therapeutic confession will lead to the realization of these values."[4] What Rosenthal did not say was that Lowell's early poetry had been written under the Eliot–Tate–New Critical influence in which the personal was largely ruled out of poetry, beginning as far back as 1917 when Eliot propounded the "Impersonal theory" of poetry in his essay "Tradition and the Individual Talent."[5] Rosenthal's countering "confessional" or "personal theory" has its roots, as Rosenthal himself suggests, in many sources; but one that is clearly at hand, native and vital, is that formulated by the poet repeatedly referred to by Lowell himself—Walt Whitman. In "A Backward Glance o'er Travel'd Roads," Whitman observed that his *Leaves of Grass* grew out of a "feeling or ambition to articulate and faithfully express in literary or poetic form, and uncompromisingly, my own physical, emotional, moral, intellectual, and aesthetic Personality, in the midst of, and tallying, the momentous spirit and facts of its immediate days, and of current America—and to exploit that Personality, identified with place and date, in a far more candid and comprehensive sense than any hitherto poem or book."[6]

But whatever Lowell might have thought about his future use of "personal history" in his 1961 interview with Frederick Seidel, in fact he turned to it more and more—almost as though he had decided to use Rosenthal (or Whitman) as a guide. In the 1970 edition of

Notebook, Lowell confessed that he couldn't seem to let go of the text, which first appeared in May 1969, and then again, revised, in July 1969, and for the third time as *Notebook*, again much revised, in early 1970. The "Afterthought" emphasizes the poet's use of his own life: "NOTEBOOK: as my title intends, the poems in this book are written as one poem, intuitive in arrangement, but not a pile or sequence of related material. It is less an almanac than the story of my life." After the "Afterthought" appears a page of "Dates," opening with "THE VIETNAM WAR, 1967," and ending with "THE VIETNAM WAR, 1968, 1969, 1970." In between appear such items as "THE PENTAGON MARCH, October 21, 1967," and "The Demonstrations and Democratic Convention in Chicago, August 25–29, 1968."[7] This end material, with its posted signs pointing to both the personal and the national, is, I think, an accurate representation of *Notebook*—or (to use the language of Whitman) an "uncompromising" articulation of the Self and at the same time a "tallying" of "current America."

Again becoming dissatisfied with *Notebook*, Lowell dumped all the poems out once more, put them through a sifting and revision, and published them in new arrangements in *For Lizzie and Harriet* (1973) and *History* (1973). It is unclear to what extent Lowell committed himself to the open form (pioneered by Whitman) and then backed off as he found himself sliding into what might have seemed to him chaos; in *History*, he confessed: "My old title, *Notebook*, was more accurate than I wished, i.e. the composition was jumbled. I hope this jumble or jungle is cleared—that I have cut the waste marble from the figure."[8] A careful reading of *Notebook* followed by a reading of *History* does not immediately clarify Lowell's purposes and aims.[9] Indeed, to a reader accustomed to the kind of open (personal as well as national) poem that *Notebook* clearly attempted to be, there is substantial loss in the more formal arrangements made in the later books. It is not my purpose here to pass judgment, however, but merely to point to Lowell's involvement with the long, loose, or open form as a part of the important changes he and modern poetry were undergoing during these decades.[10]

To what extent Lowell might have been inspired to attempt the long form by the example of John Berryman's more immediately successful *Dream Songs* is an open question (*77 Dream Songs* had appeared in 1964, the remainder in 1968). They were friends of long standing and had watched each other's work over the years. Both started at much the same point, both went through radical transformations in mid-career, and both turned to the confessional-personal form as well as the epic length. The major difference is that their popular reputa-

tions came at different times, for Lowell at the beginning, for Berryman at the end of his career—especially with his long open poem.
Lowell's uneasiness with *Notebook* might well have sprung from his
awareness of the success of Berryman's *Dream Songs*.

As with Lowell, we may pinpoint the metamorphosis in Berryman
as taking place in the late 1950s. But for Berryman we have an important critical essay that, though written in 1957, came to light only in
the posthumously published volume of essays, *The Freedom of the Poet*
(1976). The essay is entitled " 'Song of Myself': Intention and Substance." It was this extraordinary essay on Whitman that attracted
most of the reviewers of *The Freedom of the Poet*, and particularly the
British poet Donald Davie in his comments in the *New York Times Book
Review*: "It cannot be denied that at some point in mid-career Berryman momentously shifted his stance toward his art and the experience his art fed upon, just as Lowell did with his 'Life Studies' (1959).
And the shift seems to have to do, not surprisingly, with that inescapable figure in every American poet's heritage, Walt Whitman."[11]
Aside from the plain sense of this statement, two aspects are
noteworthy: it is made by an Englishman, perhaps in a better position
than Americans (too close to the subject) to detect the Whitmanian
heritage in American poetry; and its curious beginning—"It cannot be
denied . . ."—suggests that indeed there had been some kind of current refusal to accept the obvious truth.

Berryman made it plain enough, in comment after comment, that
whereas Eliot had served as a model for his earlier poetry (*Homage to
Mistress Bradstreet*), his *Dream Songs* was modeled on *Leaves of Grass*.
Pressed in one interview about what he was up to in *Dream Songs*, he
responded: "The idea was, sort of, the way Whitman puts his idea
about 'Leaves of Grass.' The idea is to record a personality, to make
him visible, put him through tests, see what the hell he's up to, and
through him, the country."[12] It is clear, now, that Berryman was here
paraphrasing one of the key passages in Whitman's "A Backward
Glance o'er Travel'd Roads," which Berryman had quoted verbatim
in his essay on "Song of Myself": " 'Leaves of Grass' . . . has mainly
been the outcropping of my own emotional and other personal
nature—an attempt, from first to last, to put *a Person*, a human being
(myself, in the latter half of the Nineteenth Century, in America,)
freely, fully and truly on record."[13]

Berryman demonstrates that he was fully aware of the extent to
which this Whitman statement was in conflict with current notions
about the nature of poetry by turning, immediately after quoting
Whitman, to Eliot: "I call your attention to an incongruity of this

formulation with Eliot's amusing theory of the impersonality of the artist, and a contrast between the mere *putting-on-record* and the well-nigh universal current notion of *creation*, or making things up. You will see that, as Whitman looks more arrogant than Eliot in the Personality, he looks less pretentious in the recording—the mere recording—poet not as *maker* but as spiritual historian." Before one has read very far in Berryman's essay, it becomes clear that the author is passionately committed to the Whitmanian views, that he speaks with the intensity and fervor of the convert writing in the midst of his visionary conversion: "The poet—one would say, a mere channel, but with its own ferocious difficulties—fills with experiences, a valve opens; he speaks them. I am obliged to remark that I prefer this theory of poetry to those that have ruled the critical quarterlies since I was an undergraduate twenty-five years ago. It is as humble as, and identical with, Keats's view of the poet as having no existence, but being 'forever in, for, and filling' other things."[14]

Berryman began his essay on Whitman with references to the "arbiters of current taste," Pound, Eliot, and Auden, in an attempt to show how his feelings about Whitman differed from theirs. His statements verge on the extravagant: "I like or love Whitman unreservedly; he operates with great power and beauty over a very wide range." " 'Song of Myself'. . . seems to me easily his most important achievement and indeed the greatest poem so far written by an American."[15] In retrospect Berryman seems to have been clarifying for himself his literary allegiances, cutting himself off from earlier commitments, and attaching himself firmly to new ones, new ones historically older than the earlier ones. There is an air of discovery running through the essay, as well as a sense of proprietary claim. Had the essay been published when written, in 1957, it would have been something of a scandal, a slap in the face of the poetic—or Eliotic—establishment. Major poets in *the tradition* did not then speak up for Whitman—it wasn't done—and the very few exceptions were usually considered eccentric or embarrassing, such as Randall Jarrell in "Some Lines from Whitman" (in his *Poetry and the Age,* 1953).

Berryman's homage to Whitman was written without documented reference to other critical or scholarly commentary on the poet—with one interesting exception. In treating of Whitman's "passionate sense of identification" in "Song of Myself," Berryman says: "I would deny that this is mystical—indeed, it is the opposite, as a writer of *PMLA* confessed (in 1955) while producing and maintaining the monstrous term 'inverted mystical.' I object to the word 'mystical' in relation to Whitman altogether."[16] Recognizing myself with some

surprise as the author of the 1955 *PMLA* essay " 'Song of Myself' as
Inverted Mystical Experience,"[17] my first reaction was not to quarrel
with the disagreement but to wonder that Berryman was formulating
his position on Whitman with some comprehension of the criticism
and scholarship extant at the time.

Donald Davie's offhand comment in his Berryman's review, linking
Berryman's shift in his "stance toward his art" with Lowell's and
connecting the two with that "inescapable figure in every American
poet's heritage, Walt Whitman," may be taken as the symbolic point
of departure for the exploration launched in this book. As the Davie
comment implies, Berryman and Lowell are not isolated cases; their
achievement and their prominence make them useful examples for
the purposes of literary history. If we take, as Lowell and Berryman at
times did, the two poles of American poetry to be symbolized by Eliot
and Whitman, with Eliot dominant from the time of *The Waste Land*
(1922) on, we may now affirm that the Eliot dominance had begun
measurably to wane by the late 1950s and continued to fade in the
1960s. There were, of course, poets like Williams who never conceded
Eliot the domination. And there were poets like Tate and Ransom
who never experienced a "shift" in their Eliotic "stance" toward their
art. And there were other poets who never pitched their tents in
either camp. The following pages have been written out of the kind of
intuition informing the Davie remark, but with a sobering sense of the
complexity of literary history and the stubborn ways in which poets
remain themselves, however much we label, classify, and categorize
them. It is their stubborn individuality and uniqueness that render
them so endlessly fascinating in the varied groupings and regroup-
ings of criticism.

A final word:
from
"For John Berryman
(After reading his last *Dream Song*)"

Robert Lowell

Something so heavy lies on my heart—
there, still here, the good days
when we sat by a cold lake in Maine,
talking about the *Winter's Tale,*
Leontes' jealousy
in Shakespeare's broken syntax.
You got there first.
Just the other day,
I discovered how we differ—humor . . .
even in this last *Dream Song,*
to mock your catlike flight
from home and classes—
to leap from the bridge.

Girls will not frighten the frost from the grave.

To my surprise, John,
I pray *to* not for you,
think of you not myself,
smile and fall asleep.[18]

Two

"The Care & Feeding of Long Poems" was Henry's title
for his next essay, which will come out when
he wants it to.
A Kennedy-sponsored bill for the protection
of poets from long poems   will benefit the culture
and do no harm to that kind lady, Mrs. Johnson.
                          John Berryman, Dream Song 354

The American Epic from Barlow to Berryman

Since the Declaration of Independence in 1776, and even before, American poets have dreamed of providing these States with a—perhaps *the*—Supreme Fiction, a delineated ideal, a set of beliefs, a model for living, a summation of the essence of what it means to be an American. This epic, sometimes anti-epic, ambition runs in the most profound currents from Timothy Dwight and Joel Barlow to John Berryman and Allen Ginsberg, with such important way stations in between as Ezra Pound, T. S. Eliot, Hart Crane, William Carlos Williams, Wallace Stevens, Charles Olson—and many more. There is one pivotal figure whose pronouncements and practice have loomed large enough to dominate—or to be elaborately rejected by—all succeeding poets, and who remains today the somewhat noisy skeleton sounding his barbaric yawp in America's poetic closet: Walt Whitman. As a saint, an embarrassment, or a joke, old Walt haunts the American poetic psyche. Every American poet must come to terms with his presence and is influenced as deeply in rejecting as in accepting him.

The New Criticism once thought that it had written Walt Whitman off, had buried him with the same finality as Fortunato is buried in

13

"The Cask of Amontillado"—bricked up deep in the dank cellars of the mind. The irrelevance of Whitman seemed permanently established when the academies and the little magazines all extolled the consciously structured, elaborately patterned, brilliantly imaged, rigorously impersonal, subtly ironic poem. All poetry was remeasured, and when it smacked of the naively celebratory, the expansively confessional, the intuitively shaped, the shamelessly personal, the improvisationally spoken or chanted, it was dismissed with amusement or contempt; the well-made poem rendered Whitman obsolete.

But like steam built up under a cap too long sealed, Whitman's long dormant live energy blew the lid off modern poetry and released new poetic energies in the land, some of them so vigorous that they swept over the New Criticism and its precious well-made poem, leaving little in their wake except some glistening, fragmentary debris. William Carlos Williams replaced T. S. Eliot as a modern touchstone some four decades after what Williams designated the "catastrophe" of American poetry: the appearance and canonization of *The Waste Land* in 1922.[1] In 1956 Allen Ginsberg "howled" in the measure of Whitman's "yawp." And like many poets of a turbulent time, Robert Lowell began his career with allegiances in one camp, but at a critical moment folded his tent and stole away to the other camp. *Life Studies* (1959) was the turning point, and *Notebook* (1970) revised into *History* (1973) represented his struggle with the new Whitmanian forms. John Berryman cut out of the Eliot path, too, and joined the journey on Whitman's open road; he confessed (in his posthumously published *Paris Review* interview, winter 1972) that he took Eliot's *Waste Land* as his model for *Homage to Mistress Bradstreet* (1956), but turned to Whitman's "Song of Myself" as his model for *The Dream Songs* (finished, more or less, in 1968).[2]

One of the marvels of the deep division that separates the two traditions in modern American poetry is that both trace their origins to identical sources. The New Criticism and its poets, such as John Crowe Ransom, Allen Tate, the early Robert Lowell, took over many of their principles, it is true, from T. S. Eliot, but all realized that these principles derived in some manner from the man who had shaped Eliot, Ezra Pound. On the other hand, such anti–New Critical poets as Charles Olson, Allen Ginsberg, and Robert Creeley came back to Pound by way of William Carlos Williams—especially the Pound of the *Cantos*, the Pound that is most like Whitman. How Pound ended up a prophet in both of two opposed poetic camps makes for one of those ambiguities sufficiently baffling to puzzle a legion of literary historians.

An even greater irony, perhaps, is Whitman's lurking presence in each of these shapers of modern American poetry. If Ezra Pound is sometimes conceived of as the father of the modern movement, and Eliot and Williams as his odd offspring often at odds, then Whitman must clearly be cast in the role of grandfather; his poetic genes flowed through Pound into both Eliot and Williams—and on beyond into those who declare their allegiance to one or the other, or even declare their independence of all, self-generated poets without ancestry (Whitman's own role, more or less).

From Whitman to Pound and from Pound to Eliot and Williams, and thus to the latest moderns of whatever school: this lineage, the focus of this book, appears to be a natural development for American literature, but the idea may come as something of a shock to those accustomed to discovering the sources of American modernism abroad, especially in France. That Pound derived from the French Symbolists (among them Stéphane Mallarmé), and Eliot also (for example, Jules Laforgue), has long been common critical knowledge if not critical commonplace. That the French Symbolists derived from an American source, Edgar Allan Poe, is a fact on which sophisticated criticism has gagged in disbelief for some time (Eliot expressed his wonder and revulsion at the notion in "From Poe to Valéry," 1948).

No one would want to deny that Pound and Eliot drew from multiple sources and were nourished by many traditions. And it is doubtful that any single context or source could illuminate all the cryptic and enigmatic lines of such a complex poem as *The Cantos*; but I believe that the American and specifically Whitmanian context will shed light on the poem's growth, method, and form—as, indeed, the American context will help us to understand what Eliot was about in *The Waste Land*, William Carlos Williams in *Paterson*, Hart Crane in *The Bridge*, and many other American poets in a multitude of long American poems. There *is* something especially American in the American poet's recurring ambition to write a long poem, sometimes a poem that takes a lifetime in the composition. The American roots of this ambition do much to explain the poem's meaning and shape. And every American poet who has written a long poem has, consciously or unconsciously, measured the length of his reach, tested the depth of his thrust, by the American poem that stands as the pivotal work for all American poetry: *Leaves of Grass*.

This theme was touched on, in part, by Roy Harvey Pearce in *The Continuity of American Poetry* (1961), in a section called "The Long View: An American Epic." Here Professor Pearce took exception to my view, expressed in the conclusion of *A Critical Guide to Leaves of Grass* (1957), that Whitman's entire work constituted (in Whitman's view as well as mine) an American epic. He defined Whitman's epic as "Song of Myself," and placed it in relation to *The Columbiad* before it and *The Cantos, The Bridge,* and *Paterson* after it.[3] Taking many hints from this seminal discussion, as well as offering some demurrers, I have endeavoured in these pages to trace some of the important implications of this almost obsessive impulse in the American poet to write a long poem: not just another long poem, but a long poem for America, that will serve as its epic, and if not its epic, then as the embodiment of its "Supreme Fiction" (in Wallace Stevens's sense), as a particularly American way of conceiving or perceiving or receiving the world.

That the impulse is obsessive seems clear enough from the beginning, especially for anyone who has tried to read either of the two versions of Joel Barlow's epic, *The Vision of Columbus* (1787) or *The Columbiad* (1807). Barlow's ambition was epic, but he found that he had to modify the form to suit his American materials (he gave up narrative in favor of sweeping vision), and the form has gone through radical transformation ever since. Whitman, at the beginning of his career as a poet, outlined in his 1855 Preface to *Leaves of Grass* a recipe for the "great psalm of the republic," whose theme "is creative and has vista."[4] In John Berryman's *Dream Songs,* published in 1969, we find in Song 354:

> "The Care & Feeding of Long Poems" was Henry's title
> for his next essay, which will come out when
> he wants it to.
> A Kennedy-sponsored bill for the protection
> of poets from long poems   will benefit the culture
> and do no harm to that kind lady, Mrs. Johnson.[5]

And in *Sphere: The Form of a Motion* (1974), A. R. Ammons wrote:

> I don't know about you,
> but I'm sick of good poems, all those little rondures
> splendidly brought off, painted gourds on a shelf: give me
> the dumb, debilitated, nasty, and massive, if that's the
> alternative: touch the universe anywhere you touch it
> everywhere.[6]

Irony sounds through Berryman's many voices, and the greatest irony is perhaps that his lines come in the middle of his most ambitious, most obsessive long poem. And Ammons writes his words in the middle of *his* long poem, tossing off what appears to be one of the assumptions basic to the American long poem: its ego-centrifugality (as well as ego-centripetality), the notion that anyone can be everyman, that the poet can represent his time, his place, his world, "touch the universe anywhere you touch it/everywhere." Ah yes, but to *touch the universe*: how is that done? The answer to this question is in some sense the answer sought through two centuries of America's quest for a Supreme Fiction.

2

Had John Berryman's Huffy Henry, who throughout the *Dream Songs* shields himself as best he can from the suffering of his "irreversible loss," and who, to the reader's delight, repeatedly discovers that he has a "sing to shay"[7]—had Henry lived to finish his essay on "The Care & Feeding of Long Poems," he could have dealt with some strange works in American literature. He might well have gone back to the beginnings to stare in amazement at that poem of cataclysmic conclusions, the Puritan epic and best-seller, Michael Wigglesworth's *Day of Doom*, published in 1662; surely he would have sympathized with the sinners who "put away the evil day, / and drown'd their care and fears, / Till drown'd were they, and swept away / by vengeance unawares."[8] And he would certainly have paused over Edward Taylor's poetic sequences, *God's Determinations* and the two series of *Preparatory Meditations*, written in the seventeenth century but not published until the twentieth; he would have wondered at the American poet's penchant from the first for the scatological image, as in Meditation 8 (First Series): "In this sad state, Gods Tender Bowells run / Out streams of Grace: And he to end all strife / The Purest Wheate in Heaven, his deare-dear Son / Grinds, and kneads up into this Bread of Life."[9] He probably would have agreed with Albert Gelpi's recent judgment (in *The Tenth Muse*, 1975) that Taylor's work "is the first instance of what may be a distinctly American genre: the open-ended poem written over years, perhaps even over a lifetime, in separate but interacting segments."[10]

Moving from the seventeenth century to the eighteenth, Henry could not avoid encountering what its author claimed to be the first epic written in America—Timothy Dwight's *The Conquest of Canaan*, begun in the early 1770s but not published until 1785 (John Trumbull's *M'Fingal*, 1782, as a *mock-epic* did not qualify for the honor). Its eleven books, written in a seemingly endless sequence of heroic couplets, was an attempt by the grandson of Jonathan Edwards to wed religion and politics by making the biblical story of Joshua's leading the Israelites into the land of Canaan suggest or symbolize George Washington's triumph over the British in the American Revolutionary War. It is not a matter of record that this epic's allegorized hero, and the man to whom the poem is, with a rhetorical flourish, dedicated—George Washington—ever got around to reading its some three hundred pages.[11] For that matter, it is not clear that anyone except the dedicated scholar has read the work in its entirety, a fate not uncommon to America's long poems.

Had Henry survived his encounter with Dwight's epic, he would next stumble up against another blockbuster, Joel Barlow's *Columbiad* (1787, 1807). Here he could test his own reaction against that of William Cullen Bryant, who said: "The plan of the work is utterly destitute of interest and that which was at first [in its 1787 form as *The Vision of Columbus*] sufficiently wearisome has become doubly so by being drawn out to its present length."[12] That length, with notes, extended over four hundred pages, or ten books of relentless heroic couplets. Barlow's epic device was to invent a guardian Genius who rescued Columbus from his old-age prison and took him to the top of the "mount of vision," whence he could witness the whole bloody history of the conquest of the American continents, the formation of the American nation, and on into the glorious future and utopian fulfillment. Clearly Columbus was enthralled by the vision of America's special destiny in the world presented by his guardian Genius, as shown in these lines closing Book the Ninth:

> As thus he spoke, returning tears of joy
> Suffused the Hero's cheek and pearl'd his eye:
> Unveil, said he, my friend [that is, Hesper, his guardian
>   Genius], and stretch once more
>
> Beneath my view that heaven-illumined shore;
> Let me behold her silver beams expand
> To lead all nations, lighten every land,
> Instruct the total race and teach at last
> Their toils to lessen and their chains to cast,
> Trace and attain the purpose of their birth
> And hold in peace this heritage of earth.
> The Seraph smiled consent; the Hero's eye
> Watcht for the daybeam round the changing sky.[13]

If Henry found himself turned off, or put to sleep, by such passages drawn out at such tedious length, in works diligently attempting to transfigure Christopher Columbus or George Washington into an epic hero, and slavishly courting the Old World muse of past epics, he might have dug out such native-seeming works as Daniel Bryan's *Adventures of Daniel Boone* (1813), with its attempt to develop a different kind of epic hero—the frontier, native-born American. But though he started with an original New World hero, the poet evoked, in startlingly elevated language, the Old World muse: "And thou my Muse! with wildly melting grace, / Strike softly from the angel-woven wires, / Of poesy's bright Harp, sweet flowing strains."[14] From lines like these, Henry might have turned quickly to Thomas Ward's *Passaic* (1842), with its attempt to embody an epic landscape, elevating to hero status an American river—later to figure importantly in a twentieth-century American epic, William Carlos Williams's *Paterson* (the Ward poem has been conveniently excerpted for the epic hunter in Mike Weaver's *William Carlos Williams: The American Background*, 1971).[15]

But if the rustic and the local might have bored Henry after a time, he could have become enthusiastic about a work that is overwhelmingly elegant and universal, Edgar Allan Poe's *Eureka: A Prose Poem* (1848). By writing his poetry in prose, Poe violated most of the tenets he had developed for the writing of poetry (such as the nonexistence of a *long poem*) and at the same time set the pattern for the prosy or prose-filled poems of the twentieth century (as in Williams, Charles Olson, Karl Shapiro, and others). Moreover, *Eureka* is suffused with the epic impulse, the impulse to "get it all together," to elevate science into metaphysics, and to erect thereon a system of belief, a myth for the mythless American. And the epic hero? It could be no other than the poem's speaker himself, Edgar Allan Poe, perceiving for his readers the unity of seemingly disparate things, reconciling the conflicts of science and religion.

What might Henry make of Henry Wadsworth Longfellow's *Song of Hiawatha*?

> Swift of foot was Hiawatha;
> He could shoot an arrow from him,
> And run forward with such fleetness,
> That the arrow fell behind him!
> Strong of arm was Hiawatha;
> He could shoot ten arrows upward,
> Shoot them with such strength and swiftness
> That the tenth had left the bow-string
> Ere the first to earth had fallen![16]

This American epic took over the hypnotic trochaic tetrameter of the Finnish epic, *Kalevala*, and appeared in that signal year of 1855 (signal because it was the year of the first edition of Whitman's *Leaves of Grass*). The one poem, Longfellow's, was hailed as a masterpiece; the other, Whitman's, almost still-born, was hailed only, or primarily, by the author's own stealthily placed reviews. Henry might raise a glass

to this inconspicuous crossing of the old and new, the one epic rush-
ing into the past and near-oblivion (at least critically), the other
wobbling uncertainly toward the future and many strange reincarna-
tions.

Henry might have paused and puzzled over the case of Emily Dickinson, like Poe the seeming genius of the short poem. He might
examine those packets in which she placed and fixed her poems,
apparently out of some obscure notion that there was an arrangement
that would turn short poems into a long poem which would penetrate
to a truth perhaps greater than the sum of the individual insights,
which by the juxtaposition of disparate subjects would make a transcendent leap to the unity behind all subjects.[17] But Henry's pause
with Emily would surely have turned into a prolonged stay with
Herman Melville if he had attempted to comprehend Melville's incredibly long poem, *Clarel: A Poem and Pilgrimage in the Holy Land*
(1876). Henry might have agreed with those who said that Melville's
greatest poetry was written in prose, that *Moby Dick* was his, and
America's, epic. But such statements do not make *Clarel* disappear,
and Henry's keen interest in the "care & feeding of long poems"
would surely impel him into a close investigation of its agonizing
search, through six hundred pages of rhyming iambic tetrameter, for
a way of belief for an American in the modern world, or, perhaps,
for an American way of belief (or an American way of living with
unbelief).

When Henry turned his attention to the early twentieth century, he
would find, in poetry as in prose, attention focused on the American
village, the small town (to turn up later in dramatic form in Thornton
Wilder's *Our Town*, 1938). Edward Arlington Robinson produced a
body of such poetry in which there lurked the long poem that was
extracted and published as *Tilbury Town* (1953).[18] But another long
poem of similar nature that Henry could add to his list is Edgar
Lee Masters's *Spoon River Anthology* (1915), which includes "The
Spooniad"[19] at the end—perhaps a tipoff to the epic (even if comic)
ambition of the book. Henry might come to speculate that *Spoon River
Anthology* was in a sense a climax in the evolution of the American
long poem—poles apart from those early attempts to find a hero in
George Washington or Christopher Columbus, stumbling instead on
a "democratic" hero in the glory of his anonymity living his anonymous life in an anonymous village—Everyman in Everytown, USA.

Beginning with Ezra Pound, Henry would find that the "care &
feeding of long poems" became something else. Something else, but
also something the same—the same, that is, as the "care & feeding"

by that pivotal poet who unobtrusively changed literary history beginning quietly—unnoticed—in 1855. Like *Leaves of Grass*, Pound's *Cantos* grew over a lifetime, assuming the shape of a life. No other long poem of the twentieth century seems to have taken so long in the writing. Though conceived earlier, the first Canto was published in 1917 (Pound was thirty-two), the last in 1969, a period of fifty-two years. Whitman, thirty-six in 1855, was to work thirty-seven years on *Leaves of Grass*—until his death and the Deathbed Edition in 1892. By comparison with such spectacular devotion to the "care & feeding of long poems," other twentieth-century poets appear to be pikers. But as Henry would surely know, a poem's excellence or impact cannot be measured by the years of its production. T. S. Eliot's *The Waste Land* was seemingly produced in a great surge of emotion and inspiration, revised by Pound, and issued at a stroke in 1922. Less sudden in execution and appearance, *The Four Quartets* appeared in 1943. If Henry examined their feeding closely, he might find both poems shaped to the poet's life more closely than anyone imagined possible on their appearance and for long after.

After Pound and Eliot, Henry's reading list would be long and arduous. One line of inquiry would carry him through long poems that grew over more or less long periods and that relate themselves more or less directly to the Whitman-Pound-Eliot patterns (or anti-patterns): Hart Crane's *The Bridge* (1930), William Carlos Williams's *Paterson* (1946–63), Charles Olson's Maximus Poems (1960–75), Henry's own John Berryman and his *Dream Songs* (1964–68), Allen Ginsberg's *Fall of America* (1972). This is the line I shall be tracking, using in addition Wallace Stevens's "Notes toward a Supreme Fiction" (1942) as a focal point for discussion of the theory of an American long poem. Wallace Stevens's long poem is divided into three sections, each of which bears a title that appears to be a rule: "It Must Be Abstract," "It Must Change," "It Must Give Pleasure."[20] And Stevens's letters reveal that he once contemplated adding a fourth section to be entitled, "It Must Be Human."[21] The antecedents of all the "Its" of these rules, although left ambiguous by Stevens, must be a work that attempts to embody a "Supreme Fiction" (a viable truth or reality, a usable myth)—that is, an epic, or a specifically American epic, in short, a Significant Long Poem (like "Notes toward a Supreme Fiction" itself).

But in tracking the American long poem, Henry might find, aside from Crane, Williams, Berryman, and Ginsberg, other possible paths to investigate, side trips to make. He (and we) might follow another line that leads through materials bearing the clear stamp of America:

Stephen Vincent Benét's *John Brown's Body* (1928), Archibald Mac-
Leish's *Conquistador* (1932), Robert Penn Warren's *Brother to Dragons*
(1953). In a way most such works struggle to connect with a narrative
epic tradition that Whitman rendered obsolete with *Leaves of Grass*.
Henry would, however, surely find ample Whitmanian echoes in a
modern master of the long narrative (and yet also intricately lyric)
poet, Robinson Jeffers, but he would just as surely note the basic
Whitmanian brightness transfigured into gloom in Jeffers's masterpiece, *The Women at Point Sur* (1927), or in his later work, *The Double
Axe* (1948).[22] And if Henry found Jeffers fascinating, he might seek
out the work of Brother Antoninus–William Everson (who has styled
himself Jeffers's "only disciple"),[23] as for example his *Man-Fate: The
Swan Song of Brother Antoninus* (1974), an account of the poet's feelings
on giving up monkhood for marriage. Or if Henry tired of the Jeffers
gloom he might prefer to immerse himself for a time in Carl
Sandburg's *The People, Yes!* (1936), a long poem that seems to out-
Whitman Whitman in its embrace of Americans "En-Masse." And if
Sandburg's expansiveness began to pall, Henry could turn to H. D.'s
more restrained *Trilogy* ("The Walls Do Not Fall," 1944; "Tribute to
the Angels," 1945; "The Flowering of the Rod," 1946), and its lyric
account of an intensely personal reaction to an overwhelming public
event, World War II. A passage from "The Walls Do Not Fall" may be
read as a kind of general motto of the American long poem:

> we know no rule
> of procedure,
>
> we are voyagers, discoverers
> of the not-known,
>
> the unrecorded;
> we have no map;
>
> possibly we will reach haven,
> heaven.[24]

Henry's ardor for "the care & feeding of long poems" might have
cooled had he become lost in the labyrinths of Louis Zukofsky's *A*,
begun in 1928, elaborated and extended for almost fifty years, and
brought ostensibly to a conclusion in 1976.[25] Or Henry might have
become bemused by the contemporary proliferation of the long poem
in a seemingly infinite variety of forms, as he spun in circles trying desperately to keep up with its hydra-headed manifestations:
Robert Duncan, *The Structure of Rime*, launched in his volume *The
Opening of the Field* in 1960; and also *Passages*, which began to appear
in his volume *Bending the Bow* in 1968; Louis Simpson, *At the End of the*

Open Road (1963), and *Searching for the Ox* (1976); Melvin B. Tolson, *Harlem Gallery* (1965); A. R. Ammons, *Tape for the Turn of the Year* (1965), and *Sphere: The Form of a Motion* (1974); John Ashberry, *The Skaters* (1966), and *Three Poems* (in prose) (1972); James Schuyler, *Hymn to Life* (1976); Edward Dorn, *Slinger* (1975); James Dickey, *The Zodiac* (1976).

Henry might have concluded, after attempting to read as many of America's recent long poems as he could find, that for a poet to choose the form of the long poem as it has evolved is to opt for many freedoms, but it also is to venture many risks. In a way, the form denudes the poet, displaying, it is true, all his genius, but mercilessly exposing, too, all his frailties. Whatever else its nature, the form offers no place to hide mediocrity, banality, conformity. In a short, well-made poem, these traits might be cleverly concealed, hidden behind the meter or metaphor or conceit; but in the American long poem, they will out, willy-nilly—and the poem can quickly become, instead of a daring adventure and journey, a colossal and predictable bore.

The risks involved and the hazards incurred Henry might find symbolized by A. R. Ammons's *Tape for the Turn of the Year* (1965), which was composed entirely on an adding-machine tape, started through the typewriter in early December and continued daily until the tape ran out in mid-January. The poem opens on 6 December:

> today I
> decided to write
> a long
>   thin
>   poem
>   employing certain
> classical considerations:
>   this
> part is called the pro-
> logue: it has to do with
>   the business of
>   getting started.
>
>   first the
>   Muse
>   must be acknowledged,
> saluted, and implored:
> I cannot
> write
>   without her help
>   but when

> her help comes it's
> water from spring heights,
> warmth and melting,
>   stream
>   inexhaustible:
> I salute her, lady
> of a hundred names—
>   Inspiration
>   Unconscious
>   Apollo (on her man side)[26]

Here, in a witty, seemingly disposable, epic, one hundred years and
more after the appearance of Whitman's *Leaves of Grass*, is a limit
reached, an extreme explored—improvisational, a free-flowing comi-
cally organic form, a poem about the writing of a poem, an anti-epic
about the writing of an epic. Henry may well look quizzical, scratch
his head, and now wander back to his own familiar habitat, *The Dream
Songs* of John Berryman, to meditate at length over the gargantuan
dimensions of the materials accumulated on "the care & feeding of
long poems."

3

Where are the beginnings of this epic impulse, this impassioned quest for a Supreme Fiction? The origins lie deep in the national psyche, and those poets who fled America in search of a more
congenial tradition (Eliot, Pound) succeeded only in demonstrating
their deepest American nature. There is one side of the American
character that shouts: throw over all tradition, cut off the past, start
and build anew; but there is the counterpart that whispers: take all
traditions as yours, connect firmly with the past, build the new only
on the old. Walt Whitman's 1855 Preface to *Leaves of Grass*, with its call
for the new, made T. S. Eliot's 1917 "Tradition and the Individual
Talent," with its praise for the past, inevitable. Both are solidly
American documents, treating of peculiarly American issues. Only a
country without much past, without long traditions, can be so self-
conscious about them, either in rejecting or in seeking them.

America needed a new literature to match the new land and the
new society, the land largely empty, the society hardly established.
This was the recurring note sounded by almost every literary and
cultural critic to comment on American literature from the time of
America's political independence on. For example, Solyman Brown, a
sometime poet, clergyman, and dentist of Connecticut, opened his

1818 "Essay on American Poetry" thus: "The proudest freedom to which a nation can aspire, not excepting even political independence, is found in complete emancipation from literary thraldom. Few nations, however, have arrived at this commanding eminence." After a sweeping survey of all civilization, Brown comes to America, and instead of finding the causes for her continuing literary dependence within, he finds the causes abroad—in a British conspiracy. "It has ever been the policy and practice of England to decry Scotch and Irish intellect and affect a sovereign contempt for all that are born on the Forth or the Liffey. As these countries have now coalesced under the crown of England, it has become less her interest to urge hostilities in those directions. America is therefore the principal object of her literary persecution." Persecution? That, indeed, is what Solyman Brown means, and he goes on to point out that this persecution is accomplished through the British reviews, through the "importation of books into the United States, often at reduced prices," and through the refusal of British men of letters to give "the smallest credit to American productions, how meritorious soever."[27] Although the specifics might and did change, the literary or intellectual hostility toward England and British literary dominance would continue for many decades, even into our own time.

William Cullen Bryant, in a review of Solyman Brown's book laying out his conspiracy theory, surveyed American poetry in 1818. Although Bryant ridiculed Brown's theories, his concern for an American poetry runs through all his comments: "Abroad, our literature has fallen under unmerited contumely from those who were but slenderly acquainted with the subject on which they professed to decide: and at home, it must be confessed that the swaggering and pompous pretensions of many have done not a little to provoke and excuse the ridicule of foreigners. Either of these extremes exerts an injurious influence on the cause of letters in our country." Bryant found Brown's boasting merely embarrassing: "We make but a contemptible figure in the eyes of the world and set ourselves up as objects of pity to our posterity when we affect to rank the poets of our own country with those mighty masters of song who have flourished in Greece, Italy, and Britain."[28]

Mighty masters of song? Would America ever have them? Henry Wadsworth Longfellow may well have had himself in mind when he posed essentially this question, at eighteen years of age, in 1825:

Is then our land to be indeed the land of song? Will it one day be rich in romantic associations? Will poetry, that hallows every scene, that renders every spot classical, and pours out on all things the soul of its enthusiasm, breathe over it that enchantment which lives in the isles of Greece, and is more than life amid the "woods, that wave o'er Delphi's steep." Yes!—and palms are to be won by our native writers!—by those that have been nursed and brought up with us in the civil and religious freedom of our country. Already has a voice been lifted up in this land, already a spirit and a love of literature are springing up in the shadow of our free political institutions.

In answering the British charge that America had no "finished scholars," Longfellow set forth in embryo the lines of a literary argument that would flourish in the twentieth century:

But there is reason for believing that men of mere learning, men of sober research and studied correctness, do not give to a nation its great name. Our very poverty in this respect will have a tendency to give a national character to our literature. Our writers will not be constantly boiling and panting after classical allusions to the vale of Tempe and the Etrurian river. . . . We are thus thrown upon ourselves: and thus shall our native hills become renowned in song, like those of Greece and Italy.[29]

It was left to Ralph Waldo Emerson to offer the classic statement that all these critics (and many more) were stammering to make. And although Emerson's 1837 "American Scholar," with its cry—"We have listened too long to the courtly muses of Europe"[30]—has come to be considered the American intellectual declaration of independence, it was not until "The Poet" (1844) that Emerson made his most eloquent plea and prophecy for American poetry:

I look in vain for the poet whom I describe. We do not with sufficient plainness or sufficient profoundness address ourselves to life, nor dare we chaunt our own times and social circumstance. If we filled the day with bravery, we should not shrink from celebrating it. Time and nature yield us many gifts, but not yet the timely man, the new religion, the reconciler, whom all things await. Dante's praise is that he dared to write his autobiography in colossal cipher, or into universality. We have yet had no genius in America, with tyrannous eye, which knew the value of our incomparable materials, and saw, in the barbarism and materialism of the times, another carnival of the same gods whose picture he so much admires in Homer; then in the Middle Age; then in Calvinism . . . . Yet America is a poem in our eyes; its ample geography dazzles the imagination, and it will not wait long for meters.[31]

From 1844 to 1855. The wait was not long for *Leaves of Grass*. In response to the copy Whitman sent him, Emerson replied in the most famous letter in American literature: "It meets the demand I am always making of what seemed the sterile and stingy nature, as if too much handiwork, or too much lymph in the temperament, were making our Western wits fat and mean. I give you joy of your free and brave thought."[32]

Emerson's role in shaping the concept of an American bard and an American epic is vital, and there is justification in recognizing him as one of the Whitmanian "Beginners": "How they are provided for upon the earth, (appearing at intervals)."[33] The relationship between Emerson and Whitman has been the subject of repeated exploration, two of the most recent commentaries, by Hyatt Waggoner and Harold Bloom, providing some of the most interesting—and debatable— conjecture.[34] It is as gross a mistake to claim that Emerson's and Whitman's ideas are identical in all respects (as Yvor Winters astonishingly claimed in attacking Hart Crane's *The Bridge*; see chapter 8, section 2, below) as it is to claim that Whitman owes nothing to Emerson. Whitman himself once said that he was "simmering, simmering" and Emerson brought him "to a boil"[35]—an image that perhaps most fairly delineates the complex relationship without diminishing the genuine originality or denying the remarkable innovation of either writer. Never would Whitman's poetry (or prose) be mistaken for Emerson's. Both were "Beginners" and both spoke with strongly individual voices. But only Whitman can lay claim to the title of America's epic poet—as Emerson himself seems to suggest in his glowing letter thanking Whitman for the gift of *Leaves of Grass*.

4

But before turning to the "free and brave thought" of Whitman's poem, we must note still one more cultural commentator—from another land—who seemed more acutely aware than most that the nature of the American democratic experiment would shape the nature and theme of American poetry in special ways: Alexis de Tocqueville, whose *Democracy in America* appeared in 1835, with an American edition in 1838 (when Whitman was nineteen years of age). Whatever Whitman took from Ralph Waldo Emerson, and it was surely a great deal, he may well have been first inspired in his ambition as a native American poet by Alexis de Tocqueville's vision. Consider, for example, the following Tocqueville comments:
On style:

Taken as a whole, literature in democratic ages can never present, as it does in the periods of aristocracy, an aspect of order, regularity, science, and art; its form will, on the contrary, ordinarily be slighted, sometimes despised. Style will frequently be fantastic, incorrect, over-burdened, and loose,—almost always vehement and bold. Authors will aim at rapidity of execution, more than at perfection of detail. Small productions will be more common than bulky books: there will be more wit than erudition, more imagination than profundity; and literary performances will bear marks of an untutored and rude vigor of thought,—frequently of great variety and singular fecundity. The object of authors will be to astonish rather than to please, and to stir the passions more than to charm the taste.

On the past:

Democratic nations care but little for what has been, but they are haunted by visions of what will be; in this direction, their un-bounded imagination grows and dilates beyond all measure.... Democracy, which shuts the past against the poet, opens the future before him.

On the subject and theme of poetry:

Amongst a democratic people, poetry will not be fed with legends or the memorials of old traditions. The poet will not attempt to people the universe with supernatural beings, in whom his readers and his own fancy have ceased to believe; nor will he coldly per-sonify virtues and vices, which are better received under their own features. All these resources fail him; but Man remains, and the poet needs no more. The destinies of mankind—man himself, taken aloof from his country and his age, and standing in the presence of Nature and of God, with his passions, his doubts, his rare pros-perities and inconceivable wretchedness—will become the chief, if not the sole, theme of poetry amongst these nations.[36]

Alexis de Tocqueville's predictions for a democratic or American poetry, in spite of their occasional quaintness of concern, of language, of focus, are remarkably accurate when measured against the poetry that America has produced and critically acclaimed. And Tocqueville is instructive too in that he brought together in his commentary many of the literary notions hanging in the air at the time and linked them to their political and cultural contexts, pointing out connections and causes where others could only express their feelings of involvement. Whether Emerson or Whitman read him is not so important as the simple fact he saw in his book of the 1830s what they were to express in the decades following, Emerson in "The Poet" in 1844, and Whit-man in his Preface and volume of poems, *Leaves of Grass*, in 1855. In his Preface Whitman announced: "The expression of the American

poet is to be transcendent and new. It is to be indirect and not direct
or descriptive or epic. Its quality goes through these to much more.
Let the age and wars of other nations be chanted and their eras and
characters be illustrated and that finish the verse. Not so the great
psalm of the republic. Here the theme is creative and has vista."[37]

A final word:
"American Poetry"

Louis Simpson

Whatever it is, it must have
A stomach that can digest
Rubber, coal, uranium, moon, poems.

Like the shark, it contains a shoe.
It must swim for miles through the desert
Uttering cries that are almost human.[38]

Three

Come Muse migrate from Greece and Ionia,
Cross out please those immensely overpaid accounts,
That matter of Troy and Achilles' wrath, and Aeneas',
    Odysseus' wanderings,
Placard "Removed" and "To Let" on the rocks of your snowy
    Parnassus,
Repeat at Jerusalem, place the notice high on Jaffa's gate and
    on Mount Moriah,
The same on the walls of your German, French and Spanish
    castles, and Italian collections,
For know a better, fresher, busier sphere, a wide, untried
    domain awaits, demands you.

Whitman, "Song of the Exposition"

She's Here, Install'd Amid the Kitchen Ware

Walt Whitman's Epic Creation

1   When Whitman wrote in the 1855 Preface to *Leaves of Grass* that the "expression of the American poet . . . is to be indirect and not direct or descriptive or epic," he used the word *epic* in its traditional meaning of an extended narrative. In a way he provided a definition to reject: "Let the age and wars of other nations be chanted and their eras and characters be illustrated and that finish the verse." Such would not be the way of the "great psalm of the republic. Here the theme is creative and has vista" (p. 413).[1] We may see here the beginning of Whitman's move to redefine rather than reject the epic and to redefine it largely in terms of his own aims and ambitions.

   We have seen how Tocqueville based his predictions of the nature of American literature on the nature of America as a democracy and on the position and fate of the individual in a democratic state. These were, for Whitman too, the bases for reconceiving the nature of a national poem. Common to both Tocqueville and Whitman was a concern for the political nature of America and how that nature actually shaped the character and lives of individuals, in conceptions of the self, and in realizations of the self. Allied to this concern was an awareness that the substance and beliefs of older poems no longer

31

served the poet because they were simply no longer believed—the "legends or the memorials of old traditions," the universe as peopled by "supernatural beings." Because both the poet and his readers have "ceased to believe," wrote Tocqueville, the poet must turn to "the destinies of mankind—man himself . . . with his passions, his doubts, his rare prosperities and inconceivable wretchedness." The old fictions would no longer do, and the poet must set out in quest of new beliefs, new fictions—or for an epic or Supreme Fiction.

Before he wrote his poem "Notes toward a Supreme Fiction," Stevens in another poem presented an image of Whitman in quest of such a fiction (although unlabeled):

> In the far South the sun of autumn is passing
> Like Walt Whitman walking along a ruddy shore.
> He is singing and chanting the things that are part of him,
> The worlds that were and will be, death and day.
> Nothing is final, he chants. No man shall see the end.
> His beard is of fire and his staff is a leaping flame.

This is the opening stanza of "Like Decorations in a Nigger Cemetery," and a few lines later (stanza V) Stevens provides a context for his dynamic, striding Whitman:

> If ever the search for a tranquil belief should end,
> The future might stop emerging out of the past,
> Out of what is full of us; yet the search
> And the future emerging out of us seem to be one.[2]

Tocqueville had written: "But the nature of man is sufficiently disclosed for him to apprehend something of himself, and sufficiently obscure for all the rest to be plunged in thick darkness, in which he gropes forever,—and forever in vain,—to lay hold on some completer notion of his being."[3] Stevens seems perfectly attuned to this view in writing "If ever the search for a tranquil belief should end, / The future might stop emerging out of the past." For Tocqueville as for Stevens, "the tranquil belief" is never in the finding but in the search: the Supreme Fiction lies in the quest itself. It cannot be fixed; a law of its nature is that "It Must Change."[4]

"Like Walt Whitman walking along a ruddy shore." Wallace Stevens's image of Whitman is not far from the self-image projected in *Leaves of Grass:*

> I tramp a perpetual journey, (come listen all!)
> My signs are a rain-proof coat, good shoes, and a staff cut
>   from the woods,
> No friend of mine takes his ease in my chair,

> I have no chair, no church, no philosophy,
> I lead no man to a dinner-table, library, exchange,
> But each man and each woman of you I lead upon a knoll,
> My left hand hooking you round the waist,
> My right hand pointing to landscapes of continents and
>   the public road.
>
> (pp. 63–64)

These are not the words of a poet who has arrived at a destination: they are the words of a poet in the midst of his quest, one who has discovered something of the exhilarating as well as definitive nature of the quest itself. The journey is all: "If ever the search for a tranquil belief should end, / The future might stop emerging out of the past."

Almost as though in response to Tocqueville's prophecies, Whitman opened *Leaves of Grass* (in the edition that finally emerged from the intricate evolution of the poem) with an announcement of his subject as it differed from the subject of traditional epics:

> One's-self I sing, a simple separate person,
> Yet utter the word Democratic, the word En-Masse.
>
> Of physiology from top to toe I sing,
> No physiognomy alone nor brain alone is worthy for the
>   Muse, I say the Form complete is worthier far,
> The Female equally with the Male I sing.
>
> Of Life immense in passion, pulse, and power,
> Cheerful, for freest action form'd under the laws divine,
> The Modern Man I sing.
>
> (p. 5)

The signs of epic intent are writ large in this opening poem, but mingled with the epic intent is epic defiance. This is an epic poet who will break all the rules for the epic form but insist on writing an epic anyway. He invokes the Muse, but then he tells her what *he* is going to do, what is good for *her*. He will violate propriety by celebrating the body, by celebrating the "Female equally with the Male."

Whitman's book, as he finally shaped it, is an epic like no other epic that had gone before. As the book grew through various editions, it took directions that Whitman could not have foreseen. Moreover, the later growths were not merely added on, but integrated with a rearrangement of the whole. The book took on a form, undeniably, but it was a form without precedent. It had more beginning, middle, and end than a merely miscellaneous collection of lyric poems. Yet it seemed more miscellaneous and less centrally focused, less directly or conventionally autobiographical, than Wordsworth's *The Prelude* (published in 1850). It had more private scope (or confessional depth) and more public purpose than Tennyson's extended elegy, *In Memoriam* (also published in 1850). These poems were not conceived as bearing the kind of special relationship to England that *Leaves of Grass* was to bear to the United States. In short, Whitman's poem was unique.[5]

Undeniably epic, *Leaves of Grass* still did not fulfill the usual definition of the epic form. An epic has traditionally been defined as a long narrative poem, written in an elevated style, relating the exploits of a truly heroic hero, whose actions are closely bound to the destiny of his country. In "Song of the Exposition," Whitman had announced the death of that kind of epic in his invitation for the Muse to migrate to America:

> Ended for aye the epics of Asia's, Europe's helmeted war-
> riors, ended the primitive call of the muses.

The epic is dead; long live the epic. But, of course, a new epic, an epic which the migrating Muse will help create for the new men in a new land:

> I say I see, my friends, if you do not, the illustrious
> emigré, (having it is true in her day, although the
> same, changed, journey'd considerable,)
> Making directly for this rendezvous, vigorously clearing a
> path for herself, striding through the confusion,
> By thud of machinery and shrill steam-whistle undis-
> may'd,
> Bluff'd not a bit by drain-pipe, gasometers, artificial fer-
> tilizers,
> Smiling and pleas'd with palpable intent to stay,
> She's here, install'd amid the kitchen ware!

This Muse, "although the same, changed, journey'd considerable," is invoked for an epic that is the "same," but "changed" because she has "journey'd considerable" in coming to the New World. "Install'd amid the kitchen ware," she is an appropriate muse to invoke for a "personal epic," for an "instant epic," for a "disposable epic," for an "anti-epic," for a "lyric epic." The Muse, like the New World epic she inspires, has been brought down into the world of common, democratic, modern *real* reality. Whitman, by his example of *Leaves of Grass*, fleshed out a definition of this new kind of epic:

1. *Form.* The traditional epic was written to a fixed measure, with a closed structure (a completed action), in a style that was awesome, elevated, elegant. The new epic is written in a "free" form, with a loose or an open structure, in a style that is familiar, colloquial, com-

mon, or earthy. Whitman wrote in his 1855 Preface: "The poetic quality is not marshalled in rhyme or uniformity or abstract addresses to
things nor in melancholy complaints or good precepts, but is the life
of these and much else and is in the soul. . . . Who troubles himself
about his ornaments or fluency is lost. This is what you shall do: Love
the earth and sun and the animals, despise riches, give alms to every
one that asks, stand up for the stupid and crazy, devote your income
and labor to others, hate tyrants, argue not concerning God" (pp.
415–16). Whitman's comments on the English language suggest the
nature of the language of the new epic: "The English language be-
friends the grand American expression . . . it is brawny enough and
limber and full enough. . . . It is the powerful language of resistance . . . it is the dialect of common sense" (p. 426).

2. *Action*. In the traditional epic there was emphasis on exterior
achievement, great and heroic deeds by great men, with a completed
and rounded action. The new epic emphasizes interior action (meditation, rumination, contemplation), with deeds scaled down to
human dimensions, and with an open, continuing, fluid action. The
action of *Leaves of Grass* is perhaps best summed up in Whitman's
short line in "Song of Myself": "I tramp a perpetual journey, (come
listen all!)." But it is suggested metaphorically, too, in the second
poem of "Inscriptions." The poet addresses defiantly the "genius of
poets of old lands":

> I too haughty Shade also sing war, and a longer and
>   greater one than any,
> Waged in my book with varying fortune, with flight, ad-
>   vance and retreat, victory deferr'd and wavering,
> (Yet methinks certain, or as good as certain, at the last,)
>   the field the world,
> For life and death, for the Body and for the eternal Soul,
> Lo, I too am come, chanting the chant of battles,
> I above all promote brave soldiers.

3. *Character*. The hero of the traditional epic was created out of
myth, a creature of superhuman strength and physical dominance,
superior to time and place. The hero of the new epic is created out of
the poet's self, and is representatively human, sensitive, a presiding
consciousness, an embodiment of his time and place. In his 1855
Preface, Whitman wrote that the "greatest poet" is "a seer . . . he is
individual . . . he is complete in himself . . . the others are as good as
he, only he sees it and they do not" (p. 415).

4. *Setting*. In the traditional epic the setting is usually mythic, na-
tionally sacred, historically charged, and the time is a heroic past of

tribal beginnings; the emphasis on the past frames and explains the present. In the new epic the setting is here and now, the place is the locale of the poet, and the time is his time, a continuous present: the emphasis on the present frames the past and the future. In the 1855 Preface Whitman wrote: "Past and present and future are not disjoined but joined. The greatest poet forms the consistence of what is to be from what has been and is. He drags the dead out of their coffins and stands them again on their feet . . . he says to the past, Rise and walk before me that I may realize you. He learns the lesson . . . he places himself where the future becomes present" (p. 417). And again: "The direct trial of him who would be the greatest poet is today. If he does not flood himself with the immediate age as with vast oceanic tides . . . and if he does not attract his own land body and soul to himself and hang on its neck with incomparable love and plunge his semitic muscle into its merits and demerits . . . and if he be not himself the age transfigured . . . let him merge in the general run and wait his development" (pp. 424–25).

5. *Subject and theme.* The inherited myths were, in the traditional epic, accepted, justified, and there was a dependence on fate and the gods; there were acceptance and endurance and achievements of great moment involving the fate of the tribe or of the state of mankind. In the new epic, new myths (Supreme Fictions) are sought, delineated, created; there is criticism, direct or implicit, that assumes possibilities of change or transcendence, and an ideal order is sketched or implied; achievements are mental or spiritual rather than physical, and bestow insight—insight that involves the "being" and awareness of the individual, nation, or mankind. From the 1855 Preface: "The poets of the kosmos advance through all interpositions and coverings and turmoils and stratagems to first principles. They are of use . . . they dissolve poverty from its need and riches from its conceit" (p. 421). First principles: these may be equated with new myths—or, Supreme Fictions.

The personal epic (anti-epic, lyric-epic) may be defined, then: a long poem whose narrative is of an interior rather than exterior action, with emphasis on successive mental or emotional states; on a subject or theme not special or superior but common and vital; related not in a literary, measured, and elevated style but in a personal, free, and familiar style; focusing not on a heroic or semidivine individual but on the poet himself as representative figure, comprehending and illuminating the age; and whose awareness, insight, being—rather than heroic actions—involve, however obliquely, the fate of the society, the nation, the human race. Such, sketched forth in rather simple terms, was Whitman's redefinition of the epic.

2

At the heart of Whitman's redefinition and re-creation of the form of the epic and his adaptation of the form for American use is the placement of the *self* in the center. Before Whitman, Alexis de Tocqueville had observed: "In democratic communities, where men are all insignificant and very much alike, each man instantly sees all his fellows when he surveys himself. The poets of democratic ages can never, therefore, take any man in particular as the subject of a piece."[6] Later, Ralph Waldo Emerson, in "The Poet," presented a description of the ideal poet and then, turning to his own time and country, observed that no poet filled the prescription outlined. One sentence stood out, and may have attracted the attention of the young Whitman (he would have been in his twenties when "The Poet" appeared in 1844): "Dante's praise is that he dared to write his auto-biography in colossal cipher, or into universality."[7] Whether or not Whitman lingered over this sentence, it is certainly true that we may apply it to Whitman's own work, *Leaves of Grass*, a work in which he "dared to write his autobiography in colossal cipher," but in ways and forms, with revelations and confessions, that neither Emerson nor Dante ever dreamed of. Whitman suggests the nature of the "cipher" in a short "Inscriptions" poem:

> Shut not your doors to me proud libraries,
> For that which was lacking on all your well-fill'd shelves,
>   yet needed most, I bring,
> Forth from the war emerging, a book I have made,
> The words of my book nothing, the drift of it every thing,
> A book separate, not link'd with the rest nor felt by the
>   intellect,
> But you ye untold latencies will thrill to every page.
>
> (p. 13)

Later in life, as Whitman ruminated over his *Leaves* in "A Backward Glance o'er Travel'd Roads," he came to define, as we have already seen, the major impulse behind his epic work in terms close in spirit to Emerson's phrase—"autobiography in colossal cipher." In a passage that cannot be too often repeated (because of its centrality to Whitman's conception), he describes the impulse that impelled him finally to write the *Leaves*. "This was a feeling or ambition to articulate and faithfully express in literary or poetic form, and uncompromisingly, my own physical, emotional, moral, intellectual, and aesthetic Personality, in the midst of, and tallying, the momentous spirit and facts of its immediate days, and of current America—and to exploit that Personality, identified with place and date, in a far more candid and comprehensive sense than any hitherto poem or book" (p. 444). Or, again: " 'Leaves of Grass' indeed (I cannot too often reiterate) has mainly been the outcropping of my own emotional and other personal nature—an attempt, from the first to last, to put *a Person*, a human being (myself, in the latter half of the Nineteenth Century, in America,) freely, fully and truly on record" (p. 454).

Lurking in these descriptions of Whitman's *Leaves* is the heart of the definition of the new epic form he brought into being and which American poets have been exploiting and elaborating ever since. Not George Washington, not Christopher Columbus, not Daniel Boone, not even Abraham Lincoln will serve this epic poet as America's epic hero: some of these national figures will make their appearance in the book, but the hero and center must be the poet himself in this democratic epic—a "simple separate person." Whitman announced as much in "Starting from Paumanok," placed after "Inscriptions," near the beginning of his book:

> Starting from fish-shape Paumanok where I was born,
> Well-begotten, and rais'd by a perfect mother,
> After roaming many lands, lover of populous pavements,
> Dweller in Mannahatta my city, or on southern savannas,
> Or a soldier camp'd or carrying my knapsack and gun, or
>   a miner in California,
> Or rude in my home in Dakota's woods, my diet meat,
>   my drink from the spring,
> Or withdrawn to muse and meditate in some deep recess,
> Far from the clank of crowds intervals passing rapt and
>   happy,
> Aware of the fresh free giver the flowing Missouri, aware
>   of mighty Niagara,
> Aware of the buffalo herds grazing the plains, the hirsute
>   and strong-breasted bull,
> Of earth, rocks, Fifth-month flowers experienced, stars,
>   rain, snow, my amaze,
> Having studied the mocking-bird's tones and the flight of
>   the mountain-hawk,
> And heard at dawn the unrivall'd one, the hermit thrush
>   from the swamp-cedars,
> Solitary, singing in the West, I strike up for a New World.

These lines are quoted by Jorge Luis Borges, in a brief essay on Whitman, and here is the way he introduces them: "The task then had required a hero, a man looming larger than his fellows: Achilles, Ulysses, Aeneas, Beowulf, Roland, the Cid, and Sigurd stand out for our admiration. Clearly this tradition would run counter to the very essence of democracy; the new society demanded a new kind of hero. Whitman's response was an amazing one: he himself would be the hero of the poem—first, as common circumstances had made him, as an American of his time; second, as magnified by hope, by joy, by exultation, and by the proud, full sail of his great verse."[8]

We might, with the suggestions of Borges, change Emerson's sentence about Dante to read: "Whitman's praise is that he dared to write his autobiography in colossal cipher, or into universality." And in doing so, we are not far from a statement by the young Ezra Pound, written in 1909, in an essay which he agreed to preserve in the *Selected Prose* published in 1973: "Mentally I am a Walt Whitman who has learned to wear a collar and a dress shirt (although at times inimical to both). Personally I might be very glad to conceal my relationship to my spiritual father and brag about my more congenial ancestry —Dante, Shakespeare, Theocritus, Villon, but the descent is a bit difficult to establish. And, to be frank, Whitman is to my fatherland...what Dante is to Italy.... Like Dante he wrote in the 'vulgar tongue,' in a new metric. The first great man to write in the language of his people."[9]

Pound here points to still other aspects of the epic form as Whitman adapted it to his own time and place. All these elements, however, flow naturally from the fundamental decision to make the self the center, and the life (or autobiography) and times the substance of the poem. As the traditional epic hero could not survive the transfiguration of the form for use in a democratic society, so the elevated style with the use of a special literary language would need to be modified, leavened. Whitman's form and language were meant to reflect the new epic conception: the free verse breaking away from the dead hand of past measures and forms, and the language itself leaving behind the musty odor of the libraries and giving off instead the odors of the open air, the woods and the streets, the land and the ocean. Whitman's conception of language was basically democratic, as he revealed in a little essay, "Slang in America": "Language, be it remember'd, is not an abstract construction of the learn'd, or of dictionary makers, but is something arising out of the work, needs, ties, joys, affections, tastes, of long generations of humanity, and has its bases broad and low, close to the ground. Its final decisions are made by the masses, people nearest the concrete, having most to do with actual land and sea.... Slang, profoundly consider'd, is the lawless germinal element, below all words and sentences, and behind all poetry, and proves a certain perennial rankness and protestantism in speech.... Considering language then as some mighty potentate,

into the majestic audience-hall of the monarch ever enters a person-
age like one of Shakespeare's clowns, and takes position there, and
plays a part even in the stateliest ceremonies."[10] And Whitman's
theory flowed into his practice: "Having pried through the strata,
analyzed to a hair, counsel'd with doctors and calculated close, / I find
no sweeter fat than sticks to my own bones" (p. 38); "Who goes
there? hankering, gross, mystical, nude; / How is it I extract strength
from the beef I eat?" (p. 38); "I sound my barbaric yawp over the roofs
of the world" (p. 68); "Limitless limpid jets of love hot and enormous,
quivering jelly of love, white-blow and delirious juice" (p. 73); "Hips,
hip sockets, hip-strength, inward and outward round, man-balls,
man-root" (p. 76).

In deciding to write his "physical, emotional, moral, intellectual,
and aesthetic"—that is, spiritual—autobiography, at the same time
"tallying the momentous spirit and facts of its immediate days, and of
current America," Whitman was committing himself to an open
form—a form that would evolve with his life, and reflect the shape of
that life. When Whitman began to write *Leaves of Grass*, he could not
have known that the Civil War would form the subject of the great
heart and center of the book, or that the assassination of Lincoln
would inspire some of the work's most moving lines. Thus the *Leaves*
remained open to whatever experience came into Whitman's field of
vision and touched his feelings, and grew organically to fill the shape
of the experience and the biography.

3

We may let Pound's and Borges's testimony stand as two
important responses to the epic nature of *Leaves of Grass*. The epic
dimension of the poem may be detected by the reader willing to give
the time to a study of the poem's structure. Before turning to the
structure, however, we must first glance briefly at the evolution of
Leaves of Grass, particularly inasmuch as some critics have declared
the poem in its best and definitive form to be, not the poem that
Whitman left at his death, but the poem in one of its earlier versions.

The dates of the several editions of *Leaves of Grass* march across the
latter half of the nineteenth century with astonishing regularity and
frequency: 1855, 1856, 1860, 1867, 1871–72, 1876, 1881, 1889, 1891–92.
Although new type was not set up for all these "editions," each one
had a shape and life of its own that deserves attention from anyone
studying the evolution of the poem. But some critics have settled on

an edition other than the last as the "true" *Leaves of Grass*. Roy Harvey Pearce gave his critical seal of approval to the third (1860) edition, primarily, he said, because it contained less of the "prophetic poet" and more of the "humane poet."[11] Malcolm Cowley chose to stick with the first (1855) edition, basically because it contained the "purest text" for "Song of Myself," which, according to him, is one of the "great inspired (and sometimes insane) prophetic works...in the western world."[12]

While both Pearce and Cowley make out a case for their choices, and do succeed in demonstrating the critical value of looking at Whitman's early editions, they also cut themselves off from some of Whitman's greatest and most interesting poetry, as in "Drum-Taps," "When Lilacs Last in the Dooryard Bloom'd," "Passage to India." They moreover fly in the face of Whitman's own last will and testament for his book, printed as a part of that last or Deathbed Edition of 1891–92: "As there are now several editions of L. of G., different texts and dates, I wish to say that I prefer and recommend this present one, complete, for future printing" (p. 1).

But of course, we might pick up Whitman's later poems individually, and read them outside their context in later editions of *Leaves of Grass*; and we might reject Whitman's testament as simply another unreliable comment by the naive poet on his work. There is, I think, a sounder reason for settling on the Deathbed Edition as the genuine *Leaves of Grass*: only in the last edition does Whitman's full major contribution to poetry and poetic form become clear, and his unique achievement stand revealed. He shaped the book to his life, the entirety of his life; to cut off the book at an early date is in a sense to cut off the life. And in so shaping the book he created a new poetic form—an open form that would follow wherever the accidents and vagaries of a life, the poet's life, might lead, encompassing whatever the poet's time and place might bring.

The life shaped the book; the book shaped the life. The interaction of the two would be difficult to disentangle. Suffice it to say that if we were persuaded to stay with the first or third or any other early edition of *Leaves of Grass*, we would be ignorant of the poem in its completeness, of what Whitman (in "A Backward Glance") called his "definitive *carte visite* to the coming generations of the New World" (p. 443). The form of *Leaves of Grass* as a personal or lyric epic is the form it assumed, finally, at the end of the poet's life, in that Deathbed Edition. To ignore that form is to ignore the form that Whitman imaginatively forged and generously bequeathed to succeeding generations of American poets—poets who have taken over the form, adopting and adapting as they have discovered their own poetic styles.

4

The three major groupings in *Leaves of Grass* are without sharp division but represent a clear shift in focus. The opening cluster of "Inscriptions" and the poem "Starting from Paumanok" are pro- grammatic, invoke the muse, describe the new form of poetry, and announce the themes that are to recur throughout the book. The first major movement of *Leaves of Grass* begins appropriately with "Song of Myself," a poem of identity more physical than spiritual, and con- tinues through "Children of Adam," "Calamus," the song section, and the seemingly miscellaneous clusters through "By the Roadside." "Drum-Taps" launches the second major movement, as the poem moves into specific historical events, the here and now of Whitman's nineteenth-century America—the tragic civil war and the assas- sination of Abraham Lincoln. This movement continues through "Memories of President Lincoln," "By Blue Ontario's Shore," and "Autumn Rivulets," providing the poet with a firm historical context and identity. But in this last cluster, the historical becomes more and more miscellaneous and fades in the next poem, "Proud Music of the Storm." Here the third major movement of *Leaves* begins, running through "Passage to India," "The Sleepers," "Whispers of Heavenly Death," and focusing on an identity more spiritual than physical in "poems bridging the way from Life to Death" (a line from the intro- ductory poem, "Proud Music of the Storm"). The last two clusters of the book, "From Noon to Starry Night" and "Songs of Parting," are poems of farewell that constitute a reprise that recalls—balances—the book's opening poems of welcome and introduction.

The three-part structure of *Leaves of Grass* may be roughly equated with the three identities explored by the poet—physical, historical, spiritual; his birth, life, death; his consciousness, involvement, dis- solution; beginning, middle, end. Although this structure might suggest Dante's three-part structure (Inferno, Purgatory, Paradise) of the *Divina Commedia*, Whitman's poem is a *Democratica Commedia*, with three parts unique and individual. But of course there are no sharp divisions between these parts, no "pure" sections uncontami- nated by secondary themes. Indeed, the physical inspires the spiritual, and the spiritual evokes the physical, as the historical lurks seen or unseen at every turn. And also at every turn, Whitman's concern for identity is something more than a uniquely personal concern: he is his own paradigm for mankind—for the reader, for you. "And what I assume you shall assume, / For every atom belonging to me as good belongs to you" (p. 25). The reader assumes a major role in *Leaves* as he is invited into an intimate relation with the poet, to accompany him on the journey: "O hand in hand—O wholesome pleasure—O one more desirer and lover!" (p. 24).

Throughout *Leaves of Grass* the central tension is played between the lyric (private) and epic (public) roles the poet has assigned himself. This tension was implicit in Whitman's first creative impulses (as he recalled them in "A Backward Glance"). He wanted to "express . . . his own physical, emotional, moral, intellectual, and aesthetic Personality," but—"in the midst of, and tallying, the momentous spirit and facts of its immediate days, and of current America" (p. 444). That word "tallying" is a Whitman favorite for describing the poetic function, and it comes closer in meaning to *embodying* or *comprehending* than to merely *listing* or *enumerating*: it lies closer to the public than to the private role of the poet. In his 1855 Preface, Whitman described the poet's double role: "The land and sea, the animals fishes and birds, the sky of heaven and the orbs, the forests mountains and rivers, are not small themes . . . but folks expect of the poet to indicate more than the beauty and dignity which always attach to dumb real objects . . . they expect him to indicate the path between reality and their souls" (p. 415). From its origin to its end, Whitman meant for *Leaves of Grass* to serve what he conceived to be the epic (or lyric-epic) function. In the first major movement of the book, beginning with "Song of Myself," the lyric voice dominates, but the poet keeps prodding himself, reminding himself of his epic role. In the second major movement, especially in "Drum-Taps," the epic voice becomes loud and even strident, but the lyric or private voice quietly intrudes. In the third major movement, in the poems clustering around "Passage to India," both the personal and public intensities appear diminished, at times inert, at times intractable, unassimilable.

Of the poems in the first part of *Leaves*, "Out of the Cradle Endlessly Rocking" is perhaps the most personal or private or lyric. The reader feels astonishingly close to the poet's key emotional experience but held back from it too by the dramatic symbolism of the mockingbirds, which both obscures and shields the personal origins of the poem. Of the other well-known poems of this section of *Leaves of Grass*, "Crossing Brooklyn Ferry" is perhaps the most philosophical, public, or epic (pointing the path for the "folks" "between reality . . . and their souls"). Both of these justly admired poems have lyric and epic voices, but in "Out of the Cradle" the poet emphasizes his unique and individual role (the searing experience that turned him into the poet of love and death), while in "Crossing Brooklyn Ferry" Whitman emphasizes his representative and public role (focusing on a common experience that mystically unites all mankind). It would be interesting in another context to look intensively at "Song of Myself," "Children of Adam," and "Calamus" in the light of the private-public tensions I have been describing. But we can note here only in passing that these three vital parts of *Leaves* have remarkably vivid sexual content—auto-, hetero-, and homo-erotic—and this content with its compelling imagery and personal reference thrusts the poems in the direction of the personal. But the poet determinedly injects the public or epic in these poems, moving the auto-erotic into the programmatically mystical, the hetero-erotic into the programmatically procreational, and the homo-erotic into the programmatically fraternal and democratic. It has often been observed that in the balanced clusters "Children of Adam" and "Calamus" Whitman's public voice seems to dominate the first, while his personal voice seems compulsively to dominate the second—perhaps contrary to the poet's own plans. However that may be, it is certainly true that "Calamus" appears strongly confessional:

> Here the frailest leaves of me and yet my strongest
> lasting,
> Here I shade and hide my thoughts, I myself do not ex-
> pose them,
> And yet they expose me more than all my other poems.
>
> (p. 95)

But at the same time, the poet seems to celebrate these painfully personal emotions as they—along with other varieties of sexuality and love—are diffused and generalized in the social fabric:

> The dear love of man for his comrade, the attraction of
> friend to friend,
> Of the well-married husband and wife, of children and
> parents,
> Of city for city and land for land.
>
> (p. 89)

In the second major movement of *Leaves of Grass*, Whitman's public voice moves clearly to the foreground. At the beginning of "Drum-Taps," the poet seems bent on becoming the national spokesman for the Union's cause, sounding the call to arms—"Mannahatta a-march

—and it's O to sing it well! / It's O for a manly life in the camp" (p. 202). Had Whitman maintained this strident tone throughout "Drum-Taps," the poems would no doubt have long since been forgotten. But almost as though in spite of the poet's purposes, the personal voice gradually begins to modulate the tone, and stridency gives way to sober sadness and a personal sense of loss, culminating in the remarkably personal and Calamus-like poem, "Vigil Strange I Kept on the Field One Night." "Drum-Taps" remains a public statement on events of great national moment, but the poems derive their quality and interest from the tension one feels, in reading them, between the public pronouncement and the private sorrow. A similar tension runs through the major poems of "Memories of President Lincoln"—but not in that most recited of Whitman's poems, "O Captain! My Captain!" The unalleviated public role of the poet renders the poem mere empty declamation for most modern readers. But "When Lilacs Last in the Dooryard Bloom'd" succeeds admirably where "Captain!" fails—in dramatizing that tension between the public and private voices. "Lilacs" is an elegy written on the occasion of a tragic national event—the assassination of Abraham Lincoln—but it is remarkable for its quality of personal feeling. Here Whitman places his most persuasive lyric voice in service of one of his most moving public (or epic) themes: he mourns the terrible loss of a great national leader (whom he had never met) with the feelings of one mourning the death of a deeply loved camerado.

With "Proud Music of the Storm" and the turn to poems "bridging the way from Life to Death," the public and private voices of the poet seem to intermingle in ways that decrease or dissipate the tensions felt in the earlier parts of *Leaves of Grass*. Such poems as "Prayer of Columbus," "To Think of Time," and the "Whispers of Heavenly Death" cluster seem to have some personal dimensions but appear in the main to be public statements, remote from the poet's intensest feelings. "The Sleepers," on the other hand (an early poem adapted for placement in this last section of *Leaves*), appears filled with a personal, almost private symbolism (not unlike "Out of the Cradle Endlessly Rocking") that is given a public dimension—in part by its very placement in this section of the *Leaves*. But the centerpiece in this part of *Leaves of Grass* is "Passage to India," a poem that juxtaposes (rather than blends) public and private emotions and experiences in fascinating and provocative ways. The poem takes its point of departure from the three great engineering achievements of the mid-nineteenth century—the Suez Canal, the transcontinental railroad, the transatlantic cable—and much of the poem is given over to sweeping views of mythic and actual history, with a call to a spiritual achievement to match the material. But underneath this public role there appears a private voice filled with an almost inexplicable (and unassimilated) intensity, which sweeps to the fore and takes over in section 8, in such lines as "Swiftly I shrivel at the thought of God, /At Nature and its wonders, Time and Space and Death," concluding with the spiritually transfigured "Calamus" emotion—"As filled with friendship, love complete, the Elder Brother found, / The Younger melts in fondness in his arms." With all its intensity, the poem for many falls flat—perhaps because Whitman has not succeeded in combining the public and personal dimensions in a single developing and convincing tension.

In this last major section of *Leaves of Grass*, Whitman introduces the national figure who had been thought by some previous poets to be the key to the American epic: Christopher Columbus. He appears first in "Passage to India," as Whitman briefly evokes the "world of 1492": "As the chief histrion, / Down to the footlights walks in some great scena." Within a few lines, Whitman traces Columbus's career, with emphasis on his "reward" as a "prisoner, chain'd," and his final days of "dejection, poverty, death." This is the Columbus of "Prayer of Columbus"—"a batter'd, wreck'd old man," living out his last days in misery full of uncertainties—

> I know not even my own work past or present,
> Dim ever-shifting guesses of it spread before me,
> Of newer better worlds, their mighty parturition,
> Mocking, perplexing me.
>
> (p. 296)

Columbus plays only a minor role in Whitman's epic, and many readers hardly remember his presence. Other national heroes or leaders make brief appearances—as Washington in his farewell to his troops in a vignette embedded in the middle of "The Sleepers"—but the individual most vividly remembered by readers is Abraham Lincoln in "Memories of President Lincoln" and especially in "When Lilacs Last in the Dooryard Bloom'd." Lincoln is evoked as the "powerful western fallen star," now "disappear'd" in the "netherward black of the night." But even Lincoln does not achieve the status of epic hero in Whitman's poem. He plays his role as it touches the country's and Whitman's life, and then Whitman himself resumes his own central and epic role.

5

Whitman's *Leaves of Grass* is a great song of affirmation of life. It is not, as has been commonly assumed by those who have read hurriedly, an unexamined and cheap affirmation of a realized American democracy. Indeed, Whitman attempted to sketch in his book the ideal that his country had not yet achieved. His opening lines—

> One's-self I sing, a simple separate person,
> Yet utter the word Democratic, the word En-Masse.
>
> (p. 5)

—offer the challenge: the challenge of a state that is fundamentally democratic yet allows for the individuality and radical self-hood of the "separate person." Whitman celebrates these idealized elements, self-hood and the "En-Masse." That he realized the strength of the forces that run counter to his idealized conceptions is evident from the very beginning of *Leaves of Grass*, in, for example, some of the lines of "Inscriptions":

> Shut not your doors to me proud libraries,
> For that which was lacking on all your well-fill'd shelves,
>   I bring.
>
> (p. 13)

Whitman knew that his book would shock the forces of "respectability" in the land, as he knew too that the ideals he celebrated would require resistance, disobedience:

> To the States or any one of them, or any city of the States,
>   *Resist much, obey little,*
> Once unquestioning obedience, once fully enslaved,
> Once fully enslaved, no nation, state, city of this earth,
>   ever afterward resumes its liberty.
>
> (p. 11)

(It is significant, perhaps, that this is one of the three Whitman poems Ezra Pound chose to publish in his anthology of lyric poetry, *Confucius to Cummings* [the other two are equally programmatic or epic— "I Sing the Body Electric" and "The Centenarian's Story"]).[13]

It is, nevertheless, true that Whitman's most severe denunciations of his time and country are to be found in his prose pieces—prose pieces that frequently were published as integral parts of his epic work, *Leaves of Grass*. The 1855 Preface and the 1856 Letter to Emerson demonstrate clearly that Whitman early understood that America did not fulfill the ideal he envisioned. In the Letter to Emerson (published at the end of the 1856 edition of *Leaves*), for example, Whitman wrote:

> To creeds, literature, art, the army, the navy, the executive, life is hardly proposed, but the sick and dying are proposed to cure the sick and dying. The churches are one vast lie; the people do not believe them, and they do not believe themselves . . . . the spectacle

is a pitiful one. I think there can never be again upon the festive earth more bad-disordered persons deliberately taking seats, as of late in These States, at the heads of the public tables—such corpses' eyes for judges—such a rascal and thief in the Presidency.[14]

In a curious way, it must be admitted that what Whitman saw in his own place and time did inspire his poetry; his disillusionment and indignation with the reality spurred him on to sketch, in his poetry, the ideal and the possibilities of its realization.

Invariably Whitman's prose denunciations of the degradations of democracy and individuality are accompanied by belief in the need for great poets—great epic poets—who by their inspired expressions of personalism and idealism will bring change and transfiguration. His most extended and brilliant statement on these themes is *Democratic Vistas* (1871), where he said bluntly: "The depravity of the business classes of our country is not less than has been supposed, but infinitely greater. The official services of America, national, state, and municipal, in all their branches and departments, except the judiciary, are saturated in corruption, bribery, falsehood, maladministration; and the judiciary is tainted" (p. 461). But all this depravity is but clear demonstration of the greater need for poets (like Whitman) and poems of persuasive impact (like *Leaves*):

> I fain confront the fact, the need of powerful native philosophs and orators and bards, these States, as rallying points to come, in times of danger, and to fend off ruin and defection. For history is long, long, long. Shift and turn the combinations of the statement as we may, the problem of the future of America is in certain respects as dark as it is vast. Pride, competition, segregation, vicious wilfulness, and licence beyond example, brood already upon us. Unwieldy and immense, who shall hold in behemoth? Who bridle leviathan? Flaunt it as we choose, athwart and over the roads of our progress loom huge uncertainty, and dreadful, threatening gloom. It is useless to deny it: Democracy grows rankly up the thickest, noxious, deadliest plants and fruits of all—brings worse and worse invaders—needs newer, larger, stronger, keener compensations and compellers. (p. 498)

Democracy grows rankly up the thickest, noxious, deadliest plants and fruits of all—Walt Whitman! This line could be placed above the writing desks of all the "native philosophs and orators and bards" to come, as the enigmatic and paradoxical challenge that Whitman threw out to America's future, to "Bards of the great Idea": come forth for your country's sake with the "newer, larger, stronger, keener compensations and compellers."

But Whitman had always known that democracy was constantly

under attack, durable in idea but fragile in the reality. He had tried to be one of the "Bards of the great Idea." In an "Inscriptions" poem at the beginning of his book, "To Thee Old Cause"—the Cause clearly democracy—Whitman wrote:

> Thou orb of many orbs!
> Thou seething principle! thou well-kept, latent germ! thou
>   centre.
> Around the idea of thee the war revolving,
> With all its angry and vehement play of causes,
> (With vast results to come for thrice a thousand years,)
> These recitatives for thee,—my book and the war are one,
> Merged in its spirit I and mine, as the contest hinged on
>   thee,
> As a wheel on its axis turns, this book unwitting to itself,
> Around the idea of thee.
>
> (p. 7)

The Old Cause—democracy—was thus at the inspirational heart in the creation of the new literary form for the New World—the lyric or personal epic, that literary form which succeeding generations of American poets would elaborate and adapt, shape and reshape, in their own attempts to create a Supreme Fiction, "a great psalm of the republic," a distinctively American epic.

A final word:
from
"Lines Written near San Francisco"

Louis Simpson

> Every night at the end of America
> We taste our wine, looking at the Pacific.
> How sad it is, the end of America!
>
> While we were waiting for the land
> They'd finished it—with gas drums
> On the hilltops, cheap housing in the valleys
>
> Where lives are mean and wretched.
> But the banks thrive and the realtors
> Rejoice—they have their America.
>
> Still, there is something unsettled in the air.
> Out there on the Pacific
> There's no America but the Marines.
>
> Whitman was wrong about the People,
> But right about himself. The land is within.
> At the end of the open road we come to ourselves. [15]

Four

There will soon be no more priests. Their work is done.
They may wait awhile...perhaps a generation or two...
dropping off by degrees. A superior breed shall take their
place...the gangs of kosmos and prophets en masse shall
take their place...Through the divinity of themselves shall
the kosmos and the new breed of poets be interpreters of men
and women and of all events and things. They shall find
their inspiration in real objects today, symptoms of the past
and future.

Whitman, 1855 Preface

There is, in fact, a world of poetry indistinguishable from the
world in which we live, or, I ought to say, no doubt, from the
world in which we shall come to live, since what makes the
poet the potent figure that he is, or was, or ought to be,
is that he creates the world to which we turn incessantly and
without knowing it and that he gives to life *the supreme fiction*
without which we are unable to conceive of it.

Stevens, "The Noble Rider and the Sound of Words"

Wallace Stevens's "Notes toward a Supreme Fiction"

If we were to reverse the order of the nineteenth and twentieth centuries, we would want to rewrite our literary histories to show that Whitman was fundamentally shaped by Wallace Stevens, and that one of the key poems in the shaping was "Notes toward a Supreme Fiction"—not an epic but, as the title indicates, suggestions and ideas for the writing of one.[1] Moreover, we might speculate that Whitman had read Stevens's words in *The Necessary Angel* and had modeled himself so as to fulfill the prophecy: "The poet who writes the heroic poem that will satisfy all there is of us and all of us in time to come, will accomplish it by the power of his reason, the force of his imagination and, in addition, the effortless and inescapable process of his own individuality."[2] And we might even conjecture that Stevens foresaw Whitman's advent and included him in a poem as an embodiment of his ideas—"Like Decorations in a Nigger Cemetery." In that poem, introduced with a vivid image of Whitman "singing and chanting," Stevens wrote: "If ever the search for a tranquil belief should end, / The future might stop emerging out of the past." Whitman in the Stevens poem is on that search, as he was through all the editions of *Leaves of Grass*. Stevens throughout his work was on the same quest. His second "rule" in "Notes toward a Supreme Fiction" is, after all: "It Must Change" (*CP*, p. 389).[3] The quest can never end, or can only end with life itself. One Stevens critic, Joseph Riddell, has likened the whole of Stevens's work to Whitman's epic: "Like Whitman's *Leaves of Grass*, but in a modern, non-transcendental context, Stevens' canon becomes something else again than a collection of separate poems, and his development something other than casual changes of style."[4] Another Stevens critic, Harold Bloom, has claimed that " 'Notes toward a Supreme Fiction' can be termed the *Song of Myself* of our time."[5]

Like Pound and Williams, Stevens had ambivalent feelings about Whitman. In 1955 he was invited to contribute to a symposium on Whitman in the *Hudson Review* commemorating the centenary of *Leaves of Grass*. His answer is, as we might expect, full of surprises. He did not have time to write an essay, but his short letter provides the ideas for one never written. He begins with what looks like a compliment: "The poems in which he collects large numbers of concrete things, particularly things each of which is poetic in itself or as part of the collection, have a validity which, for many people, must be enough and must seem to them all opulence and elan" (*L*, pp. 870–71).[6] But then he took it back: "For others, I imagine that what was once opulent begins to look a little threadbare and the collections seem substitutes for opulence even though they remain gatherings-together of precious Americana, certain to remain precious but not certain to remain poetry. The typical elan survives in many things" (*L*, p. 871). Stevens then added enigmatically: "It seems to me, then, that Whitman is disintegrating as the world, of which he made himself a part, disintegrates. *Crossing Brooklyn Ferry* exhibits this disintegration" (*L*, p. 871). In that poem Whitman had written: "The simple, compact, well-join'd scheme, myself disintegrated, every one disintegrated yet part of the scheme." Surely Stevens had some such notion of "disintegration" as this—which leads into the fusing and merging and unification that is the essence of "Crossing Brooklyn Ferry."

But perhaps the most interesting opinion expressed by Stevens is hidden in the poems he chose to name next: "The elan of the essential Whitman is still deeply moving in the things in which he was himself deeply moved. These would have to be picked out from compilations like *Song of the Broad-Axe, Song of the Exposition*" (*L*, p. 871). But whoever reads those poems—except Wallace Stevens on a long Sunday afternoon browsing through the whole of *Leaves of Grass*? Well, what parts of these poems would Stevens have picked out for exhibit, had he ever written his essay? The poems are side by side in the song section of *Leaves of Grass*. "Song of the Broad-Axe" begins with a single symbolic object and projects an entire mythos of America, primarily in imagistic terms of construction and making—the work of ordinary (but really extraordinary) human beings, not very different, really, in method or procedure from Stevens's method in "The Man with the Blue Guitar," with all its themes and variations. "Song of the Exposition," an occasional poem read at an industrial exposition, projects an industrial or technological mythos of America (not "merely for products gross or lucre," but for the "soul in thee, electric, spiritual!" [p. 150]),[7] and includes that celebrated invitation to the Old World muse to migrate to America and to install herself by "thud of machinery and shrill steam-whistle," "by drain-pipe, gasometers, artificial fertilizers," "amid the kitchen ware" (p. 144): a serious poem that is filled with the kind of imagistic and linguistic wit not unlike Stevens's own in "Notes toward a Supreme Fiction"— which might, indeed, have included, had it grown longer, a stanza on the Whitman-christened "illustrious emigré." Both poets had a penchant for the use of foreign languages, especially French; and although Stevens clearly knew more French than Whitman did, the effect at times isn't appreciably different in the two poetries.

1

Before turning to "Notes toward a Supreme Fiction," a word of explanation: I am fully aware that in distilling a recipe for an epic, or personal epic, from Stevens's poem, I am going beyond mere interpretation, beyond the intentions of Stevens himself. My main purpose is to explore areas in which Stevens's notions about poetry in some way parallel Whitman's. In the main, these notions have to do not just with the epic but with poetry of whatever kind. But Stevens through the suggestiveness of his title invites the kind of imaginative extensions I attempt with his notions. I accept his invitation to use his "notes" as the basis for elaborating themes and variations which he never follows through himself. Such a way of reading I assume to be well within the spirit of his theory of the interaction of imagination and reality—in this case the imagination of the reader as it is inspired by, yet anchored in, the reality of the poem.

Rule one of "Notes toward a Supreme Fiction": "It Must Be Abstract." Indeed? But American poetry had been struggling from the beginning of the century to rid itself of the old meaningless abstractions—honor, beauty, fate. Shouldn't it be the other way (as

Pound and others had long said): "It must be concrete"? But of course Stevens is not saying that the poet must choose between two kinds of languages, one concrete, the other abstract; he is saying, à la Wittgenstein, that the poet must choose language, which is by its very nature *abstract*, an abstracting from life, an inventing of life, not life itself. Stevens put it this way in his 1942 essay, "The Noble Rider and the Sound of Words": the measure of a poet "is the measure of his power to abstract himself, and to withdraw with him into his abstraction the reality on which the lovers of truth insist. He must be able to abstract himself and also to abstract reality, which he does by placing it in his imagination."[8] This ability to abstract reality is basic for the poet. And thus at the beginning of his poem, Stevens sends "ephebe," beginning poet, to the world itself—or reality—for a beginning: "You must become an ignorant man again / And see the sun again with an ignorant eye." Why? Because all the gods are dead— "Phoebus is dead, ephebe." And moreover, "Phoebus was / A name for something that never could be named." Whitman (in "Song of the Exposition") had put it this way, more crudely, but still, rather wittily, in his wooing of the muse: "Placard 'Removed' and 'To Let' on the rocks of your snowy Parnassus" (p. 142).

Stevens's call throughout the opening of "Notes toward a Supreme Fiction" for ephebe to abandon the past mythologies for the reality itself, is reminiscent of Whitman's declaration in "A Backward Glance o'er Travel'd Roads": "Without stopping to qualify the averment, the Old World has had the poems of myths, fictions, feudalism, conquest, caste, dynastic wars, and splendid exceptional characters and affairs, which have been great; *but the New World needs the poems of realities* and science and of the democratic average and basic equality, which shall be greater" (p. 449; italics mine). Whitman's phrase— "poems of realities"—might well apply to the motivating impulse in Stevens's entire poem, which could have been entitled "Notes toward the Imaginative Creation of Poems of Realities." Stevens has in mind that ephebe must establish (in Emersonian terms) an "original relation with the universe";[9] and ephebe must understand (in Whitman's admonition) that poems (or Supreme Fictions) "distilled from other poems will probably pass away" (p. 426).

In stanza II, Stevens tells us: "It is the celestial ennui of apartments / That sends us back to the first idea, / the quick of this invention." Whitman felt the "ennui" of those apartments at the beginning of "Song of Myself": "Houses and rooms are full of perfumes, the shelves are crowded with perfumes"; and he went "to the bank by the wood" to "become undisguised and naked," in order to "permit to speak at every hazard / Nature without check with original energy." Out in the sun, with clothes off—but alone, breathing only the "odorless" atmosphere, Whitman pursued that "first idea."

Stanza III: "The poem refreshes life so that we share, / For a moment, the first idea." Whitman said: "For every atom belonging to me as good belongs to you." And further: "Stop this day and night with me and you shall possess the origin of all poems" (pp. 25–26), the "first idea" surely. Stevens again: "An elixir, an excitation, a pure power, / The poem, through candor, brings back a power again / That gives a candid kind to everything." Whitman's candor shocked his age (but excited too): "Welcome is every organ and attribute of me, and of any man hearty and clean, / Not an inch nor a particle of an inch is vile, and none shall be less familiar than the rest" (p. 27). In stanza IV, Stevens gets to the heart of the matter: "There was a myth before the myth began, / Venerable and articulate and complete. / From this the poem springs." Whitman (and Emerson before him) would recognize the lineage here, and would approve.

In stanza V Stevens turns to the animals and observes how they have their own, not a secondary, relationship to their universe, their environment. "The lion roars at the enraging desert," "The elephant / Breaches the darkness of Ceylon with blares," "The bear . . . snarls in his mountain / At summer thunder and sleeps through winter snow." Only ephebe writhes, clutching "the corner / Of the pillow," pressing "bitter utterance from" his "writing, dumb, / Yet voluble dumb violence." Ephebe has been bred "against the first idea," but the animals create their sounds in direct response to it; they experience it bare, through nobody's senses but their own. Whitman said, "I think I could turn and live with animals, they are so placid and self-contain'd." By saying what the animals do *not* do, Whitman appears to image forth Stevens's ephebe: "They do not sweat and whine about their condition, / They do not lie awake in the dark and weep for their sins," "They do not make me sick discussing their duty to God" (p. 47). After all, the gods are dead; when one died, they all died. Whitman, Stevens, and the animals, unlike poor witless ephebe, live in harmony with, in response to, "the first idea," without intermediaries, without obstructing myths.

In the concluding stanzas of "It Must Be Abstract," stanzas VI–X, Stevens begins to develop the idea of "major man," whom we may for the moment conceive as the epic hero for this epic recipe. Abstraction alone is not enough, but (stanza VI) "An abstraction blooded, as a man by thought." In stanza VII, we learn that "The truth depends on a walk around the lake, / A composing as the body tires, a stop / To see hepatica," "a rest / in the swags of pine-trees bordering the lake." And what happens? The mystic, the intuitive moment comes, a time of "inherent excellence," not "balances / That we achieve but balances that happen." Stevens is tentative in his assertion of the nature of this phenomenon: "Perhaps there are moments of awakening, / Extreme, fortuitous, personal, in which / We more than awaken, sit on the edge of sleep, / As on an elevation, and behold / The academies like structures in a mist." *Perhaps*. As many critics have asserted, Stevens differed from Whitman markedly in this: he was not transcendental. Therefore, he could not believe in, portray, the mystic vision. Then what is this curious *awakening*, those strange "academies like structures in a mist"? Are they *merely* a psychological phenomenon? But "truth depends" on them. And what is truth but the "supreme fiction"? That vision of "academies like structures in a mist": are they the familiar institutions, perceived in a new meaning, a new complexity, a new imaginative apprehension, a new truth? Or are they the conventional academies, here perceived surrounded by the fog generated by their own pedantic intellectualism—the kind of fog Whitman must have meant by his "talkers" and the "trippers and askers" (pp. 26, 27)? In any case, there is vision, transcendental or no, in Stevens's epic recipe.

Stevens next asks (stanza VIII): "Can we compose a castle-fortress-home, / Even with the help of Viollet-le-Duc, / And set the MacCullough there as major man?" (Viollet-le-Duc, refurbisher of the noble monuments of Europe.) Stevens has written: "The gist of this poem is that the MacCullough is MacCullough: MacCullough is any name, any man. The trouble with humanism is that man as God remains man, but there is an extension of man, the leaner being, in fiction, a possibly more than human human, a composite human. The act of recognizing him is the act of this leaner being moving in on us" (*L*, p. 434). The answer to Stevens's poetic question is no. MacCullough taken from his environment and placed in a castle in the midst of the monumental would not thus be transfigured into the grand epic hero. But MacCullough himself, "lounging by the sea, / He might take habit, whether from wave or phrase, / Or power of the wave, or deepened speech, / Or a leaner being, move in on him, / Of greater aptitude and apprehension." The result then, even with a MacCullough, is deeper insight, epic vision: "As if the waves at last were never broken, / As if the language suddenly, with ease, / Said things it had laboriously spoken."

MacCullough, "any man," every man, an epic hero. Stanza IX:

"The romantic intoning, the declaimed clairvoyance / Are parts of apotheosis, appropriate / And of its nature, the idiom thereof." This "declaimed clairvoyance" differs from "reason's click-clack, its applied / Enflashings." "Major man" does not have his origin in "apotheosis," but he comes "Compact in invincible foils, from reason, / Lighted at midnight by the studious eye, / Swaddled in revery, the object of / The hum of thoughts evaded in the mind, / Hidden from other thoughts, he that reposes / On a breast forever precious for that touch." This creature, not of reason but of reason and revery—imagination—may be the proper subject of a modern epic. Stevens addresses his muse with a Whitmanian epithet: "My dame, sing for this person accurate songs." He is a "foundling of the infected past" (infected, perhaps, by false notions of myth and the heroic, thus dismissing or disowning an ordinary man like MacCullough), and "The hot of him is purest in the heart."

Stevens's MacCullough could be named Walt Whitman, "lounging by the sea," letting the language say things "it had laboriously spoken"—in "Out of the Cradle Endlessly Rocking." Or to shift to the poem Stevens admired (at least in part), "Song of the Broad-Axe," Whitman presents an everyman, an ordinary man, as major man: "How beggarly appear arguments before a defiant deed! / How the floridness of the materials of cities shrivels before a man's or woman's look!" Clearly Whitman's epic hero of the saga of the broad-axe is the handler of the axe himself, not the occupant of the mansion or castle built by him. When the "leaner being" moves in "on him," then everything is changed: "All waits or goes by default till a strong being appears; / A strong being is the proof of the race and of the ability of the universe, / When he or she appears materials are overaw'd / The dispute on the soul stops, / The old customs and phrases are confronted, turn'd back, or laid away" (p. 139). Stevens put it this way (stanza X): "The major abstraction is the idea of man / And major man is its exponent, abler / In the abstract than in his singular." Though he plays "an heroic part," he is "of the commonal. / The major abstraction is the commonal." Ephebe, then, must begin with the reality of the "one, in his old coat, / His slouching pantaloons, beyond the town, / Looking for what was, where it used to be." Out of such a one, ephebe must "confect / The final elegance, not to console / Nor sanctify, but plainly to propound." From slouching pantaloons to elegance? He may be major man, because he is "beyond the town," looking, questing, maybe in his search for "what was," really on his way to one of those "moments of awakening."

2

Rule two: "It Must Change." Whitman put it this way, in "Eidólons": "Ever the dim beginning, / Ever the growth, the rounding of the circle, / Ever the summit and the merge at last, (to surely start again,) / Eidólons! eidólons. / Ever the mutable, / Ever materials, changing, crumbling, re-cohering, / Ever the ateliers, the factories divine, / Issuing eidólons" (p. 8). Although Whitman's vision contains elements of the transcendental, and Stevens's does not, the transience of all things provides similar realities for both. In stanza I of "It Must Change," an old Italian painting, with its seraphs and doves and Italian girls, is presented as a "withered scene" and placed in contrast with the reality of pigeons that "clatter in the air." Stevens wrote of stanza II: "We cannot ignore or obliterate death, yet we do not live in memory. Life is always new; it is always beginning. The fiction is part of this beginning" (L, p. 434). And this renewal, this new beginning, is its own reality: "when in golden fury / Spring vanishes the scraps of winter, why / Should there be a question of returning or / Of death in memory's dream? Is spring a sleep?" Whitman said (in the 1855 Preface): the poet "places himself where the future becomes present," he floods himself "with the immediate age as with vast oceanic tides" (pp. 417, 424). In spring he lives and loves in the spring. In stanza III (of section two), Stevens describes the "great statue of the General Du Puy," which, on Sundays, is surrounded by those who come to "study the past." But, "There never had been, never could be, such / A man." The general's false statue was a denial, defiance of change. Thus the "General was rubbish in the end."

With stanza IV Stevens begins a sequence of stanzas celebrating the two interdependent elements of the Supreme Fiction: imagination and reality: "Two things of opposite natures seem to depend / On one another, as a man depends / On a woman, day on night, the imagined / On the real." And this, we are told, is "the origin of change," worth a deeper exploring. Stanza V portrays a "planter" on an exotic "blue island," who, Stevens admitted, is "a symbol of change. He is, however, the laborious human who lives in illusions and who, after all the great illusions have left him, still clings to one that pierces him" (L, p. 435). In stanza VI, we enter a world of insistent change, a garden of birds all singing their songs of transience, the sparrow saying "Bethou me"—thus, as Stevens says, expressing "one's own liking for change" (L, pp. 437–38). The birds "are of minstrels lacking minstrelsy, / Of an earth in which the first leaf is the tale / Of leaves."

Thus the birds are (as Stevens says) subject to a change that "destroys them utterly.... In the face of death life asserts itself" (L, p. 438).

In stanza VII, the real and the imagined are again opposed: "After a lustre of the moon, we say / We have not the need of any paradise, / We have not the need of any seducing hymn." Far preferable to inaccessible is "accessible bliss": "The lover sighs as for accessible bliss"; "For easy passion and ever-ready love / Are of our earthy birth and here and now / And where we live and everywhere we live." But the "bliss" is "accessible" also in other areas of experience, "As in the courage of the ignorant man, / Who chants by book," and "in the heat of the scholar, who writes / The book." Passion, love, courage, heat—these abstractions have their human realities in the here and now. In stanza VIII, a little drama is played out by Nanzia Nunzio, who travels around the world and confronts Ozymandias—Shelley's king whose mind was futilely fixed on the endurance of his magnificance into the future. Nanzia Nunzio presents herself divested of all array, including even her "burning body," presenting herself as the "contemplated spouse," she asks to be clothed "entire in the final filament," so that she will "tremble with love." And Ozymandias says "the spouse, the bride / Is never naked. A fictive covering / Weaves always glistening from the heart and mind." The imagination interacts with reality to create the fiction we apprehend. Stevens comments: "If we are willing to believe in fiction as an extension of reality, or even as a thing itself in which we must believe, the next consideration is the question of illusion as value. Under the name of escapism this is one of the problems that bothers people. The poem about Ozymandias is an illustration of illusion as value" (L, p. 431).

In the examination of language in stanza IX, Stevens moves back and forth, again, between imagination and reality, between the "poet's gibberish" and the "gibberish of the vulgate." Stevens asks: "Is the poem both peculiar and general?" By nature, yes, he answers: the poet "tries by a peculiar speech to speak / The peculiar potency of the general, / To compound the imagination's Latin with / The lingua franca et jocundissima." The poet's language is a combining—of reality's "peculiar" language with imagination's "general." The scene shifts in stanza X to a man in a park on a bench, an audience of one in a trance ("A bench was his catalepsy," "a place of trance" [L, p. 435]) observing the "Theatre of Trope"—the theatre of change and transfiguration. "The lake was full of artificial things," "in which swans / Were seraphs, were saints, were changing essences." The imagination interacts with reality. Throughout the scene in the park, there was "a will to change," "a kind / Of volatile world." Change is not only inevitable, but good: "The freshness of transformation is / The freshness of a world." Indeed, this freshness is ultimately "the freshness of ourselves." Whitman celebrated such a theatre of change in "Crossing Brooklyn Ferry," and exhorted change itself to continue: "Flow on, river! flow with the flood-tide, and ebb with the ebb-tide! / Frolic on, crested and scallop-edg'd waves! / Gorgeous clouds of the sunset! drench with your splendor me, or the men and women generations after me! / Cross from shore to shore, countless crowds of passengers!" (p. 119). For Whitman the scene of the crossing of Brooklyn Ferry was indeed a "Theatre of Trope."

3

Rule three: "It Must Give Pleasure." An odd rule, come to think of it. Is it, by any chance, related to the impulse that caused Whitman to remove from *Leaves of Grass* some of his pessimistic poems—those that did not make a turn back to hope? True, Stevens's poetry does not portray the earth's agonies. And here in this poem, he is struggling to put death itself in a context of "change" that will remove its sting. So . . .

It is "facile exercise," Stevens notes in stanza I, to sing hymns of joy and celebration ("jubilas"). Then the "pleasure" given must be something more? Yes—in the challenge of the "difficultest rigor": "to catch from that / Irrational moment its unreasoning, / As when the sun comes rising, when the sea / Clears deeply, when the moon hangs on the wall / Of heaven-haven." Although these "are not things transformed," we are "shaken by them as if they were," and we "reason about them with a later reason." The pleasure, then, is in probing to the source (out there, in here) of the "unreasoning" in those "irrational moments" of life. The "blue woman" in stanza II, Stevens tells us, "was probably the weather of a Sunday morning" (*L*, p. 444): at "her windows," this blue woman "did not desire that feathery argentines / Should be cold silver, neither that frothy clouds / Should foam, be foamy waves." The reality was enough in itself, without metamorphosis. The blue woman "remembered" the argentines (cotton thistle) and the frothy clouds as what they actually (in reality) were. Stevens commented: "In the memory, (the past, the routine, the mechanism) there had always been a place for everything, free from change, and in its place everything had been right" (*L*, p. 444). Thus the woman observed the "corals of the dogwood" from her window—"cold and clear, / Cold, coldly delineating, being real, / Clear and, except for the eye, without intrusion." Stevens explained:

"One of the approaches to fiction is by way of its opposite: reality, the truth, the thing observed, the purity of the eye" (L, p. 444). A statement like that might well recall to mind the long catalogs of Whitman, naming things for what they are as observed, not as transfigured by metaphor into something else, direct engagement by the imagination with the multiplicity of reality.

Stevens presents a predominantly static scene in stanza III—a weather-worn statue of a god, and places it in contrast with (at the end of the stanza) a "dead shepherd" that "brought tremendous chords from hell / And bade the sheep carouse." Stevens said that the "dead shepherd was an improvisation" (L, p. 438). Movement, and thus change, was needed to restore a lost reality: "Children in love with them brought early flowers / And scattered them about, no two alike." Life (reality) enters the dead scene. Stanza IV opens: "We reason of these things with later reason"—thus ferreting out the source of their irrationality. The stanza is devoted to a "mystic marriage in Catawba" between "a great captain and the maiden Bawda." The one appears to be imagination, the other (the maiden) reality. The poem makes the reason for the marriage clear: first, *not* because of "his high, / His puissant front nor for her subtle sound"; but rather—"Each must the other take as sign, short sign / To stop the whirlwind, balk the elements." Not because of the mutual attractiveness—but in mutual defence from the threatening elements: the imagination *must*, on threat of destruction, engage and take to bed reality. The captain identifies Bawda with "the ever-hill Catawba," and "Bawda loved the captain as she loved the sun"; "They married well because the marriage-place / Was what they loved. It was neither heaven nor hell. / They were love's characters come face to face." Imagination; reality.

Canon Aspirin enters the poem in stanza V and shapes its meaning almost to the end. Canon Aspirin, Stevens tells us, has a name that is "supposed to suggest the kind of person he is" (L, p. 427). He eased pain, especially of the head, quickly? He is "the sophisticated man: the Canon Aspirin, (the man who has explored all the projections of the mind, his own particularly) comes back, without having acquired a sufficing fiction,—to, say, his sister and her children. His sister has never explored anything at all and shrinks from doing so" (L, p. 445). Canon Aspirin sees his sister as ecstatically sensible—she saw her children "as they were," and she held them "closelier to her by rejecting dreams," demanding that the sleep of her children be "only the unmuddled self of sleep." But in stanza VI, when the Canon himself "came to sleep," he soared out on "ascending wings" and descended "to the children's bed." And then, indeed, "Straight to the utmost crown of night he flew. / The nothingness was a nakedness, a point / Beyond which thought could not progress as thought." Confronted with a choice, not between excluding things, not "between, but of," "He chose to include the things / That in each other are included, the whole, / The complicate, the amassing harmony." Stevens commented on this difficult passage: "If he is to elude human pathos, and fact, he must go straight to the utmost crown of night: find his way through the imagination or perhaps to the imagination. He might escape from fact but he would only arrive at another nothingness, another nakedness, the limitation of thought. It is not, then, a matter of eluding human pathos, human dependence. Thought is part of these, the imagination is part of these, and they are part of thought and of imagination. In short, a man with a taste for Meursault, and lobster Bombay, who has a sensible sister and who, for himself, thinks to the very material of his mind, doesn't have much choice about yielding to 'the complicate, the amassing harmony'"(L, p. 445). This yielding, Stevens implies, was a part of the Canon's mistake: he might have chosen "of" both reality and imagination, not an "amassing harmony" beyond reach of either.

In stanza VII, we contemplate the Canon's shortcomings: "He imposes orders as he thinks of them," and thus has instinctive affinities with the fox and snake. But to "impose is not / To discover," as, for example, "To discover winter and know it well." In the search, "It must be that in time / The real will from its crude compoundings come," like a "beast disgorged." The goal then: "To find the real, / To be stripped of every fiction except one, / The fiction of an absolute" reality. The confused reader may sympathize with the opening exclamation of the poet in stanza VIII: "What am I to believe?" If the angel "in his cloud," gazing into the "violent abyss," "grows warm" in his flight through the "evening's revelations," "Am I that imagine this angel less satisfied?" It is the imaginer, not the imagined, who is filled with "expressible bliss," clearly, and thus "majesty is a mirror of the self": "I have not but I am and as I am, I am." A kind of song of the self, this: the self as source of wonders, the self as source of ultimate, feelable satisfactions. Those "external regions" we ourselves fill with "reflections, the escapades of death, / Cinderella fulfilling herself beneath the roof?" How can a reflection be more than its imaginative creator? In stanza IX, the poet boasts: "Whistle aloud, too weedy wren. I can / Do all that angels can. I enjoy like them, / Like men besides, like men in light secluded, / Enjoy angels." Stevens exhorts: to the wren, "whistle aloud"; to the cock bugler, "whistle

and bugle"; to the red robin, "stop in your preludes, practicing /
Mere repetitions." Almost like Whitman's, this advice, at the end of
"Crossing Brooklyn Ferry"—"flow on, frolic on, cross, stand up,
throb, suspend, gaze." These "things," these functions and activities,
exercises, works, comprise "A thing final in itself and, therefore,
good: / One of the vast repetitions final in / Themselves and, therefore, good." The functions of reality, the cyclic activities of creatures
involved in creature's work, is "good"—"the merely going round, /
Until merely going round is a final good, / The way wine comes at a
table in a wood." What's that again? So now we're at a picnic—and
there is the wine, indeed a "final good." We enjoy "like men," as we
look with pleasure at a leaf above the table as it "spins its constant
spin." And a hero for this epic of the daily, cyclic? "Perhaps, / The
man-hero is not the exceptional monster, / But he that of repetition is
most master." Master, that is, of all those "final goods," and therefore hero for this modern kind of epic of reality.

The fat girl of stanza X, Stevens tells us, "is the earth" (L, p. 426):
"Fat girl, terrestrial, my summer, my night, / How is it I find you in
difference, see you there / In a moving contour, a change not quite
completed?" Sitting under a tree (suggesting reflection, and sym-
bolizing "fixity, permanence, completion" [L, p. 426]), the poet addresses the fat-girl earth: "You / Become the soft-footed phantom,
the irrational / Distortion," "the more than rational distortion, / The
fiction that results from feelings." The world is a "moving contour,"
in its reality the source of the Supreme Fiction, but apprehendable
finally in its constant change only by "irrational distortion." One day,
all this will be straightened out at the academy (the Sorbonne), and it
will be stated that "the irrational is rational, / Until flicked by feeling." Thus the poet's poem to the fat-girl world becomes a love poem:
"I call you by name, my green, my fluent mundo. / You will have
stopped revolving except in crystal."

Stevens's insistence on the reality of the physical (as in his term
"accessible bliss") is reminiscent of Whitman's constant insistence on
the physical (and sexual) reality. Stevens's love poem to his "fat-girl
world" recalls Whitman's claim: "The known universe has one complete lover and that is the greatest poet" (p. 416). And Stevens's
emphasis on transience ("change") and bliss or happiness ("pleasure") recalls Whitman's similar emphasis on flux and flow and on the
affirmative aspects of experience (engaging in simple activities, re-
petitive, cyclic). In Stevens's view of physical reality as basic, he
dispenses with death by envisioning it as a natural part of the tran-
sient physical process, or "moving contour" (or as in stanza II of

section two, sees "death in memory's dream" as an unnatural intrusion in the advent of the "golden fury" of spring as it "vanishes the scraps of winter"). Similarly, but with a radically different rhetoric, Whitman finds death a natural part of the flow of life (as in section 49 of "Song of Myself"): "And as to you Death, and you bitter hug of mortality, it is idle to try to alarm me"; "And as to you Corpse, I think you are good manure, but that does not offend me"; "And as to you Life I reckon you are the leavings of many deaths." Stevens's "fluent mundo" (another term of affection for his fat-girl world) has some affinities with Whitman's "monde" in "Salut au Monde!": "I see a great round wonder rolling through space" (p. 101). And also the globe in "A Song of the Rolling Earth": "Whoever you are! motion and reflection are especially for you, / The divine ship sails the divine sea for you. / Whoever you are! you are he or she for whom the earth is solid and liquid, / You are he or she for whom the sun and moon hang in the sky" (p. 163).

In the closing (unnumbered) stanza, the poet sees a relationship between the soldier and the poet, the latter engaged in the war between the "mind and sky," between "thought and day and night": between, that is, imagination and reality. "It is / For that the poet is always in the sun, / Patches the moon together in his room." Old reality, sun; pale imagination, moon. The soldier's war ends, the poet's never. But the "soldier is poor without the poet's lines"—those "sounds that stick, / Inevitably modulating, in the blood." Thus, the "fictive hero becomes the real": the soldier reading the poet who through imagination has made a genuine engagement with reality. "How gladly with proper words the soldier dies, / If he must, or lives on the bread of faithful speech." The Supreme Fiction, then, serves life or death, death or life, supreme because it has imaginatively embraced fundamental reality, expressed in "proper words," "faithful speech." A Supreme Fiction, then, is not simply pretty poetry—but a matter, in a basic sense, of life and death. Whitman said (in "As I Ponder'd in Silence"): "Lo, I too am come, chanting the chant of battles, / I above all promote brave soldiers" (p. 6). And in "When Lilacs Last in the Dooryard Bloom'd": "I float this carol with joy, with joy to thee O death" (p. 238).

Stevens warned: "The *Notes* [*toward a Supreme Fiction*] are a miscellany in which it would be difficult to collect the theory latent in them" (*L*, pp. 430–31). We have emphasized the *Notes toward* of the title. Here, then, is the material (or part of the material) for perhaps building a theory—not the theory itself. And Stevens's method is playful, not systematic. He is charmed, and he charms his reader, by the play of ideas. Like a frisky puppy with a bone, he grabs an idea and shakes it, he runs with it, he hides it, he guards it or buries it—only to dig it up again. And as readers we are constantly surprised and enchanted on seeing the energy and enthusiasm the bone inspires at each appearance, and the renewed delight. There are few readers who have not been puzzled by some "meaning" of a Stevens line, and even Stevens himself in his voluminous commentary on his poem in his letters seems at times to stumble; but the interest in the way that bone is tossed, tumbled, and chewed seldom flags.

Stevens knew he was "playing" with ideas that many consider too weighty for poetry to comprehend. Uncertainty was part of his plan. He did not even want to say definitely that the Supreme Fiction was poetry: "I don't want to say that I don't mean poetry; I don't know what I mean. The next thing for me to do will be to try to be a little more precise about this enigma. I hold off from even attempting that because, as soon as I start to rationalize, I lose the poetry of the idea. In principle there appear to be certain characteristics of a supreme fiction *and the Notes is confined to a statement of a few of those characteristics.* As I see the subject, it could occupy a school of rabbis for the next few generations. In trying to create something as valid as the idea of God has been, and for that matter remains, the first necessity seems to be breadth" (L, p. 435; Stevens's italics). Indeed, yes. A school of rabbis or a gaggle of epic poets—the poets that Whitman envisioned arising in America in "By Blue Ontario's Shore." Stevens's unwillingness to define precisely the "Supreme Fiction" of his title gives us the leeway to play with the idea (and his ideas) as they relate to the epic poetry of the kind developed in the tradition that flows out of Whitman.

Stevens's poem was, he believed, open-ended (like other American lyric-epics). In 1954 he wrote of his 1942 poem: "For a long time, I have thought of adding other sections to the *Notes* and one in particular: *It Must Be Human.* But I think it would be wrong not to leave well enough alone" (L, pp. 863–64). But of course. Seeing the words on paper seems to endow them with inevitability. And they mean something more than that the old epic gods no longer serve (as Whitman proclaimed in "Song of the Exposition"). In "Song of the Broad-Axe" (that poem Stevens thought had possibilities), Whitman wrote: "What do you think endures? / Do you think a great city endures? / Or a teeming manufacturing state? or a prepared constitution? or the best built steamships? / Or hotels of granite and iron? or any chef-d'oeuvres of engineering, forts, armaments? / Away! these are not to be cherish'd for themselves, / They fill their hour, the dancers dance,

the musicians play for them, / The show passes, all does well enough
of course, / All does very well till one flash of defiance. / A great city
is that which has the greatest men and women, / If it be a few ragged
huts it is still the greatest city in the world" (p. 138).

Yes, surely, *It* must be human. And taking a hint from Stevens's
own view of the openness of "Notes toward a Supreme Fiction," we
may add this as Rule four to our recipe for a modern American epic.
And in the spirit of much modern art, we'll let the rule stand by itself
for the reader to fill in the details—with his own play of mind over his
own images and words. In brief, we'll leave it to his imagination to
engage the reality of his human-ness.

4

Rule four: "It Must Be Human."

5

The man in old coat and drooping pantaloons, his imagination roaming reality, conceives he has discovered a lost Stevens
manuscript:

> Conclude, ephebe, by turning to the wall
> On which there hangs a mirror to the world
> And step between to gaze into the glass.
>
> The light rays out in endless buzzing beams
> Like bees around a radiating form
> That puzzles and attracts and fills a void
>
> That never was a void until the form
> Stepped forward in its progress through the room
> To make a space and fill it out forthwith.
>
> Never avoid, ephebe, the figure in the glass
> Whose gaze engages yours in fixed return,
> Whose smile replies to yours in sly amaze.
>
> The form you see is seen by you alone.
> Observe its place at center of its space,
> And take the measure of its length and breadth.
>
> For there is major man, or leaner being,
> Being human there as must a human being,
> As must all human beings beginning to be human.
>
> Say, ephebe, which is the real ephebe?
> The mirror's form or form before the glass.
> Both forms, aroused, reply: "It's I," "It's I."

Part Two   *Branches*

Are you he who would assume a place to teach or be a poet here in
    the States?
The place is august, the terms obdurate.

Who would assume to teach here may well prepare himself body and
    mind,
He may well survey, ponder, arm, fortify, harden, make lithe
    himself,
He shall surely be question'd beforehand by me with many
    and stern questions.

"By Blue Ontario's Shore"
Walt Whitman

Five

I find in [Whitman] what...I should...call our American keynote.... It is, as nearly as I can define it, a certain generosity; a certain carelessness, or looseness, if you will; a hatred of the sordid, an ability to forget the part for the sake of the whole, a desire for largeness, a willingness to stand exposed. "Camerado, this is no book; / Who touches this touches a man."

Pound, "Patria mia"

An Epic Is a Poem Containing History

Ezra Pound's "Cantos"

And Ezra Pound emerged from Hailey, Idaho—but not really, having moved with his family at the age of four to Philadelphia. He remembered later (in an interview of March 1962) that he had "begun" his *Cantos* when he would have been only nineteen or twenty: "I began the Cantos about 1904, I suppose. I had various schemes, starting in 1904 or 1905. The problem was to get a form—something elastic enough to take the necessary material. It had to be a form that wouldn't exclude something merely because it didn't fit."[1] A neat form, that—one "that wouldn't exclude something merely because it didn't fit." There is other evidence that Pound had a long poem on his mind during his early years[2] up to the first publication in 1917 of a Canto, which, after revision, was to become Canto 3.

What was on Pound's mind during this formative period? Dante, Provençal poetry, Cavalcanti, Anglo-Saxon poetry, and much more that has been the focus of a growing body of scholarship and criticism. It is with some trepidation that I introduce Whitman's barbaric yawp in such august literary company, especially in view of a hostility to Whitman manifest in many Pound commentators—T. S. Eliot, for example, in his 1928 Introduction to Pound's *Selected Poems*: "Now

Pound's originality is genuine.... Whitman's originality is both genuine and spurious.... It is spurious in so far as Whitman wrote in a way that asserted that his great prose was a new form of verse. (And I am ignoring in this connexion the large part of clap-trap in Whitman's content.)"[3] Hugh Kenner, in his enormously learned and encyclopedic *The Pound Era* (1971), finds no room for mention of Whitman except as Pound himself forces the name on the lips of anyone commenting on Canto 82 (although Emerson comes in by way of Ernest Fenollosa). It is perhaps important, then, to emphasize that in my necessary concentration on the presence of Whitman in *The Cantos*, I have no intention of excluding others whose attendance has been so well documented, often by Pound himself. But I must confess, too, that the position I claim for Whitman is central, not peripheral.

1

Whitman's claim is central, I believe, because of his presence in both the form and content of *The Cantos*. Pound himself, in an essay written during those early, formative years—"What I Feel about Walt Whitman," dated 1909 but not published until 1955— sorted through his relationships with Whitman in an astonishing confession:

> Mentally I am a Walt Whitman who has learned to wear a collar and a dress shirt (although at times inimical to both). Personally I might be very glad to conceal my relationship to my spiritual father and brag about my more congenial ancestry—Dante, Shakespeare, Theocritus, Villon, but the descent is a bit difficult to establish.
> And, to be frank, Whitman is to my fatherland (*Patriam quam odi et amo* [the fatherland I love and hate so much] for no uncertain reasons) what Dante is to Italy and I at my best can only be a strife for a renaissance in America of all the lost or temporarily mislaid beauty, truth, valor, glory of Greece, Italy, England and all the rest of it.

I would not attempt to make any greater claim for Whitman's presence in Pound's work than Pound himself confesses in this passage. But Pound's critics tend to discount Pound's confession, and point to his negative comments. And it is true that Pound's little essay is critical of Whitman: "He *is* America. His crudity is an exceeding great stench, but it *is* America. He is the hollow place in that rock that echoes with his time. He *does* 'chant the crucial stage' and he is the 'voice triumphant.' He is disgusting. He is an exceedingly nauseating pill, but he accomplishes his mission." Here as elsewhere in the essay, the negative comment is followed by an all-important *but*—and the negative becomes (at least partially) itself negated; the fault turns out to be the inevitable obverse of a great virtue: "He is content to be what he is, and he is his time and his people. He is a genius because he has vision of what he is and of his function. He knows that he is a beginning and not a classically finished work."

The remarkable note struck in this essay is Pound's acute personal involvement—there is no pretense here of an objective assessment of Whitman. It is almost as though Pound had, in 1909, recognized that Whitman had usurped the position in his nation's poetry that Pound himself coveted, and that Pound had reluctantly come to the conclusion that since he could not be America's Dante (or epic poet), he must somehow work out his relationship with the poet who held that position. Thus the essay is as much about Pound as about Whitman, and particularly Pound's job of work as a poet. With a flourish he said of Whitman, "I honor him for he prophesied me while I can only recognize him as a forebear of whom I ought to be proud." And he said: "As for Whitman, I read him (in many parts) with acute pain, but when I write of certain things I find myself using his rhythms. The expression of certain things related to cosmic consciousness seems tainted with this maramis."

But the "rhythms" of Whitman are the bearers of his "message." And Pound, in his eulogistic arrogance, testifies backhandedly to its endurance in himself: "I am (in common with every educated man) an heir of the ages and I demand my birth-right. Yet if Whitman represented his time in language acceptable to one accustomed to my standard of intellectual-artistic living he would belie his time and nation. And yet I am but one of his 'ages' and ages' encrustations' or to be exact an encrustation of the next age. The vital part of my message, taken from the sap and fibre of America, is the same as his." There could be no better expression, I think, for the continuity of the American epic impulse from Whitman to Pound than the one Pound himself has here formulated. Even as he asserts his equal immortality, Pound sounds almost wistful that the Dante role for America has been filled by Whitman: "I am immortal even as he is, yet with a lesser vitality as I am the more in love with beauty (If I really do love it more than he did). Like Dante he wrote in the 'vulgar tongue,' in a new metric. The first great man to write in the language of his people."

What, then, is left for Pound to do? The end of his essay is given over to his role: "It seems to me I should like to drive Whitman into the old world. I sledge, he drill—and to scourge America with all the old beauty. (For Beauty *is* an accusation) and with a thousand thongs from Homer to Yeats, from Theocritus to Marcel Schwob." Pound seems here to have his own epic in mind, seeing it in the context of (as a continuity with) Whitman's. Pound concludes: "It is a great thing, reading a man to know, not 'His Tricks are not as yet my Tricks, but I can easily make them mine' but 'His message is my message. We will see that men hear it.'"[4] Pound's earlier claim that he is but one of Whitman's "ages' and ages' encrustations" evokes by direct quotation Whitman's late poem in the "Goodbye my Fancy" cluster, "Long, Long Hence":

> After a long, long course, hundreds of years, denials,
> Accumulations, rous'd love and joy and thought,
> Hopes, wishes, aspirations, ponderings, victories,
>   myriads of readers,
> Coating, compassing, covering—after ages' and ages'
>   encrustations,
> Then only may these songs reach fruition.[5]

Pound and his *Cantos* a Whitmanian encrustation? Pound did say, *His message is my message.* Not even Hart Crane or Allen Ginsberg would later claim a stronger identification.

After "What I Feel about Walt Whitman," Pound's scattered references to Whitman reveal a struggle to come to terms with the feelings expressed in this early confession. In *The Spirit of Romance* (1910), in his discussions of his major continental masters, Pound curiously uses Whitman for key points of comparison, always to Whitman's detriment. In his essay on Dante, Pound links Whitman's name with Wordsworth, but only to show that both are inferior to Dante in expression of "'pantheism' or some such thing," as found in the opening lines of the *Paradiso* (as translated by Pound):

> The glory of him who moveth all
> Penetrates and is resplendent through the all
> In one part more and in another less.

Pound comments: "The disciples of Whitman cry out concerning the 'cosmic sense,' but Whitman, with all his catalogues and flounderings, has never so perfectly expressed the perception of cosmic consciousness as does Dante in the canto just quoted." Pound then adds two lines particularly apt, perhaps, for a comparison with the author of *Leaves of Grass*:

> As Glaucus, tasting of the grass which made him
> sea-fellow of the other gods.[6]

Pound again turns to Whitman as a point of comparison in his essay on Villon, and again to emphasize Whitman's inferiority:

If [Villon] sings the song of himself he is, thank God, free from that horrible air of rectitude with which Whitman rejoices in being Whitman. Villon's song is selfish through self-absorption; he does not, as Whitman, pretend to be conferring a philanthropic benefit on the race by recording his own self-complacency. Human misery is more stable than human dignity; there is more intensity in the passion of cold, remorse, hunger, and the fetid damp of the mediaeval dungeon than in eating water melons. Villon is a voice of suffering, of mockery, of irrevocable fact; Whitman is the voice of one who saith: Lo, behold, I eat water-melons. When I eat water-melons, I partake of the world's water-melons.

This somewhat lame parody runs for eight more lines, and can only inspire a close reader of Whitman to rebuttle: Whitman's "Song of Myself" devotes some major sections to suffering and mockery: "I am the man, I suffer'd, I was there. . . . Hell and despair are upon me. . . . Agonies are one of my changes of garments. . . . I project my hat, sit shamefaced, and beg." But rebuttle is not the point, except as shocked recognition that Pound did not give his fellow American poet the care in reading that his own poetry demands: Pound seems to share a prudish distortion of Whitman common among his would-be censors: "Whitman, having decided that it is disgraceful to be ashamed, rejoices in having attained nudity."[7] The main point is that Whitman serves repeatedly for points of comparison with Pound's literary models, and the very vigor of Pound's attack suggests the depth of Whitman's lodgement in Pound's poetic psyche.

Pound handed a curious work, "Patria mia," over to a publisher in 1913, but for complicated business reasons (among them, the financial failure of the publisher), the book did not appear until 1950. The book is an examination of American culture (rather thin) and an elaborate exploration of Pound's own relationship to it, in the context of Pound's insistence on his own inevitable American-ness: "If a man's work require him to live in exile, let him suffer, or enjoy, his exile gladly. But it would be about as easy for an American to become a Chinaman or a Hindoo as for him to acquire an Englishness, or a Frenchness, or a European-ness that is more than half a skin deep." In this book, Pound makes some of the same points he made in his early essay on Whitman: "Whitman established the national *timbre*. One may not need him at home. It is in the air, this tonic of his. But if one is abroad; if one is ever likely to forget one's birth-right, to lose faith, being surrounded by disparagers, one can find, in Whitman, the reassurance. Whitman goes bail for the nation."

Just as the Anglo-Saxon poems "The Seafarer" and "The Wanderer" reveal the "English national chemical," so, Pound asserted, Whitman provides the "American keynote": "It is, as nearly as I can define it, a certain generosity; a certain carelessness, or looseness, if you will; a hatred of the sordid, an ability to forget the part for the sake of the whole, a desire for largeness; a willingness to stand exposed. 'Camerado, this no book; / Who touches this touches a man.' The artist is ready to endure personally a strain which his craftsmanship would scarcely endure."[8] Pound's formulation here seems much closer to the mark than in *The Spirit of Romance,* as it seems also much closer, too, to Pound's great long work yet to come, *The Cantos.* Indeed, as Albert Gelpi has suggested (in *The Tenth Muse*), Pound's characterization of Whitman here comes uncannily close to the mark in identifying those distinctively American traits that distinguish American poetry—and the American epic tradition.[9]

Pound's poem on Whitman, "A Pact," first published in 1916, acquires a depth of richer meaning in the context of the foregoing—almost like the final resolution of a long struggle, a public acknowledgment after long postponement:

> I make a pact with you, Walt Whitman—
> I have detested you long enough.
> I come to you as a grown child
> Who has had a pig-headed father;
> I am old enough now to make friends.
> It was you that broke the new wood,
> Now is a time for carving.
> We have one sap and one root—
> Let there be commerce between us.[10]

The acknowledgment seems almost painful—that "one sap and one root" (like the "sap and fibre of America" of the early essay) which Pound shares with Whitman. But if painful, also therapeutic: the proclamation of the "pact" will perhaps free Pound to set about in earnest on his own epic poem. It was about this time that Pound would have been formulating the first of *The Cantos.*

We may pass over for the moment Whitman's dramatic appearance in the "Pisan Cantos" (Canto 82) and turn briefly to that curious anthology that Pound edited with Marcella Spann, *Confucius to Cummings,* published near the end of his career, in 1964. Among the oddities of this book is the devotion of fifteen pages to Whitman, as compared with four to Dante and seven to Villon, a fact that is diminished in importance the moment one notices the inclusion of Bret Harte and James Whitcomb Riley. The Whitman poems number only three: "I Sing the Body Electric," "The Centenarian's Story," and "To the States" (from "Inscriptions"), all poems distinguished by turning up on almost nobody's list of Whitman's finest poems. The eccentricity of choice stamps it, I think, as Poundian. Moreover, the poems may all be placed in what I would call Whitman's epic (or public) voice. After writing *The Cantos*, we may assume, this is the Whitmanian voice that Pound remembers. The brief note that Pound adds to the Whitman section is striking: "The U.S. during the first century of its existence as an independent nation was full of exhilarating ferment. . . . Whitman took a place in world literature, proclaiming himself American and not mentioning Asiatic components of his outlook."[11]

Not mentioning Asiatic components of his outlook. For one who earlier had repeatedly emphasized the American-ness of Whitman, this statement seems a considerable advance. And from one who labored much of his life to introduce "Asiatic components" into his own epic, especially Confucianism, this sounds like a major modification or revision of that 1916 pact.

2

What did Pound write in *The Cantos*? What did Pound think he was writing in *The Cantos*? There are, perhaps, two different answers to these similar questions. But any serious attempt to understand the long poem ought to begin with some contemplation of Pound's view of what it is. From the beginning to the end, Pound clearly was attempting to write an *epic*, a word that he used over and over in relation to *The Cantos*, and which he conveniently defined for his readers in his 1962 interview: "An epic is a poem containing history. The modern mind contains heteroclite elements. The past epos has succeeded when all or a great many of the answers were assumed, at least between author and audience, or a great mass of audience. The attempt in an experimental age is therefore rash." The attempt *to write an epic* in an experimental age is indeed rash. Pound's definition of the *epic* ("a poem containing history") is loose enough to suit his purposes—to get in all those "heteroclite" (abnormal, anomalous) elements of the (his) "modern mind."

Pound found himself insisting that there *were* epic subjects: "The struggle for individual rights is an epic subject. . . . The nature of sovereignty is epic matter, though it may be a bit obscured by circumstance." Sovereignty? Pound clarifies by more Poundianism: "The nature of the individual, the heteroclite contents of contemporary consciousness." Sovereignty, then, is selfhood? Song of the self? Pound is representative? His consciousness he takes for "contemporary consciousness"? He explains: "It's the fight for light versus subconsciousness; it demands obscurities and penumbras." That's a tangle to untangle. At first Pound seems to be on the side of the light; but those beloved "obscurities and penumbras" seem to place him on the side of "subconsciousness." Come to think of it, wouldn't those "heteroclite contents" hover somewhere near or in the "subconscious"?

Pound is accommodating in his interview. He wants not only to define his form but to convey his substance; "I am writing to resist the view that Europe and civilization are going to Hell. If I am being 'crucified for an idea'—that is, the coherent idea around which my muddles accumulated—it is probably the idea that European culture ought to survive, that the best qualities of it ought to survive along with whatever other cultures, in whatever universality. Against the propaganda of terror and the propaganda of luxury, have you a nice simple answer? One has worked on certain materials trying to establish bases and axes of reference." An epic intent, that, within the great tradition, certainly. And didactic without apology. That last sentence, with its oblique "one has," tells us surely that *The Cantos* attempt to establish the "bases and axes of reference" on which the "best qualities" of "European culture ought to survive."

Pound's brief description of his epic reaches from one extreme to the other: from the finely restricted lyric end to the freely unbounded epic end, from the individual to society, from consciousness to country, from self to civilization. When pressed by his interviewer, Pound denies Dante as his model: "I was not following the three divisions of the Divine Comedy exactly. One can't follow the Dantesquan cosmos in an age of experiment."[12] Twice now Pound has reminded his interviewer that he writes his epic in an "age of experiment," a "rash" act indeed because clearly the form must be experimental, not traditional. Moreover, Pound had long ago asserted that Whitman had done for America (already, alas) what Dante did for Italy, and Pound certainly did not think *Leaves of Grass* followed the form of the *Divine Comedy*. Pound thus can be somewhat (not *exactly*) like Dante by being like Whitman, by writing a work that relates significantly to his time and place the way Dante and Whitman did.

Pound's insistence that his subject "demands obscurities and penumbras" raises the central question in Pound criticism: his readability. When Pound describes one of *The Cantos'* major themes as "the coherent idea around which my muddles accumulated," he is perhaps being ironic but he seems very close to some of the most telling criticism of his poem. Pound is the only poet I know whose most devoted admirers at some time or other throw up their hands in despair at ever penetrating all those *obscurities* or illuminating all those *penumbras;* of coming to terms with the successive *muddles.* Anyone who has experienced bafflement in trying to make some sense out of a page of *The Cantos* is likely to grab to his bosom such comment as the following from Robert Graves, placed after a passage quoted from Canto 50: "Even Whitman's barbaric yawp was hardly as barbaric as that. But remove the layers and layers of cloacinal [sewer-like] ranting, snook-cocking, pseudo-professorial jargon and double-talk from Pound's verse, and what remains? Longfellow's plump, soft, ill-at-ease grand-nephew remains."[13] This may be fun, but it is hardly fair. One of Pound's hardest critics, and one of his most pene-trating, George Dekker, has warned us that many of Pound's most distinguished critics have not earned the credentials (by reading *The Cantos*) to denounce him as they have, among them F. R. Leavis, Edmund Wilson, Yvor Winters.

But George Dekker presents his admirable credentials, along with his illuminations, in *The Cantos of Ezra Pound* (1963), and then, having clearly earned the right, asserts his belief that *The Cantos,* "as a poem, is a colossal failure." And the failure, he seems to say throughout his book, lies in the "characteristic obscurity" of the poetry.[14] In his influ-ential 1964 work (*Ezra Pound: Poet as Sculptor*), Donald Davie devotes much space to a sympathetic account of *The Cantos,* but he is often overcome by exasperation—as, for example, when discussing the American history and Chinese history cantos: "The whole plan of them is absurdly, even insanely, presumptuous; there is simply too much recorded history available for anyone to offer to speak of it with such confidence as Pound does." Davie concludes: "Pound seems to have had before him, as one main objective, the baffling and defeat-ing of commentators and exegetes. If so, he has succeeded, for the *Cantos* defeat exegesis by inviting it so inexhaustibly."[15]

Another of Pound's long-term interpreters, Noel Stock, presents his conclusion in *Reading the Cantos* (1965): "*The Cantos* . . .do not con-stitute a poem, but a disjointed series of short poems, passages, lines and fragments, often of exceptional beauty or interest, but unin-formed, poetically or otherwise, by larger purpose."[16] This cannot be said to be the attitude of Hugh Kenner, the most devoted, the most dedicated, the most patient, and the most persistent of all Pound critics. But even Kenner, in *The Pound Era,* finally admits to some frustration in reading *The Cantos.* In his discussion of the "Fifth

Decad" of Cantos, Kenner sets about straightening out Pound's enigmatic, cryptic, recurrent use of the Bank of Siena (Monte dei Paschi,
Mountain of the Grazing Lands), and pauses to remark: "For just
here we encounter a kind of difficulty that will bulk larger and larger
as the Cantos progress." This difficulty is Pound's omission from *The
Cantos* of any real clue as to why he sets up the Siena Bank as a
paradigm. Kenner finds the explanation in one of Pound's pamphlets
on economics, and laments: "But it is not explained in the Canto, but
in a pamphlet on Social Credit. In the Canto it is virtually hidden
amid the picturesque details, and while the facts are all present it is
doubtful if an uninstructed reader could be sure he had assembled
them correctly."[17] Cautious, yes; but criticism, indeed. And from the
most ardent of Poundians.

After twice reading *The Cantos* straight through in two periods of
sustained application, and spending much time with individual Cantos in private and with students (but without devoting my life to the
task); after much consultation of the indispensable *Annotated Index*[18]
and browsing through the bulging shelves of Poundiana; after puzzling over periods of darkness and exulting over illuminations (especially when I brought my own light), I think I have accumulated a
modest set of credentials that earns me the right to the opinions I
have formed. And these opinions are very close to Pound's own
conceptions and doubts—his conception of the poem as an epic, and
his uneasiness with the poem's obscurities and muddlements.

3

At the beginning of *Leaves of Grass* (in "Starting from
Paumanok"), Whitman invites the reader to join him on his
journey—"to haste firm holding—to haste, haste on with me." He
says in "Song of Myself," "I tramp a perpetual journey, (come listen
all!)."[19] At the beginning of *The Cantos*, Pound introduces his
Odysseus-self, who (as Tiresias predicts) "Shalt return through spite-
ful Neptune, over dark seas, / Lose all companions." And Canto 1
closes with an image of Odysseus-Pound sailing—"outward and
away" (p. 5).[20] The journey-voyage image, common both to (and
used throughout) *Leaves of Grass* and *The Cantos*, is the overall formal
base on which the epics are constructed. Both poets started their
works before they knew where they would go: they knew only that
the journey was the form, and, in a way, that the journey-form was
the message.

Whitman's by now familiar—and certainly fundamental—

description of his own achievement in "A Backward Glance" may stand for the achievement of both poets: "This was a feeling or ambition to articulate and faithfully express in literary or poetic form, and uncompromisingly, my own physical, emotional, moral, intellectual, and aesthetic Personality, in the midst of, and tallying, the momentous spirit and facts of its immediate days, and of current America—and to exploit that Personality, identified with place and date, in a far more candid and comprehensive sense than any hitherto poem or book."[21] Implicit in this statement is darkness on direction; only as events unfold can they enter a poem already structured and open to contain them—the Civil War for Whitman, for example; and World War II (and internment at Pisa) for Pound. Both poets revealed themselves perhaps more than they knew or intended in their epics, and for better and worse: "uncompromisingly." And herein lies their achievement, their very failures becoming a valuable revelation for their countrymen and readers.

Pound himself seemed to recognize this nature of *The Cantos* when, in 1966 (with only fragments of the final Cantos left to be published), he wrote in his Foreword to *Selected Cantos* (his selections): "The best introduction to the *Cantos* and to the present selection of passages might be the following lines from the earlier draft of a Canto (1912) . . . .

> Hang it all, there can be but one "Sordello"!
> But say I want to, say I take your whole bag of tricks,
> Let in your quirks and tweeks, and say the thing's an
>   artform,
> Your Sordello, and that the modern world
> Needs such a rag-bag to stuff all its thoughts in;
> Say that I dump my catch, shiny and silvery
> As fresh sardines slapping and slipping on the marginal
>   cobbles?
> (I stand before the booth, the speech; but the truth
> Is inside this discourse—this booth is full of the marrow
>   of wisdom.)"[22]

Note the ease with which the speaker moves from *I* to *you*, and to the *modern world* and its *thoughts*: the ease with which Pound assumes the role of modern man, representative of mankind, his thoughts the thoughts of the *modern world*. This, too, was the role Whitman assumed. Pound says he will include in his "rag-bag" even the *quirks* and *tweeks*; perhaps what Pound thought only a quirk the world would come to recognize as a sizable flaw. Still, Pound apparently wanted, like Whitman, to level with his reader. Pound's endorsement of this passage near the end of his career ("the best introduction to the *Cantos*") appears to cancel his omission (suggesting rejection) of some of these lines when he included the passage in Canto 3.

Perhaps one of the best witnesses to this conception of the form of the *Cantos* is Allen Ginsberg, whose Jewishness might have made him feel a victim—or worse—of one of Pound's "quirks" or "tweeks." When Ginsberg heard the news of Pound's death, 1 November 1972, his spontaneous response was extravagant tribute: "The one poet who heard speech as spoken from the actual body and began to measure it to lines that could be chanted rhythmically without violating human common sense, without going into hysterical fantasy or robotic metronomic repeat, stale-emotioned echo of an earlier culture's forms, the first poet to open up fresh new forms in America after Walt Whitman—certainly the greatest poet since Walt Whitman."

Pressed on the point of Pound's demonstrable anti-Semitism in his poetry, Ginsberg responded with a combination of eulogy and analysis both moving and persuasive:

> Pound told me he felt that the Cantos were "stupidity and igno-
> rance all the way through," and were a failure and a "mess," and
> that his "greatest stupidity was stupid suburban anti-semitic prej-
> udice," he thought—as of 1967, when I talked with him. So I told
> him I thought that since the Cantos were for the first time a single
> person registering over the course of a lifetime all of his major
> obsessions and thoughts and the entire rainbow arc of his images
> and clingings and attachments and discoveries and perceptions,
> that they were an accurate representation of his mind and so
> couldn't be thought of in terms of success or failure, but only in
> terms of actuality of their representation, and that since for the first
> time a human being had taken the whole spiritual world of thought
> through fifty years and followed the thoughts out to the end—so
> that he built a model of his consciousness over a fifty-year time
> span—that they were a great achievement. Mistakes and all, natu-
> rally.

The questioner says at this pause, "Like *Leaves of Grass*, again, isn't it. Like Whitman again, where he did that in making *Leaves of Grass*." And Ginsberg answers, "Yes, he did."[23]

In a remarkably brief span, and extemporaneously, Ginsberg has covered the scope of Pound's form, from detail to whole, from word to structure, and has pronounced it fresh and innovative, the essence of Pound's contribution. But there is more to be said, outlines to fill in. Although with both Whitman and Pound the major form grows organically out of the journeys of their lives, the voyages of their spirits, they succeeded in giving shape through language and imagination to the lives they embodied in their works. Moreover, their voices are contained in their lines, not single monotonous voices, but the voices of a lifetime, sounding in the very words on the page; they themselves are embodied in their form and language.

Is it possible to find a shape in *The Cantos*? The report from most readers—the few who persist through the full eight hundred pages—is mixed, but mainly negative, even from Pound's admirers. But there are exceptions. In his first work on Pound (1951), Hugh Kenner reported: "It was Pound's discovery that the logical end of conscientious rendering was an epic without (in the usual sense) a plot. . . . In the *Cantos* the place of a plot is taken by interlocking large-scale rhythms of recurrence."[24] This sounds remarkably like some of the early criticism of Whitman. By the time that Kenner wrote *The Pound Era* (1971), he detected a succession of subjects or themes in *The Cantos*: "Each group of Cantos, it grows clear, has its special plane of attention: the first 16, we may say, perspective, all things in the mind simultaneous; the next group [17–30] journeyings; 31–41, letters and documents; 42–51, money and fertility; 52–71, history and biography; the Pisan sequence [74–84], memory; 85–95, vegetable growth; and finally, Thrones, 96–109, philology."[25]

Daniel D. Pearlman has proposed, in *The Barb of Time* (1969) that there are three major "phases" in *The Cantos*—considering them as complete through Canto 84 (the "Pisan Cantos"). The organizing theme is Time: Time as Disorder dominates Cantos 1–30 but runs to Canto 46; Time as Order begins to overlap as early as Canto 31, but becomes clearly dominant by Cantos 47–71; Time as Love dominates Cantos 74–84 (Cantos 72–73 have never been published), the "Pisan Cantos." These themes are not embodied in a plot or action but rather in Pound's consciousness or perception—the "poet-hero of the Cantos." Another way of stating this three-part division is to say that the poet at first focuses on war, usury, decay of civilization; next on order within the individual and within the society, as formulated by Confucianism and represented in Chinese history and in John Adams (second President of the United States); and finally on the transcendentally mystical—paradise apprehended intuitively in the Pisan prison—"He conquers by undergoing a profound mystical experience which reveals to him the illusory nature of historical time and place, and consequently of his own ego. . . . In his direct, subjective contact with the abundant goodness of the cosmos, Everyman-Pound experiences on his pulses the metaphysical *essence* of the earthly paradise of all his poetical and polemical visions."[26]

Many readers will grant these successive "phases" in *The Cantos*, agreeing that there are no sharp divisions (though they might take exception to the weight of mystical meaning that Pearlman places on the "Pisan Cantos"). *A Draft of XXX Cantos*, though in preparation perhaps for some two decades and published variously before, appeared in 1930, and was followed rather quickly by *Eleven New Cantos XXXI–XLI* (1934), and *The Fifth Decad of Cantos XLII–LI* (1937). These first fifty-one Cantos seem to be rather much of a piece, with much churning and many varied themes, mostly negative, coming to the surface: the personal voice of Ezra Pound the voyager appears at the fore, even when he immerses himself in the details of Sigismundo Malateste's time in fifteenth-century Italy (as in the Malateste Cantos, 8–11) or of Thomas Jefferson's time in early American history (as in Cantos 21–34). But some kind of transition does seem to be taking place in "The Fifth Decad," with the memorable *usura* Canto (45) and the brilliant procreational Canto (47); in between, in Canto 46, Pound seems to be announcing the end of Part I of his work: phrases appear as though subliminal flashes—"nineteen / Years on this case"—and then: "This case, and with it / the first part, draws to a conclusion, / of the first phase of this opus."

In 1940 appeared Cantos 52–71. The opening of Canto 52 presents a brief summary, vitriolic and bizarre (reference to "yitts," "goyim," and "neschek" [usury]) of previous Cantos: "And I have told you of how things were." After about one and a half pages, we seem to enter a different world with "Know then"—the world of Chinese history, a Confucian-perspective "survey" that runs for only a little less than a hundred pages (Cantos 52–61). Then there is a leap in time to the days of the early American republic and the career of John Adams, America's Confucian man, covering as many Cantos (62–71) and as many pages as the Chinese stretch. There is a concentration of focus in these twenty Cantos that can be found nowhere else in the poem. Pound's public or epic voice is at the fore, but even here there are "quirks" of language ("booze in the bamboo grove," "goddam bhuddists," "Jap sailors drove chinks to embargo") that constantly remind the reader of a personal bias and eccentrically personal voice behind the sweeping review of history, a bias that can relegate the "eunuchs, taozers and hochang [Buddhists]" (p. 312) to the role of villain recurrently in China, and that can elevate an assumed Confucianist, John Adams, to the sainted position among America's Founding Fathers. But whereas the previous Cantos had tended to be caught up in their most vivid moments in violence and decay, the dishonesty and disaster of civilization and life, the Chinese-Adams Cantos concentrate with determination and steadiness on Confucian ideals that thread their way delicately through Chinese history and through John Adams's writings and deeds, the one focus clearly meant to counter the other, a move from the negative to the affirmative, from chaos to order, from hell to reality to the possibilities of an ideal.

Some eight years, a world war, and a scarring imprisonment after Cantos 52–71, Pound published the "Pisan Cantos," 74–84 (1948). And in these Cantos there is a clear shift away from the public voice of the middle Cantos and a return to the personal voice, but a voice not nearly so arrogantly self-assured as in the early Cantos. For the first time Pound seems to be caught in history—like Whitman in the "Drum-Taps" section of *Leaves of Grass*, but with a voice more nearly like Whitman's in the "Passage to India" section, a voice that speaks a poem "bridging the way from Life to Death." The "Pisan Cantos" appear to move toward an extraordinary understanding or illumination, especially in Canto 81 ("What thou lovest well remains") in a vision of life and in Canto 82 ("the loneliness of death came upon me") in a vision of death. The whole of the "Pisan Cantos" seems to weave the many previous themes of the Cantos together and to bring them to some kind of resolution (or unresolved balance) in these climactic insights. But the image that emerges finally is not of Pound mercilessly exposing civilization, or of Pound triumphantly revealing the energies of history, but of Pound painfully sifting through the fragments of his life searching for what remained, what meaning they might reveal, what finally he could hesitatingly assert. There is some swagger here, but it tends to get lost in the inundation of memory.

After the "Pisan Cantos," there appeared *Section: Rock-Drill de los Cantares LXXXV–XCV* (1955) and *Thrones de los Cantares XCVI–CIX* (1959); and the *Drafts and Fragments of Cantos CX–CXVII* (1969) and "Canto CXX" (1969)—end. Pound's own comments on *Rock-Drill* and *Thrones* suggest their supplementary nature in the structure of *The Cantos*. Asked if these collections were "attacking particular problems," Pound answered: "No. *Rock Drill* was intended to imply the necessary resistance in getting a certain main thesis across—hammering.... The Thrones in the *Cantos* are an attempt to move out from egoism and to establish some definition of an order possible or at any rate conceivable on earth. One is held up by the low percentage of reason which seems to operate in human affairs. *Thrones* concerns the states of mind of people responsible for something more than their personal conduct."[27] Introducing nothing new in either technique or theme, these sections serve very much as do the closing sections of *Leaves of Grass* ("Songs of Parting") or even the Annexes ("Sands at Seventy," "Goodbye My Fancy"), harmonious with but not integral to the basic developmental structure of the poem; that is not to say, however, that their poetry is less important, than that of the other Cantos, for their poetry.[28]

In a discussion of "The Ideogrammic Method" in his 1934 volume, *ABC of Reading* (drawing, of course, on Ernest Fenollosa's "Essay on the Chinese Written Character," written in 1906 but not published until 1919—and then under Pound's sponsorship), Pound wrote somewhat cryptically: "A general statement is valuable only in REFERENCE to the known objects or facts."[29] One of Pound's critics (Daniel Pearlman) has defined the method as "a procedure which dispenses with grammatical logic as a means of connecting a string of poetic images, depending, instead, upon a logic of association by which juxtaposed images elucidate one another through patterns of similarity and contrast that are capable of a full range of ironic and symbolic suggestiveness."[30] Any reader of *The Cantos* will attest to the use of this method and will probably have mixed feelings about the degree of its success in the poem; the abrupt shift from what often appears private symbol or reference to other private symbols and references has left many a reader floundering, splashing, gasping for meaning or direction. Some of the same questions that have been raised about Pound's ideogrammic method have been raised about Whitman's catalogs and images and his clusters of poems in *Leaves of Grass*. Some of the abrupt shifts in the poems of the "Sea-Drift" section, for example, or the catalogs of "Song of Myself," or in the swiftly succeeding images of "The Sleepers," are hard to interpret or explain in neat generalizations, yet they achieve some of the same intensifying or ironic effects available with the ideogrammic method. In both Whitman and Pound, at times this method approaches something in the nature of associational meditation or stream of consciousness—Whitman in "The Sleepers," for example, and Pound in the "Pisan Cantos." The method is perhaps used at its best when it seems to dramatize the flow of the mind, as in these poems.

Pound's language, like Whitman's, is closely associated with voice. Pound's early praise of Whitman singled out language for special comment: "Like Dante he wrote in the 'vulgar tongue,' in a new metric. The first great man to write in the language of his people."[31] This statement may reveal as much about Pound's language as Whitman's. It certainly seems plausible that Pound deliberately made it a part of his epic intent to use the "vulgar tongue" and write in the "language of the people." Passages of common American street "vulgarity" are abundant: Canto 15, "a clerical jock strap hanging back over the navel / his condom full of black beetles"; Canto 50, "S..t on the throne of England, s..t on the Austrian sofa / . . . Pus was in Spain, Wellington was a jew's pimp"; Canto 75, "but a snotty barbarian ignorant of T'ang history need not deceive one." *The Cantos* displays, of course, a whole range of language levels, depending on the voice the poet assumes. There are those moments of intense feelings of beauty or grief in which the language becomes more formal and special: Canto 47, "Falleth, / Adonis falleth. / Fruit cometh after"; Canto 81, "What thou lovest well remains, / the rest is dross / What thou lov'st well shall not be reft from thee." Like Whitman in such poems as "When Lilacs Last in the Dooryard Bloom'd," when the occasion or feeling calls for it, Pound shifts to a voice which the American reader recognizes as more formal, more traditional (even biblical), more (in some sense) elevated, a language for those special ceremonial and often sacred moments of life.

4

Walter Whitman's first statement to the world as Walt Whitman was the opening sentence of the 1855 Preface: "America does not repel the past or what it has produced under its forms or amid other politics or the idea of castes or the old religions." One of Whitman's last great poems was entitled "Passage to India,"— containing a "cry with thee O soul, / The Past! the Past! the Past!": a poem groping its way into the future by way of the past's myths and "primitive fables," "deep diving bibles and legends."[32] Ezra Pound's opening Canto is a modern translation (using many Anglo-Saxonisms) of a Renaissance Latin version of a Greek epic poem. This condensation of the past placed in the context of the modern is a recurrent method and technique of Pound, and, in spite of Whitman's occasional use and embrace of the past, sets Pound apart. More frequently than not, Whitman affirmed the time and place of the poet as the present and America, the here and now; Pound seems to have got caught up in the past and other cultures for many Cantos at a stretch.

Indeed, for many readers, the most un-American element of Pound is his propensity for other times, other places. Ancient China, Imperial Rome, Homeric Greece, Anglo-Saxon England, Medieval France, Renaissance Italy: can this be an *American* writer, who lived so much of his life in England, France, and Italy? Along with Henry James and T. S. Eliot, Pound takes his place as one of America's "foreign writers," non-native—in the view of some readers. But is this possible—that an American turn himself into a "foreign writer"? The myth persists, but the reality seems otherwise. Listen to two

Englishmen on Pound. Here is Stephen Spender, remembering the early Pound: "The persona was that of the rebel and raw genius from Idaho who knew about Provençal literature.... There was a parallel between the Whitmanish Ezra Pound and the working class D. H. Lawrence. Both produced an impression of bringing in mud onto the carpet."[33] And here is Wyndham Lewis: "Pound is, was always, is, must always remain, violently American. Tom Sawyer is somewhere in his gait, the *Leaves of Grass* survive as a manly candour in his broad and bearded face."[34] And Pound himself indicated his own feelings when he said in "Patria mia" (1913): "It would be about as easy for an American to become a Chinamen or a Hindoo as for him to acquire an Englishness, or a Frenchness, or a European-ness that is more than half skin deep."[35] And in his later life (as in his 1962 interview), Pound insisted on his American-ness. Asked about Europe, he answered: "There is incomprehension, Europe's incomprehension, of organic America. There are so many things which I, as an American, cannot say to a European with any hope of being understood. Somebody said that I am the last American living the tragedy of Europe."[36]

But with Whitman in the here and now, and Pound in the there and then, how can both be American, embody America and express America and portray America in epic poems—poems in which they themselves, old Walt and Old Ez, are the epic heroes? The answer may be more simple than it seems: they represent two responses to the American dilemma of American identity. Both Whitman and Pound launch journeys in quest of this knowledge, the one remaining at home, the other going abroad, the one searching intensively through his own time, the other through all time. This is perhaps a bit exaggerated, but nevertheless true; Whitman and Pound are simply reverse responses to a single challenge, the one response by its very oppositeness affirming the other—as American.

Both in the singleness of their responses go overboard. The single most common criticism of Whitman is his provincialism, his imaginative imprisonment in mid-nineteenth-century America, interpreted by some as chauvinism and barbarous ignorance. The single most common criticism of Pound is his alienation from his country and age, his imaginative imprisonment in the foreign and the past. However distorted these views (and both *are* considerably distorted), they represent tendencies in the poets and feelings in readers and critics that are typically American, clearly related to the brevity of American traditions, the elusiveness of an American identity, the absence of an uncontested American belief, myth, or Supreme Fiction. Indeed, the epic impulse in these two poets is to fill the void, to discover the lacking and needed, to recover the misplaced or lost. Thus the travel metaphor that they both use in common; though their routes are different, they travel to the same purpose and with the same destination in mind.

5

Is it possible to say what Pound discovers on his journey, and how it relates to Whitman's findings? Although the explicators have not yet read *The Cantos* in all their depth and complexity, it is possible now to detect broad lines of meaning, recurring and emphasized themes. Pound himself, though often cryptic, has made clear enough outside the poem many of its opaque meanings.

It is perhaps best to begin with what Pound recurrently laments, criticizes, curses, condemns, since the reader of *The Cantos* is most likely to carry away from them the most vivid impressions of the negative. The first extensive condemnatory Cantos are the Hell Cantos, Cantos 14, 15, and 16, with strong denunciation of war and particularly the disaster of World War I. But later scenes of the idle rich, the vacuous middle class, and meaningless activity of contemporary man all suggest the decline and decay of modern civilization. As the Cantos gather detail and momentum, it becomes clear that though the manifestations of the problem are many, the root cause may be resolved into one, indicated by Pound's most emotionally charged, overworked word: *usura*. The concept and name of usura appear and reappear throughout *The Cantos*, from beginning to end, and the word seems to come eventually to symbolize all past and present evil for Pound—the Moby Dick to his Ahab. And the word accumulates such charged meaning for him and the enduring reader that as the Cantos go by, Pound need only drop the word on the page to elicit the angry response.

Although there are many places in *The Cantos* where usura receives extended attention, Canto 45 appears the definitive if not classic statement in the poem. And Pound appends to this Canto a handy definition: "N.B. Usury: A charge for the use of purchasing power, levied without regard to production; often without regard to the possibilities of production (Hence the failure of the Medici Bank)." To clarify this definition would require a treatise on Pound's economic theories, which recur fragmentarily throughout *The Cantos*. Suffice it to say that from the beginning of time, with rare exceptions, those who have created the money supply for a society have unjustly received interest on it, thereby creating the basis for most economic (and human) problems. Most of Canto 45 is given over to a catalog of what usura precludes in life: with usura, no man has "a house of good stone," or "a painted paradise on his church wall," or "mountain wheat," or "strong flour." There is heavy emphasis on usura as destroyer or denier of man's art throughout the Canto, but at the end it broadens out:

> Usura slayeth the child in the womb
> It stayeth the young man's courting
> It hath brought palsy to bed, lyeth
> between the young bride and her bridegroom
>   CONTRA NATURAM
> They have brought whores for Eleusis
> Corpses are set to banquet
> at behest of usura.

In short, usura violates the selfhood of the individual, even in his procreational identity and sacred sexuality. In an old-age amendment of his views (in his 1972 Foreword to his *Selected Prose, 1909–1965),* Pound says: "Re usury: I was out of focus, taking a symptom for a cause. The cause is AVARICE."[37] This amendment seems hardly worth the trouble, for in *The Cantos* usura gradually gathers to itself the meaning of avarice, of money-lust. As such, it was a key evil in Whitman's view also. But since Whitman had a programmatic design for *Leaves of Grass* which diminished or eliminated the negative when it could not be embraced in a larger vision (see for example his negative rejected poems), he tended to confine his criticisms of contemporary life to his prose (this, of course, is not to deny the recurring anti-materialism theme in *Leaves of Grass,* in poems like "Song of the Open Road" and "Passage to India"). Perhaps his most vivid statement about money-lust, in language vying with Pound's in its intensities, appeared in the 1855 Preface:

> Beyond the independence of a little sum laid aside for burial-money, and of a few clapboards around and shingles overhead on a lot of American soil owned, and the easy dollars that supply the year's plain clothing and means, the melancholy prudence of the abandonment of such a great being as a man is to the toss and pallor of years of moneymaking with all their scorching days and icy nights and all their stifling deceits and underhanded dodgings, or infinitesimals of parlors, or shameless stuffing while others starve ...and all the loss of the bloom and odor of the earth and of the flowers and atmosphere and of the sea and of the true taste of the women and men you pass or have to do with in youth or middle age, and the issuing sickness and desperate revolt at the close of a

life without elevation or naivete, and the ghastly chatter of a death
without serenity or majesty, is the great fraud upon modern civilization and forethought, blotching the surface and system which
civilization undeniably drafts, and moistening with tears the immense features it spreads and spreads with such velocity before the
reached kisses of the soul.[38]

Pound's introduction—in Canto 45—of sexuality as one of the dimensions of man whose vitality is destroyed by usura suggests the
importance of the sexual theme in the Cantos as a whole. If the reader
is likely to carry away usura as the most vivid evil in Pound's poem,
he is likewise likely to carry away sexuality as the most vivid of his
affirmations. One critic (George Dekker) has devoted a principal part
of his work to tracking the "Theme of Eros in the Cantos."[39] I do not
wish to repeat his findings; nor do I wish to deny the important
influence of writers other than Whitman—such as Remy de Gourmont, whose *The Natural Philosophy of Love* (*Physique de l'amour*)
Pound translated in 1922.[40] But I would like to place Pound's sex
themes in the context of the Whitmanian epic tradition. Any full
account of Pound's treatment of sex would need to dwell at some
length on his presentation of women in Canto 29 ("the female / Is an
element, the female / Is a chaos / an octopus / A biological process")
and his use of Cavalcanti in Canto 36 ("Sacrum, sacrum, inluminatio
coitu": sacred, sacred, the illumination in coition).

But the most remarkable (and key) Canto on this theme is Canto 47.
In this Canto Pound reintroduces Odysseus, sailing "after knowledge," uniting with Circe, but "freed from the one bed / that thou
may'st return to another." The sexual or generative imagery is drawn
from all realms—"begin thy plowing," "wheat shoots rise," "the bull
runs blind on the sword"—and the Canto rises to rapturous sexual
climax:

> Hast thou found a nest softer than cunnus
> Or hast thou found better rest
> Hast'ou a deeper planting, doth thy death year
> Bring swifter shoot?
> Hast thou entered more deeply the mountain?
>
> The light has entered the cave. Io! Io!
> The light has gone down into the cave,
> Splendour on splendour!
> By prong have I entered these hills:
> That the grass grow from my body,
> That I hear the roots speaking together,
> The air is new on my leaf,

The forked boughs shake with the wind.
Is Zephyrus more light on the bough, Apeliota
more light on the almond branch?
By this door I have entered the hill.
Falleth,
Adonis falleth.
Fruit cometh after.

(p. 238)

Indeed, "sacrum, sacrum, inluminatio coitu": the image of the light
entering the cave suggests sexual penetration and, simultaneously,
illumination of darkness. The passage is remarkable for its mixture of
sexual and natural imagery, much in the highly suggestive way that
Whitman combined them.

There are several passages in Whitman evoked by Pound's Canto.
Section 28 of "Song of Myself" comes to mind, beginning "Is this
then a touch? quivering me to a new identity," and leading on to
sexual climax. And there is "Scented Herbage of My Breast" (in the
"Calamus" cluster), with such lines as: "O slender leaves! O blossoms
of my blood! I permit you to tell in your own way of the heart that is
under you"; "Yet you are beautiful to me you faint tinged roots, you
make me think of death." But perhaps the most clear evocation is
from a "Children of Adam" poem, "I Sing the Body Electric" (a poem
which Pound selected for his 1964 anthology):

Bridegroom night of love working surely and softly into
    the prostrate dawn,
Undulating into the willing and yielding day,
Lost in the cleave of the clasping and sweet-flesh'd day.

This the nucleus—after the child is born of woman, man
    is born of woman,
This the bath of birth, this the merge of small and large,
    and the outlet again.[41]

It is difficult to believe that Pound did not derive some of his
ingenuity in combining natural with sexual imagery, charging the
entire universe with sexuality, from his early reading of Whitman. And his introduction of the grass imagery ("That the grass
grow from my body") may well be taken, like many of the indirect allusions and references in The Cantos, as an oblique tribute
to and evocation of Whitman.

Usura, sexuality: these themes thread their way through all the
Cantos, continuing even after their full presentation in Cantos
45 and 47. Another recurring theme closely related to these is

political: if usura can destroy the individual in his sexuality, it can also destroy the body politic, the society, civilization. How should a man live, how should men live together? Pound found his guide in Confucius, introduced into *The Cantos* as early as Canto 13. The wisdom of Kung (Confucius) is presented in a remarkably direct manner:

> And Kung said, and wrote on the bo leaves:
>   If a man have not order within him
> He can not spread order about him;
> And if a man have not order within him
> His family will not act with due order;
>   And if the prince have not order within him
> He can not put order in his dominions.
> And Kung gave the words "order"
> And "brotherly deference"
> And said nothing of the "life after death."
> And he said
>   "Anyone can run to excesses,
> It is easy to shoot past the mark,
> It is hard to stand firm in the middle."
>
> (p. 59)

This rather simple set of principles may be taken as one of the foundation stones of *The Cantos*. Kung reappears frequently in *The Cantos*, along with references to him—such as the Chinese character meaning "balance."

In a sense, *The Cantos* may be read as a quest to discover the Confucian men of the past who might serve as models for the chaotic present. The Malatesta Cantos, Cantos 8–11, portray Sigismundo Malatesta of Renaissance Italy (Rimini) as what Pound called in *Guide to Kulchur* a "factive personality. . . an entire man."[42] In Cantos 31–34, Thomas Jefferson, John Adams, and James Madison emerge as a kind of pantheon of Confucian men, but it is John Adams who was to become the principal of these American heroes, the center of Cantos 62–71, some of the longest, and some would say dullest, of the Cantos. There are other individuals who are singled out for attention— Mussolini in Canto 41 and elsewhere—but Pound more or less rests his case on Malatesta and Adams. Clearly a critical test for a Poundian Confucian man is his ideas on money and banking: if he shares or seems to share some of Pound's (and C. H. Douglas's) ideas on social credit, he may be a leading candidate. But of course, he must also exhibit the simple principles of Confucius. Pound's Cantos devoted to these men and their historical periods tend to be the most disappointing in the poem: personalities become submerged in miscellaneous detail that accumulates at such a rapid rate and in such zig-zag fashion that continuity as well as poetry is dissipated in trivia.

The Confucian theme appears elsewhere throughout *The Cantos*, and becomes of first importance in the Chinese Cantos, 52–61. Here Pound covers Chinese history beginning 2837 B.C. and running to A.D. 1736. Dynasties come and dynasties go, but Pound persists through it all in search of the Confucian emperors, actions, and periods. The effect of these Cantos is a sense of the flow and panoramic sweep of history that is hard to define, but which is introduced in Canto 52, with Pound's partial translation of the Li Ki: "Toward summer when the sun is in Hyades / Sovran is Lord of the Fire / to this month are birds." The lines in their entirety give a rhythmic sense of the passage of time, and in addition, of a life lived in harmony with the seasonal and daily rhythms: the kind of harmony that might be called Confucian—order within the individual in tune with the great cosmic order of the universe.

Like most readers of *The Cantos*, I find the "Pisan Cantos" (though bristling with obscurities like the other Cantos) the most moving of the poem, and I am convinced, too, as Daniel Pearlman has persuasively argued, that they develop toward a climax—the climax of transcendent awareness in Canto 81, and the resulting reconciliation to death in Canto 82. Both of these Cantos, I believe, share a great many elements with the poetry of *Leaves of Grass*.

It is perhaps significant that Whitman's name is evoked three times in Canto 80—passing references, true, but perhaps foreshadowing. Before Canto 81, the "Pisan Cantos" have portrayed a man held in the Pisa DTC (Disciplinary Training Center), without books, with the barest of necessities, a crate for a desk placed in a "cage," his mind wandering over the historical past, his own personal past, dwelling on the deaths of friends, but coming back insistently and repeatedly in a kind of anguish to the present hell of imprisonment and humiliation. The body fixed, the mind wanders, sifting, sorting, searching, back and forth, back and forth, a mind pacing the body's cage, looking for an opening; and then, in Canto 81, the opening appears; there is a breakthrough, but not a breakout; there is a freeing of the mind, but not of the body. The mind soars out and up triumphantly, in an illumination new to the poem. The key passage begins: "Ed ascoltando al leggier mormorio" ("And listening to the light murmur"):

> there came new subtlety of eyes into my tent,
>   whether of spirit or hypostasis,
>   but what the blindfold hides
>   or at carnival

nor any pair showed anger
Saw but the eyes and stance between the eyes,
colour, diastasis,
careless or unaware it had not the
whole tent's room
nor was place for the full Εἰδὼς
interpass, penetrate
casting but shade beyond the other lights
sky's clear
night's sea
green of the mountain pool
shone from the unmasked eyes in half-mask's
space.

(p. 520)

There is clearly here a visitation—a visitation from the deeper self, bringing a "knowing" that has been too long hidden.

The self-knowledge is both reassuring and devastating:

What thou lovest well remains,
the rest is dross
What thou lov'st well shall not be reft from thee
What thou lov'st well is thy true heritage
Whose world, or mine or theirs
or is it of none?
First came the seen, then thus the palpable
Elysium, though it were in the halls of hell,
What thou lovest well is thy true heritage
What thou lov'st well shall not be reft from thee
The ant's a centaur in his dragon world.
Pull down thy vanity, it is not man
Made courage, or made order, or made grace,
Pull down thy vanity, I say pull down.

(pp. 520–21)

There is more along the same line—"Thou art a beaten dog beneath the hail, / A swollen magpie in a fitful sun"; "How mean thy hates / Fostered in falsity"—leading to a bit of recouping of self-assurance at the end—

To have gathered from the air a live tradition
or from a fine old eye the unconquered flame
This is not vanity.
Here error is all in the not done,
all in the diffidence that faltered . . .

(p. 522)

This Canto is remarkable from almost any point of view. It does appear in some sense a summary vision, a scathing self-illumination that Pound is finally able to endure. It appears almost like a final assessment, in preparation for an end that is near.

Perhaps the closest thing in Whitman appears in section 8 of "Passage to India," a poem in which Whitman's mind ranges over all history in a kind of fitful search until the sudden freeing comes: "Swiftly I shrivel at the thought of God, / At Nature and its wonders, Time and Space and Death." But there are similar visionary moments in other poems, such as the one that comes in section 15 of "When Lilacs Last in the Dooryard Bloom'd," introduced with the lines: "While my sight that was bound in my eyes unclosed, / As to long panoramas of visions."[43] Or the one that comes to the boy in "Out of the Cradle Endlessly Rocking," as he listens to the bird's song by the seaside, seeking the missing clue (death) from the whispering sea.

The passage evoking Whitman's "Out of the Cradle Endlessly Rocking" in Canto 82 stands in relation to the whole Canto much as the visionary lines of Canto 81 stand in relation to that Canto: they come at the end, after Pound's mind has wandered some leagues from the subject:

> Till forty years since, Reithmuller indignant:
> "Fyy! in Tdaenmarck efen dh' beasantz gnow him,"
>   meaning Whitman, exotic, still suspect
>   four miles from Camden
>
> (pp. 525–26)

It is perhaps characteristic that Pound would introduce Whitman by way of R. H. Reithmueller, who vividly emphasized his significance to Pound, many years before, at the University of Pennsylvania, where Riethmueller, author of *Walt Whitman and the Germans* (1906), was an instructor of German. Dredged from memory, Whitman comes to Pound by way of a foreigner concerned for the American poet's reputation at home—in America.

The Whitman that Pound evokes is the Whitman as poet of death in "Out of the Cradle Endlessly Rocking":

> "O troubled reflection
> "O Throat, O throbbing heart"
> How drawn, O GEA TERRA,
>   what draws as thou drawest
>   till one sink into thee by an arm's width
> embracing thee. Drawest,
>   truly thou drawest,
> Wisdom lies next thee,
>   simply, past metaphor.
>
> (p. 526)

Clearly Pound is feeling, like Whitman in the poem, the pull of earth, the pull of death: "man, earth: two halves of the tally / but I will come out of this knowing no one / neither they me." Amidst a flood of other associations, there emerge several lines in a reminder of Whitman's poem: "strong as the undertow / of the wave receding / but that a man should live in that further terror, and live / the loneliness of death came upon me / (at 3 P.M., for an instant)." The personal reference here is startling in its particularity, like the presence of death itself. Whitman's boy-bird drama was played out at the seashore, climaxing with an almost sexual interchange between the boy and the sea: the sea "Creeping thence steadily up to my ears and laving me softly all over," "hissing melodious"—"Death, death, death, death, death." The Canto ends with a reminder of the bird's song in "Cradle":

> three solemn half notes
>   their white downy chests black-rimmed
>   on the middle wire
>   periplum
>
>   (p. 527)

Whitman's mockingbird had sung his aria in groups of three notes—first in the happy song, "Shine! shine! shine!" and then in the sad song of death, "Soothe! soothe! soothe!"[44] The bird of Pound's Canto sounds his notes, surely, of "solemn" knowledge of "death, death, death." Pound at the end of the Canto, like Whitman's boy at the end of "Cradle," is ready for continuation of the journey, endowed now with a new and vital knowledge and experience of death. I tramp a perpetual journey—periplum—circumnavigation.[45]

The reader who has experienced intense frustration in reading *The Cantos* (and I put myself, along with most readers, in this category) is likely to overvalue the older poet's statements criticizing and even dismissing the younger poet's work. Neither Pound nor Whitman gained the readers they must have envisioned for their work, and Whitman reconciled himself (in "Long, Long Hence," the poem Pound referred to in his early essay on Whitman) to a postponed assessment or recognition: "after ages' and ages' encrustations, / Then only may these songs reach fruition."[46] Pound had as a young man envisioned himself as one of Whitman's "encrustations," and his feelings at the end of his career must have been very close to Whitman's. Pound's late "Drafts and Fragments" reveal a poet beset by self doubts. Canto 116 is perhaps typical:

> Came Neptunus
>   his mind leaping

> like dolphins,
> These concepts the human mind has attained.
> To make Cosmos—
> To achieve the possible—
>
> (p. 795)

Is this "Neptunus" the young Pound, full of the possibilities of making his epic—or "Cosmos" (a favorite Whitmanian word)? The spirit and energy of youth is there in the image of the "mind leaping, / like dolphins." But—

> But the record
>   the palimpsest—
> a little light
>   in great darkness—
>   (p. 795)

But the obscured tablets do not yield their messages: too many texts, too many erasures, only a "little light." Pound asks:

> I have brought the great ball of crystal;
>   who can lift it?
> Can you enter the great acorn of light?
>   But the beauty is not the madness
> Tho' my errors and wrecks lie about me.
> And I am not a demigod,
> I cannot make it cohere.
> If love be not in the house there is nothing.
> The voice of famine unheard.
>   (p. 796)

Few indeed can lift Pound's "great ball of crystal" or enter his "great acorn of light"; the "errors and wrecks" are formidable, the incoherence frustrating. But something, something remains:

> but about that terzo
>   third heaven,
>   that Venere,
> again is all "paradiso"
>   a nice quiet paradise
>   over the shambles,
> and some climbing
>   before the take-off,
> to "see again,"
> the verb is "see," not "walk on"
> i.e. it coheres all right
>   even if my notes do not cohere.
> Many errors,

                    a little rightness,
              to excuse his hell
                    and my paradiso.
                         (pp. 796–97)

If Pound could not create the Paradiso he had envisioned in his
youth, at least he could proclaim its existence: Paradiso coheres, even
though Pound's notes (*The Cantos*) do not: it is there to be seen, not
walked on. The Canto concludes:

        To confess wrong without losing rightness
        Charity I have had sometimes,
              I cannot make it flow thru.
        A little light, like a rushlight
              to lead back to splendour.
                         (p. 797)

   Canto 116 is a confessional Canto that will disarm some of Pound's
severest critics. But the question persists: what is the Paradiso about
which he seems so upset, frustrated. Early in the "Pisan Cantos"
(Canto 74, dated 1948), he wrote: "le Paradis n'est pas artificiel / but
spezzato apparently" (p. 438). Paradise is not artificial, but broken
apparently; "it exists only in fragments unexpected excellent
sausage, / the smell of mint, for example" (p. 438). In Canto 92 (*Rock
Drill*, dated 1955), he wrote in similar vein:

        Le Paradis n'est pas artificiel
                         but is jagged,
        For a flash,
                 for an hour.
        Then agony,
                 then an hour,
                         then agony.
                         (p. 620)

And in the last Canto (120), published in 1969, clearly only a fragment, but also something of a last testament, Pound confessed:

        I have tried to write Paradise

        Do not move
           Let the wind speak
              that is paradise.

        Let the Gods forgive what I
              have made
        Let those I love try to forgive
              what I have made.
                         (p. 803)

These lines at the end of *The Cantos* may be viewed as something of an oasis by the reader who has made his way through the bewilderments of eight hundred pages of the poem. They are lucid, they are wise, they are human, and they are moving. It is perhaps a small knowing that Pound has led to, but it is also perhaps a deep one: how many restless readers have attained the wisdom to remain still to listen, to "let the wind speak"?

A final word:
"Walt's Reply"

Irving Layton

I make a peace with you, Ezra Pound—
I have ignored you long enough.
I come to you as a father
Who has had a pig-headed son;
I am ghost enough now not to grieve.
The obstinacy was yours, not mine;
Insolence and folly brought you low.
Too late you learned humility and love.
Let mankind judge between us.[47]

Six

Beneath all the declamation there is another tone, and behind all the illusions there is another vision. When Whitman speaks of the lilacs or of the mocking-bird, his theories and beliefs drop away like a needless pretext.

Eliot, "Whitman and Tennyson"

T. S. Eliot's "Waste Land"

One of the several handbooks on *The Waste Land* has characterized it as "something like the modern epic," but with a difference: "If an epic is 'that rich vessel which contains the ideals and aspirations of the race,' this poem is a mirror of a certain modern fatigue and dismay."[1] Earlier, I. A. Richards categorized *The Waste Land* as an epic in defending its density of literary allusions: "Allusion in Mr. Eliot's hands is a technical device for compression. *The Waste Land* is the equivalent in content to an epic. Without this device twelve books would have been needed."[2] Whether the reader agrees with the effect claimed for allusion, he is likely to feel *The Waste Land* is in some obscure sense "epic." But in what sense?

In the Whitmanian sense? It is difficult to find two more unlike poets than Eliot and Whitman. But their very unlikeness may be the clue to their community of aim: to express an age through expression of self. Of course, if we take Eliot at his word in "Tradition and the Individual Talent," he would have none of any "expression of the self."[3] But in fact, with what we know now after the publication of the earlier version of *The Waste Land*, and with Eliot's critical comments later in life that seem to refer to *The Waste Land*, we may easily envision Eliot bent on "expression of self" in his most famous poem (as, indeed, we might argue easily that Whitman found his "objective correlative" in such "personal" poems as "Song of Myself" or "When Lilacs Last in the Dooryard Bloom'd").

M. L. Rosenthal, in one of the most perceptive analyses of the *Waste Land* manuscripts (*"The Waste Land* as an Open Structure"), intuitively reached back to Whitman via D. H. Lawrence for a major point of comparison:

> . . .because of certain different emphases while the poem [*The Waste Land*] was still in the making, the sense of improvisation at the high pitch of genius that struck the first readers of the printed text is reinforced. One almost does well to forget Pound and think of someone as unlikely as Lawrence, with his idea of Whitman as the poet of the "open road," and of a poetry "of the present"; Lawrence wrote in 1918 of "the poetry of that which is at hand: the immediate present. In the immediate present there is no perfection, no consummation, nothing finished. The strands are all flying, quivering, intermingling into the web, the waters are shaking the moon . . . . This is the unrestful, ungraspable poetry of the sheer present, poetry whose very permanency lies in its wind-like transit. Whitman's is the best poetry of this kind."[4]

In examining the passages Eliot (often on Pound's advice) discarded from the original version of *The Waste Land*, Rosenthal astutely observed:

> And yet Eliot, had he kept these passages, would have committed himself to a much more confessional and vulnerable role in the structure of the poem. He would have had to set his own finicky and precious attitudes, and his abysmal feelings about female physicality, into the scale with other predominant motifs. These were possibilities of commitment toward which he went a fairly long way. In the era of Robert Lowell and Allen Ginsberg, he might well have gone the whole distance. Neither his nor Pound's taste was ready to be confident about doing so in 1922, and doubtless the best available reading public for poetry would not have been ready either.[5]

The implications that flow from the revelation that the deep or original (or originating) structure of *The Waste Land* was "open" and "confessional" in this Whitmanian-Lawrentian sense will be traced out below.[6] It is enough now to suggest that Whitman's so-called optimism and Eliot's pessimism are two sides of the same poetic coin, that both outlooks derived from personal sources and were projected onto worlds that accepted the outlooks as confirming their own.

Eliot's earliest comments on Whitman might well give pause to anyone seeking a link between the two. In fact, Eliot's references to Whitman are such as to raise questions of deeper connections than those admitted. One book has argued the case strongly for a pervasive unconscious influence of Whitman on Eliot.[7] Is it possible that Eliot was so strong in his denunciation because he felt touched, swayed, even influenced? In his Introduction to the 1928 edition of Ezra Pound's *Selected Poems*, Eliot wrote: "I did not read Whitman until much later [than 1908, 1909] in life and had to conquer an aversion to his form, as well as to much of his matter, in order to do so."[8]

One of the strange aspects of Eliot's attitude toward Whitman is his repeated insistence that Whitman could not have influenced Pound—strange, that is, in view of Pound's own admission in his early essay on Whitman (written 1909, published 1955) of just such an influence ("Mentally I am a Walt Whitman who has learned to wear a collar"). In "Ezra Pound: His Metric and Poetry" (1917) Eliot wrote: "Whitman is certainly not an influence; there is not a trace of him anywhere; Whitman and Mr. Pound are antipodean to each other."[9] *Not a trace* is the kind of extreme statement to inspire a contrary critic to find a trace—the kind of statement, in fact, that calls itself by the very nature of its flamboyance into question; and indeed, some critics have found several traces of Whitman in Pound, as for example Donald Davie in his 1964 work, *Ezra Pound: Poet as Sculptor* (referring to the early poetry: "The only poetic voice that [Pound] can command . . . is the voice of Whitman.")[10] Eliot would not let the matter lie, and returned to it in his Introduction to *Ezra Pound: Selected Poems* (1928): "I am . . . certain—it is indeed obvious—that Pound owes nothing to Whitman"; "Now Pound's originality is genuine in that his versification is a *logical* development of the verse of his English predecessors. Whitman's originality is both genuine and spurious. It is genuine in so far as it is a *logical* development of certain English prose; Whitman was a great prose writer. It is spurious in so far as Whitman wrote in a way that asserted that his great prose was a new form of verse. (And I am ignoring in this connection the large part of clap-trap in Whitman's content.)"[11] It is somewhat surprising to find Eliot here resurrecting a disreputable theory that Whitman's poetry was really not poetry, but prose instead. And the parting shot, especially that "clap-trap," betrays an intensity of feeling that the critical point seems hardly to call for. What in Whitman inspired such passionate response?

In a 1926 review of Emory Holloway's biography of Whitman, which had raised a question about Whitman's ambivalent sexuality following Holloway's discovery that a "Children of Adam" poem addressed to a woman had been in manuscript originally addressed to a man, Eliot perhaps touched on the matter that made him so intense in his feeling about Whitman: "Whitman had the ordinary desires of the flesh; for him there was no chasm between the real and the ideal, such as opened before the horrified eyes of Baudelaire. But this, and the 'frankness' about sex for which he is either extolled or mildly reproved, did not spring from any particular honesty or clearness of vision: it sprang from what may be called either 'idealization' or a faculty for make-believe, according as we are disposed. There is, fundamentally, no difference between the Whitman frankness and the Tennyson delicacy, except in its relation to public opinion of the time." This is a strange statement indeed in the context of the revelations of the Holloway book; and the attempt to equate the "Whitman frankness and the Tennyson delicacy" seems far-fetched: clearly Eliot saw himself closer to the Baudelaire "horror." In spite of its general negative thrust, his review of the Whitman biography concluded with a positive assessment, however backhanded: "Beneath all the declamations there is another tone, and behind all the illusions there is another vision. When Whitman speaks of the lilacs or of the mocking-bird, his theories and beliefs drop away like a needless pretext."[12] This last sentence has the passionate ring of one who has been deeply moved by Whitman's major poetry—perhaps even in spite of himself.

In something of a final assessment of Whitman in 1953, in "American Literature and the American Language," Eliot singled him out along with Poe and Twain as "landmarks" of American literature: "To Walt Whitman . . . a great influence on modern poetry has been attributed. I wonder if this has not been exaggerated. In this respect he reminds me of Gerard Manley Hopkins—a lesser poet than Whitman, but also a remarkable innovator in style. Whitman and Hopkins, I think, both found an idiom and a metric perfectly suited for what they had to say; and very doubtfully adaptable to what anyone else has to say."[13] In view of Eliot's previous views of Whitman, this statement is nothing short of amazing, and seems to pay homage to both Whitman's form and content. To place Whitman above Hopkins, whose religious poetry would by its very nature have attracted Eliot's deep appreciation, and whose dazzling metrics and sound patterns would have held his deep interest, is astonishing. And to conclude of Whitman that he found "an idiom and a metric perfectly suited" for what he had to say is a long, long way from his early view that both his form and content were suspect. Can we detect here, perhaps, the genuine view of a poet now secure in his own style and reputation, with no longer a need to deny his precursors?

Although it would serve no purpose to go through Eliot's poetry tracking every Whitmanian echo,[14] there are one or two highly relevant to my purposes here. The first, little noticed, appears in "Ode," a poem that Eliot published in *Ara Vos Prec*, 1920 limited edition, never reprinted; thus it does not appear among his collected poems, and has escaped the attention of most of his critics. Space does not permit full analysis of this poem (for my reading of it as a confessional poem see *T. S. Eliot's Personal Waste Land*), but the second stanza appears intelligible only in a Whitmanian context:

> Misunderstood
> The accents of the now retired
> Profession of the calamus.[15]

Eliot's pervasive technique of literary allusion renders it inevitable that, on encountering "calamus," the reader recall the only literary use of the word—in Whitman's *Leaves of Grass*. "Calamus" is a cluster of poems devoted to comradeship, "adhesive" love, and man-man relationships, coming directly after and in contrast to the "Children of Adam" cluster of procreational, sexual, or man-woman poems. (*Calamus* was the title, too, given to a volume of Whitman's passionately intense letters to his "Young Friend," Peter Doyle, published in 1897.) Eliot would surely never have used the word without expecting his readers to make the Whitman connection. We can only assume, then, that the speaker of "Ode" has been a writer whose work has been "misunderstood"—the previous work that was written with the "accents" of the "profession of the calamus." The "accents" of comradeship, man-man love? "Ode" was probably written in 1918, and Eliot had published in 1917 *Prufrock and Other Observations*, a book containing such poems as "The Love Song of J. Alfred Prufrock," and "Portrait of a Lady"—poems portraying (among other things) men who cannot love women.

Another important echo of *Leaves* appears in a passage of *The Waste Land* that Eliot designated as his favorite—what he called the "30 good lines" of the poem, lines of "the water-dripping song in the last part" ("What the Thunder Said"). Among these lines appear the following:

> If there were the sound of water only
> Not the cicada
> And dry grass singing
> But sound of water over a rock

Where the hermit-thrush sings in the pine trees
Drip drop drip drop drop drop drop
But there is no water.

(p. 144)[16]

In view of Eliot's own appreciation of "When Lilacs Last in the Dooryard Bloom'd" (as in the comment quoted above concluding his review of the Holloway biography), the Whitman connection here can be missed only at peril of misreading the meaning. The hermit thrush is an American bird, and Whitman made it his own in his Lincoln elegy. We might even take the "dry grass singing" as an oblique allusion to *Leaves of Grass*, where the grass image evoked is usually green, not dry. There is no "sound of water," there is no green grass growing, there is no hermit thrush singing in the pine trees. What is missing, then, is not merely a set of sounds, but what the sounds vitally imply; and what they imply can be fully comprehended only in the context of Whitman's "Lilacs." Whitman's hermit thrush becomes the source of his reconciliation to Lincoln's death, to all death as the "strong deliveress." The poet follows the bird to hear "Death's outlet song of life" as he goes "Down to the shores of the water, the path by the swamp in the dimness, / To the solemn shadowy cedars and ghostly pines so still." Lincoln is never mentioned by name in "Lilacs," but references to him are very much in the "calamus" spirit—the poet mourns for his "comrade lustrous," for the dead he "loved so well."[17] If we follow out all the implications of Eliot's evocation of Whitman's "Lilacs" at this critical moment in *The Waste Land*, we might assume that the modern poem has its origins, too, in a death, in a death deeply felt, the death of a beloved friend. But unlike the Whitman poem, Eliot's *Waste Land* has no retreat on the "shores of the water," no hermit thrush to sing its joyful carol of death; rather, "Only a cock...on the rooftree" to sound mockingly its ambiguous "Co co rico co co rico" (p. 145).

2

When Valerie Eliot edited and published *The Waste Land: A Facsimile and Transcription of the Original Drafts* in 1971, she prefaced the materials with one of Eliot's few comments about the poem's meaning: "Various critics have done me the honour to interpret the poem in terms of criticism of the contemporary world, have considered it, indeed, as an important bit of social criticism. To me it was only the relief of a personal and wholly insignificant grouse against life; it is just a piece of rhythmical grumbling." Critics have tended to ignore or discount this statement, primarily because they have been unwilling to reconsider the long tradition of interpreting the poem as primarily social criticism. I wish to take Eliot's statement seriously, and, moreover, I would like to link it to the by now familiar description, in "A Backward Glance," of Whitman's aim in *Leaves of Grass*, "to articulate and faithfully express in literary or poetic form, and uncompromisingly, my own physical, emotional, moral, intellectual, and aesthetic Personality, in the midst of, and tallying, the momentous spirit and facts of its immediate days, and of current America."[18]

In making this link with Whitman, I shall not follow the practice of critics of looking back from the 1922 published *Waste Land* to the 1917 essay "Tradition and the Individual Talent," with its ambiguous "Impersonal theory of poetry" (later strongly modified by Eliot); but instead will look forward to the Eliot who would describe his own *Waste Land* as a "personal...grouse," and who could write of Tennyson's *In Memoriam*: "It is unique: it is a long poem made by putting together lyrics, which have only the unity and continuity of a diary, the concentrated diary of a man confessing himself." In this same 1936 essay on Tennyson, Eliot appeared to have his own *Waste Land* in mind when he wrote: "It happens now and then that a poet by some strange accident expresses the mood of his generation, at the same time that he is expressing a mood of his own which is quite remote from that of his generation."[19] The thrust behind such language as this is very close to that in Whitman's remark quoted above: whether expressing a "Personality" (emotional, moral, intellectual), or expressing his own mood, Whitman, Tennyson—and Eliot himself in *The Waste Land*—seem to be embarked on obscurely related enterprises.

But how is it that critics have for so long missed the personal "mood" in *The Waste Land* that Eliot seems to claim repeatedly as prior and fundamental?[20] The answer, I think, is that there are two *Waste Lands*, the one published in 1922, heavily shaped by Ezra Pound; the other, the original set of manuscripts that Eliot handed over to Pound. It is possible that this "original" poem is the one that Eliot is remembering when he speaks of his relation to the poem. It is, after all, closer to the original sources, feelings, and impulses out of which the poem came. Moreover, there is evidence that Eliot felt the poem slipping out of his grasp as he saw it revised by Pound and as he sometimes reluctantly acquiesced in the revision; as he saw it, in other words, become something other than he had set out to write and had actually written.

Let us take one example, but an important one—the epigraph of the original poem, from Joseph Conrad's *Heart of Darkness:* "Did he live his life again in every detail of desire, temptation, and surrender during that supreme moment of complete knowledge? He cried in a whisper at some image, at some vision—he cried out twice, a cry that was no more than a breath—'The horror! the horror!'" (p. 3). The words are, of course, those of Marlow describing the death of Kurtz, speculating on Kurtz's own awareness of complicity and self-involvement. Pound wrote to Eliot: "I doubt if Conrad is weighty enough to stand the citation." Eliot replied: "Do you mean not use the Conrad quote or simply not put Conrad's name to it? It is much the most appropriate I can find, and somewhat elucidative." At this slight complaint, Pound gave his reluctant permission on the epigraph: "Ditto re Conrad; who am I to grudge him his laurel crown?"[21] But of course, Pound's acquiescence is phrased in such a way as to encourage Eliot to change the quotation—which he did, adopting the now famous passage in Latin and Greek, without indication of its source from Petronius's *Satyricon* (chapter 48): "Yes, and I myself with my own eyes saw the Sibyl of Cumae hanging in the cage; and when the boys cried at her: 'Sibyl, what do you want?', she used to reply, 'I want to die' " (p. 133).

   As in instance after instance in the revision, Pound succeeded here in diffusing one dimension of the poem on behalf of another, a "public" or "social" meaning which he perhaps succeeded in making dominant. Indeed, in a letter written in July 1922 Pound defended the social criticism of his own poetry, spoke out for a "profounder didacticism" in art ("It's all rubbish to pretend that art isn't didactic"), and then revealingly referred to *The Waste Land* in a proprietary tone: "Eliot's Waste Land is I think the justification of the 'movement,' of our modern experiment, since 1900. It shd. be published this year."[22] The context makes it clear that Pound saw *The Waste Land* as an example of that "profounder didacticism" which he was defending—the kind of didacticism that would seriously confront the "foeter" of England and the "rotting" of the "British Empire." It takes little imagination, in the light of Eliot's later disclaimers of any major intent of "social criticism," to assume that *The Waste Land*'s author and *The Waste Land*'s reviser were working at odds, consciously or unconsciously, in giving final birth to the poem. The reviser made the poem over into a Poundian poem.

   The shift of the epigraph from Conrad to Petronius may be taken as representative. The shift is out and back, to foreign (even "dead") languages and the distant past. And the shift is from the human to the mythic—it is the Sybil who wants to die. The possible personal relevance is highly ambiguous. But the Conrad quotation is another matter. Eliot's remark to Pound—"It is the most appropriate I can find, and somewhat elucidative"—has gone almost unnoticed by *Waste Land* critics. *Appropriate* and *elucidative:* the very fact that Eliot saw the Conrad quotation in this way, and that Pound simply wondered about its "weightiness," suggests a major difference in approach, in comprehension. Moreover, Eliot would seem to be right. There are words and phrases in the Conrad epigraph that are echoed in the poem: "Did he live his life again in every detail of desire, temptation, and surrender during that supreme moment of complete knowledge?" Desire: "memory and desire, stirring / Dull roots with spring rain." Temptation and surrender: "The awful daring of a moment's surrender / Which an age of prudence can never retract." A "supreme moment of complete knowledge": Then spoke the Thunder; "Datta, dayadhvan, damyata": "give, sympathise, control" (pp. 145–46). In *Heart of Darkness*, Kurtz "cried in a whisper at some image, at some vision—he cried out twice, a cry that was no more than a breath—'The horror! the horror!' " The whole of *The Waste Land*, especially as it exists in the manuscripts, appears to be scenes from a life lived over again, scenes flashing by during a "supreme moment of complete knowledge," scenes that make up an interior "image" or "vision," evoking "The horror! the horror!"

In short, the Petronius quotation points outside while the Conrad points inside the consciousness of the poem: indeed, the state of consciousness and self-awareness of Kurtz in *The Heart of Darkness* may be taken as a paradigm for a similar state of consciousness lying behind and unifying *The Waste Land*. It announces (or suggests) that *The Waste Land* is focused not on the world but on an individual's consciousness as he is perceiving himself and the world—in a state of emotional-spiritual crisis. Marlow's statement about Kurtz, then, offers a kind of outline of the "action" of *The Waste Land*, and is indeed, as Eliot told Pound, "appropriate" and "elucidative." This "action" is not an objective statement of social criticism about the world become waste land. Rather, it is a dramatization of an individual consciousness in a precarious state of balance living "his life again in every detail of desire, temptation, and surrender" as he works his way to that "supreme moment of complete knowledge" out of the Thunder's voice (at the end of "What the Thunder Said"). The knowledge is self-knowledge. The final vision is a vision of the self broken and shattered, shoring some literary-intellectual fragments against his "ruins." *The Waste Land* lies within. It may lie within us all.

We may, then, read the original *Waste Land* as a dreamlike recapitulation of a life, all the scenes connected with that one life, the characters melding into each other as in a dream, but resolving into figures connected with the life represented by that central consciousness. All of the original poem fits easily into this frame, and the parts form a sequence that moves with a kind of directness and inevitability to the vision brought by the Thunder's voice at the end. With this frame in mind, we may more easily understand those sections of the manuscripts, excised by Pound and Eliot, that had direct connection with Eliot's life—the opening scene of debauchery, for example, which came out of Eliot's Harvard days, or the long sea scene of Part IV, that related to Eliot's youth and his summer vacations in Massachusetts near the Dry Salvages. In presenting a consciousness reliving his moments of "desire, temptation, and surrender," Eliot felt free to draw (or perhaps unconsciously drew) on moments and details of his own life, some of the most clear-cut of which did not survive revision. With the publication of *The Waste Land* facsimile, Valerie Eliot revealed more and more of the poem's "characters" as originating in Eliot's own life (as, for example, the Marie of the opening section, and Stetson at its close).[23]

3

In contrast with most analyses of *The Waste Land*, we might heed Eliot's observations that in his end is his beginning: we shall begin with the "moment" which the original epigraph indicated was in the poem, and to which all the rest of the poem is directed: a life relived up to a moment of "complete knowledge." Since the epigraph indicated that the "details" of the life relived were details of "desire, temptation, and surrender," we might expect the knowledge achieved to have something to do with these matters. And, indeed, this proves to be the case.

Eliot directs our attention in his footnotes to the *Brihadaranyaka Upanishad*, 5, 1, for the source of his "Datta, dayadhvam, damyata," and for the "fable of the meaning of the Thunder." In the *Upanishad*, the god Prajāpati is asked by his sons—gods, men, and Asuras—to instruct them, and he does so through the voice of the Thunder, always in a single syllable. First he says "Da," and the gods understand him to advise self-control; his next "Da" to the men they take to mean "give"; and his third "Da" to the Asuras (Hindu evil deities) they understand to mean "have compassion." As the commentator on this *Upanishad* points out, the uttering of the one syllable forced each group in turn to discover his own weakness within. In other words, the god's advice turns out to be self-advice that is elicited through self-awareness.[24]

Eliot departs from the *Upanishad*, as he inverts the order from *control yourselves, give*, and *have compassion* to *give, sympathize, control*, and as he subtly modulates the meaning to suit his own purposes. The first "Da" the poet hears he takes to be "Datta": give. Whereas the men in the *Upanishad* take this advice to mean "distribute your wealth to the best of your might, for you are naturally avaricious," Eliot applies it in an entirely different context. This should be sufficient signal to the reader that the poet is not simply reproducing the incident from the *Upanishad* but is adapting it to his situation in *The Waste Land*. When the Thunder says "Da," the poet-protagonist responds with a genuine confrontation with the interior self—and the intrusive memory that has haunted him throughout the poem.

The manuscript is helpful in clarifying the nature of that memory. At one time (in probably the earliest version), Eliot had written (italicized words later revised):

> Datta. *we brother,* what have we given!
> My friend, *my friend, beating in* my heart,
> The awful daring of a moment's surrender
> Which an age of prudence *cannot* retract—
> By this, and this only, we have existed,
> Which is not to be found in our obituaries,
> *Nor* in memories *which will busy* beneficent spiders
> Nor *in documents eaten* by the lean solicitor
> In our empty rooms.
>
> (p. 77)

The partner is unmistakably masculine, the moment is a "moment of surrender," a giving of the self to a friend—a surrender and a giving that "an age of prudence cannot retract." In revising the passage, the meaning was not changed, but slightly dispersed or diffused. The first line dropped the direct address, "we brother." The second line became "My friend, blood shaking my heart"; in the original, it is clearly the friend "beating in" the poet's heart that has been the origin of his passionate intensity.

The meaning of this passage appears to me lucid, and the tone not ironic but deeply moved, deeply moving. It is a confrontation that is also self-confession. The poet and his friend have experienced the "awful daring of a moment's surrender." An age, or lifetime, of "prudence" cannot "retract" that moment, cannot replace it; it exists in time, it endures in the memory. Moreover, this moment has been the essence of their existence, this memory shaping their very selves, giving them their essential, their emotional identity. When they die, this shaping event will not even be listed in their obituaries, nor will it be found in "memories" (mementoes, "treasures") that the spiders will take over, nor in the documents, "under seal," opened after their death by their lawyers (solicitors) going through their "empty rooms." Clearly this passage is clarification for the self, and an affirmation, a confrontation with the truth that the poet-protagonist must learn to live with, not evade, not suppress, not deny, not duplicate or attempt to duplicate.

The second "Da" of the Thunder becomes in the poet's understanding "Dayadhvam," "sympathize." The manuscript version is again helpful (italicized words later revised):

> Dayadhvam. *friend, my friend* I have heard the key
> Turn in the door, once and once only.
> We think of the key, each in his prison,
> Thinking of the key, each *has built* a prison.
> Only at nightfall, aetherial murmurs
> *Repair* for a moment a broken Coriolanus.
>
> (p. 79)

Once again, Eliot's revisions have slightly diffused the meaning. And his quotations in the footnotes from Dante and F. H. Bradley have deflected the critics from the continuity of meaning in the Thunder passage. It is significant, as revealed in the manuscript, that the passage begins in direct address to the friend. The key that has turned in the door "once and once only" is surely related to the previous "awful daring of a moment's surrender." The self has been genuinely penetrated only once—during that surrender with the friend. The rest of existence has been a memory of that moment, and a contemplation of the key that was once turned. But each is in his prison, a prison (as in the manuscript) "each has built." Though we long for that human or spiritual intermingling, for the soul-sharing that might come with the turn of the key, it does not turn, and we remain alone. *Sympathize. Have compassion.* In a world in which we all exist behind barriers, in fearful isolation, that we ourselves have created, where the very nature of existence itself helps create the prisons we built for ourselves, there is abundant need of sympathy and compassion. The proud Coriolanus may be a supreme example of a man isolated in his own prison. Eliot changed the *repair* to *restore*, and then to *revive the spirits of*. Finally the line read: "Revive for a moment a broken Coriolanus." The precise meaning of these references to Coriolanus may remain obscure,[25] but the general meaning is clear: only occasionally and perhaps transcendentally (or imaginatively) is his (or the poet's, or our) isolation dispelled—and then only momentarily, "aetherially."

The third "Da" spoken by the Thunder evokes from the poet "Damyata," control. In the *Upanishad*, the control is clearly self-control. In Eliot, the control is expanded in meaning. Again, the original manuscript gives us more details with which to construct the meaning (italicized words later revised):

> Damyata: *the wind was fair, and* the boat responded
> Gaily, to the hand expert with sail and *wheel.*
> The sea was calm, *and* your *heart responded*
> Gaily, when invited, beating *responsive*
> To controlling hands. *I left without you*
> *Clasping empty hands I sit upon the shore*
> *Fishing, with the desolate sunset behind me*
> *Which now at last . . . .*
>
> (p. 79)

These lines went through several changes, and were finally published:

> Damyata: The boat responded
> Gaily, to the hand expert with sail and oar
> The sea was calm, your heart would have responded
> Gaily, when invited, beating obedient
> To controlling hands.
>
> (p. 146)

In the published *Waste Land*, there is a distinct break at this point, as the image of the poet become fisher king begins the concluding section of the poem.

Given the sequence we have been following in the "Thunder" passages of the manuscripts, there is every reason to believe that the poet is addressing his friend in this sea scene, and it may, in the original version, have been a reconstruction of that moment of daring surrender. In the original manuscript, the moment is consummated: "your heart responded / Gaily, when invited, beating responsive / To controlling hands." By the time the passage is published, the moment is an opportunity passed by: "your heart *would have* responded"; and the beating of the heart would not have been *responsive* but *obedient.* The "controlling hands" are curiously retained. Moreover, the original manuscript describes a separation: "I left without you / Clasping empty hands I sit upon the shore." That "desolate sunset" is clearly the poet's own desolation in the separation from his friend, symbolized by the "clasping empty hands" that once were "controlling."

The third "Da" completes the Thunder's message, and completes, too, the poet's vivid confrontation with the realities of his life that have heretofore evaded him. Though he has not resolved the causes of his agony, he has come to a full recognition of its sources, and he can now set about shaping his life to live as he can with this "complete knowledge." We might summarize the section devoted to the "fable of the meaning of the Thunder"—give, sympathize, control— thus: the poet-protagonist confesses that he has given himself in surrender in a moment whose meaning is beyond calculation; he asks for understanding and sympathy in his impenetrable isolation, an imprisonment that is part of the common human predicament; and he pledges an exchange of one kind of control (of another individual) into self-control, changing controlling hands into clasped hands.

In arriving at this "supreme moment of complete knowledge," the poet presumably relived his life in every detail of "desire, temptation, and surrender." The scenes of *The Waste Land* leading up to this climactic moment should, if we are right, reveal something of these details.

4

We may assume that we are closer not only to the poem's sources but also to its profoundest meanings in reading it through the manuscripts, in the structure it had before the Pound revisions. The various scenes, episodes, or images we may take as flashing fleetingly through the mind of the poet-protagonist on his way to the vision evoked by the Thunder's voice. The original title of the work, "He Do the Police in Different Voices," suggests such a continuity: that is, that all the voices of the poem are those of the poet himself, that the entire drama is interior, that the self of the poet comes forth in the many roles in which he had previously lived his life. In editing the manuscripts, and subsequently, Valerie Eliot has emphasized the biographical sources of the poem. Her persuasive revelations, often coming originally from the poet himself, show the poem as much less independent of its author than once assumed. Indeed, the "I" of the poem appears now to have the kind of connection with the author that Whitman's "I" has in his *Leaves*, or Pound's in *The Cantos*, or (in a complicated way) John Berryman's various "I's" in *The Dream Songs*. Thus in quickly reading through the poem, we shall repeatedly note a biographical dimension.

Perhaps the most biographical of all the lines are those Eliot placed first, a scene of one night's debauchery (or hell-raising) by college youth in a night out on the town in the Boston of Eliot's own college days. Drinking and sex are the aim, but there seems to be more of the first than the latter. By the end of the passage, an "I" has separated out from the various characters, an "I" whom we might identify with the "I" of *The Waste Land*. As his companions race off in a meaningless romp, this individual gets out of the cab and goes off alone: "So I got out to see the sunrise, and walked home." There is an essential inno- cence to this episode that is part of its tone, a merry boys-will-be-boys fun. Clearly this scene comes from the life of the poet *before* the events that are the focus of the episode of the Thunder's voice, the subject of his "complete knowledge." His instantaneous review of his life be- gins with a period of innocence when so much of what he will later view with a kind of horror or revulsion, especially sex, is evoked in a comic context (drunken college boys refused admission to Myrtle's brothel). Moreover, the image of the sunrise at the end of this open- ing episode, viewed clearly with anticipation and pleasure, provides a strong contrast with the "desolate sunset" to which the "fisher king" turns his back at the very end of the manuscript version of the poem. But by the time Eliot and Pound had finished their revision, both sunrise and sunset had disappeared from *The Waste Land*.

The next passage after this opening college scene is the now famous one that opens the published *Waste Land*: "April is the cruellest month, breeding / Lilacs out of the dead land, mixing / Memory and desire, stirring / Dull roots with spring rain." We may assume that with these lines we are much closer in time to the poet on his way to complete knowledge, the poet who has clearly been severely wounded in the time between those innocent college days and the "now" of the poem. April and lilacs stir "memory and desire," car- rying the poet back to the period abroad—a time that we might iden- tify as 1910–11, when Eliot left Harvard for a year to study at the Sorbonne, followed by a summer of travel through Europe, including northern Italy and Munich. All the details fit (Königssee, Hofgarten), including the conversation of Marie—who is, according to Valerie Eliot, Countess Marie Larisch, whom Eliot actually met and whose "description of the sledding, for example, was taken verbatim" from the conversation (pp. 125–26). Although we are not told when this encounter took place, we might assume it to be during that summer trip in Germany. But the important detail of these lines comes in "Winter kept us warm"; "Summer surprised us"; "we stopped in the colonnade." The plural pronoun reveals that the poet is remembering the time with his friend—the friend revealed by the Thunder's voice—but here in the midst of their fulfilled friendship; a friend perhaps met at the Sorbonne who may have accompanied Eliot on his summer travels, the two together encountering the "niece and confidante of the Austrian Empress Elizabeth" and hearing her idle conversation of an idle life.

After the break of the asterisks (in the manuscript only), the poet has slipped from memory back into the agonizing present—"What are the roots that clutch, what branches grow / Out of this stony rubbish?" The lifeless scene ("dead tree," "dry stone," "red rock") is highly evocative of death, and the concluding line of the cluster—"I will show you fear in a handful of dust"—suggests (in line with the title of this section, "The Burial of the Dead") that death is the root cause of the present agony. Another set of asterisks indicates the taking over of "memory and desire" once again, confirmed by the Wagnerian love lyric, followed by recollections of a moment in the past, associated with hyacinths, of transcendent love—"I was neither / Living nor dead, and I knew nothing, / Looking into the heart of light, the silence." The closing Wagnerian fragment for this cluster ("Desolate and empty the sea") again shifts the poem from memory to the present.

Are we to assume that the accompanying friend remembered in the present opening of *The Waste Land* is the "hyacinth girl" of these lines? There are many reasons not to so assume. Perhaps the strongest is that the Thunder fable refers clearly to a masculine friend. Moreover, the only reference to the "hyacinth girl" in these lines is placed in a quotation: "You give me hyacinths first a year ago; / They called me the hyacinth girl." With emphasis on *girl*, we might see that the speaker need not be feminine (it was the poet who had presented the hyacinths to the speaker). In addition, there is the classical association of the hyacinth with the calamus-like relationship between Apollo and Hyacinthus, a handsome boy accidentally killed when the two were throwing the disk: in his memory, Apollo created the flower bearing his name as an eternal reminder of his love. Further, the "hyacinth girl" recurs no place else in *The Waste Land* or in the memory of the poet-protagonist, nor does "she" turn up in the hand dealt by Madame Sosostris in the lines next following in "Burial of the Dead." And finally (and perhaps conclusively), the manuscripts of "A Game of Chess" provide a masculine association with the hyacinth image: "I remember / The hyacinth garden. Those are pearls that were his eyes, yes!" (p. 13). Though the "hyacinth garden" reference disappeared in revision, Eliot put in a footnote to the remainder of the line: "Cf. Part I, 1. 37, 48" (p. 147). The first of these contains the "hyacinth garden" image, the second contains the first appearance of the line, "Those are pearls that were his eyes" (parenthetically inserted in Madame Sososostris's speech). Thus Eliot seemed determined that the reader would associate memory of the hyacinth garden with a haunting memory of the drowned sailor.

With Madame Sosostris the poet-protagonist returns from memory to the present, and an ironic assessment of his present condition. The cards dealt by this "famous clairvoyant" are the cards fate has dealt the poet. It is significant that the first is that of the "drowned Phoenician Sailor," causing a momentary catch in the memory of the poet, who meditates to himself as he listens to the Madame: "(Those are pearls that were his eyes. Look!)." Although Pound marked this line for excision, it remained; and it surfaces repeatedly elsewhere in the published *Waste Land* and appears to be a line evoking the friend who is now lost, incarnated in the poem as Phlebas the Phoenician. This first card of fate, then, reveals the basic cause of the poet's present agony: the loss of his companion and friend through drowning, subject of Part IV of the poem. The next card dealt is that of "Belladonna, the Lady of the Rocks, / The lady of situations." This card appears to refer to the woman in the poet's life, and the epithets applied to her suggest her hardness, her craft; we may assume that the poet has become linked to her, probably through marriage, and the relationship has developed into a major source of grief for him. "Belladonna," then, is the second basic fact to account for the poet-protagonist's present critical state, and is a primary subject in Part II of the poem. Grieving for the death of an intimate and beloved friend, trapped in a loveless marriage with a scheming woman, the poet may well view his situation with despair. The next card dealt him is himself and the life he may look forward to: "Here is the man with three staves, and here the Wheel." In the manuscript Eliot had tried "King fishing" and "fisher king" for the "man with three staves" (p. 9), finally settling on the latter. It is the impotent "fisher king" role that the poet-protagonist will later assume, especially in Part III and in the final Part V of the poem. And the "Wheel" symbolizes the tortured, meaningless suburban life that his present plight had bound him to; the figure of the wheel appears in "The Death of the Duchess," a manuscript poem that yielded many of its lines for Part II of *The Waste Land*—"The inhabitants of Hampstead are bound forever on the wheel" (p. 105).

We may take the first three cards of Madame Sosostris as the cards delineating the poet's present fate. But what of his future? The next cards are not reassuring. "And here is the one-eyed merchant, and this card, / Which is blank, is something he carries on his back, /

Which I am forbidden to see." In his footnote to the Sosostris section, Eliot points out that this merchant (like the Phoenician sailor) appears later in the poem—as in fact he does, in Part III, making what appears to be a homosexual proposition ("a weekend at the Metropole") in his "demotic French" (p. 140). But what is suggested by the blank card signifying something he carries on his back— something that even Madame Sosostris is forbidden to see? Could it be the burden that the proposition carries with it, if accepted? And its sordidness as well as its indeterminateness or vagueness keeps it out of Madame Sosostris's vision? This, then, could be a possible future? Madame Sosostris says (in the manuscript): "I look in vain / For the Hanged Man" (p. 9). Eliot's note tells us: "The Hanged man...fits my purpose in two ways: because he is associated in my mind with the Hanged God of Frazer, and because I associate him with the hooded figure in the passage of the disciples to Emmaus in Part V" (p. 147). Had Madame Sosostris found the Hanged Man, the poet-protagonist might have had the kind of hope found in the traditional elegy—the hope of resurrection and renewal, the trust in spiritual reuniting with the beloved lost friend. But since this card is not found, the poet can look forward to no surcease of his sorrow and despair. Madame Sosostris advises, "Fear death by water": death will bring no release from the pain the poet feels.

In the closing lines of Part I of *The Waste Land*, we see the poet in his present state greeting a friend in the street, one Stetson (who, according to Valerie Eliot, is based on a real bank-clerk acquaintance),[26] with the kind of badinage friends share, but with a serious undercurrent— "That corpse you planted last year in your garden, / Has it begun to sprout? Will it bloom this year?" Corpses buried in the garden, like memories hidden in the psyche, will out no matter what. In the Madame Sosostris section of the poem, the poet has just reviewed in the cards of his fate all those buried corpses of his past that will not lie quietly buried: but principal among them is the real corpse buried, the lost sailor and friend who haunts the poet and appears to be the moving spirit haunting *The Waste Land*.

In Part II of *The Waste Land*, "A Game of Chess," the poet relives the essence of his relation with his wife. The original title of the section, "In the Cage," after the Henry James story of a telegraphist, offered a kind of specific preparation for the second command of the Thunder—sympathize—with the poet's meditation on each creating his own prison: all the characters who appear in "A Game of Chess" are imprisoned within selves that no turning key can reach. In the first half of the section, the poet and his wife have a talk, but without communication: the wife's voice dominates throughout with a kind of nervous staccato; the only answers she receives are the silent meditations of her husband. She demands: "Do you know nothing? Do you see nothing? Do you remember / Nothing?" He replies (but to himself only): "I remember / The hyacinth garden. Those are pearls that were his eyes, yes!" (p. 13). He is on that Wheel of Madame Sosostris's card. The second half of Part II, the scene in the pub, shifts to a level lower in the social order, but the emptiness of relations between the sexes does not markedly differ: everywhere the poet turns, he sees a reflection of his own agonized state, his own imprisonment. We may take the final voice of the section—"Good night, ladies, good night, sweet ladies, good night, good night"—as the poet's own, the poet in delicate psychic balance, making an ironic comment on a scene overheard, a scene that he has translated into the language of his own personal anguish.

Part III of *The Waste Land*, "The Fire Sermon," consists of a medley of scenes, each of which works some variation of "desire, temptation, and surrender," and each of which connects directly or subterraneously with the poet's own particular spiritual malaise. The opening lines on Fresca, marked for deletion by Pound, may be read as some of the most flagrantly misogynistic of the entire poem, dramatically justified by the total vacuity of the poet's marriage as presented in the preceding section. Fresca may represent a composite portrait of all women for the poet—with her "hearty female stench," her "wit of natural trull" (prostitute), she is reduced by the "same eternal and consuming itch" to the role of "plain simple bitch" (pp. 23, 27). It is no accident that immediately after this devastating portrait, the poet appears as the impotent fisher king fishing "in the dull canal," and soon afterwards he receives his invitation from the Smyrna merchant for a "weekend at the Metropole." And shortly thereafter, he becomes the slightly voyeuristic Tiresias, witnessing at the "violet hour" seduction of the bored typist by the "young man carbuncular." Elizabeth and Leicester float into view next, and their gilt trappings are placed in contrast with the sordid scenes of seduction of three modern maidens, all variations in some sense of the bored typist. The section ends with what seems to be both a confession and a prayer: a confession by the poet that he remains caught up in his desires, temptations, surrenders—he is "burning burning burning burning" —and a prayer to be released: "O Lord thou pluckest me out."

In Part IV of *The Waste Land*, "Death by Water," the poet is carried back further into his past than even his college days at Harvard. The sea narrative that once opened this section begins with a journey starting from the Dry Salvages—a cluster of dangerous rocks off Gloucester, Massachusetts, the vacation home of the Eliots during T. S. Eliot's boyhood (and, of course, the title of the third of "Four Quartets"). There are several indications ("A porpoise snored upon the phosphorescent swell," "the sea rolled asleep" [p. 55]) that this narrative is some kind of dream sequence in which the poet is reliving his life symbolically up to the death of his beloved friend. The ship started out with "kingfisher weather," and nearly "everything went wrong," with the food spoiled and the crew becoming quarrelsome. But then the fish came, and the voyage suddenly turned into a happy one, as the men began to count their earnings. Just as suddenly the voyage again turned threatening—this time into a nightmare, the ship sailing beyond the "farthest northern islands," and ultimately into an iceberg—and total destruction. At a critical point the poet confessed, "I thought, now, when / I like, I can wake up and end the dream." But the dream continued to its nightmare conclusion—and death. It is at this point that the lines (on Phlebas the Phoenician), that survived revision, appear; the drowned sailor is described in his death as in some ways reenacting the experience of the poet in the structure of the poem: "He passed the stages of his age and youth / Entering the whirlpool." Memory of Phlebas lies at the heart of the "memory and desire" of the poem: "Consider Phlebas, who was once handsome and tall as you" (pp. 55–61).

If Part IV of *The Waste Land* presents a sea journey to a confrontation with death, ending with the vivid scene of the drowned sailor disintegrating beneath the waves, Part V ("What the Thunder Said") presents a land journey to a similar confrontation—at the Chapel Perilous in the mountains, amidst the "tumbled graves": "There is the empty chapel, only the wind's house, / It has no windows, and the door swings, / Dry bones can harm no one." The journey has been long and arduous for such an empty discovery; but of course this is not *the* discovery of the section, but a requisite preliminary to it. The realization that "dry bones can harm no one" brings a "damp gust," and then the speech of the Thunder. The discovery brought by the Thunder is a discovery about life that could come only after the confrontation with death, the discovery that we have already examined above, embodied in the Thunder's speech: give, sympathize, control. In confronting the sailor's death, the poet can finally confront the meaning of his relationship with him in life, that "awful daring of a moment's surrender." Our final view of the poet is in his role as impotent fisher king, picking through the pieces that constituted his life ("These fragments I have shored against my ruins"), yearning for

"Shantih, shantih, shantih"—"The Peace which passeth understanding." But he has made his journey to confrontation, and has probed the obscure and elusive meaning of his existence. He does have fragments to work with to shore against his "ruins."

5

Validity of the above reading does not hang on identification of Phlebas the Phoenician in Eliot's life. But as a matter of fact, there is some reason to believe that he was one Jean Verdenal, a French medical student who wrote poetry and lived in Eliot's *pension* in Paris during Eliot's year (1910–11) of study at the Sorbonne. (It should be noted parenthetically that the first critic to make this suggestion, John Peter, was earlier the author of an essay reading *The Waste Land* [without benefit of the manuscripts] along the lines outlined above; and he was threatened by Eliot with a lawsuit and as a result withdrew the article until after Eliot's death, at which time he resurrected it and presented his theory about Jean Verdenal; this fascinating chapter in *Waste Land* criticism requires its own separate treatment.)[27] Eliot's dedication of his first volume of poems, *Prufrock and Other Observations* (1917), to him tells us most of what we know about him: "For Jean Verdenal, 1889–1915 / mort aux Dardanelles." The Dante quotation which came to be included in the dedication is from Canto XXI of the *Purgatorio*, and may be translated—"Now you are able to comprehend the quantity of love that warms me toward you, / When I forget our emptiness / treating shades as if they were solid."[28] Eliot's only other reference to Verdenal is to be found in the editor's column of *Criterion* for April 1934 in a passage in which Eliot was reminiscing about the Paris of his youth: "I am willing to admit that my own retrospect is touched by a sentimental sunset, the memory of a friend coming across the Luxembourg Gardens in the late afternoon, waving a branch of lilac, a friend who was later (so far as I could find out) to be mixed with the mud of Gallipoli."[29]

With the sparse facts that are known, we might construct the following plausible account of the Eliot-Verdenal relationship: At the age of twenty-two, Eliot went to Paris and found living in his same *pension* a charming young Frenchman his own age who was studying medicine and who wrote poetry. Loneliness impelled Eliot into friendship, and proximity made close attachment possible and even probable. It would have been natural for the two to travel in Italy and Germany during the summer (especially Munich, where Eliot completed "Prufrock"), and it is possible that their relationship was renewed in 1914 on Eliot's return to Paris. World War I forced Eliot's departure from Germany to England in 1914 and led to Verdenal's enlisting or being drafted in the French forces. Caught in the campaign to take the Dardanelles in 1915, he was one of the countless young Frenchmen, Englishmen, and Australians who were lost in "the mud of Gallipoli."

According to his military records, he was cited for bravery in evacuating the wounded by sea on 30 April 1915, and he was "killed by the enemy on the 2nd May 1915 in the Dardanelles." A notation on the record indicates he was killed "while dressing a wounded man on the field of battle." There appears to be no record of disposition of the body by land or by sea.[30] Eliot would have heard of his death in May, or at the latest in early June, and his dismay and anguish may well have impelled him into a hasty marriage that was largely meaningless except as an irrational response to his bitter loss. The marriage turned out to be catastrophic; the deeply wounded Eliot seems to have felt revulsion at the thought of intimacy with a woman—a woman that all his friends (and apparently he) found "vulgar";[31] finding himself unstimulated sexually, he seems to have attempted to fill Vivienne's physical needs only some six months after the marriage by sending her off alone on a beach holiday with Bertrand Russell, something of a satyr. But as Vivienne's mental health deteriorated, caused in part at least by the frustrations of an unsatisfying, perhaps unconsummated, marriage, Eliot's health also began to deteriorate, and his ability to write poetry to decline. The critical point was reached in 1921, when he found his only refuge from a breakdown was to take leave from his job (and Vivienne), consult a nerve specialist, or psychologist, in Lausanne, Switzerland, and write a long poem which had been under contemplation for some time—The Waste Land.[32]

If this version of Eliot's early years is approximately right, there can be no doubt that the voice of The Waste Land is his voice, the spiritual crisis of the poem's protagonist his crisis. What we have in The Waste Land, then, is not an "impersonal" poem, nor yet an autobiographical poem, but a poem much closer in form to such poems of Whitman's Leaves of Grass as "Out of the Cradle Endlessly Rocking" or "When Lilacs Last in the Dooryard Bloom'd," poems in which biography has been transfigured into poetic drama. Or, indeed, much closer than formerly thought to Eliot's own later Four Quartets, where the spiritual quest has always been assumed to be Eliot's own. We might say of The Waste Land what Eliot wrote of Whitman's two poems: "Beneath all the declamations there is another tone, and behind all the illusions there is another vision. When Whitman speaks of the lilacs or of the mocking-bird, his theories and beliefs drop away like a needless pretext."[33]

The reality of Jean Verdenal, or the actual biographical nature of his relationship with Eliot, does not determine the meaning we have been exploring in *The Waste Land*. What Eliot made imaginatively of the reality of some such relationship has determined the meaning deposited in the poem itself. It is along this line of thought that we might be led to say that if Jean Verdenal did not exist, we would have to invent him: *The Waste Land* insists on it and demands of us the invention.[34] In a similar vein, we could say of Milton's "Lycidas" that it demands we invent Edward King, or of Tennyson's *In Memoriam* that we invent Arthur Hallam, or of Whitman's "When Lilacs Last in the Dooryard Bloom'd" that we invent Abraham Lincoln. The parallels are not exact, but they are close enough to render comparison meaningful: each of these poems begins with a private grief and moves out through an ever widening view to a public perspective. The first has shaped the latter, but the latter is shared by the poem's readers in ways that the first could never be. Thus a private and personal anguish becomes the means through poetic experience to a general or universal insight. The poet begins with himself, but ends with the world. *The Waste Land* lies within, but it leads to the world in waste.

6

In 1933 Eliot asserted: "But what a poem means is as much what it means to others as what it means to the author: and indeed, in the course of time a poet may become merely a reader in respect to his own works, forgetting his original meaning—or without forgetting, merely changing."[35] Here Eliot seems to be acknowledging that in spite of his protests, *The Waste Land* has continued to be and will continue to be read as social criticism—and the readers who thus interpret the poem have their right to do so.

We have already noted how the American personal epic, though it begins with individual experience, reaches out to a public or political dimension. Even in his "Calamus" or most "confessional" poems, Whitman projected a political ideal, a state of democratic brotherhood. The pattern of movement from personal to public, from private to political, is repeated in all the American long poems ambitious to be epic. As Eliot implies, it would be foolish to deny that this "meaning" exists in the poem. Any "personal grouse" against life is, to be persuasive, necessarily involved with some of the probably unpleasant realities of life as it objectively "is." There *is* sterility in modern urban life, there *is* spiritual desiccation in modern religious belief, there *is* a deep sense of futility in contemporary experience, meaninglessness in much of modern activity, emptiness in many human relationships and institutions, including marriage.

The Waste Land, then, like Whitman's *Leaves* before it or John Berryman's *Dream Songs* after, does have a dimension of "social criticism" that is important to its totality of meaning. But as in the other poems, it is not independent but dependent—and dependent on that "personal" dimension that is central to the poem's meaning and structure. Of all the American long poems with which we are dealing here, it is in some ways most like Berryman's *Dream Songs*. The secret of Berryman's sequence is the recurring nightmarish memory of the father's suicide—a suicide committed in the young son's presence. This very private, very personal experience is the unspoken event around which the *Dream Songs* revolve; they often take their meaning from this private anguish even when they contain no reference to it. The father's suicide may be said to haunt *The Dream Songs* just as Jean Verdenal's death haunts *The Waste Land*. But both long poems radiate out from this private source, and take a jaundiced view of the world and human experience that exerts its universal appeal.

But *The Waste Land*'s early readers, without benefit of the manuscripts published in 1971, tended to read the poem as social criticism without awareness of the personal dimension. They saw the poem's unrelieved anguish as a supposedly objective view of the world as it "really is," and they struggled to interpret the poem's odd attitude toward sex and women as compatible with the poem's social and religious themes. Ezra Pound helped in his revisions to give the poem this unrelieved look, closer in spirit to those Cantos that often are unrelieved invective or diatribe against some social ill or wrong.

Both Hart Crane and William Carlos Williams took dark views of this dark poem, and their reactions were important in shaping *The Bridge* and *Paterson*—poems that were in some ways "answers" or "replies" to *The Waste Land*. But one of the elements of these "answers" is the personal dimension they include, as much as to say: if Eliot would take poetry down an "impersonal" path, they would remain relentlessly "personal"—but still dedicated to austere art. They did not live to know the manuscripts of Eliot's poem—and just how intimately "personal" Eliot's poem was. Crane saw it as a poem of "complete renunciation" that was "so damned dead," and he saw his "vision" in *The Bridge* as in some way countering Eliot's.[36] Williams believed that *The Waste Land* "gave the poem back to the academics," and returned poetry "to the classroom."[37] Both poets reflected Eliot's influence in their poems, including his dark "vision": but both poets labored to write their poems as in some sense a corrective to the unrelieved darkness of Eliot's vision.

Very often in the history of American poetry, Walt Whitman and T. S. Eliot have been presented as two possible polarities, the two extremes: of the personal and the impersonal; of the optimistic and the pessimistic. They have been painted in unrelieved colors, and poets have taken one or the other as model, or have attempted to thread their way through the straits between. In reality, neither poet is so unrelieved. And they have more in common than has often been thought—in the way they exploit poetically their emotional experience, and in the way they use themselves and their feelings as representative of their time and place. It seems unlikely that Eliot's long poem, in the form in which it was first conceived and written, would have been possible without the precedence of Whitman's own experiments in similar forms. In what he derived from Whitman consciously or unconsciously, and in the way he shaped the poems that came after him, T. S. Eliot must assume a prominent place in the succession of America's poets of the personal epic. And *The Waste Land* must be viewed with double vision: the poem as it exists in history (the 1922 published version) and the poem as it escapes history (as it is glimpsed in manuscript), as it is in and of itself.

> *A final word:*
> *from*
> "Fifty Years of American Poetry"
>
> *Randall Jarrell*
>
> Won't the future say to us in helpless astonishment:
> "But did you actually believe that all those things about
> objective correlatives, classicism, the tradition, applied to
> *his* poetry? Surely you must have seen that he was one of
> the most subjective and daemonic poets who ever lived,
> the victim and helpless beneficiary of his own inexorable
> compulsions, obsessions? From a psychoanalytical point of
> view he was far and away the most interesting poet of your
> century. But for you, of course, after the first few years,
> his poetry existed undersea, thousands of feet below that
> deluge of exegesis, explication, source listing, scholarship,
> and criticism that overwhelmed it. And yet how bravely,
> and personally it survived, its eyes neither coral nor
> mother-of-pearl but plainly human, full of anguish.[38]

Seven

Williams is part of the great breath of our literature. *Paterson* is our *Leaves of Grass*.

Robert Lowell, "William Carlos Williams"

1   In the poem that stands first in his *Collected Earlier Poems,* in Whit-
    manesque lines that Williams first published in 1914, he says:

> But one day, crossing the ferry
> With the great towers of Manhattan before me,
> Out at the prow with the sea wind blowing,
> I had been wearying many questions
> Which she had put on to try me:
> How shall I be a mirror to this modernity?
>
> (*CEP*, p. 3)[1]

The "she" of these lines, "old, painted— / With bright lips," looks
startlingly like a descendant of Whitman's muse which he discovered
"install'd amid the kitchen ware!" The ferry on which Williams rides
in these lines may not be Whitman's Brooklyn ferry, but it conjures
up some of the same kinds of poetic vision.

   The road from the 1914 "Wanderer" to the first Book of *Paterson* in
1946 is a long and open one, and it is not easy to assess the extent to
which Whitman was a camerado in arms. In his *Autobiography* (1951),
Williams freely confessed the unhealthy influence of Keats on his

127

early poetry, an influence that he was able to lay to rest rather quickly under the scathing criticism of his friend Ezra Pound. But at the same time that he acknowledged the obsessions with Keats, Williams said: "For my notebooks, however (which I don't think anyone ever saw), I reserved my Whitmanesque 'thought,' a sort of purgation and confessional, to clear my head and my heart from turgid obsessions" (*A*, p. 53). Of his first book of poetry, Williams wrote: "The poems were bad Keats, nothing else—oh well, bad Whitman too. But I sure loved them" (*A*, p. 107).

Although Keats seemed to drop out of Williams's vocabulary rather early without much problem, Whitman remained in it over the years, as a focus of discussion or a point of reference. As early as 1917 Williams attempted to disentangle Whitman's significance for poetry and for him: "Whitman created the art [of poetry] in America.... There is no art of poetry save by grace of other poetry. So Dante to me can only be another way of saying Whitman. Yet without a Whitman there can be for me no Dante." Whitman was the "rock," the "first primitive," and modern poets could not "advance" until they had "grasped Whitman and then built upon him." But straight imitation was wrong: "The only way to be like Whitman is to write *unlike* Whitman. Do I expect to be a companion to Whitman by mimicking his manners?"[2] The line that Williams established in this little essay was one that he elaborated repeatedly in a variety of places. At times he was more, at times less, critical of Whitman—in a way carrying on a love-hate relationship not unlike that of Pound in his "Pact," and seeing himself (as did the early Pound) as one of Whitman's "encrustations" to come in "ages and ages." One of the most interesting of Williams's comments on Whitman came in that strange, early book, *Spring and All* (1923), filled with some of Williams's finest early poems together with seemingly random comments on the art and nature of poetry: "Whitman's proposals are of the same piece with the modern trend toward imaginative understanding of life. The largeness which he interprets as his identity with the least and the greatest about him, his 'democracy' represents the vigor of his imaginative life" (*I*, pp. 112–13).

This aspect of Whitman was perhaps the most enduring in its impact on Williams, in both his poetry and fiction. But it was Whitman's technical innovation that inspired Williams's most extensive and complicated commentary. In "Against the Weather: A Study of the Artist" (1939), Williams identified Whitman as "a key man to whom I keep returning ... tremendously important in the history of modern poetry" (*SE*, p. 218). Whitman's importance is dramatically identifiable: "He broke through the deadness of copied forms which keep shouting above everything that wants to get said today drowning out one man with the accumulated weight of a thousand voices in the past—re-establishing the tyrannies of the past, the very tyrannies that we are seeking to diminish. The structure of the old is active, it says no! to everything in propaganda and poetry that wants to say yes. Whitman broke through that. That was basic and good" (*SE*, p. 218). But Whitman's innovation, however remarkable, was beyond his own full understanding: "Whitman was never able fully to realize the significance of his structural innovations. As a result he fell back to the overstuffed catalogues of his later poems and a sort of looseness that was not freedom but lack of measure. Selection, structural selection was lacking" (*SE*, p. 212). In brief, Whitman "broke the new wood"; now is the "time for carving" (as Pound had written in "A Pact").

By the 1950s, Williams's view of Whitman as the great innovator who somehow fell short of his own discoveries became a recurring theme, with variations. In 1954: "Whitman was right in breaking our bounds but, having no valid restraints to hold him went wild.... Whitman, great as he was in his instinctive drive, was also the cause of our going astray. I among the rest have much to answer for. No verse can be free, it must be governed by some measure, but not by the old measure. There Whitman was right but there, at the same time, his leadership failed him. The time was not ready for it. We have to return to some measure but a measure consonant with our time and not a mode so rotten that it stinks" (*SE*, p. 339). In 1955 (in "An Essay on *Leaves of Grass*"): "Whitman's so-called 'free verse' was an assault on the very citadel of the poem itself: it constituted a direct challenge to all living poets to show cause why they should not do likewise. It is a challenge that still holds good after a century of vigorous life during which it has been practically continuously under fire but never defeated." Yes, but: "He had seen a great light but forgot almost at once after the first revelation everything but his 'message,' the idea which originally set him in motion, the idea on which he had been nurtured, the idea of democracy—and took his eye off the words themselves which should have held him."[3] By the time Williams wrote these comments, he himself was in process of exploiting the new "variable foot" and "triadic line" which he had hit upon in the writing of Book II of *Paterson* (1948).

Later, Williams's view of Whitman became somewhat more expansive. In an important little essay entitled "The American Idiom" (1961), he wrote: "The American idiom is the language we speak in the United States. It is characterized by certain differences from the language used among cultured Englishmen, being completely free from all influences which can be summed up as having to do with 'the Establishment.' This, pared to essentials, is the language which governed Walt Whitman in his choice of words. It constituted a revolution in the language." Williams asserted that the revolution is continuing, and the modern reply to the "fixed foot of the ancient line" is "the variable foot which we are beginning to discover after Whitman's advent. . . . Whitman lived in the nineteenth century but he, it must be acknowledged, proceeded instinctively by rule of thumb and a tough head, correctly, in the construction of his verses. He knew nothing of the importance of what he had stumbled on, unconscious of the concept of the variable foot."[4]

It is clear from these scattered comments on Whitman that Williams felt affinities and at the same time felt the necessity of declaring his independence; after all, in his drive to discover the new, Williams could not give over his allegiance totally to any poet of the past—not even Whitman. But there is one more significant comment on Whitman to be noted. In all of *Paterson*, Whitman's name is not to be found (except in one of the Allen Ginsberg letters—"I do have a whitmanic mania & nostalgia for cities and detail & panorama and isolation in jungle and pole, like the images you pick up") (*P*, p. 213). But Williams goes out of his way to inject Whitman's name in a brief commentary on *Paterson* at the end of his *Autobiography*. Williams published what he assumed to be then the final book, Book IV, of *Paterson* that same year (1951): the poem fulfilled his plans as publicly announced and he saw it as finished. His brief comments in his *Autobiography*, in the final chapter entitled "The Poem Paterson," are mostly of a general nature, but one of the few paragraphs turns almost interpretive: "In the end the man rises from the sea where the river appears to have lost its identity and accompanied by his faithful bitch, obviously a Chesapeake Bay retriever, turns inland toward Camden where Walt Whitman, much traduced, lived the latter years of his life and died. He always said that the poems, which had broken the dominance of the iambic pentameter in English prosody, had only begun his theme. I agree. It is up to us, in the new dialect, to continue it by a new construction upon the syllables" (*A*, p. 392). This is a remarkable comment, hardly to be derived from the poetic text itself, but clearly earnest and almost defiant (earlier in the passage Williams addresses his critics); at this critical final (final as of 1951) moment in his poem, Williams's imagination evokes Whitman—as Pound had done in Canto 82, as Crane had done in Part IV of *The Bridge*.

2

But before attempting to fathom Williams's meaning here ("It is up to us . . . to continue" the theme which Whitman "had only begun"), we must trace in outline the emergence of Williams's *Paterson*. For this, two other poets are of considerable importance. If Whitman was a poet with whom Williams connected and of whom he felt himself a continuation, the expatriates T. S. Eliot and Ezra Pound (the latter a lifelong friend) constituted poets against whom he felt himself in reaction. There is no need here to trace out the relations in detail—these have been illuminatingly explored in Louis Simpson's *Three on the Tower*[5]—but Williams's strong feelings against some aspects of their poetry shaped his own ideas of *Paterson*. Williams came to view *The Waste Land* as "the great catastrophe to our letters" (*A*, p. 146), and he wrote with passionate intensity of his memory of the poem's publication:

> Then out of the blue *The Dial* brought out *The Waste Land* and all our hilarity ended. It wiped out our world as if an atom bomb had been dropped upon it and our brave sallies into the unknown were turned to dust.
> To me especially it struck like a sardonic bullet. I felt at once that it had set me back twenty years, and I'm sure it did. Critically Eliot returned us to the classroom just at the moment when I felt that we were on the point of an escape to matters much closer to the essence of a new art form itself—rooted in the locality which should give it fruit. I knew at once that in certain ways I was most defeated.
> Eliot had turned his back on the possibility of reviving my world. And being an accomplished craftsman, better skilled in some ways that I could ever hope to be, I had to watch him carry my world off with him, the fool, to the enemy. (*A*, p. 174)

Although Williams's relationship with Pound was much more complex (as, for example, note Williams's appreciative review of *A Draft of XXX Cantos* [1931]), his reservations about Pound's epic were deep. He wrote in 1939:

> The truth is that news offers the precise incentive to epic poetry, the poetry of events; and now is precisely the time for it since never by any chance is the character of a single fact ever truthfully represented today. If ever we are to have any understanding of what is going on about us we shall need some other means for discovering it.
> The epic poem would be our "newspaper," Pound's cantos are the algebraic equivalent but too perversely individual to achieve the universal understanding required. The epic if you please is what

we're after, but not the lyric-epic sing-song. It must be a concise
sharpshooting epic style. Machine gun style. Facts, facts, facts, tear-
ing into us to blast away our stinking flesh of news. Bullets.[6]

When Williams wrote in the italicized epigraph to *Paterson*—"a reply
to Greek and Latin with the bare hands"—he was pitting his epic
against the long poems of Eliot and Pound; and throughout *Paterson*
Williams continued his response to them (as at the end when Paterson rises from the sea they followed to Europe and turns back to the
land, Camden, and Whitman).

Although the first book of *Paterson* appeared in 1946, when
Williams was sixty-three, and other books appeared in 1948, 1949,
1951, and 1958 (when he was seventy-five; notes for Book VI were
found at his death in 1963), some of the lines were written as early as
1914, in the poem "The Wanderer," when he was only thirty-one.
From 1914 to 1958 is forty-four years—a long time to live with a poem.
And that thirty-two-year lag (a minimal period, since we don't have a
complete record of Williams's mind) from embryonic idea to first
execution surely constitutes the kind of "long foreground" which
Emerson detected behind *Leaves of Grass* on its appearance in 1855.
The 1939 comment quoted above (on the nature of the "epic poem")
appears to have been made by a man who had long since determined
not only what constituted an epic but also that he was going to write
one. The first line from a strange prose piece entitled "Notes in Diary
Form" and dated 1927 flashes out to arrest attention: "I will make a
big, serious portrait of my time" (*SE*, p. 62). In 1927 Williams also
published a poem entitled "Paterson," in which for the first time he
introduces a Mr. Paterson who has some of the aspects of a city
("Inside the bus one sees / his thoughts sitting and standing" [*CEP*,
p. 233]), and in which he reiterates: "Say it, no ideas but in things"
(*CEP*, p. 233). Both lines and ideas from this poem ended up in the
later epic: by 1927 the embryo had developed recognizable features,
but still had to wait out a long gestation.

In 1937 appeared "Paterson: Episode 17," the very title suggesting a
long poem well along in progress, if not in fact at least in conception.
If this conception was to change considerably over the next nine years
before the publication of Book I, there would still be room in Book III
(1949) for many lines and the main themes of "Paterson: Episode 17":
"Beautiful Thing," detected in the form of a maid beating a rug, a
comely girl with a mixed sexual history who, in spite of violence and
violation, retains a kind of innocence and purity, her rhythmic action
containing the beat of poetry itself:

> The stroke begins again—
>   regularly
> automatic
>   contrapuntal to
> the flogging
> like the beat of famous lines
> in the few excellent poems
>   woven to make you
>   gracious
> and on frequent occasions
>   foul drunk
>   Beautiful Thing
> pulse of release
>   to the attentive
> and obedient mind.
>   (*CEP*, pp. 441–42)

Inasmuch as *Paterson* is a poem portraying a quest for beauty, and specifically Beautiful Thing, and particularly since in the long poem the poet finds Beautiful Thing in essentially the same embodiment as he did in this 1937 poem, we might assume that by this year Williams had brought into focus an important part of his epic's scope and meaning. As fragments of "Paterson: Episode 17" appear in Book III of *Paterson* (contrapuntally with the burning of the library), the phrase Beautiful Thing takes on resonance and almost visionary meaning—a meaning worthy of exploration in its proper place in the poem.

Of Williams's many works that might be cited as important milestones on the road to *Paterson*, two prose volumes must be singled out for mention. The first of these is *In the American Grain* (1925), an extraordinary exploration of the American past through the accounts and histories of America's discoverers, explorers, founders, adventurers, warriors, leaders, and writers. The cumulative picture is not a pretty one, and is filled with cruelty and violence, as Williams permits many of the personages to condemn themselves through their own incredible narratives—as, for example, Cotton Mather does in his accounts of the witches of Salem in chapters from *Wonders of the Invisible World*. Williams reveals something of his purpose in the book when he records his reply to a question (in Paris) as to why Americans don't speak more often of the things he has just recounted (much like the things of this book): "Because the fools do not believe that they have sprung from anything: bone, thought and action. They will not see that what they are is growing on these roots. They will not look. They float without question. Their history is to them an enigma"

(*IAG*, p. 113). If this unromantic examination of the American past brought Williams closer to his epic vision, his volume of short stories published in 1938, *Life along the Passaic River*, brought him still closer. In the former book Williams located himself as an American in time (in relation to the past); in the latter he found himself in place (in relation to locality and the local). The stories of *Life along the Passaic River* are sketches of ordinary, mostly humble people with whom Williams has shared some experience in his role as family doctor delivering babies and caring for children. Williams not only finds his material in the locality where he lives and works, but he also finds his values there—material and values that were to figure prominently in the epic then shaping.

3

Williams's "long foreground" gave him time to work out, change, and work out again many plans for *Paterson*, but his conception of a Mr. Paterson seems to have endured from his first appearance in the 1927 poem. Paterson is a shifting identity: the city, but also a man, everyman, modern man, a poet, a doctor, and, of course, William Carlos Williams himself. If there is ambiguity as to the "I" or speaker in the poem, it is no doubt intentional and is in the tradition of ambiguity that Whitman established in *Leaves of Grass*, where the "I" may be any one of a number of identities, not unlike many of those *Paterson* assumes. Although the identity of Paterson may sometimes be confusing when we first enter the poem, as we move into the later books the speaker of the poem becomes more and more clearly identifiable as William Carlos Williams. Like *Leaves of Grass*, *Paterson* contains a great deal of autobiography, all put in the service of the poetry.

Like other epics we are examining, the basic structure of *Paterson* is the structure of the journey or voyage, the inner or spiritual quest in search of—what? Knowledge? Awareness? Beauty? Language? All these, and perhaps more. The opening lines of the poem's "Preface" state bluntly: "Rigor of beauty is the quest. But how will you find beauty / when it is locked in the mind past all remonstrance?" (*P*, p. 3). At one time, Williams had added to these lines: "It is not in the things nearest us unless transported there by our employment. Make it free, then, by the art you have, to enter these starved and broken pieces."[7] The beauty is there, in the local, but only art can *make it free*. These are words to remember as we pursue (with Williams) Beautiful Thing in Book III of *Paterson*.

But if Paterson the man is an Odysseus figure (and the metaphor is used on occasion, as at the end of Book IV), he is an Odysseus who travels at home, his highest adventure a Sunday walk in the park, a dunking in the ocean near the shore. *Paterson* is rigorously local, and only by so being could it become American or universal: "The first idea centering upon the poem, *Paterson*, came alive early: to find an image large enough to embody the whole knowable world about me. The longer I lived in my place, among the details of my life, I realized that these isolated observations and experiences needed pulling together to gain 'profundity'" (*A*, p. 391). But the "whole knowable world" could not be embodied in a poem about the universe, the globe, the country, but only about a specific locale: "That is the poet's business. Not to talk in vague categories but to write particularly, as a physician works, upon a patient, upon the thing before him, in the particular to discover the universal. John Dewey had said (I discovered it quite by chance), 'The local is the only universal, upon that all art builds.'" (*A*, p. 391). *Paterson*, then, conceived in these terms and with these purposes, provides far larger boundaries for the imagination than the geographic. We do not want to use the term "symbolic" because it was a term that Williams avoided, condemned as a grasping after that universal without the local. But neither do we want to mistake *Paterson* as providing locale for the purpose of mere local color. Williams put it: "If it rose to flutter into life awhile—it would be as itself, locally, and so like every other place in the world. For it is in that, that it be particular to its own idiom, that it lives" (*A*, p. 392).

The basic form, the quest. Then what? After only a few pages into the poem, the poetry is interrupted by fragments of prose—letters, historical accounts, statistics, advertisements, recorded interviews, and so on—some of them quite long, interrupting the poetic flow for several pages, or standing at important junctures, as, for example, the eight-page letter at the end of Book II. What kind of "poetry" can this be? In response to Wallace Stevens's suggestion that the prose passages were "anti-poetic," Williams wrote:

All the prose, including the tail which would have liked to have wagged the dog, has primarily the purpose of giving a metrical meaning to or of emphasizing a metrical continuity between all word use. It is *not* an anti-poetic device, the repeating of which piece of miscalculation makes me want to puke. It *is* that prose and verse are both *writing*, both a matter of the words and an interrelation between words for the purpose of exposition, or other better defined purpose of *the art*. Please do not stress other "meanings." I want to say that prose and verse are to me the same thing, that verse (as in Chaucer's tales) belongs *with* prose, as the poet belongs with "Mine host," who says in so many words to Chaucer, "Namoor, all that rhyming is not worth a toord." Poetry does not *have* to be kept away from prose as Mr. Eliot might insist, it goes *along with* prose and, companionably, by itself, without aid or excuse or need for separation or bolstering, shows itself by *itself* for what it is. *It belongs* there, in the gutter. Not anywhere else or wherever it is, it is the same: the poem. (*SL*, p. 263)

In the gutter?

Williams's explanation verges on the irrational—a term that he himself evoked in another attempt on his part to explain the prose insertions in *Paterson*:

. . . one fault in modern compositions . . . is that the irrational has no place. Yet in life (you show it by your tolerance of things which you feel no loss at not understanding) there is much that men exclude because they do not understand. The truly great heart *includes* what it does not at once grasp, just as the great artist includes things which go beyond him. . . . The irrational enters the poem in those letters, included in the text, which do not seem to refer to anything in the "story" yet do belong somehow to the poem—how, it is not easy to say. (*SL*, p. 309)

Here Williams seems to be as puzzled about the prose in *Paterson* as some of his readers, who might take Williams's reaction as an invitation to discover their own rationale for the presence of the prose in the poem. In the first place, the prose is a way of extending the poem beyond its poetic boundaries—in the direction of the comprehensive. Elements are injected—an Indian massacre, letters of a quasi-neurotic poetess, a handbill on social credit—that extend the reach of the poem suddenly, forcefully, and with an immediacy that would be hard to achieve in a rational introduction of the subject into the verse. The prose pieces are all intensely "local" artifacts whose grounding in feeling and passion, time and place, is indisputable. They provide, then, through their supreme particularity, much of the poem's reach for universality. In this way they resemble the long catalogs in *Leaves of Grass*—those lists of items, persons, scenes, activities, thoughts, all of which, by near-exhaustion of possibilities, convey the sense of totality: all of life is included here, Whitman and Williams seem to say, and belongs here and cannot be excluded, the poetic and the anti-poetic, the rational and the irrational, the important and the trivial, the poetry and the prose of life.

Allied perhaps to this purpose of comprehensiveness is the attempt to keep the poem close to reality—the real reality of life as daily experienced by all of us. We have read such accounts, we have heard of such massacres, we have talked of such sensational behavior, we have feared such violence, and we have received or written such letters. We recognize the painful reality of the exposures, and we perhaps squirm a bit in discomfort. Williams must have thought: the poem in its poetry, at such length, is likely to wander away from reality too easily (language is tricky, deceptive); the way to keep it near things as they are is to have these periodic injections of prose, real prose, taken out of my life as I live it in this place, from these people I know, from these books I read, from these handbills I receive, from these statistics I ponder. Some such reasoning, conscious or unconscious, we might imagine on Williams's part. And he might have thought, too, that since his theme is importantly about language, the varieties of language introduced by the prose would reinforce his theme in subtle ways. There is a wide range of usage, tone, level in the language of the prose—nearly always jarring, striking, or puzzling. There is language that is groping, language that is inarticulate, salty language, stilted language, passionless and impassioned language, language that cries and language that laughs—and it is all language that brings to the reader the shock of recognition, of reality. Has the poem drifted too far in its measured language? Then tear out a page from daily life and stick it in to bring it back close to earth; the language will signal its reality. And since the poet works intuitively, to his own rhythmic sense of pacing—the prose appearing rhythmically spaced—there will be reverberations, resonance, ironic echoes and reechoes. The theme is art or poetry? Then the letters will be from artists and poets; the reader may test the poem's reality directly in its interwoven stream of quotidian reality in subjects and themes openly or subterraneously related.

Such must have been some of the unformulated theory that lay behind the prose passages. They are compatible—meld—with what is perhaps the poem's geographic centerpiece, the falls: "Paterson lies in the valley under the Passaic Falls." (Williams remarked of his choice of the city Paterson in 1951, "It has . . . a central feature, the Passaic Falls which as I began to think about it became more and more the lucky burden of what I wanted to say.")[8] The ears of the man-city are the rocks that lie under the falls. Williams wrote in his *Autobiography*: "The Falls let out a roar as it crashed upon the rocks at its base. In the imagination this roar is a speech or a voice, a speech in par-

ticular: it is the poem itself that is the answer" (A, p. 392). The first full
description of the falls comes after a prose insert (fragment of a letter
from a frustrated woman poet):

> Jostled as are the waters approaching
> the brink, his thoughts
> interlace, repel and cut under,
> rise rock-thwarted and turn aside
> but forever strain forward—or strike
> an eddy and whirl, marked by a
> leaf or curdy spume, seeming
> to forget
>
> (P, p. 7)

Here Paterson's thoughts and, implicitly, the letter's pleading, are
mixed in the waters that move to the edge to—

> fall, fall in air! as if
> floating, relieved of their weight,
> split apart, ribbons; dazed, drunk
> with the catastrophe of the descent
> floating unsupported
> to hit the rocks: to a thunder,
> as if lightning had struck
>
> (P, p. 8)

"Catastrophe of the descent": here is the lost history of Paterson that
has cried out in descent only to "hit the rocks," the deaf ears of
mankind. "The language, the language / fails them / They do not
know the words / or have not / the courage to use them" (P, p. 11).
Only in the local may be found the universal: the lost history of
Paterson, the lost history of America, the lost history of mankind has
poured with thunder over those falls, falling on stone ears. The poet
sets himself the task of "combing out" the language of the falls—and
that includes watching, listening, observing language from its every
direction as it pours down on the poet. What is the significance of
"insignificant" lives; what is the meaning of the "meaningless" flow
of events in the voiceless currents of ceaseless experience? Book I
concludes: "Earth, the chatterer, father of all / speech." The poet
struggles to unstop his stone ear.

4

Readers of Paterson quickly realize that they are not reading
a traditional narrative, but they soon begin to catch glimpses of a
fugitive narrative. Paterson's journey through the local does, finally,

reach some kind of awareness. And the arrangements of the books of *Paterson* represent to some extent stages on that journey to aware- ness. The form is open-ended inasmuch as such journeys are never concluded until the death of the poet; thus *Paterson* has its concluding fragments, just as *The Cantos* has its and *Leaves of Grass* the Annexes. But the open-endedness does not preclude conclusion. In a sense, each book of *Paterson* is a conclusion, and the first four books espe- cially lead to a conclusion, but Book V carries the reader further along to another stage in the poet-Paterson's insight or vision, combing further the language of the falls.

There are abundant suggestions of an elemental organization of *Paterson*, especially in the various descriptions that Williams drew up for the poem. One of the earliest available of these is the poem, "Paterson: The Falls," which appeared in the 1944 volume, *The Wedge*:

> What common language to unravel?
> The Falls, combed into straight lines
> from the rafter of a rock's
> lip. Strike in! the middle of
> some trenchant phrase, some
> well packed clause. Then . . .
> This is my plan. 4 sections:
>
> (*CLP*, p. 10)

The poem's remaining eight stanzas give an outline of the poem as Williams planned it. "First, / the archaic persons of the drama." Here will be "an eternity of bird and bush," and "an unraveling: / the confused streams aligned, side / by side, speaking!" Next, "The wild / voice of the shirt-sleeved / Evangelist rivaling," his voice "echoing / among the bass and pickerel." And then, "Third, the old town: Alexander Hamilton / working up from St. Croix," but "stopped cold / by that unmoving roar." And finally,

> Fourth,
> the modern town, a
>
> disembodied roar! the cataract and
> its clamor broken apart—and from
> all learning, the empty
> ear struck from within, roaring.
>
> (*CLP*, p. 11)

This early conception of the poem is clearly comprehensive at the same time that it omits much vital to the finished poem. And if the plan for Part Four—"the empty / ear struck from within, roaring"— was for some climactic interior vision, the plan was not apparently fulfilled, until, perhaps, Part Five with its vision of death as "a hole," through which the "imagination / escapes intact" (*P*, p. 212).

When Book I appeared in 1946, Williams wrote: "Part One introduces the elemental character of the place. The Second Part comprises the modern replicas. Three will seek a language to make them vocal, and Four, the river below the falls, will be reminiscent of episodes—all that any one man may achieve in a lifetime" (*P*, p. 1). The epigraph to *Paterson* suggests seasonal analogies: *"spring, summer, fall and the sea"* (*P*, p. 2). Writing on the publication of Book III, Williams said: "From the beginning I decided there would be four books following the course of the river whose life seemed more and more to resemble my own life as I more and more thought of it: the river above the Falls, the catastrophe of the Falls itself, the river below the Falls, and the entrance at the end into the great sea." Williams then defined the poem's structure in terms of a quest: "The brunt of the four books is a search for the redeeming language by which a man's premature death . . . might have been prevented. Book IV shows the perverse confusions that come of a failure to untangle the language and make it our own as both man and woman are carried helplessly toward the sea (of blood) which, by their failure of speech, awaits them. The poet alone in this world holds the key to their final rescue."[9]

In 1951, Williams reviewed his plans for *Paterson*, and confessed:

> There were a hundred modifications of this general plan as, following the theme rather than the river itself, I allowed myself to be drawn on. The noise of the Falls seemed to me to be a language which we were and are seeking, and my search, as I looked about, became the struggle to interpret and use this language. This is the substance of the poem. But the poem is also the search of the poet after his language, his own language which I, quite apart from the material theme, had to use to write at all. I had to write in a certain way to gain a verisimilitude with the object I had in mind.

Williams's own intuitive way of working is suggested by his statement: "So the objective became complex. It fascinated me, it instructed me besides." The concluding book then became a challenge:

> And I had to think hard as to how I was going to end the poem. It wouldn't do to have a grand and soul-satisfying conclusion, because I didn't see any in my subject. Nor was I going to be confused or depressed or evangelical about it. It didn't belong to my subject. It would have been easy to make a great smash up with a "beautiful" sunset at sea, or a flight of pigeons, love's end and the welter of man's fate. Instead, after the little girl gets herself mixed up at last in the pathetic sophisticate of the great city, no less de-

feated and understandable, even lovable, than she is herself, we come to the sea at last. Odysseus swims in as a man must always do, he doesn't drown, he is too able, but, accompanied by his dog, strikes inland again (toward Camden) to begin again. [10]

Book V of *Paterson* never figured in the early planning of the poem, but it was not long after the publication of Book IV in 1951 that Williams began musing on the possibility of Book V. In 1953 he remarked to John Thirlwall: "At first I didn't have any plans. It ends with the river mingling with the ocean. You come to the ocean and that's the end of all life; that's the end of the river and the end of everything that concerns the river. But the fifth book, well, you might logically say there shouldn't be an end. But, as you recollect, as you look back to find a meaning, nobody knows anything about death and whether it is an end. It possibly isn't an end. It's a possibility that there's something more to be said." In this same conversation, Williams remarked of the earlier books: "It's a man in his own life going through, not revealing very much of his own life, but telling of the region which he's inhabited for a certain number of years and what it meant to him so far as it can be told. Many things are to be inferred." [11]

Whatever Williams's plans, and whatever his remembrance of *Paterson*, the achieved poem escapes the outlines. As someone has said of linguistics—all grammars leak. All the structures of any complex poem, even those of the maker, leak: there are elements, depths, dimensions that escape the net. *Paterson* may be viewed as a sequence of stages on the way (an endless way) to knowing. The dominant elements of each of the books then come to focus in patterns and relationships that begin to make a whole:

Book I, "The Delineaments of the Giants": blockage and divorce as Paterson's historical inheritance. The two most vivid examples, Sam Patch (Noah Faitoute Paterson) who jumps to his death (in 1829) in the Genesee River falls, his body later found in a cake of ice; and Mrs. Sarah Cumming, recently married to the Reverend Hopper Cumming, who fell without a word, probably deliberately, over the Passaic Falls in 1812. Appearing contrapuntally with these two vivid and recurring images of language failure is the image of an old *National Geographic* picture of the nine women of an African chief, a picture that speaks of something enigmatic in spite of its silence.

Book II, "Sunday in the Park": the book of place—here; the shoddy and the sordid; deformity and drunkenness. The Sunday walk in the park above the falls presents a sequence of vignettes that might at first glance constitute a wasteland of modern urban industrial life; Hamilton's "great beast," the common people, in meaningless and purposeless Sunday relaxation and torpor. There are two contrapuntal threads of action that vividly mark the walk: a pair of lovers caught sleepily in their desire, frustrated, dozing; and an itinerant minister who has given over all his riches in order to preach salvation. The dominant prose injection of this book is the sequence of letters from the anxiety-ridden female poet, and the book ends in a long denunciation of Paterson by the poetess.

Book III, "The Library": the book of time—now; the library's stench, purified by storm, fire, flood. As Book II was a walk in the park, Book III is a walk in the past, through books. "The library is desolation, it has a smell of its own / of stagnation and death" (P, p. 100). The contrapuntal theme is the search for Beautiful Thing, found in a Negress beating a rug—far from the environment or concerns of the books of a library. The prose passages inject considerable violence, particularly historical accounts of the killing of Indians (juxtaposed to Beautiful Thing).

Book IV, "The Run to the Sea": "perverse confusions"; the Lesbian poetess and Paterson vie for Phyllis in an ironic modern Idyl. Images of blockage and divorce dominate—the atom bomb, Billy Sunday, usury, violence (especially in the prose accounts of murder); but there are contrapuntal themes, particularly in the account of Madame Curie's discovery of radium and in Paterson's vigorous return from the "sea of blood" ("the sea is not our home") at the end and striding off inland with refreshed spirit for a new beginning.

Book V: bridging the way from life to death; the Unicorn tapestries and the immortal vision of art. Out of the tapestries at the Cloisters museum in New York City, Paterson weaves a final poem of discovery beyond the Paterson of Book IV: he discovers a "hole" through the bottom of death—the imagination of art. But this book of death is filled with a lively life: the life of love triumphant over blockage and divorce. Love walks the bridge of imagination (and art) to and *through* death. The poet advises himself (and his reader), "keep your pecker up." The book ends with the "measured dance," a dance of life made up (like the serpent with its tale in its mouth) of both the joyous and the painful, of love and death; "dance to a measure / Satyrically, the tragic foot."

In this summary view of *Paterson*, much has leaked away that is vital to the poem. But the overview might serve as the basis for a longitudinal approach which will constitute a kind of combing out of the major languages of the poems as they thread and entangle their way through all the books of *Paterson*. Williams repeatedly asserted that his poem constituted a search for a redeeming language. The question remains, Did he find it? The answer to this question involves us in passages of the poem passed over in the above summary view. Of the poem's many languages, there is first and foremost the Language of Chaos: there is the unmistakably less robust Language of Beauty; and there is the more fragile Language of Redemption. As we comb out these languages we shall simplify, but they will immediately re-entangle themselves in the poem where they shall remain inviolate.

5

The loudest language of *Paterson* is the language of chaos, of criticism, the language which the poet finds as the reality of Paterson, the reality of America. Indeed, a first reading of the poem might well leave the impression that it is the only language because it is so dominant. The voiceless drownings of Sam Patch (who used the symbolic name of Noah Faitoute Paterson, thus enabling the poet to identify with him) and Mrs. Cumming offer a paradigm for a languageless, perishing America, suffering from "blockage" (it's there but it's dammed up, blocked) and from "divorce," a failure of connecting humanly because of a failure of language. But the Patch-Cumming episodes are only the most vivid of a large cluster of related images of failure:

> The language, the language
>   fails them
> They do not know the words
>   or have not
> the courage to use them   .
>   —girls from
> families that have decayed and
> taken to the hills. no words.
> They may look at the torrent in
>   their minds
> and it is foreign to them.   .

> They turn their backs
> and grow faint—but recover!
>   Life is sweet
> they say: the language!
>   —the language
> is divorced from their minds,
> the language   .   .   the language!
>   (*P*, pp. 11–12)

It is not, of course, that there is no language at all: worse, there is abundant language (or sound) that misleads and betrays:

> A false language. A true. A false language pouring—a
> language (misunderstood) pouring (misinterpreted) with-
>   out
> dignity, without minister, crashing upon a stone ear.
> (*P*, p. 15)

By divorce Williams does not of course have reference simply to matrimony: his notion of divorce goes much deeper, with profounder consequences:

> a bud forever green,
> tight-curled, upon the pavement, perfect
> in juice and substance but divorced, divorced
> from its fellows, fallen low—
>
>   Divorce is
> the sign of knowledge in our time,
> divorce! divorce!
>
>   with the roar of the river
> forever in our ears (arrears)
> inducing sleep and silence, the roar
> of eternal sleep .   .   .   challenging
> our waking—
>
> (*P*, p. 18)

This divorce is a severance from the fruition of life itself. In divorce "from its fellows," the bud remains "forever green." Thus Williams suggests a profound immaturity characteristic of America, with the energy and potential present but unrealized. And the divorce is clearly related to the "roar" which communicates nothing but its uncombed sound, rendering genuine human connection difficult if not impossible. Life roars by and leaves nothing in its wake but a trailing silence, "the roar / of eternal sleep," death, the final and lasting divorce.

In Book II of *Paterson*, the poet-protagonist's Sunday walk through the park brings into focus some of the causes of blockage and divorce. There is, first of all, the people—Alexander Hamilton's "great beast"— coarsened by a life of hard work:

> ... the ugly legs of the young girls,
> pistons too powerful for delicacy!
> the men's arms, red, used to heat and cold,
> to toss quartered beeves and   .
>
> (*P*, p. 44)

Their Sunday relaxation suggests the nature of the other days of their lives—days in the factories and businesses of Paterson earning the money for survival. In what is potentially an Eliotic *Waste Land* scene, the "great beast" of the people ignoring the traditional meaning of Sunday and wasting their time in meaningless activities, drinking beer, playing ball, quarreling and napping, we encounter a vision closer to Whitman's than to Eliot's: there is sympathy and under-standing and searching as Paterson walks through the park. "Cash is mulct of them that others may live / secure /   . .   and knowledge restricted" (*P*, p. 72). A significant part of the poet's vision comes in a prose passage: "Even during the Revolution Hamilton had been im-pressed by the site of the Great Falls of the Passaic. His fertile imagi-nation envisioned a great manufacturing center, a great Federal City, to supply the needs of the country. Here was water-power to turn the mill wheels and the navigable river to carry manufactured goods to the market centers: a national manufactury" (*P*, p. 69). Williams had been attracted to Paterson and its Passaic Falls precisely because of Hamilton's historical involvement, his vision of great material wealth, prototype of the American dream. Somewhere, back in the past, in the visionary planning of such as Hamilton, lies the cause of the wastes on display on Sunday in the park.

There is one man in the park who speaks a torrent of words: Klaus, the "Protestant! protesting—as / though the world were his own." In telling his story to the Sunday park strollers, he reveals himself the victim of the American dream—victim in the sense that he came to America, made the riches he dreamed of, and discovered in a visita-tion from "our blessed Lord" that he was not happy. He followed the injunction to give away all his money and found finally in his evangelism the way to happiness: "There is no / end to the treasures of our Blessed Lord who / died on the Cross for us that we may be saved" (*P*, p. 73). We no sooner read the "Amen" to Klaus's familiar revival sermon than we find ourselves in a prose passage describing the Federal Reserve System in the U.S., a private enterprise that creates money and lends it at high interest, forcing the people to "pay interest to the banks in the form of high taxes" (*P*, p. 73). Usury, a familiar theme from Ezra Pound's *Cantos*, here divulged as lying obscurely behind the ugliness of Sunday in the park: "The Federal Reserve Banks constitute a Legalized National Usury System." (*P*, p. 74). Klaus's torrent of words misses the economic reality. The people comprehend neither him nor the system his mythology distorts and veils. The roar goes on, unattended, uncombed.

The Library, in Book III, turns out to be the repository not of the wisdom of the past, but of the cumulative horrors of history. Accumulated newspapers reveal that the past is simply more of the present:

> Old newspaper files,
> to find—a child burned in a field,
> no language. Tried, aflame, to crawl under
> a fence to go home. So be it. Two others,
> boy and girl, clasped in each others' arms
> (clasped also by the water) So be it. Drowned
> wordless in the canal. So be it.
>
> (P, pp. 97–98)

From newspapers Paterson turns to the books: "A library—of books! decrying all books / that enfeeble the mind's intent" (P, p. 102). It is soon clear that the books do not contain the revelation for which the poet seeks:

> The place sweats of staleness and of rot
> a back-house stench   .   a
> library stench
>
> (P, p. 103)

Paterson realizes that the books "cannot penetrate and cannot waken, to be again / active but remain—books / that is, men in hell, / their reign over the living ended"(P, p. 115). In the midst of this awareness, one of the most violent of the prose inserts relates the story of the torture and murder of innocent Indians by American colonists, witnessed by "leaders" who "stood laughing heartily at the fun" (P, p. 102). The reader muses: where are the books in this library that reveal the reality of this American pioneer past? By the time the tornado strikes, followed by the fire and the flood, the reader yearns with Paterson for the cleansing of the past to make way for a new beginning.

Book III concludes with some of the most Whitmanian lines of *Paterson*. Unlike Eliot and Pound, very much like Emerson and Whitman, Paterson learns from the Library experience—

> The past above, the future below
> And the present pouring down: the roar,
> the roar of the present, a speech—
> is, of necessity, my sole concern   .
>
> (P, p. 144)

Whitman put it this way in his 1855 Preface: "The direct trial of him who would be the greatest poet is today. If he does not flood himself with the immediate age as with vast oceanic tides . . . and if he be not

himself the age transfigured . . . let him . . . wait his development."[12]
Paterson seems determined to be the Whitmanian poet:

> I cannot stay here
> to spend my life looking into the past;
>
> the future's no answer. I must
> find my meaning and lay it, white,
> beside the sliding water: myself—
> comb out the language—or succumb
>
> —whatever the complexion. Let
> me out! (Well, go!) this rhetoric
> is real!
> (*P*, p. 145)

Whitman always declared that his rhetoric was of the flesh: "Camerado, this is no book, / Who touches this touches a man."[13]

Book IV, which was once thought to complete *Paterson*, pleased almost nobody, and even Williams felt moved to add another book. No doubt a major reason for the critical displeasure with the book is the dominance of the language of chaos, with vignettes and images of perversion, sexual frustration, violence and death. Readers have not known how to interpret the opening section, portraying a Lesbian poetess vying with Dr. Paterson for the sexual favors of a beautiful nurse. Critics have tended to be more condemnatory morally than Williams himself, who commented: "The little girl gets herself mixed up at last in the pathetic sophisticate of the great city, no less defeated and understandable, even lovable, than she is herself."[14] Clearly Williams did not intend the episode in an Eliotic sense—sexual perversion as emblematic of moral and spiritual perversion. His sympathies for all the frustrated participants come through the long sketch, and his admiration for the girl shines brightly in the poetry. What has not been much noticed about the narrative is its mixture of languages. The poetess in the "Idyl" is a creature out of the library of Book III, her version of reality framed by poetic visions from the past, classical or modern; she forces her life into the unreal form of a pastoral, and she writes Phyllis a poem with lines that even she recognizes from Yeats. Paterson, too, sees his experience with Phyllis framed in an Eliotic vision: "Oh Paterson! Oh married man! / He is the city of cheap hotels and private entrances" (*P*, p. 154). As he departs from a rendezvous, he remembers that there is something he wanted to say—"but I've forgotten / what it was   . something I wanted / to tell you. Completely gone! Completely" (*P*, p. 154). The only entirely genuine language in this frustrated triangle is the language of the down-to-earth letters that Phyllis writes to her alcoholic father, reeking with a refreshing reality that points up the phoniness of the rest: "Look, Big Shot, I refuse to come home until you promise to cut out the booze" (P, p. 150).

Book IV presents other images of chaos, images of the atomic bomb, of "the cancer, usury," and of violence. Perhaps the most impressive of these are the prose accounts (in Part Three) of several murders, one the story of a young man killing his own infant daughter when "her crying annoyed him," and another the story (1850) of one John Johnson, a sometime hired hand (an inverse of Robert Frost's), who killed his former employer and wife, and then "was hung in full view of thousands who had gathered on Garrett Mountain and adjacent house tops to witness the spectacle" (P, p. 203). What gives this passage authority is its position within five short lines of the conclusion of Book IV (and one time the end of the poem). It is, indeed, the final image of the book, and is almost like a slap in the face for readers who have smiled affirmatively as they have just witnessed Paterson wade out of the "sea of blood" and strike inland for what seems to be a new beginning. The closing lines: "This is the blast / the eternal close / the spiral / the final somersault / the end." Thus readers are not permitted a sentimental conclusion; they are reminded of the reality of violence as it exists not only in Johnson but also in the crowds come to witness, among whom the reader might even, if he looks hard enough, discover himself.

In Book V of *Paterson*, the images of chaos decrease considerably, and they are integrated almost inseparably with images of renewal—the unicorn suffers death, but transcends death. In Part Two, Paterson exclaims:

> I saw love
> > mounted naked on a horse
> > > on a swan
> > the tail of a fish
> > > the bloodthirsty conger eel
> > > > and laughed
> > recalling the Jew
> > > in the pit
> > > > among his fellows
> > when the indifferent chap
> > > with the machine gun
> > > > was spraying the heap
> > he had not yet been hit
> > > but smiled
> > comforting his companions

> comforting
>   his companions.
>   (*P*, p. 223)

Paterson does not evade evil and horror, but seems now to see it in a totality that balances: there is the man who shoots, but there is also the man who comforts—a Whitmanian figure bringing succor to the suffering (as in "Song of Myself"). The serpent with its tail in its mouth; evil begetting good, good begetting evil, evil begetting good: "the river has returned to its beginnings" (*P*, p. 233). Paterson goes on—

> Dreams possess me
>   and the dance
>   of my thoughts
> involving animals
>   the blameless beasts
>   (*P*, p. 224)

Whitman said: "I think I could turn and live with animals, they are so placid and self-contain'd, / I stand and look at them long and long."[15] Paterson's dance, the dance of his thoughts and the dance that ends the poem, is a dance of acceptance that embraces (as "all we know") both the joyous and the tragic.

6

Paterson's Preface opens, "Rigor of beauty is the quest. But how will you find beauty when it is locked in the mind past all remonstrance" (*P*, p. 3). At one time, Williams had added: "It is not in the things nearest us unless transposed there by our employment."[16] Language must be used in explorations for beauty, and much of *Paterson* is given over to its discovery and delineation, its tenuous embodiment in an elusive language. Paterson does indeed find beauty in "the things nearest us," but it is only by employment of his art that it is "transposed there."

The first extended probing for beauty comes in Book I, with minute examination in memory of an old photograph from the *National Geographic*:

> I remember
> a *Geographic* picture, the 9 women
> of some African chief semi-naked
> astraddle a log, an official log to
> be presumed, head left:
>   (*P*, p. 13)

Paterson's eye of memory moves from the youngest, most recent wife along the line to the "last, the first wife, / present! supporting all the rest growing up from her." Her breasts sag "from hard use," but on her face there is a "vague smile, / unattached, floating like a pigeon / after a long flight to his cote." After presenting the examples of Sam Patch and Mrs. Cumming (blockage and divorce), Paterson's mind returns to this enigmatic woman:

> Which is to say, though it be poorly
> said, there is a first wife
> and a first beauty, complex, ovate—
> the woody sepals standing back under
> the stress to hold it there, innate
>
> a flower within a flower whose history
> (within the mind) crouching
> among the ferny rocks, laughs at the names
> by which they think to trap it. Escapes!
> Never by running but by lying still—
>
> (*P*, p. 22)

Beauty locked—or lurking—in the mind? An unlikely place, this—an old African woman with sagging breasts—to begin the search for beauty. But for the African chieftain, the beauty of his first wife crouches there among the "ferny rocks" of *his* mind, and is obscurely translated through the eight successors. Paterson will seek—and find—beauty in the most unlikely of places.

In "Sunday in the Park" (Book II), Paterson spots two lovers in a "grassy den," the woman "lies sweating" at the side of a dozing man—

> She stirs, distraught,
> against him—wounded (drunk), moves
> against him (a lump) desiring,
> against him, bored
>
> flagrantly bored and sleeping, a
> beer bottle still grasped spear-like
> in his hand   .
>
> (*P*, p. 59)

Small boys peer down on the frustrated lovers. The woman moves nearer the man, "her lean belly to the man's backside," but he does not waken:

> —to which he adds his useless voice:
> until there moves in his sleep

a music that is whole, unequivocal (in
his sleep, sweating in his sleep—laboring
against sleep, agasp!)
                    —and does not waken.

Sees, alive (asleep)
            —the fall's roar entering
his sleep (to be fulfilled)
                            reborn
in his sleep—scattered over the mountain
severally

            —by which he woos her, severally.
                                (*P*, p. 60)

Later in the day, Paterson passes by once again and notices that "the drunken lovers slept, now, both of them" (*P*, p. 62).

Later, after listening to the evangelist Klaus, Paterson ponders and puzzles over beauty—"These women are not / beautiful and reflect / no beauty but gross . . / Unless it is beauty / to be, anywhere, / so flagrant in desire" (*P*, p. 71). *Unless, unless.* Before presenting the frustrated Sunday park lovers, Paterson remembered a scene from an Eisenstein film in which an old peasant is drinking with abandon in a kind of sexual celebration: "the female of it facing the male, the satyr— / (Priapus!)" (*P*, p. 58). The priapus principle of life has been frustrated in the lovers in the park—but affirmed by the poet. These lovers are not re-creations of Eliot's typist and "young man carbuncular," but rather, perhaps, anwers to them. Their desire is healthy and life-affirming, not sordid and meaningless. It is the beauty that the poet seeks, and he works to "transpose" it there without falsifying or sentimentalizing or satirizing. Many readers have been misled by this passage, seeing it in the context of Eliot's *Waste Land* view of sex. But Williams has made it clear, both in the poem and out of it, that he is on the side of the frustrated lovers. He remarked in 1954: "I was always concerned with the plight of the young in the industrial age who are affected by love. It's a classic theme because a tragic theme—because love is much thought about and written about. It's tragedy when it is realized by an artist and comes out in a form like this. I love the impassioned simplicity of young lovers. When it's thwarted, and they don't know it's thwarted, then the vulgarity is lifted to distinction by being treated with the very greatest art which I can conceive." Williams saw the "love" scene as vital to the poem: "It's easy to miss, but the whole theme of *Paterson* is brought out in this passage, the contrast between the mythic beauty of the Falls and Mountain and the industrial hideousness . . . . so in this scene love has triumphed."[17] Beauty locked in the mind— released.

In Book III, "The Library," the quest for beauty surges to the fore, flashing in Paterson's (and the reader's) mind in the strangely vague refrain, "Beautiful Thing." But the vagueness perhaps suits the poet's purposes in appearing rather common (and undistinguished) language but suggesting reverberations that go beyond any specific attachment. The refrain has a long history in the conception of *Paterson*. It appeared first at the end of the Columbus chapter, "The Discovery of the Indies," in *In the American Grain* (1925): Columbus has sent his men off for water in the new land of his discovery, and during the two hours he contemplates this new world: "During that time I walked among the trees which was the most beautiful thing which I had ever seen" (*IAG*, p. 26). Williams inserted this passage in *Paterson* IV, ii (*P*, p. 178) (changing only the last word to *known*), himself calling attention to the historic and national dimension of the refrain: Beautiful Thing was there for the simple viewing, not locked away in the mind, not hidden deep within the sordid surfaces—in the beginning of the American experience. What had become of it (or what we had done to it) in the centuries since was a different matter.

As we have already observed, Beautiful Thing figured centrally in Williams's 1937 poem, "Paterson: Episode 17," and many of the passages of this poem turn up in Book III of Paterson. The idea and the phrase embodying it, then, seem to have been an important part of the poem's beginning. Throughout Book III, Beautiful Thing seems to be set over against the library, offering a meaning and vitality that the books of the dead past cannot match. The Beautiful Thing of the original poem is a beautiful Negro servant girl, loved and violated by many, caught in the lively moment of beating a rug. But in *Paterson* she seems raised to mythic level—"tall / as you already were— / till your head / through fruitful exaggeration / was reaching the sky and the / prickles of its ecstasy / Beautiful Thing!" (*P*, pp. 126–27). In this role, she reaches back in the poem to Book I to connect with the old (first) wife of the African chieftain of the *National Geographic* picture and to Book II to connect with the girl filled with frustrated desire in the park; and she reaches forward in the poem to connect with Phyllis of the Idyl and with Madame Curie (Book IV) and with the "whore and virgin" of Book V: the mystery of woman, the mystery of sex, the mystery of love, the mystery of creativity—themes of Whitman throughout *Leaves of Grass*, but especially in the sex poems of "Children of Adam."

For a time in Book III, Paterson seems to hold the "answer" in his mind:

> What end but love, that stares death in the eye?
> A city, a marriage—that stares death
> in the eye
> the riddle of a man and a woman
>
> For what is there but love, that stares death
> in the eye, love, begetting marriage
> not infamy, not death
>
> (P, p. 106)

The line turns almost Whitmanian in the midst of this new awareness:

> Sing me a song to make death tolerable, a song
> of a man and woman: the riddle of a man
> and a woman.
>   What language could allay our thirsts,
> what winds lift us, what floods bear us
>   past defeats
> but song but deathless song   ?
>
> (P, p. 107)

Language, love, death: beauty is the key, beauty locked in the mind released, beauty "transposed" to the simple scene of Beautiful Thing in all her vitality and appeal:

>   Beautiful thing, your
> vulgarity of beauty surpasses all their
> perfections!
>
>   Vulgarity surpasses all perfections
> —it leaps from a varnish pot and we see
> it pass—in flames!
>
>   (P, pp. 119–20)

The books cannot substitute for the reality, however "vulgar":

>   But you are the dream
> of dead men
>
>   Beautiful Thing!
>
> Let them explain you and you will be
> the heart of the explanation. Nameless,
> you will appear
>   Beautiful Thing
> the flame's lover—
>
>   (P, pp. 122–23)

It was the Emersonian-Whitmanian transcendental tradition to reject books (and the past) when experience itself offered directly what the books could offer only indirectly. Williams clearly places himself in this tradition.

Beautiful Thing appears (as we noted above) in numerous incarnations in *Paterson*, but perhaps receives her apotheosis in Book V in the fused vision of the virgin and the whore. "The moral / proclaimed by the whorehouse / could not be better proclaimed / by the virgin, a price on her head, / her maidenhead!" (*P*, p. 208). Again: "The whore and the virgin, an identity: / —through its disguises" (*P*, p. 210). And again: "the virgin and the whore, which / most endures? the world / of the imagination most endures" (*P*, p. 213). The Unicorn legend woven into the tapestries of the Cloisters invites this fusion of identities, as it brought together both religious and secular meanings, the Unicorn itself representing Christ, but also, with his phallic horn, the lover-bridegroom. Thus the poet allies himself to a long tradition in seeing the two designations—virgin and whore—based on a single identification of sexuality, evocative of fundamentally identical creative sexual energy: "every married man carries in his head / the beloved and sacred image / of a virgin / whom he has whored" (*P*, p. 234). And he can assert paradoxically: "no woman is virtuous / who does not give herself to her lover / —forthwith" (*P*, p. 229).

In Part Two of Book V of *Paterson* there appears what seems to be an independent poem, beginning:

> There is a woman in our town
> walks rapidly, flat bellied
> in worn slacks upon the street
> where I saw her.
> > neither short
> nor tall, nor old nor young
> her
> > face would attract no
> adolescent.
> > > (*P*, p. 219)

This woman could be Beautiful Thing in another guise. Her appearance is not extraordinary, but her effect on the poet is: "She stopped / me in my tracks—until I saw / her / disappear in the crowd." And he exclaims, "if ever I see you again / as I have sought you / daily without success / I'll speak to you, alas / too late!" The poem might be read as an updated version of a Whitman "Children of Adam" poem ("A Woman Waits for Me," perhaps), and the poet adds at the end: "have you read anything that I have written? / It is all for you" (*P*, pp. 255–56).

Beautiful Thing, sexual-creative energy, the phallic-priapus principle, love against death: these themes intermingle and become vital in *Paterson*, culminating in Book V: "The Unicorn roams the forest of all true lovers's minds. They hunt it down. Bow wow! sing hey the green holly!" (*P*, p. 234). The poet admonishes himself: "Paterson, / keep your pecker up / whatever the detail!" (*P*, p. 235). Sexuality and creativity, like the virgin and whore, fuse, and the energy of the "pecker" is as important to creating poetry as for making love. For "to measure is all we know, / a choice among the measures /   . .   / the measured dance." And this "measure" is made up of the eternal satyr in man as well as the eternally tragic—"to dance to a measure / contrapuntally, / Satyrically, the tragic foot" (*P*, p. 239).

7

Paterson's search for a redeeming language turns up a language of redemption, but it is a delicate thread winding its way through the poem. In the first book the emphasis is on descent, as Paterson himself identifies with Sam Patch in his leap into Passaic Falls, ending up in a cake of ice. Paterson hovers near the edge—

> The thought returns: Why have I not
> but for imagined beauty where there is none
> or none available, long since
> put myself deliberately in the way of death?
>
> (*P*, p. 20)

The imagination as man's redeemer? Possibly, as we shall see in Book V. But meanwhile, the nul and the descent must be faced. Part Three of Book II opens with the admonition: "Look for the nul / defeats it all." This "nul" is "the N of all / equations," "the blank / that holds them up." It is "that nul / that's past all seeing / the death of all that's past / all being" (*P*, p. 77). This blankness and nullity appear to be very close to that palsied whiteness that Melville's Ishmael (in *Moby-Dick*) saw in the heart of all matter, the whiteness that "shadows forth the heartless voids and immensities of the universe, and thus stabs us from behind with the thought of annihilation."[18]

Then Paterson suddenly breaks off from contemplation of the nul: "But Spring shall come and flowers will bloom / and man must chatter of his doom." This is self-admonition, a turning away from abstract ideas of nullity and blankness to the apprehendable realities of spring

and flowers ("no ideas but in things"). There follows the justifiably
famous passage in which Williams discovered his beloved triadic
line—as well as affirmation in nullity:

> The descent beckons
>   as the ascent beckoned
>   Memory is a kind
> of accomplishment
>   a sort of renewal
>   even
> an initiation, since the spaces it opens are new
> places
>   inhabited by hordes
>   heretofore unrealized,
> of new kinds—
>   since their movements
>   are towards new objectives
> (even though formerly they were abandoned)
>
> No defeat is made up entirely of defeat—since
> the world it opens is always a place
>   formerly
>   unsuspected. A
> world lost,
>   a world unsuspected
>   beckons to new places
> and no whiteness (lost) is so white as the memory
> of whiteness   .
>
> (P, pp. 77–78)

The vision here may be reminiscent of Ezra Pound's descent described in the "Pisan Cantos," resulting in the unanticipated new
awareness on Pound's part—"What thou lov'st well remains,"[19] a
reservoir of the memory that is "a kind of accomplishment," "a sort of
renewal." Like Pound, Paterson finds in descent a reversal—

> The descent
>   made up of despairs
>   and without accomplishment
> realizes a new awakening   :
>   which is a reversal
>   of despair.
>
> (P, p. 78)

The nul, the blank, the descent, confronted in their reality, open up
new spaces for the imagination.

In contrast with Eliot's wasteland negativism, Williams's vision might be called creative despair—that which brings reversal not by sentimental avoidance but by inhabiting the new spaces revealed. It is very much like the reversal that comes in Whitman's "Song of Myself," where the poet has come (in section 33) to identify with all the miserable of the world—"Hell and despair are upon me," "Agonies are one of my changes of garments." But as he reaches the nadir of his despair ("I project my hat, sit shame-faced, and beg"), he also reaches one of those open spaces, and he experiences reversal of despair in a new awareness. He cries out "Enough! enough! enough!" as he remembers the "overstaid fraction," discovering new spiritual or imaginative energy which he can share through his poetry.[20]

This theme of renewal through despair is echoed throughout *Paterson*, as, for example, in Book III, in the midst of the burning of the library—

> An old bottle, mauled by the fire
> gets a new glaze, the glass warped
> to a new distinction, reclaiming the
> undefined. A hot stone, reached
> by the tide, crackled over by fine
> lines, the glaze unspoiled
> Annihilation ameliorated:
>
> (*P*, p. 118)

In the renewal of the bottle (found in its "new space") there is vital reversal—

> the flame that wrapped the glass
> deflowered, reflowered there by
> the flame: a second flame, surpassing
> heat   .
>
> (*P*, 118)

Deflowered: reflowered. Despair, reversal of despair. Descent: renewal. Paterson contemplates the example of the reflowered bottle:

> Hell's fire. Fire Sit your horny ass
> down. What's your game? Beat you
> at your own game, Fire. Outlast you:
> Poet Beats Fire at Its Own Game! The bottle!
> the bottle! the bottle! the bottle! I
> give you the bottle! What's burning
> now, Fire?
>
> (*P*, p. 118)

It is the poet's language of redemption that has beaten the fire at its own game, turning destruction into creation, resurrecting (and preserving) the bottle in its new incarnation.

In Book IV, Madame Curie's discovery of radium constitutes a similar reversal—

> A dissonance
> in the valence of Uranium
> led to the discovery
> Dissonance
> (if you are interested)
> leads to discovery
>
> (P, p. 176)

At a critical moment in the Curie investigations, there appeared the nul, the blankness—but

> a stain at the bottom of the retort
> without weight, a failure, a
> nothing. And then, returning in the
> night, to find it
>
> LUMINOUS
>
> (P, p. 178)

The luminosity derives from the assumed nothing—the blank space that gave room for the new awakening.

The pattern of descent and renewal is the pattern of the central action of the poem. Paterson takes on the identity of Sam Patch fallen to his doom and encased in a cake of ice in the opening of the poem. If the doom is final, Patch-Paterson should disappear in the sea at the end of the descent of the falls as the river runs to the sea—the "sea of blood"—in the conclusion of Book IV:

> the nostalgic sea
> sopped with our cries
> Thalassa! Thalassa!
> calling us home   .
> I say to you, Put wax rather in your
> ears against the hungry sea
> it is not our home!
>
> (P, p. 201)

With the recurring cry, "the sea is not our home," Paterson wades out of the "blood dark sea" at the end of Book IV and has a refreshing nap on the beach. All the imagery in the closing lines describing Paterson's action is the imagery of life—the dog who accompanies him, the girls he notices playing on the beach, the beach plums he samples (spitting out the seed, emblem of renewal), his striking out energetically inland.

The language of redemption moves to the central position in Book V of *Paterson*, inherent in the very nature and narrative of the Unicorn tapestries. The story is a story of death and resurrection. The most magnificent of all the tapestries is the last, in which the Unicorn appears alone, chained to a tree, surrounded by a wooden fence in an incredibly beautiful field of multicolored flowers. Here the Unicorn may be the risen Christ in Paradise, or he may be the lover finally secured by his lady-love, a fusion of sexual-religious symbolism that goes to the heart of Williams's purposes:

> in a field crowded with small flowers
> .   . its neck
>   circled by a crown!
>   from a regal tapestry of stars!
> lying wounded on his belly
>   legs folded under him
> the bearded head held
>   regally aloft   .
>
> (*P*, p. 211)

The risen (erect?) unicorn "has no match / or mate," just as "the artist / has no peer": "Death / has no peer." The Unicorn has been killed, yet lives—

> We shall not get to the bottom:
> death is a hole
> in which we are all buried
> Gentile and Jew.
>
> The flower dies down
> and rots away   .
> But there is a hole
> in the bottom of the bag.
>
> It is the imagination
> which cannot be fathomed.
> It is through this hole
> we escape   .   .
>
> So through art alone, male and female, a field of
> flowers, tapestry, spring flowers unequaled
> in loveliness.
>
> (*P*, pp. 211–12)

The descent of death is the final descent: but there are new spaces

even here, and a reversal of despair: the imagination finds the hole at
the bottom of death through which to escape—as the resurrected
Unicorn has escaped in the tapestry.

> Through this hole
> at the bottom of the cavern
> of death, the imagination
> escapes intact.
>
> he bears a collar round his neck
> hid in the bristling hair.
>
> (*P*, p. 212)

Immediately following this defiant assertion appears a letter from the
young, then unknown poet Allen Ginsberg, setting out to dedicate
his life to the poetic imagination. The letter thanks Williams for writing his introduction (to *Howl!*), and proclaims his "whitmanic mania":
"In any case Beauty is where I hang my hat. And reality. And
America" (*P*, p. 213). Williams-Paterson's Unicorn, perhaps? Redemption, resurrection, through the imagination, of Whitman's "ages'
and ages' encrustations." But of course, Williams's Unicorn of the
seventh tapestry is the poem *Paterson* itself. It has handsomely escaped through the hole at the bottom of death. And many readers
would conclude with Robert Lowell's judgment, in proclaiming
Williams as "part of the great breath of our literature, that "*Paterson* is
our *Leaves of Grass*."[21]

A final word:
from
"An Elegy for W. C. W., the lovely man"

John Berryman

Henry in Ireland to Bill underground:
Rest well, who worked so hard, who made a good sound
constantly, for so many years:
your high-jinks delighted the continents & our ears:
you had so many girls your life was a triumph
and you loved your one wife.

At dawn you rose & wrote—the books poured forth—
you delivered infinite babies, in one great birth—
and your generosity
to juniors made you deeply loved, deeply:
if envy was a Henry trademark, he would envy you,
especially the being through.[22]

Eight

For all I know, the *Bridge* may turn into something like
the form of "Leaves of Grass," with a number of editions,
each incorporating further additions.

Hart Crane, 1929

Hart Crane's "Bridge"

1 Although Hart Crane's short life did not permit him the long gestation period for his epic, *The Bridge*, that Pound had for *The Cantos* or Williams for *Paterson*, there is evidence that he conceived it some seven years before its final and complete parturition in 1930. And moreover, there is evidence that from the beginning of his conception, Walt Whitman figured prominently. In the early months of 1923, when he had the first idea of writing the poem, he wrote to his close friend Gorham Munson: "The more I think about my *Bridge* poem the more thrilling its symbolical possibilities become, and since my reading of you and [Waldo] Frank (I recently bought *City Block*) I begin to feel myself directly connected with Whitman. I feel myself in currents that are positively awesome in their extent and possibilities" (*L*, p. 128).[1] This confession that *The Bridge* and Whitman were, from the outset, inextricably mixed, is not news to the poem's readers, inasmuch as the finished poem includes an extravagant and structurally vital "ode" to Whitman which reveals Crane's feelings for and imaginative dependence on the first genuinely epic American poet. But the confession I take as a basis for a claim I wish to push: that

163

Whitman is a much more pervasive presence in *The Bridge* than its commentators have revealed.

Crane's allegiance to Whitman was to prove, in a sense, the temporary critical undoing of *The Bridge* on its appearance. For a while during the 1920s, Crane was able to straddle two poetic camps. Although the poetic politics of the time should not be exaggerated, they cannot be discounted. Crane's emotions were with one camp, his style (in some aspects) with another. There were the Whitmanites (not Whitmaniacs) Gorham Munson and Waldo Frank, with eclectic mystic P. D. Ouspensky assuming the role of a kind of culture hero. And there were the classicist anti-Whitmanites, Allen Tate and Yvor Winters, with eclectic pessimist T. S. Eliot as culture hero. Crane's chief connections with these two strong currents of the period were Gorham Munson and Allen Tate. One of the ironies of Crane's career is that his early, important poem, "For the Marriage of Faustus and Helen" (whose theme was the initial inspiration for *The Bridge*), attracted praise from the two poetic camps, which both hailed it as among the most important of modern poems. Munson and Tate were extravagant in their comments in letters to Crane.[2] Yvor Winters called the poem "one of the great poems of our time, as great as the best of Stevens, or Pound, or Eliot."[3] Waldo Frank, who had praised the poem in letters to Crane, concluded his review of *White Buildings* in which the poem appeared: "*White Buildings* gives us enough to justify the assertion, that not since Whitman has so original, so profound and—above all, so important a poetic impulse come to the American scene."[4] The fact that this conclusion was deleted by *New Republic* editors did not diminish its impact on Crane, who had a copy of the original review.

Crane had read Whitman with great care, and he had also read Waldo Frank's *Our America* (1919) with its eulogy of Whitman. From Whitman directly and from Frank's conception of a mystical Whitman, Crane derived much of his inspiration for *The Bridge*.[5] He even considered his universally admired "Faustus and Helen" as in some sense in the Whitmanian-Frank tradition. He wrote to Gorham Munson (whose *Waldo Frank: A Study* appeared in 1923): "And I am even more grateful for your very rich suggestions best stated in your *Frank Study* on the treatment of mechanical manifestations of today as subject for lyrical, dramatic, and even epic poetry. You must already notice that influence in 'F and H.' It is to figure even larger in *The Bridge*" (*L*, p. 125). Crane clearly and early linked his lyric "Faustus and Helen" with his epic *Bridge*, structurally and thematically. In his first reference to *The Bridge* in his correspondence, 6 February 1923, he wrote to Gorham Munson: "I am ruminating on a new longish poem under the title of *The Bridge* which carries on further the tendencies manifest in 'F. and H.' " (*L*, p. 118). And again to Munson (18 February 1923): "The form [of *The Bridge*] will be symphonic, something like 'F. and H.' with its treatment of varied content" (*L*, p. 125).

How was it that a Whitmanian poem like "For the Marriage of Faustus and Helen" could attract intense praise from critics like Tate and Winters, who would later take exception to the Whitmanian dimension of *The Bridge*? The ready answer is, of course, that on the surface "Faustus and Helen" looked much more like an Eliotic than a Whitmanian poem, and did not make the mistake (like *The Bridge*) of dramatically incorporating Whitman in the structure. Indeed, by all appearances, "Faustus and Helen" was the kind of classical poem that both Tate and Winters aspired to write, with its classical title, its Eliot-like epigraph, its dense obscurities. But though *The Waste Land* had appeared in 1922, the year before Crane completed "Faustus and Helen," the latter was not a "Waste Land" poem. Although Crane's poem included the modern sordid scene, it was by no means so negative or so seemingly pessimistic as Eliot's poem. It was, though not all its readers may have realized it, a poem of praise, of celebration. Crane himself explained, in "General Aims and Theories" (written some time in 1924–26): "When I started writing 'Faust & Helen' it was my intention to embody in modern terms . . . a contemporary approximation to an ancient human culture. . . . And in so doing I found that I was really building a bridge between so-called classic experience and many divergent realities of our seething, confused cosmos of today, which has no formulated mythology yet for classic reference or for religious exploitation" (*CP*, p. 217). The key word here (in many senses) is "bridge": Crane thinks of his poem not as contrasting a barren and sterile present with a mythic and fruitful past (the method of *The Waste Land*), but rather as building a bridge between past and present to emphasize vital continuities beneath surface contrasts.

Crane wrote: "So I found 'Helen' sitting in a street car; the Dionysian revels of her court and her seduction were transferred to a Metropolitan roof garden with a jazz orchestra; and the *katharsis* of the fall of Troy I saw approximated in the recent World War. The importance of this scaffolding may easily be exaggerated, but it gave me a series of correspondences between two widely separated worlds on which to sound some major themes of human speculation—love, beauty, death, renascence" (*CP*, p. 217). Underline *renascence*. Crane, or his persona, is the Faustus of the poem who, on finding Helen on the streetcar, becomes so devoted to her beauty that, though "the earth may glide diaphanous to death," will lift his arms to her and offer "one inconspicuous, glowing orb of praise." In Part II of the poem, the frenzied orgy of sound and movement does not conclude with rejection but acceptance of this modern promiscuous flapper-version of Helen: "she is still so young, / We cannot frown upon her as she smiles." And Part III of "Faustus and Helen," with its dominant imagery of war and destruction and a "religious gunman," "eternal gunman," with whom the speaker identifies in his innocent destructiveness, concludes:

> Distinctly praise the years, whose volatile
> Blamed bleeding hands extend and thresh the height
> The imagination spans beyond despair,
> Outpacing bargain, vocable and prayer.

(CP, 33)

All the modern images are, in a way, Eliot's, and the classical frame is Eliot-like, but instead of irony of contrast we find a *bridge* of identity. Somewhere in these modern materials is the vitality, the meaning, the redemptive imagination of the long past: "The imagination spans beyond despair." Crane's jazz-mad, seductive Helen has less to do with Eliot's tired typist (seduced by the "young man carbuncular" in Part III of *The Waste Land*) than with (to come later) William Carlos Williams's Beautiful Thing of Book III of *Paterson*, a violated Negress beating a rug. Or rather, where Eliot could see only the sordid, Crane and Williams penetrated imaginatively to a redeeming beauty. And the Dionysian Helen of "Faustus and Helen" clearly has important imaginative connections with Pocahontas and the Eve-Magdalene-Virgin songs of *The Bridge*.

2

What enabled Crane to affirm in defiance of the sordid and destructive nature of the modern materials he chose to treat in his poetry? It is impossible to say with certainty, inasmuch as many experiences must have gone into the shaping of Crane's imagination. But it should not be overlooked that he early became familiar with P. D. Ouspensky's *Tertium Organum*, and was urging it on Gorham Munson in 1922.[6] This book is devoted to the notion of a "higher consciousness" attainable by mankind (a fourth dimension), and concludes with a long extract from R. M. Bucke's *Cosmic Consciousness* (1901), a book which takes Walt Whitman as its primary modern example (Bucke, a Canadian alienist or psychoanalyst, had known Whitman well and had earlier written the first biography of the poet).

Clearly Crane had known Whitman before encountering the version presented in the Bucke extract included in Ouspensky's book, but he may not have known (or conceived) so spiritual or mystical a version of the American poet. Bucke's Whitman (and Ouspensky's ideas) may have sent Crane back to a deeper reading of the *Leaves*.

In Bucke's view, there were three kinds of consciousness: the lower consciousness characteristic of animals; self-consciousness characteristic of mankind; and cosmic consciousness characteristic only of a few of mankind's most advanced specimens, including the Buddha, Christ, and, among a few poets, Walt Whitman. Cosmic consciousness endowed its possessor with a transcendent vision that enabled him to detect the order in the chaos, the spiritual in the material, the good buried seedlike within evil. Although Whitman had never reduced his belief to such a neat formula, he did define the "cosmic poet" in seerlike terms, and his own greatest poetry characteristically rose to a visionary level of affirmation—*through* rather than *around* the negative aspects of experience (as, for example, in the poetry of Blake).

That Crane was strongly attracted by the mystical-spiritual dimension in Whitman and in visionary poetry generally is suggested strongly in a letter he wrote to Gorham Munson, 18 June 1922, concerning his own mystical experience:

> Did I tell you of that thrilling experience this last winter in the dentist's chair when under the influence of aether and *amnesia* my mind spiraled to a kind of seventh heaven of consciousness and egoistic dance among the seven spheres—and something like an objective voice kept saying to me—"You have the higher consciousness—you have the higher consciousness. This is something that very few have. This is what is called genius"? A happiness, ecstatic such as I have known only twice in "inspirations" came over me. I felt the two worlds. And at once. As the bore went into my tooth I was able to follow its every revolution as detached as a spectator at a funeral. O Gorham, I have known moments of eternity. I tell you this as one who is a brother. I want you to know me as I feel myself to be sometimes. I don't want you to feel that I am conceited. But since this adventure in the dentist's chair, I feel a new confidence in myself. (*L*, pp. 91–92)

Clearly this experience and perhaps others like it flowed into the writing of "Faustus and Helen" and into the initial conception of *The Bridge*. It is important to note that the mystical transcendence comes not in the midst of contemplation of beauty or of the apprehension of ecstasy, but paradoxically in the drug-induced experience in a mundane dental (*dental!*) chair: the modern paradigm? From the sordid,

beauty? Through common experience to vision and pleasure? Whatever the case, it is important also to note that the year of Crane's
dental chair mystical experience, 1922, was also the year of Eliot's
Waste Land. The reading and personal experiences impelling him in a
positive way toward the writing of *The Bridge* were supplemented
by a negative compulsion: to counter the pessimism of *The Waste
Land*.

Crane had been an early reader of Eliot, but his experience of *The
Waste Land* was similar to William Carlos Williams's: a sense of set-
back, a sense of defeat, and, finally, a challenge. We find him commenting first in a 20 November 1922, letter to Gorham Munson:
"What do you think of Eliot's *The Wasteland?* I was rather disap-
pointed. It was good, of course, but so damned dead. Neither does it,
in my opinion, add anything important to Eliot's achievement"
(*L*, p. 105). In early 1923 (5 Jan. 1923), at a time when he was flooded
with the first inspiration for *The Bridge,* he wrote again to Gorham
Munson:

> There is no one writing in English who can command so much
> respect, to my mind, as Eliot. However, I take Eliot as a point of
> departure toward an almost complete reverse of direction. His
> pessimism is amply justified, in his own case. But I would apply
> as much of his erudition and technique as I can absorb and assem-
> ble toward a more positive, or (if [I] must put it so in a sceptical
> age) ecstatic goal. I should not think of this if a kind of rhythm and
> ecstasy were not (at odd moments, and rare!) a very real thing to
> me. I feel that Eliot ignores certain spiritual events and possibilities
> as real and powerful now as, say, in the time of Blake. Certainly
> the man has dug the ground and buried hope as deep and dire-
> fully as it can ever be done. (*L*, pp. 114–15)

Shortly after this ebullient letter, on 27 February, Crane wrote to
Waldo Frank in response to Frank's understanding of and praise for
"Faustus and Helen":

> I can feel a calmness on the sidewalk—where before I felt a de-
> fiance only. And better than all—I am certain that a number of us
> at last have some kind of community of interest. And with this
> communion will come something more vital than stylistic ques-
> tions and "taste," it is vision, and a vision alone that not only
> America needs, but the whole world. We are not sure where this
> will lead, but after the complete renunciation symbolized in *The
> Wasteland* and, though less, in *Ulysses* we have sensed some new
> vitality. Whether I am in that current remains to be seen,—but I
> am enough in it at least to be sure that you are definitely in it
> already. (*L*, pp. 27–28)

From the very beginning of his conception of *The Bridge*, then, Crane saw himself as in some sense answering Eliot's pessimism with a mysticism or cosmic consciousness derived from Frank, Ouspensky, Whitman, Blake (or personal experience). But his answer was to be (as it had been in "Faustus and Helen") in Eliot's own "erudition and technique." It is possible that, had Crane avoided writing the "Cape Hatteras" (Whitman) section of *The Bridge*, he might have succeeded in keeping the allegiance of Tate and Winters that he had paradoxically gained with "Faustus and Helen." (Eliot himself published "The Tunnel" section in *Criterion*.) But Whitman's appearance in "Cape Hatteras" as a kind of Virgil-guide to Crane-as-Dante was to prove the poem's critical undoing, delaying its just assessment for many years because of the vagaries of literary history. But of course, Crane could no more have left Whitman out of *The Bridge* than Eliot could have dropped the fisher king from *The Waste Land*. Whitman was central to the conception, and his presence pervasive even when he remained unnamed (as in his unseen presence in "Faustus and Helen").

Crane's original idea for Whitman's role in *The Bridge* makes fairly clear Crane's conception of the strong link between "Faustus and Helen" and his epic. Crane originally thought of the Whitman section as representing "The Spiritual body of America" (in contrast with "Pokahantus—The Natural body of America-fertility, etc." [L, 241]), and he conceived a highly dramatic scene:

Whitman approaches the bed of a dying (*southern*) soldier—scene is in a Washington hospital. Allusion is made to this during the dialogue. The soldier, conscious of his dying conditions, at the end of the dialogue asks Whitman to call a priest, for absolution. Whitman leaves the scene—deliriously the soldier calls him back. The part ends here before Whitman's return, of course. The irony is, of course, in the complete absolution which Whitman's words have already given the dying man, before the priest is called for. This alternated with the eloquence of the dying man, is the substance of the dialogue—the emphasis being on the symbolism of the soldier's body having been used as a *forge* toward a state of Unity. His hands are purified of the death they have previously dealt by the principles Whitman hints at or enunciates (without talking upstage, I hope) and here the "religious gunman" motive returns much more explicitly than in F & H. The agency of death is exercised in obscure ways as the agency of life. Whitman knew this and accepted it. The appeal of the scene must be made as much as possible independent of the historical "character" of Walt.[7]

Crane himself provides the Whitmanian generalizations (the "religious gunman motive") that links his two poems: "The agency of death is exercised in obscure ways as the agency of life."

This mystical, deeply spiritualized Whitman was the Whitman Crane clearly wanted to embody in his poem, in his essence as well as in his person. Although he ultimately changed the nature of Whitman's presence in the poem, his appearance remained vital to the poem's structure and meaning. And some of the critics who had hailed "Faustus and Helen" as one of the greatest poems of the century found themselves gagging on *The Bridge*'s obvious allegiance to the Whitmanian spirit. The Winters-Tate commentary on *The Bridge* established an infectious critical "line" that has yet to be fully comprehended. Yvor Winters's review of *The Bridge* (in the June 1930 *Poetry*)[8] was a prefiguration of the influential line he was to take in his essay, "The Significance of *The Bridge*, by Hart Crane, or What Are We to Think of Professor X?" (*Anatomy of Nonsense*, 1943). In the latter, he assigned Whitman the villainous role of corrupting a talented poet, and amazingly blamed Whitman's beliefs (which he derives, in an astonishing sleight of hand, from Emerson, asserting that Emerson's and Whitman's ideas were exact equivalents) for Hart Crane's suicide![9] Rarely has such outrageous and irresponsible critical rant had such profound influence on a poet's reputation (it is echoed even in R. W. B. Lewis's 1967 study of Crane [*The Poetry of Hart Crane*], in which he perpetuates the practice of linking Crane to Whitman through explicating Emerson, and refers to the Whitman poem he thinks most important to *The Bridge*, "Passage to India," as a "tiredly turgid work").[10] Crane's reputation, particularly his *Bridge*, and its shaping and disfigurement by the New Critical establishment criticism, beginning with the Winters-Tate line of 1930, constitutes an important chapter in modern poetic history yet to be written.

When Crane read Yvor Winters's review of *The Bridge*, he wrote to Allen Tate, whose review had not yet appeared, expressing his surprise and concern. Tate replied with what was essential agreement with Winters: "I too felt that your tribute to Whitman was, while not excessive, certainly sentimental in places, particularly at the end of Cape Hatteras. But more than this I could not say except that in some larger and vaguer sense your vision of American life comes from Whitman, or from the same sources in the American consciousness as his. I am unsympathetic to this tradition, and it seems to me that you should be too. The equivalent of Whitmanism in the economic and moral aspect of America in the last sixty years is the high-powered industrialism that you, no less than I, feel is a menace to the spiritual life in this country. In the end, this is all I can see in him; though he did write some great poetry."[11] Tate in his review said that *The Bridge* represented "a sentimental muddle of Walt Whitman and the pseudo-primitivism of Sherwood Anderson and Dr. W. C. Williams, raised to a vague and transcendental reality." And he concluded: "Crane follows the main stream of romanticism in the last hundred years. . . . If this impulse is dying out, it is as fortunate for its reputation as it is remarkable that it should be represented at the end by a poetry so rich, finely wrought, and powerful as Hart Crane's."[12]

Tate's elaborate compliment took some of the sting out of his criticism, but nevertheless Crane's reply (13 July 1930) defended Whitman and Whitman's role in *The Bridge* and tried to correct Tate's misunderstanding of that role: "It's true that my rhapsodic address to him in *The Bridge* exceeds any exact evaluation of the man. I realized that in the midst of composition. But since you and I hold such divergent prejudices regarding the value of the materials and events that W. responded to, and especially as you, like so many others, never seem to have read his *Democratic Vistas* and other of his statements sharply decrying the materialism, industrialism, etc., of which you name him the guilty and hysterical spokesman, there isn't much use in my tabulating the qualified, yet persistent reasons I have for my admiration of him, and my allegiance to the positive and universal tendencies implicit in nearly all his best work. You've heard me roar at too many of his lines to doubt that I can spot his worst, I'm sure" (*L*, pp. 353–54). In a short essay entitled "Modern Poetry" and published in 1930, Crane concluded with perhaps his final assessment of Whitman: "The most typical and valid expression of the American *psychosis* seems to me still to be found in Whitman. His faults as a technician and his clumsy and indiscriminate enthusiasm are somewhat beside the point. He, better than any other, was able to coordinate those forces in America which seem most intractable, fusing them into a universal vision which takes on additional significance as time goes on. He was a revolutionist beyond the strict meaning of Coleridge's definition of genius, but his bequest is still to be realized in all its implications" (*CP*, p. 263). Like Pound, like Williams, Crane perhaps saw himself as one of those, prophesied by Whitman, to come "after ages' and ages' encrustations."

But a postscript needs to be added to the Whitman connection: whatever the impact of Whitman on Crane's vision, there are some aspects of his style closer to Eliot's, and some which he attempted to describe as peculiarly his own, particularly what he came to call the "logic of metaphor." He treats this subject in a famous letter to Harriet Monroe in 1926, and in "General Aims and Theories" (written around 1924–26). He said in the latter: "As to technical considerations: the motivation of the poem must be derived from the implicit emotional dynamics of the materials used, and the terms of expression employed are often selected less for their logical (literal) significance than for their associational meanings. Via this and their metaphorical inter-relationships, the entire construction of the poem is raised on the organic principle of a 'logic of metaphor,' which antedates our so-called pure logic, and which is the genetic basis of all speech, hence consciousness and thought extension" (CP, p. 221). Crane is anxious to explain "these dynamics," he says, because of the alleged difficulties in understanding his poems: he defends his method as "at times the only means possible for expressing certain concepts in any forceful or direct way whatever" (CP, p. 221). The example he presents is useful: "In 'Voyages (II), I speak of 'adagios of islands,' the reference is to the motion of a boat through islands clustered thickly, the rhythm of the motion, etc. And it seems a much more direct and creative statement than any more logical employment of words such as 'coasting slowly through the islands,' besides ushering in a whole world of music" (CP, p. 221). This Cranean principle of "logic of metaphor" is not, of course, peculiar to Crane, though he made it a central element of his language. It had been used by other poets before, and it would be used by poets after—as, for example, Allen Ginsberg (who rediscovered the "logic of metaphor" by studying the paintings of Cezanne; see chapter 11).

3

Through Crane's letters it is fairly simple to trace the evolution of *The Bridge* from its conception in 1923 until publication in 1930. With all the changes that the idea underwent, it is astonishing how the initial conception held firm. Crane wrote to Gorham Munson about *The Bridge*, 18 February 1923: "Very roughly, it concerns a mystical synthesis of 'America.' History and fact, location, etc., all have to be transfigured into abstract form that would almost function independently of its subject matter. The initial impulses of 'our people' will have to be gathered up toward the climax of the bridge, symbol of our constructive future, our unique identity, in which is included also our scientific hopes and achievements of the future. The mystic portent of all this is already flocking through my mind (when I say this I should say 'the mystic possibilities,' but that is all that's worth announcing, anyway) but the actual statement of the thing, the marshalling of the forces, will take me months, at best; and I may have to give it up entirely before that; it may be too impossible an ambition. But if I do succeed, such a waving of banners, such ascent of towers, such dancing, etc., will never before have been put down on paper! The form will be symphonic" (*L*, pp. 124–25). Crane's prophecy of difficulty in completing his poem was borne out in reality over the next seven years of struggle. When he turned to the philanthropist Otto H. Kahn for subsidy, he described *The Bridge* as aiming "to enunciate a new cultural synthesis of values in terms of our America" (*L*, p. 223). The words *mystical* and *synthesis* were his most frequently used words in getting at the essence of his idea.

But punctuating the periods of elation were times of despair, one of the deepest occurring in 1926, poured out in a letter to Waldo Frank:

> The form of my poem rises out of a past that so overwhelms the present with its worth and vision that I'm at a loss to explain my delusion that there exist any real links between that past and a future destiny worthy of it. The "destiny" is long since completed, perhaps the little last section of my poem is a hangover echo of it—but it hangs suspended somewhere in ether like an Absalom by his hair [Crane had finished first the last part of *The Bridge*, the visionary "Atlantis"]. The bridge as a symbol today has no significance beyond an economical approach to shorter hours, quicker lunches, behaviorism and toothpicks. . . . If only America were half as worthy today to be spoken of as Whitman spoke of it fifty years ago there might be something for me to say—not that Whitman received or required any tangible proof of his intimations, but that time has shown how increasingly lonely and ineffectual his confidence stands. (*L*, pp. 261–62)

Such self-doubts are probably natural for any large-scale poetic enterprise. Crane here seems to be testing some of Tate's ideas (they were in close association during this period) on Frank to discover what kind of response he might elicit. Crane's own later reply to Tate appears to be the best reply to Crane's own self-questioning in this letter (especially his reminder of Whitman's *Democratic Vistas*).

The detailed account of Crane's writing of *The Bridge* need not be traced here, but there is abundant evidence in the John Unterecker biography, *Voyager*, that the work almost did not get finished. There were endless problems in the writing, and there was a general reluctance in Crane to let the poem go. Had not Caresse Crosby suggested to Crane that the Crosbys' Black Sun Press publish what he had written already, with the notion that a second edition would contain revisions and additional materials, it is doubtful that Crane would ever have agreed to publication when he did, catching himself up in the commitment to a deadline that forced him to turn the poem loose. But Crane did commit himself, writing to Caresse Crosby in 1929: "As you say, there can always be a second edition incorporating additions. For all I know, the *Bridge* may turn into something like the form of 'Leaves of Grass,' with a number of editions, each incorporating further additions."[13]

The *form* of *The Bridge* had been on Crane's mind from the moment he conceived the idea for the poem. It is surely significant that here in 1929, when he is almost finished, he thinks of the form in connection with Whitman's book and its organic growth. By this time Crane had already outlined for his benefactor, Otto Kahn, his conception of the comprehensive form of his work in what is perhaps its most acute definition: "I am really writing an epic of the modern consciousness, and indescribably complicated factors have to be resolved and blended" (*L*, p. 308). Crane's juxtaposition of the two words, *epic* and *modern consciousness*, was no accident. His scope *was* epic, but the epic he was writing was not the traditional narrative—which would, after all, have been much simpler structurally. His hero was not the conventional epic hero but himself, as representative man of his time, his own consciousness as the key to the modern consciousness. No wonder the difficulty in resolving and blending the "complicated factors." He did not hesitate to classify his poem by comparison: "*The Aeneid* was not written in two years—nor in four, and in more than one sense I feel justified in comparing the historic and cultural scope of *The Bridge* to this great work. It is at least a symphony with an epic theme, and a work of considerable profundity and inspiration" (*L*, p. 309).

Crane had used "symphonic" (*L*, p. 125) to describe the form of "Faustus and Helen," a term which suggests movements, the appearance, disappearance, and reappearance of themes, variations on themes ("symphonic" was a term applied to *Leaves of Grass* also). But Crane did not leave the form entirely to intuitive development. He had a keen sense of the poem as a whole, and he planned sections in sequence to reach a designed end. In two letters that he wrote to Otto Kahn about one and a half years apart (18 March 1926 and 12 September 1927) we find Crane spelling out specific intentions and providing outlines for his work. In the first of these he described the poem in its basic intention: "There are so many interlocking elements and symbols at work throughout *The Bridge* that it is next to impossible to describe it without resorting to the actual metaphors of the poem. Roughly, however, it is based on the conquest of space and knowledge. The theme of 'Cathay' (its riches, etc.) ultimately is transmuted into a symbol of consciousness, knowledge, spiritual unity. A rather religious motivation, albeit not Presbyterian" (*L*, p. 241). The transmutation of the material into the spiritual is, of course, precisely the plan of Whitman's "Passage to India," a poem clearly vital in the conception of *The Bridge*.

In his 1926 letter to Kahn, Crane revealed a clear conception of where the poem would begin and where it would end: "Right now I'm supposed to be Don Cristobal Colon returning from 'Cathay,' first voyage. For mid-ocean is where the poem begins" (*L*, p. 240). It is noteworthy that Crane sees *himself* in the role of Columbus, suggesting his own partaking of all the "characters" in the poem. He goes on: "It concludes at midnight—at the center of Brooklyn Bridge. Strangely enough that final section of the poem has been the first to be completed—yet there's logic to it, after all; it is the mystic consummation toward which all the other sections of the poem converge. Their contents are implicit in its summary" (*L*, p. 240). The end, then, provided Crane his beginning—and a fixed goal toward which to aim all his movements.

As the letter to Kahn reveals, Crane's conception of the poem in March 1926 is somewhat different from its final form. He outlines six sections (in contrast with the poem's ultimate eight):

    I   Columbus—Conquest of space, chaos
   II Pokahantus—The natural body of America-fertility, etc.
 III Whitman—The spiritual body of America
        (A dialogue between Whitman and a dying soldier in a
        Washington hospital; the infraction of physical death, dis-
        unity, on the concept of immortality)
 IV John Brown
        (Negro porter on Calgary Express making up berths and
        singing to himself (a jazz form for this) of his sweetheart
        and the death of John Brown, alternately)
  V Subway—The encroachment of machinery on humanity; a
        kind of purgatory in relation to the open sky of last
        section
 VI The Bridge—a sweeping dithyramb in which the Bridge be-
        comes the symbol of consciousness spanning time and
        space   (*L*, p. 241)

In the final poem, the "Pokahantus" section was to grow to five subparts, quite complex in design. The "Whitman" section was to change content entirely and fuse with material on the newly developed airplane. The "John Brown" section was to disappear and the Proem and three new sections to appear—"Cutty Sark," "Three

Songs," and "Quaker Hill." Observing the plans for *The Bridge* in midstream, we might well imagine that Crane would come to think of the structure as open, like *Leaves of Grass;* his direction fixed, his conclusion set, he might add to and subtract from, shape and re-shape, almost infinitely, the major body of his work. Crane's 1926 plans for *The Bridge* offer many hints of the general thrusts of the various sections of the finished poem. It is significant, for example, that in this early conception Crane thought of the poem in terms of people—Columbus, Pocahontas, Whitman, John Brown—not culture heroes, precisely, but symbolic American figures. It is perhaps useful to know that in their original conception, the "Pokahantus" section was to portray the "natural body of America," while the Whitman section presented the "spiritual body of America."

By the time he wrote his 1927 letter to Kahn, Crane had brought his poem much closer to its final shape. He was able to list for Kahn many of the poems that had been accepted by various little magazines, and to present in detail his notion of what he had meant each of his poetic parts to mean. He was concerned that Kahn might not understand the nonchronological approach he was making to American history (his first outline for Kahn suggested a kind of straight chronology), particularly in the "Powhatan's Daughter" section. He wrote: "It seemed altogether ineffective from the poetic angle—beginning with, say, the landing of 'The Mayflower,' continuing with a résumé of the Revolution through the conquest of the West, etc. One can get that viewpoint in any history primer. What I am after is an assimilation of this experience, a more organic panorama, showing the continuous and living evidence of the past in the inmost vital substance of the present" (L, p. 305). Not simply *portrayal* of experience, but *assimilation*—constituting an "organic panorama," the past as some-how experienced in the "vital substance of the present"—through a "modern consciousness" (Crane's own). Crane explained: "Consequently I jump from the monologue of Columbus in 'Ave Maria'—right across the four intervening centuries—into the harbor of 20th-century Manhattan. And from that point in time and place I begin to work backward through the pioneer period, always in terms of the present—finally to the very core of the nature-world of the Indian. What I am really handling, you see, is the Myth of America" (L, p. 305). Not the events of the past but their assimilation; not the history but the myth. Thus there is no narrative in the usual epic sense. But the sections of the poem all have intricate interconnections. "Each is a separate canvas, as it were, yet none yields its entire significance when seen apart from the others. One might take the Sistine Chapel as an analogy" (*L*, p. 305). Michelangelo? A religious theme? Well, why not? A genuine epic ought to aspire to be in that league.

4

Crane's descriptions of his epic poem are sufficient to prepare us to find his own consciousness, as a representative "modern consciousness," providing the frame for the cultural synthesis or assimilation he is attempting. In short, he is (like Whitman before him) his own epic's hero. His consciousness is the presiding consciousness of the poem, and we must turn to it for the poem's ultimate structure. In the frame of that consciousness, the poem's duration is one day— from the dawn of the "Proem" (or of "The Harbor Dawn") to the night of "The Tunnel" and midnight of "Atlantis." In this structure, the high noon of the poem is, then, the Whitman section, "Cape Hatteras." Crane mentioned in a letter to Caresse Crosby (26 Dec. 1929) that he wanted a photograph of barges and a tug to come between "Cutty Sark" and "Cape Hatteras": "That is the 'center' of the book, both physically and symbolically" (*L*, p. 347). But of course, there are many days and nights in the poem, and the structure can be envisioned as one day only if the poem is taken as a meditation, an imaginative re-creation in the consciousness of the poet as he himself goes through one day of life in New York, ending at midnight in the middle of Brooklyn Bridge.

But though the poet's meditative or spiritual journey is for one day, in a sense it is forever (in the open form of the poem) and in intention it is out of space, out of time, into eternity—via the poet's cosmic consciousness. As in other personal epics, the journey itself is the destination; voyaging is its own excuse for being. In the tour I shall make of the poem now, I shall attempt to keep my direction in relation at all times to the larger structure (and in so doing will use as much as possible Crane's own guideposts) but I shall focus on connections with America's paradigmatic epic poet, Walt Whitman— particularly as he enters the poem dramatically in the "Cape Hatteras" section and as his spirit pervades the poem from beginning to end.[14]

"To Brooklyn Bridge"

In a letter to Waldo Frank (24 July 1926), Crane wrote: "That little prelude, by the way, I think to be almost the best thing I've ever written, something steady and uncompromising about it. Do you notice how its construction parallels the peculiar technique of space and detail division used by El Greco in several canvasses—notably *Christus am Olberg?*" (*L*, p. 267). Crane's note points up the visual or picturelike quality of his Proem, as it moves from detail to detail of the New York harbor at dawn through the crowded business and cinematic world of the city to Brooklyn Bridge itself, and the first action identified with it is a suicide—a "jest" falling from "the speechless caravan"—an action recalling Crane's generalization for what he called his "religious gunman" motive: "the agency of death is exercised in obscure ways as the agency of life."[15] Crane's Proem is, of course, the epic invocation to the muse—the bridge itself filling the role of muse, clearly a near relation to that Whitmanian muse "by thud of machinery and shrill steam-whistle undismay'd" (*CPSP*, p. 144).[16] The bridge thus serves not as the actual subject of the poem but rather as (like the muse) its inspiration. The skimming traffic lights of the cars highlight the bridge's "Unfractioned idiom, immaculate of stars, / Beading thy path—condense eternity." The language of the bridge has remained "unfractioned," as it is the language of eternity. The word recalls a like use at a critical juncture in "Song of Myself" (section 38), at the moment when the poet turns from his nadir of despair crying "Enough! enough! enough!" and cries out a new, or newly remembered knowledge or language: "I remember now, / I resume the overstaid fraction, / The grave of rock multiplies what has been confided to it, or to any graves, / Corpses rise, gashes heal, fastenings roll from me" (*CPSP*, p. 56). Whitman continues with the mystic vision of the "overstaid fraction"; Crane suggests that his epic will attempt to "fraction" that idiom of eternity from the bridge, bestow on it a new reality. He concludes with an appeal, "descend / And of the curveship lend a myth to God." God has run out of myths, and is thus in need of a loan from a bridge? Perhaps yes—a peculiarly modern, peculiarly American idea. A country without beliefs, without established traditions, must find its God where it can, and must find the myths (or The Myth) for that God. The bridge, then, will be America's St. Peter's or Notre Dame, doing for God and belief what these structures did in their time and place. That is—if Crane can "fraction" that idiom . . . if the bridge will help . . .

There are other, looser connections with Whitman which should not be overlooked. Crane's Proem functions for *The Bridge* much like the "Inscriptions" section for *Leaves of Grass*, with invocation and introduction to themes. But Crane's Brooklyn Bridge is surely meant, by its location and nature, to remind the reader of one of Whitman's most famous poems, "Crossing Brooklyn Ferry," another poem in which Whitman "fractioned" the "unfractioned idiom" of a ferry boat, transcending time and space to "fuse" with the reader.

"Ave Maria"

As the opening invocation to the bridge-muse ends by asking the bridge to "lend a myth to God," "Ave Maria" opens with a prayer by Columbus to God asking for reassurance and protection on his return from his first voyage of discovery of America. We need no greater reminder that ours is an age without faith or myth, in contrast with that other era, the era of "our" (America's) beginning, when there were both faith and myth, as well as mystery. If the opening Proem in some sense evoked "Crossing Brooklyn Ferry," "Ave Maria" is suggestive of two Whitman poems, "Passage to India" and the poem that follows it in *Leaves of Grass*, "Prayer of Columbus." In the former, Columbus makes a brief appearance in Whitman's historic sweep from the past to the present; in the latter, a "batter'd, wreck'd old man," imprisoned, he offers up a prayer: "That Thou O God my life hast lighted, / Light rare untellable, lighting the very light, / Beyond all signs, descriptions, languages" (*CPSP*, p. 296). "Unfractioned idiom" of God? Perhaps. Whitman's Columbus appears in the latter sections of *Leaves of Grass*. It is doubtful, with the example of the lifeless *Columbiad* so fresh in mind, that Whitman or anyone else of his time would have thought of starting an epic, especially an experimental new form, with Columbus. But Crane places Columbus at the beginning without flinching.

Of course, he knows at the outset that he will not present a narrative of Columbus's voyage. And he has the example of the Columbus chapter in *In the American Grain* (1925), excerpts from Columbus's journals (Crane took his Pocahontas epigraph for "Powhatan's Daughter," from the same book). William Carlos Williams ended his Columbus chapter with Columbus's exclamation about America—"I walked among the trees which was the most beautiful thing which I had ever seen"[17]—a passage which he incorporated later in *Paterson*, using Beautiful Thing as a central quest-refrain. Writers of the 1920s, disenchanted as they generally were with contemporary America, showed uncommon interest in how the first sight of America must have struck the beholders—as, for example, F. Scott Fitzgerald in the lyrical close of *The Great Gatsby*. Clearly a primary purpose of Crane's "Ave Maria" is to incorporate the wonder of that original view of

America which will contrast so sharply with his contemporary America of "Quaker Hill" and "The Tunnel." His Columbus meditates on his discovery:

> I thought of Genoa: and this truth, now proved,
> That made me exile in her streets, stood me
> More absolute than ever—biding the moon
> Till dawn should clear that dim frontier, first seen
> —The Chan's great continent. . . . Then faith, not fear
> Nigh surged me witless. . . . Hearing the surf near—
> I, wonder-breathing, kept the watch,—saw
> The first palm chevron the first light hill.
>
> (CP, p. 48)

Beautiful Thing, indeed, genuine cause for "wonder-breathing." But Columbus is bearer on this first homeward journey of more than news of an innocent, fresh, and indescribably beautiful land: his voyage has proved that the seas surround, "enclose / This turning rondure whole, this crescent ring / Sun-cusped and zoned with modulated fire." His belief that he had discovered Cathay, China, India—the Orient—does not affect the meaning and impact of what he had truly discovered. Full of this divine knowledge (part of the "unfractioned idiom" fractioned), Columbus prays that he and his ship may be spared destruction by the sea so that he may bear this knowledge to mankind. His prayer ends, "O Thou Hand of Fire" (fire of the corposants he has seen, divine fire both destructive and purifying), a phrase repeated by the protagonist at the end of "The Tunnel," after he has experienced the modern urban hazards (of a subway-hell) not unlike the sea hazards of Columbus's 1492 voyage home.

II. "Powhatan's Daughter"

If Crane thought of himself in the role of Columbus (as his letters suggest), there is no doubt that he enters his poem directly in his own identity in "Powhatan's Daughter." Crane described the five subsections of "Powhatan's Daughter" thus: "The love-motif (in italics) carries along a symbolism of the life and ages of man (here [in 'Harbor Dawn'] the sowing of the shed) which is further developed in each of the subsequent sections of 'Powhatan's Daughter,' though it is never particularly stressed. In 2 ('Van Winkle') it is Childhood; in 3 ['The River'] it is Youth; in 4 ['The Dance'], Manhood; in 5 ['Indiana'] it is Age. This motif is interwoven and tends to be implicit in the imagery rather than anywhere stressed" (L, p. 306). Crane's "ages of

man" turn out to be close in biographical data to his own sequence of
ages, and thus Crane gives us specific reason to see him (his "modern
consciousness") transfigured into the various characters that appear,
including the Indian brave, Maquokeeta, of "The Dance."

But before glancing at the separate sections, it is useful to get some
perspective on Crane's conception of the entire sequence. He wrote
to Kahn: "Powhatan's daughter, or Pocahontas, is the mythological
nature-symbol chosen to represent the physical body of the continent, or the soil. She here takes on much the same role as the traditional Hertha of ancient Teutonic mythology" (*L*, p. 305). As indicated
in the "ages of man" quotation above, Crane thought of the sequence
as embodying a "love-motif," beginning with "the sowing of the
seed" in "Harbor Dawn" and continuing throughout. As the protagonist moves out across the continent and back in time, he seems recur-
ringly to engage in a love that is part physical, part visionary (with the
land), and always mystical—as, for example, in "The River": "But I
knew her body there, / Time like a serpent down her shoulder,
dark, / And space, an eaglet's wing, laid on her hair." In "The
Dance" (as in the jazz orgy of Part II, "Faustus and Helen") Pocahontas appears to yield herself to the poet become Indian brave
Maquokeeta: but of course, she is as much the fertile land as he is the
seasons of time and procreation. And at the end of "Indiana," the
pioneer woman relates the story to her now grown son of holding him up when a baby as she exchanged some mystic sign
with a "homeless squaw" who "cradled a babe's body" on her
back.

The epigraph of "Powhatan's Daughter" comes from an early history by William Strachey, but no doubt by way of William Carlos
Williams's chapter in *In the American Grain* entitled "The May-Pole at
Merry Mount." The secondary source is interesting inasmuch as it
provides us a context for judging Crane's aims. The quotation that
Crane took from Strachey via Williams is clearly orgiastic or wanton
in nature: "—Pocahuntus, a well-featured but wanton young girle
...of the age of eleven or twelve years, get the boyes forth with
her into the market place, and make them wheele, falling on their
hands, turning their heels upwards, whom she would followe, and
wheele so herself, naked as she was all the fort over." Williams is
clearly sympathetic to the free ("wanton") spirit of the young Indian
girl, as his entire chapter is written to redeem the reputation of
Thomas Morton, the libertine who was expelled from the colonies by
the Puritans because of the pagan revels he inspired by raising the
clearly phallic maypole of Merry Mount[18]—around which there is

performed a Dionysian dance similar to that celebrated in Part II of "Faustus and Helen" and in "The Dance" later in *The Bridge*. By taking over as his epigraph this particular passage describing the young Pocahontas, Crane was clearly evoking this pagan, Dionysian dimension of the American past as against the Puritan suppression of the physical, reclaiming the lost physical body of America as he would reclaim the spiritual through Whitman—a poet who also celebrated the physical as the conduit to the spiritual.

Indeed, the first half of *The Bridge* (through "Cutty Sark") may be likened in many respects to the opening sections of *Leaves of Grass*, beginning with "Song of Myself" and running through the procreational poems of "Children of Adam" and the comradeship poems of "Calamus." In many ways these sections provide the "physical body" of *Leaves of Grass*, as the emphasis is on sexual identity throughout. The acceptance of the body and all its complex erotic feelings is a major theme running through "Song of Myself," suggested by the line, "Is this then a touch? quivering me to a new identity" (*CPSP*, p. 45). And the world itself is identified in sexual terms, as in "Press close bare-bosom'd night—press close magnetic nourishing night!" (*CPSP*, p. 39). The "Children of Adam" poems are celebrations of phallic energy and procreational relationships—of the kind that Pocahontas evokes and suggests in her youthful wantonness. Whitman sings "the body electric," and celebrates the "Bridegroom night of love working surely and softly into the prostrate dawn" (*CPSP*, p. 73), not unlike the cosmic coupling suggested in the opening stanzas of "The Dance" ("The swift red flesh, a winter king— / Who squired the glacier woman down the sky?"). Whitman's "Calamus" poems are evoked by Crane with the specific mentioning of a "Calamus" poem ("Recorders Ages Hence") in the later "Cape Hatteras" section, but the "Calamus theme as experienced directly by the poet appears to be the subject of "Cutty Sark," opening: "I met a man in South Street, tall— / a nervous shark tooth swung on his chain." Crane has already, in the poems of "Powhatan's Daughter," inserted aspects of his childhood and youth. There seems no reason not to see, then, "Cutty Sark" as one of his real-life "Calamus" experiences—chance male acquaintances—in a waterfront bar finding sailor comradeship and "adhesiveness" (Whitman's term, taken from phrenology, for the "Calamus" emotion). Crane's "Voyages," of course, had already obliquely celebrated such a relationship. These parallels are not exact, to be sure, but they are suggestive of the endurance of deep imaginative connections with Whitman that Crane began to feel when he first conceived *The Bridge*.

"Harbor Dawn"

The "Powhatan's Daughter" sequence opens appropriately with an act of love, a sexual act of "merging" of seed, in the "Harbor Dawn" of modern New York, the fog itself acting as a kind of protective or shielding enwrapment for consciousness against the modern industrial city waiting outside the window. Crane wrote of this section to Kahn: "Here the movement of the verse is in considerable contrast to that of the 'Ave Maria,' with its sea-swell crescendo and the climacteric vision of Columbus. This legato, in which images blur as objects only half apprehended on the border of sleep and consciousness, makes an admirable transition between the intervening centuries" (*L*, p. 306). The transition is psychological, in the consciousness of the protagonist—who (if we insist on credible continuity) might well have dreamed himself into the Columbus role and prayer. Now Columbus's discovery of America is brought into modern focus in the shape of a fog-enwrapped act of fertile love in a teeming industrialized world. The question Crane provided in the margin sends the protagonist on his quest out in space, back in time: "Who is the woman with us in the dawn? . . . whose is the flesh our feet have moved upon?"

"Van Winkle"

No better gloss has been written on this section than Crane's:

> The protagonist has left the room with its harbor sounds, and is walking to the subway. The rhythm is quickened; it is a transition between sleep and the immanent tasks of the day. Space is filled with the music of a hand organ and fresh sunlight, and one has the impression of the whole continent—from Atlantic to Pacific—freshly arisen and moving. The walk to the subway arouses reminiscences of childhood, also the "childhood" of the continental conquest, viz., the conquistadores, Priscilla, Capt. John Smith,etc. These parallelisms unite in the figure of Rip Van Winkle who finally becomes identified with the protagonist, as you will notice, and who really boards the subway with the reader. He becomes the "guardian angel" of the journey into the past. (*L*, p. 306)

It may startle the reader to learn that it is he boarding the subway with Rip, but no matter. Like Whitman fusing with his reader, the protagonist of *The Bridge* is Crane but Crane as American, Crane as modern man, Crane as the reader. Memory is at the center of this section, memory of the country's history and legends (Priscilla, Captain Smith, Rip Van Winkle) as well as memory of Crane's personal past, his childhood, his father and mother (with her "Sabbatical" smile). Movement: on to the subway, into the past.

"The River"

Whitman opened "Song of the Open Road": "Afoot and light-hearted I take to the open road, / Healthy, free, the world before me." The sense of movement that Whitman achieved is also achieved in "The River," as the protagonist strides out across the American continent. The hoboes he encounters seem to embody the "open road" theme of Whitman. Crane explained this section to Kahn:

> The subway is simply a figurative, psychological "vehicle" for transporting the reader to the Middle West. He lands on the railroad tracks in the company of several tramps in the twilight. The extravagance of the first twenty-three lines of this section is an intentional burlesque on the cultural confusion of the present—a great conglomeration of noises analogous to the strident impression of a fast express rushing by. The rhythm is jazz.
>
> Thenceforward the rhythm settles down to a steady pedestrian gait, like that of wanderers plodding along. My tramps are psychological vehicles, also. Their wanderings as you will notice, carry the reader into interior after interior, finally to the great River. They are the left-overs of the pioneers in at least this respect—that their wanderings carry the reader through an experience parallel to that of Boone and others. I think [I] have caught some of the essential spirit of the Great Valley here, and in the process have approached the primal world of the Indian, which emerges with a full orchestra in the succeeding dance. (*L*, pp. 306–7)

In a letter to his "Aunt Sally" (who appears in the poem, as he tells her; she is actually Mrs. T. W. Simpson, housekeeper at the Crane house on the Isle of Pines), Crane was perhaps even more explicit about his intention: "I'm trying in this part of the poem to chart the pioneer experience of our forefathers—and to tell the story backwards, as it were, on the 'backs' of hoboes. These hoboes are simply 'psychological ponies' to carry the reader across the country and back to the Mississippi, which you will notice is described as a great River of Time. I also unlatch the door to the pure Indian world which opens out in 'The Dance' section, so the reader is gradually led back in time to the pure savage world, while existing at the same time in the present" (*L*, p. 303). The river carries the protagonist—and the reader—back in time, out in space: "a mustard glow / Tortured with history, its one will—flow!" In this section the protagonist's immersion in time and space, the past and geography of America, is a necessary prelude to the transcendence to come in the next section.

"The Dance"

In "The Dance" Crane presents the most intensely physical experience of *The Bridge*—its ecstatic transcendence matching in many ways the visionary transcendence in the closing "Atlantis." (A similar comparison might be made, in Whitman's "Song of Myself," between the sections on touch, particularly sections 28–29, and the visionary soaring of section 33 or sections 44–45.) Crane explained to Kahn:

> Here one is on the pure mythical and smoky soil at last! Not only do I describe the conflict between the two races in this dance—I also become identified with the Indian and his world before it is over, which is the only method possible of ever really possessing the Indian and his world as a cultural factor. I think I really succeed in getting under the skin of this glorious and dying animal, in terms of expression, in symbols, which he himself would comprehend. Pocahontas (the continent) is the common basis of our meeting, she survives the extinction of the Indian, who finally, after being assumed into the elements of nature (as he understood them), persists only as a kind of "eye" in the sky, or as a star that hangs between day and night—"the twilight's dim perpetual throne." (*L*, p. 307)

As he was Columbus, the poet becomes one with Maquokeeta in the sexual-fertile frenzy of his dance, dancing "us back the tribal morn!" As Maquokeeta dies and blends with the changing seasons of nature, he begins his eternal gaze on his bride Pocahontas, now the continent, "immortal in the maize!" She is "virgin to the last of men," and her "breasts are fanned / O stream by slope and vineyard—into bloom!" Maquokeeta and Pocahontas represent nature, procreation, fertility—life itself, the pagan (natural) and continental heritage of America. "The Dance" concludes:

> We danced, O Brave, we danced beyond their farms,
> In cobalt desert closures made our vows . . .
> Now is the strong prayer folded in thine arms,
> The serpent with the eagle in the boughs.
>
> (*CP*, p. 75)

Already in "The River" Crane had introduced the serpent and the eagle in a sexual-cosmic scene ("But I knew her body there, / Time like a serpent down her shoulder, dark, / And space, an eaglet's wing, laid on her hair"). And in an earlier stanza of "The Dance" he had portrayed Maquokeeta laughing as "pure serpent, Time itself." In this last stanza of "The Dance," the "strong prayer" folded in Maquokeeta's (nature's) arms is that the serpent of time might somehow be reconciled with the eagle of space to apprehend or experience transcendence of both—a prayer that is answered at the end of the poem, in the closing lines of "Atlantis." Crane's imagery of the serpent and eagle comes significantly not from Christian but from pagan sources. He mentions in a letter to Gorham Munson of 5 March 1926, that he has read D. H. Lawrence's *The Plumed Serpent*, but adds: "Only my interest in Maya and Toltec archaeology led me to order Lawrence's book. It was poor in this—at least regarding the details I had hoped for" (*L*, p. 236). Mexican and other Indian mythologies could have provided an analogue for Crane's symbolism: "Out of the earth came the serpent, from whose dwelling place came the water that sustained life. . . . The enemy of the serpent was the eagle. This giant bird dominated the heavens. . . . The conflict between these representatives of the two primary natural forces could only be resolved if they became one god of earth and sky. So the *quetzal* (bird) and the *coatl* (snake) became one, Quetzalcoatl, the feathered serpent, the most revered and most impressive of the ancient gods."[19] In Maya mythology, the snake was "associated with time," and the quetzal bird, a "shy forest dweller," was "capable of releasing man from time."[20] But Crane's eagle and serpent seem also to evoke the Norse legend of Yggdrasil—the tree of the world, with an eagle at the top, a serpent at the base.

"Indiana"

The protagonist had set off from "Harbor Dawn" to find the woman "with us in the dawn," the one whose "flesh our feet have moved upon"—in short, Pocahontas or the physical body of America. He had encountered and achieved physical union with her in "The Dance" through becoming one with the Indian brave, Maquokeeta. In "Indiana" (as we are told in the marginal note) he reads "her in a mother's farewell gaze." Crane had originally planned (as he told Kahn) to make this section a father's farewell to this son setting out to sea, the mother having died on the way back from the California gold rush (her death implying her "succession to the nature-symbolism of

Pocahontas") (*L*, p. 307). The transformation from the male into a female monologue perhaps enabled Crane to point up the Pocahontas relationship more clearly. Crane wrote of the "Indiana" section: "The symbolism of Indiana (metamorphosis of Pocahontas [the Indian] into the pioneer woman, and hence her absorption into our 'contemporary veins' [)] is, I hope, sufficiently indicated without too great sacrifice of poetic values. . . . It does round out the cycle, at least historically and psychologically—one leaves the continent surrounded by water (pure space) as one found it in the first place (Harbor Dawn), and Cutty Sark quite logically follows as 'space' again."[21]

The most interesting part of the Indiana mother's monologue delivered to her departing, sea-destined son Larry is the story of lifting him up when a baby to a passing "homeless squaw," whose eyes were "sharp with pain" until they saw the pioneer woman and then "their violet haze / Lit with love shine":

> I held you up—I suddenly the bolder,
>   Knew that mere words could not have brought us
> nearer.
> She nodded—and that smile across her shoulder
>   Will still endear her
>
>   (*CP*, p. 78)

This mystic communion is very close to that suggested in Whitman's "The Sleepers," in which the poet's mother tells about the time when she was a girl on the old homestead and a red squaw came to the place, and "She look'd at the freshness of her tall-borne face and full and pliant limbs, / The more she look'd upon her she loved her" (*CPSP*, p. 300). The strange communion was experienced for only a day, and the poet's mother was "loth" to have the squaw go away; but the event endured through the years—endured in the memory of the listening poet-son. Crane's episode is very similar in nature and meaning to Whitman's.

Moreover, Crane's use of the state of Indiana as the scene of this last of the Pocahontas sequence suggests other Whitmanian connections, particularly with "Starting from Paumanok," a poem in which the protagonist moves out from "Mannahatta my city" across the American continent, to "strike up for a New World." Whitman's vision embraces both space and time also—"See, vast trackless spaces, / As in a dream they change, they swiftly fill, / Countless masses debouch upon them" (*CPSP*, p. 15). But most notable, perhaps, is Whitman's way of incorporating the Indian past in his vision:

> The red aborigines,
> Leaving natural breaths, sounds of rain and winds, calls
>   as of birds and animals in the woods, syllabled to us
>   for names,
> Okonee, Koosa, Ottawa, Monongahela, Sauk, Natches,
>   Chattahoochee, Kaqueta, Oronoco,
> Wabash, Miami, Saginaw, Chippewa, Oshkosh, Walla-
>   Walla,
> Leaving such to the States they melt, they depart, charg-
>   ing the water and the land with names.
>
> (*CPSP*, p. 23)

Whitman's vision is of an Indian presence in the land, in the air, very close to Crane's vision throughout "Powhatan's Daughter." This heritage both poets would claim as vital to the American identity, giving it a dimension rendering it unique: "A world primal again" (*CPSP*, p. 23), as Whitman said; and Crane wrote "The Dance" to re-create the "primal world of the Indian," a world "charging" the very air and earth of America in the names that endure.

III. "Cutty Sark"

A scene in a waterfront bar, some rambling drunken talk with a wandering sailor, a persistent nickelodeon repeating over and over again one song, "O Stamboul Rose," separation, farewell, a dawn walk across "the bridge," and a fantasy vision of old clipper ships: these are the unlikely elements Crane chose to conclude the first half of *The Bridge*. What did he think he was doing? He told Kahn:

> The next section, "Cutty Sark," is a phantasy on the period of the whalers and clipper ships. It also starts in the present and "progresses backwards." The form of the poem may seem erratic, but it is meant to present the hallucinations incident to rum-drinking in the South Street dive, as well as the lurch of a boat in heavy seas, etc. So I allow myself something of the same freedom which E. E. Cummings often uses.
>
> "Cutty Sark" is built on the plan of a *fugue*. Two "voices"—that of the world of Time, and that of the world of Eternity—are inter-woven in the action. The Atlantis theme (that of Eternity) is the transmuted voice of the nickel-slot pianola, and this voice alternates with that of the derelict sailor and the description of the action. The airy regatta of phantom clipper ships seen from Brooklyn Bridge on the way home is quite effective, I think. It was a pleasure to use historical names for these lovely ghosts. Music

still haunts their names long after the wind has left their sails.
(*L*, pp. 307–8)

If we glance on the page before "Cutty Sark," we find the last words
of "Indiana" suspended at the end, followed by a dash: suggesting
that the sailor of "Cutty Sark" is a reincarnation of the son Larry of
"Indiana," and that the theme is friendship, comradeship, the
"Calamus" theme of Whitman—counterbalancing the love (or "Children of Adam") theme dominant in "Powhatan's Daughter." The
"derelict sailor's" eyes press "through green grass," that is, "green
glasses": the imagery associated with him tends vaguely to the phallic, from the "nervous shark tooth" swinging on his chain to his
mention of the Mexican volcano Popocatepetl and the spiracle of the
whale: "he shot a finger out the door... / 'O life's a geyser—
beautiful.' " The protagonist says:

> I saw the frontiers gleaming of his mind;
> or are there frontiers—running sands sometimes
> running sands—somewhere—sands running...
> Or they may start some white machine that sings
> Then you may laugh and dance the axletree—
> steel—silver—kick the traces—and know—
>
> > ATLANTIS ROSE drums wreathe the rose,
> > the star floats burning in a gulf of tears
> > and sleep another thousand—
> >
> > > (*CP*, p. 83)

The syntax is rum-dense, the meaning obscure, but I sense here
lurking the "Calamus" theme, the flickering possibility of depth in
relationship, the passing potential of ecstatic vision. The "frontier" of
the sailor's mind gives way to the imagery of time—"running
sands"—which in turn gives way to machine imagery, but a "white
machine that sings" and that inspires laughing and dancing on the
"axletree" and a kicking "the traces," ending in knowledge—
knowledge of "Atlantis Rose": a prefiguring glimpse of the vision of
the final "Atlantis" section.

The sailor departs, almost hit by a "wharf truck" ("I can't live on
land—!"), and the protagonist-poet walks home across the Bridge at
dawn and has his vision of the mid-nineteenth-century clipper ships,
ca. 1845–70, and the poem turns into a listing of the names of these
swift-sailing ships, the *Cutty Sark* (surviving as the contemporary
name of the poet's favorite scotch), *Rainbow, Leander, Nimbus, Taeping,
Ariel*. The evocation is much like that of the title of "Indiana," or of
Whitman's evocation of "what the air holds of the red aborigines" in

the listing of the musical Indian names that survive in the land. Again in this passage, the poet moves out in space and time, out into the seas of the world and into the middle of the last century: the sea imagery connecting with that of "Ave Maria" and "Harbor Dawn." Most important, however, this movement out into the sea counterbalances the movement into the continent of the "Powhatan's Daughter" section, making *The Bridge*, like *Leaves of Grass*, "ocean's poem" (as in Whitman's "In Cabin'd Ships at Sea"): "Here are our thoughts, voyagers' thoughts, / Here not the land, firm land, alone appears" (*CPSP*, p. 8).

IV. "Cape Hatteras"

The second half of *The Bridge* begins with the epigraph to "Cape Hatteras" from Whitman's "Passage to India": "The seas all crossed, / weathered the capes, the voyage done." The epigraph applies in a literal sense, in that the poet's voyage out in space and back in time is finished. The remaining sections of *The Bridge* ("Cape Hatteras," "Three Songs," "Quaker Hill," "The Tunnel," and "Atlantis") will be devoted to the here and now of contemporary America. But as the first half of *The Bridge* was devoted to a physical journey, in physical space, in physical time, so the second half is devoted to a spiritual journey and exploration, a search for the possible sources of the Whitmanian faith in the unpromising industrialism and urbanism of twentieth-century America.

Whitman is evoked at the beginning of this journey so that he may serve as a guide, as Virgil for Dante. "Passage to India" seized on the then (1871) technological achievements that "rounded" the globe (Suez Canal, the transoceanic cable, and the transcontinental railroad) to call for like spiritual or religious or mystical achievement on the part of mankind. Crane's "Cape Hatteras" in a sense begins with similar twentieth-century achievements—the airplane, the radio— and calls for a similar mystical feat to parallel (and spiritualize) the technical or scientific "advances." But "Cape Hatteras" is much more than an updating of Whitman's "Passage to India." It is, indeed, a synthesis of the complex themes of Whitman's *Leaves of Grass*, and proposes a reclamation by America of the Whitman vision and myth.

The poem opens with evolutionary imagery ("the mammoth saurian / ghoul," "the dorsal change / Of energy") reminiscent of that used by Whitman in section 31 of "Song of Myself" ("I find I incorporate gneiss, coal, long-threaded moss, fruits, grains, esculent roots / And am stucco'd with quadrupeds and birds all over" [*CPSP*,

p. 46]) or in section 44: "My embryo has never been torpid, nothing could overlay it. / For it the nebula cohered to an orb, / The long slow strata piled to rest it on, / Vast vegetables gave it sustenance, / Monstrous sauroids transported it in their mouths and deposited it with care" (*CPSP,* p. 62). Crane's opening lines come to focus (line 10) on "we," who have been back in that evolutionary past and who have been round all the capes of the world, now "return home to our own / Hearths," there to "eat the apple" (of modern knowledge) and "to read you, Walt." For it is Walt who knows that we are "in thrall / To that deep wonderment, our native clay": the "eternal flesh of Pocahontas" (*CP,* p. 88). This native spot, as well as any foreign, "Is veined by all that time has really pledged us," and the air above, too, with its "thin squeaks of radio static," brings "whisperings of far watches on the main / Relapsing into silence." We peer through time's periscope to glimpse "joys or pain," but time "deflects" us to a "labyrinth submersed / Where each sees only his dim past reversed" (*CP,* p. 88).

Whisperings, time. These recall the *Leaves of Grass* cluster, "Whispers of Heavenly Death" and the poem "To Think of Time," in the latter part of the book huddled near "Passage to India"—poetry "bridging the way from Life to Death." "Whispers of heavenly death murmur'd I hear, / Labial gossip of night, sibilant chorals, / Footsteps gently ascending, mystical breezes wafted soft and low, / Ripples of unseen rivers, tides of a current flowing, forever flowing" (*CPSP*, p. 309). In contrast, Crane's "radio static" is bleak indeed. "To Think of Time" for Whitman meant to conclude: "I swear I think there is nothing but immortality! / That the exquisite scheme is for it, and the nebulous float is for it, and the cohering is for it!" (*CPSP,* p. 309). For Crane, time directs each of us into a labyrinth where our vision is limited to our own dim past.

At this point, Crane changes direction, explaining the elusiveness of the Whitmanian faith: "But that star-glistered salver of infinity, / The circle, blind crucible of endless space, / Is sluiced by motion,— subjugated never" (*CP,* p. 89). Even Whitman's gleanings of infinity or eternity or immortality were just that—gleanings, momentary forays, a motion in and out: he never "subjugated" it any more than man, now the "master" of space with his new technological advance of the airplane, will subjugate it. Crane turns to Whitman:

> "—Recorders ages hence"—ah, syllables of faith!
> Walt, tell me, Walt Whitman, if infinity
> Be still the same as when you walked the beach

> Near Paumanok—your lone patrol—and heard the wraith
> Through surf, its bird note there a long time falling.
>
> (*CP*, p. 89)

The Whitman title is a "Calamus" poem, and of course, Paumanok is the Indian name Whitman used for Long Island, his home, which figures in "Starting from Paumanok" and (here especially) "Out of the Cradle Endlessly Rocking." "Recorders Ages Hence" and "Out of the Cradle Endlessly Rocking" share the theme of love, its potential loss in the one, its actual loss in the other. "Recorders ages hence, / Come I will take you down underneath this impassive exterior, I will tell you what to say of me, / Publish my name and hang up my picture as that of the tenderest lover, / The friend the lover's portrait, of whom his friend his lover was fondest," one "Who oft as he saunter'd the streets curv'd with his arm the shoulder of his friend, while the arm of his friend rested upon him also" (*CPSP*, pp. 89–90). This poem's title recurs a few lines before the end of "Cape Hatteras," making its "Calamus" content an important part of the vision of *The Bridge*. The love theme of "Out of the Cradle" is attached inseparably to the theme of death, a word that the sea whispers to the poet-boy as he asks for the "clew" to the experience of the grief of lost love: the "clew" offered by the "old crone" of the sea rocking the cradle, symbol of birth. Crane provides his own answer to the question addressed to Whitman by establishing him as directly in the modern world:

> O Saunterer on free ways still ahead!
> Not this our empire yet, but labyrinth
> Wherein your eyes, like the Great navigator's without
>   ship,
> Gleam from the great stones of each prison crypt
> Of canyoned traffic.
>
> (*CP*, p. 89)

As Columbus filled the role of patron saint of the first half of *The Bridge*, the physical journey, Whitman becomes the patron saint of this second half, the spiritual journey. His image is firmly fixed in the modern world (and in the poem): "Sea eyes and tidal, undenying, bright with myth!"

With Whitman's myth-bright eyes firmly fixed on the action of the poem, Crane next turns to modern technology; Cape Hatteras is, of course, the site of the testing of the airplane by the Wright Brothers. The marvelous advances have created a power that "whips a new universe," and the next few pages of the poem are devoted to delineation of that universe. Crane begins with the wonders of the modern engine-machine, where "power's script" is "stropped to the slap of belts on booming spools," and where there is a "giggling in the girth / Of steely gizzards," and the "bearings glint" in "oilrinsed circles of blind ecstasy!" (*CP*, p. 90). The satyric thrust of the language is unmistakable, turning the machine itself into a live object of worship—clearly antithetical to the spiritual meaning of the poem (although some readers have been seduced by the ingenuity of the language into believing Crane meant it straight).

Crane moves quite quickly from the invention and development of the airplane at Cape Hatteras to its destructive use in World War I, the pilots sowing "doom" in the "alcohol of space." He addresses the "Falcon-Ace": "Thou hast there in thy wrist a Sanskrit charge / To conjugate infinity's dim marge— / Anew." The reference, like the later characterization of Whitman as "Vedic Caesar" (emperor of the Vedas), is to "Passage to India":

> Passage to more than India!
> Are thy wings plumed indeed for such far flights?
> O soul, voyagest thou indeed on voyages like those?
> Disportest thou on waters such as those?
> Soundest below the Sanscrit and the Vedas?
> Then have thy bent unleash'd.
>
> (*CPSP*, p. 294)

Whitman, through contemplation and penetration of the technological marvels of his day, had "conjugated" (not "subjugated") infinity before; now with the still more marvelous technology, man might "conjugate infinity's dim marge— / Anew." But instead he is using the technology to destroy, not only others but himself: Crane arranges his lines to suggest the falling and crashing of an airplane—into "mashed and shapeless débris."

Following the crash, Crane evokes Whitman again. At "junctions elegiac" he wields the "rebound seed," and like the "probable grass" answers "deepest soundings": "O, upward from the dead / Thou bringest tally, and a pact, new bound, / Of living brotherhood!" (*CP*, p. 93). The passage has links with many parts of *Leaves of Grass*, including "Song of Myself" (the grass imagery), the elegy to Lincoln, "When Lilacs Last in the Dooryard Bloom'd" ("To the tally of my soul, / Loud and strong kept up the gray-brown bird"), the "Calamus" comradeship poems, and the "Drum-Taps" poems on the Civil War, specifically suggested in the following lines linking the "fraternal massacre" with World War I: "What memories of vigils."

One of Whitman's most moving "Drum-Taps" poems was "Vigil Strange I Kept on the Field One Night," the all-night communion of a soldier with his slain comrade on the battlefield, expressing the "Calamus" (brotherhood) emotion in its most intensely spiritual dimension.

The next passage in "Cape Hatteras" describes Crane's first experience in reading Whitman, one spring amid "cowslip and shad-blow," and the exhilaration he felt as "early following" Whitman, he went out to experience nature directly, with nature to serve as glosses or duplications of Whitman's lines. Beginning with the direct address, *Panis Angelicus,* "Cape Hatteras" concludes with an odelike appreciation of America's epic poet. Crane's characterizations of Whitman pyramid—"near," "onward yielding," "familiar," "evasive," and "Our Meistersinger, thou set breath in steel; / And it was thou who on the boldest heel / Stood up and flung the span on even wing / Of that great Bridge, our Myth, whereof I sing!" (*CP,* p. 94). Whitman was a builder of that bridge—the American myth—which Crane himself is attempting to reclaim: his breath was set in the "steel" (permanence) of *Leaves of Grass.* From this point on, allusions to Whitman's poetry abound. "Years of the modern" is in the concluding cluster, "Songs of Parting," a poem of prophecy ("I see tremendous entrances and exits, new combinations, the solidarity of races" [*CPSP,* p. 339]). "Beyond all sesames of science was thy choice" suggests section 23 of "Song of Myself": "Hurrah for positive science! long live exact demonstrations!" "Your facts are useful, and yet they are not my dwelling, / I but enter by them to an area of my dwelling" (*CPSP,* p. 41). Crane explains that dwelling: "Thou, Vedic Caesar, to the greensward knelt!" (*CP,* p. 95).

Crane envisions "vast engines outward veering with seraphic grace / On clarion cylinders pass out of sight / To course that span of consciousness thou'st named / The Open Road—thy vision is reclaimed!" (*CP,* p. 95). In "Song of the Open Road," the journey was a spiritual journey of "consciousness," as Crane indicates, reminding us at the same time that his poem is meant to be an "epic of the modern consciousness" —as Whitman's *Leaves* was for his time. Crane's lines are in effect (and in the spirit of "Passage to India") a call for a spiritual soaring (or soaring of cosmic consciousness) to match the physical flight into space of the modern airplane. In the final lines of the section, Crane repeats the title "Recorders Ages Hence," a "Calamus" poem evoking the "Calamus" emotion that Crane's own feelings for Whitman parallel, as he starts the journey by his side, "afoot again" and with his hand in Walt Whitman's, an acceptance of the offer extended at the end of "Song of the Open Road":

> Camerado, I give you my hand!
> I give you my love more precious than money.
> I give you myself before preaching or law;
> Will you give me yourself? will you come travel with me?
> Shall we stick by each other as long as we live?
>
> (*CPSP*, p. 115)

As the poem closes—"My hand / in yours, / Walt Whitman— / so"—we may assume that Whitman accompanies the poet throughout the rest of the journey of *The Bridge*, supporting him through the sordidness of the modern American scene, standing by his side in that final ecstatic vision of "Atlantis."

V. "Three Songs"

The role of "Three Songs" in the structure of *The Bridge* has always puzzled readers, and there is evidence that Crane himself was uncertain of their placement.[22] Critics have tended to conclude that they were a mistake or that they were Eliot-like portrayals of women meant ironically to show the absence in the modern world of the Pocahontas ideal delineated in the first half of *The Bridge*. In view, however, of Crane's tendency to reject Eliot's pessimism, and particularly in view of his portrayal of the modern Helen in "Faustus and Helen" as a jazz-mad orgy-prone flapper, and in view of his adoption of the Pocahontas epigraph for "Powhatan's Daughter" portraying her as a wanton young girl driving all the boys to turning sexual cartwheels—it seems unlikely that Crane would include Eliotic female portraits in his epic.

And indeed, there is not the revulsion in these poems we feel in Eliot's portrayal of, say, the bored typist of *The Waste Land*. Crane's modern Eve, Magdalene, and Virgin Mary are, ultimately, celebratory in nature, finding even within the sordid modernity a sexual-procreational energy that is ultimately redeeming. In this celebratory quality these poems link with such Whitmanian poems as "To a Common Prostitute" ("Be composed—be at ease with me—I am Walt Whitman, liberal and lusty as Nature, / Not till the sun excludes you do I exclude you" [*CPSP*, p. 73]) and look forward to such William Carlos Williams conceptions as "Beautiful Thing" (found in a probably "promiscuous" Negress beating a rug). In "Southern Cross," the protagonist's sexual longing enables him to evoke a Whitmanian scene of cosmic coupling ("The Southern Cross takes night / And lifts her girdles from her, one by one" [*CPSP*, p. 98]), but his call for a woman in the flesh "falls vainly on the wave." Eve is evoked in what appear to be negative terms, but is finally affirmed, though not realized ("Yes, Eve—wraith of my unloved seed!"). The poem closes in what seems to be masturbatory loneliness, the "unloved seed" scattered in the ocean as the Southern Cross itself drops "below the dawn": "Light drowned the lithic trillions of your spawn."

In "National Winter Garden" Magdalene is reincarnated in the "common prostitute" of a modern burlesque queen, with the protagonist in the audience, picking a "blonde out neatly through the smoke." As the dance reaches a climax of lewdness, the protagonist says: "We flee her spasm through a fleshless door." But the poem concludes in affirmation: "Yet, to the empty trapeze of your flesh, / O Magdalene, each comes back to die alone. / Then you, the burlesque of our lust—and faith, / Lug us back lifeward—bone by infant bone." Lust and faith; sexual energy and cosmic consciousness. Even the vulgarity of the burlesque cannot negate the vitality. And the vitality is present too in the mundane business-office world of "Virginia," with the protagonist singing the song of his Mary ("And I'm still waiting you") and elevating her commonplace attributes into tower-dwelling mythological and shining "Cathedral Mary," a miracle of imaginative transfiguration through sexual energy.

VI. "Quaker Hill"

Whitman's Quaker background may lurk in "Quaker Hill," or at least the mystical Quaker doctrine of the inner light, but the poem is a savage exposure of the emptiness of life in the resort-hotel that the modern age has made out of the old Quaker Meeting House in upstate New York. The tourists are the living dead "playing" in what was ironically the "Promised Land." In this scene, the protagonist sees "death's stare" from all four horizons, and the poem turns from the modern scene to the past, as the poet asks not "scalped Yankees" but "slain Iroquois to guide." The poet tells us that we must descend "from the hawk's eye stemming view" to "worm's eye" in order to "construe" death (and love):

> Yes, while the heart is wrung,
> Arise—yes, take this sheaf of dust upon your tongue!
> Listen, transmuting silence with that stilly note
>
> (*CP*, p. 106)

A "throbbing throat" that transmutes silence is highly evocative of

Whitman's hermit thrush in "When Lilacs Last in the Dooryard Bloom'd"—who sang the "Song of the bleeding throat, / Death's outlet song of life." But Crane later introduces his own bird—"That triple-noted clause of moonlight— / Yes, Whip-poor-will, unhusks the heart of fright." Triple-noted, much like that other songbird of death in Whitman, the mockingbird of "Out of the Cradle Endlessly Rocking." As in the Whitman poems, it is the bird in "Quaker Hill" that "breaks us and saves," that "shields / Love from despair—when love foresees the end" (*CP*, p. 106).

VII. "The Tunnel"

While writing "The Tunnel," Crane reported to Waldo Frank: "It's rather ghastly, almost surgery—and, oddly almost all from the notes and stitches I have written while swinging on the strap at late midnights going home" (*L*, pp. 274–75). And Crane described "The Tunnel" to Kahn: "Subway—The encroachment of machinery on humanity: a kind of purgatory in relation to the open sky of last section" (*L*, p. 241). The section does seem to be made up of a miscellany of scraps and pieces of subway-hurried, night-driven lives. It is a place where love is "A burnt match skating in a urinal," and where Death stares "gigantically down / Probing through you—toward me, O evermore!" Poe is the muse invoked. Crane wrote to Waldo Frank (of William Carlos Williams's *In the American Grain*): "I was so interested to note that he puts Poe and his "character" in the same position as I had symbolized for him in 'The Tunnel' section" (*L*, p. 278). The only sign of Columbus in this nadir of Crane's epic appears near the end of the subway ride as the poet addresses a "Wop washerwoman, with the bandaged hair," going home after her night of scrubbing the floors of sky-scrapers: "O Genoese, do you bring mother eyes and hands / Back home to children and to golden hair?" The dream in the Columbus prayer at the beginning of *The Bridge*, in "Ave Maria," appears reduced, in "The Tunnel," to this submission or obeisance to the "Daemon," the subway itself, as symbol of all the machinery that has reduced or diminished life: "O caught like pennies beneath soot and steam, / Kiss of our agony thou gatherest" (*CP*, p. 111). "The Tunnel" ends: "Kiss of our agony thou gatherest, / O Hand of Fire / gatherest—" (*CP*, p. 112). The "kiss of our agony" caught for a time in the soot and steam and death-dealing subway is liberated at the end by the "Hand of Fire"—much like the "Hand of Fire" of Columbus's prayer in "Ave Maria," related to the corposants that burned like signals from God at the tops of the ship's masts. The protagonist emerges from the depths of the subway to the open air and the exhilarating, liberating view of the city and the river.

VIII. "Atlantis"

Crane's movement from "The Tunnel" to the bridge—from a "dark night of the soul" to a state almost of ecstatic "union," from depression to euphoria, from blindness to vision—has at least three parallels in Whitman. There is, first, the movement in "Song of Myself" from the latter part of section 33 ("Hell and despair are upon me"; "Agonies are one of my changes of garments"; "I am the man, I suffer'd, I was there") through deepening gloom in sections 34, 35, 36, 37—until a sudden burst through to light, beginning with "Enough! enough! enough!" in section 38 ("I remember now, / I resume the overstaid fraction"; "I troop forth replenish'd with supreme power" [*CPSP*, p. 36]). Thereafter, vision, cosmic consciousness, a transcendence achieved not by evasion of reality but by direct encounter with its horror, as suggested by the Blake epigraph Crane used for "The Tunnel": "To Find the Western path / Right thro' the Gates of Wrath." A similar movement occurs in Whitman's poetry in "Crossing Brooklyn Ferry" and in "Passage to India." In "Crossing Brooklyn Ferry" there is a kind of rising or spiraling movement to the climactic breaking through the bonds of time and space into the ecstatic union with the reader (and mankind) in section 8. In "Passage to India," the movement is from the historical sweep of the earlier sections to the soaring out into mystic vision and merge of section 8: "Thou matest Time, smilest content at Death, / And fillest, swellest full the vastnesses of Space."

Crane described "Atlantis" to Kahn: "The Bridge—A sweeping dithyramb in which the Bridge becomes the symbol of consciousness spanning time and space" (*L*, p. 241). The language of the section is taut and tense, even vibrant, transfiguring the Bridge into a dynamic creator of cosmic unity and harmony—a "steeled Cognizance whose leap commits / The agile precincts of the lark's return," that "like an organ," leads "from time's realm / As love strikes clear direction for the helm" (*CP*, p. 116). The Bridge leads to the lost mythological continent "Atlantis," beyond time and space—to that eternity only glimpsed in previous sections of *The Bridge* (in "The Dance," "Cutty Sark"). The poem concludes:

> —One Song, one Bridge of Fire! Is it Cathay,
> Now pity steeps the grass and rainbows ring

The serpent with the eagle in the leaves . . . ?
Whispers antiphonal in azure swing.

(*CP*, p. 117)

Much of *The Bridge*'s main thrust is caught up in the closing lines—
Columbus's prayer, the divine Hand of Fire (corposants), the New
World Columbus took to be Cathay. The final lines evoke
Whitman—that grass (his) and those leaves (his, too). The serpent
and the eagle, the subject of the prayer left folded in the arms of
Maquokeeta at the end of "The Dance," find themselves a prayer
finally realized, the serpent of time and the eagle of space reconciled
"beyond time," in the "leaves" of "infinity." Those "whispers"
Crane hears at the very end of his epic connect with the whispers
heard in *Leaves of Grass*: "Whispers of heavenly death murmur'd I
hear, / Labial gossip of night, sibilant chorals." "Mystical breezes,"
"ripples of unseen rivers" (*CPSP*, p. 309). Like Whitman before him,
Crane is attuned to the cosmic whispers "swinging" beyond sound.

A final word:
"Words for Hart Crane"

Robert Lowell

"When the Pulitzers showered on some dope
or screw who flushed our dry mouths out with soap,
few people would consider why I took
to stalking sailors, and scattered Uncle Sam's
phoney gold-plated laurels to the birds.
Because I knew my Whitman like a book,
stranger in America, tell my country: I,
Catullus redivivus, once the rage
of the Village and Paris, used to play my role
of homosexual, wolfing the stray lambs
who hungered by the Place de la Concorde.
My profit was a pocket with a hole.
Who asks for me, the Shelley of my age,
must lay his heart out for my bed and board."[23]

Part Three   Leaves

For the great Idea,
That, O my brethren, that is the mission of poets.

Songs of stern defiance ever ready,
Songs of the rapid arming and the march,
The flag of peace quick-folded, and instead the flag we know,
Warlike flag of the great Idea.

> "By Blue Ontario's Shore"
> Walt Whitman

Nine

o Whitman,
let us keep our trade with you
Olson, "I, Mencius, Pupil of the Master"

Making a Mappemunde to Include My Being
Charles Olson's Maximus Poems

Charles Olson described an essay in progress[1] in February 1952 as "using these States as counters / & arguing a proper predecession / a sort of backhanded salute to Walt Whitman, for his unhappinesses" (*LO*, p. 90).[2] Such cryptic references to Whitman, scattered throughout Olson's poetry and prose, do not in themselves reveal the depth of his debt to Whitman. Moreover, among America's nineteenth-century writers, Olson's primary public allegiance was to Herman Melville, subject of his first book, *Call Me Ishmael*. It was published in 1947, when Olson was thirty-seven years old, one year beyond Whitman when he published his first edition of *Leaves of Grass*. In it Olson adapted Whitmanian forms to praise Melville's evocation of space. In the Melville book Olson staked out literary territory he was never to relinquish, turning himself into a ferocious watch dog snapping at anyone, especially academic, who happened to stray on to his claim—as in "Letter for Melville 1951" (the members of the Melville Society "scratch each other's backs with a dead man's hand") (*AM*, pp. 32–38).

Although Olson had early immersed himself in *Leaves of Grass*, and had obviously taken much from it, he seems never to have been self-conscious in his relationship with (or in his borrowings from) Whitman. Indeed, one of his students has described a buildup in class through "three baffling weeks," to a "magnificent reading" of Whitman's "Crossing Brooklyn Ferry"—a reading so powerful that "Olson and Whitman were suddenly one."[3] But though Olson could freely become Whitman, he could not so easily identify with his more immediate precursors. As a self-styled representative of a post-Modernist generation, he felt a fundamental anxiety in working out for himself and his readers his relationship with Ezra Pound, William Carlos Williams, and T. S. Eliot. Of these three, Eliot was the easiest to dismiss as irrelevant. Olson is consistently hostile in all his several references to Eliot: "T. S. (G I) Eliot" (*LO*, p. 6), "O. M. Eliot" (*SW*, p. 26). But he is consistently uneasy in his abundant references to Pound and Williams, always worrying the question of how, given all the clear continuities, he actually differs from his immediate predecessors.

In 1951, at a time when his own ambitions to write an epic were taking form (*Maximus Poems | 1–10* appeared in 1953) he demonstrated for himself (in one of his "Mayan Letters") that both Pound and Williams had deficiencies which he himself would avoid: "Ez's epic solves problem by his ego: his single emotion breaks all down to his equals or inferiors (so far as I can see only two, possibly, are admitted, by him, to be his betters—Confucius, & Dante. Which assumption, that there are intelligent men whom he can outtalk, is beautiful because it destroys historical time, and thus creates the methodology of the Cantos, viz, a space-field where, by inversion, though the material is all time material, he has driven through it so sharply by the beak of his ego, that, he has turned time into what we must now have, space & its live air" (*SW*, pp. 81–82). Pound made all history contemporary by bringing historical periods into the present for ruthless examination and evaluation. Olson sees this "inversion" as Pound's major defect, but he sees the resultant methodology (of the "space-field") as a major contribution.

Williams in *Paterson* avoided Pound's "ego" pitfall, but fell into a trap of his own: "The primary contrast, for our purposes, is, BILL: his Pat is exact opposite of Ez's, that is, Bill HAS an emotional system which is capable of extensions & comprehensions the ego-system (the Old Deal, Ez as Cento Man, here dates) is not. Yet by making his substance historical of one city (the Joyce deal), Bill completely licks himself, lets time roll him under as Ez does not, and thus, so far as what is the more important, methodology, contributes nothing, in fact, delays, deters, and hampers, by not having busted through the very problem which Ez has so brilliantly faced, & beat" (SW, pp. 82–83). Thus Olson clears the space for his own Maximus Poems, somewhere between Pound's ego-dominance and Williams's ego-submission: "Each of the above jobs are HALVES, that is, I take it (1) that the EGO AS BEAK is bent and busted but (2) whatever it is that we can call its replacement (Bill very much a little of it) HAS, SO FAR, not been able to bring any time so abreast of us that we are in this present air, going straight out, of our selves, into it" (SW, p. 83). Olson will forgo Pound's ego, but he will not allow himself to be inundated (as did Williams) by history: he will, like Pound, bring history into the present and will show how we might, "going straight out, of our selves, [go] into it." What precisely this movement might mean is perhaps not clear even to Olson at this point as he appears to grope his way to his own poetic territory. But it is significant that he is writing from Mexico's Yucatan, where he has become enamored of past and current Mayan life, and where he is discovering for himself his fundamental cultural position in a civilization in which past and present exist side by side.

Some two years later, after his first Maximus Poems had been written and published, Olson again tried to sort out his relation to Pound and Williams: "if i think EP gave any of us the methodological clue: the RAG-BAG; bill gave us the lead on the LOCAL." Here the thinking is more sure of itself, the expression more direct: "Or put it that pat: EP the verb, BILL the NOUN problem. To do. And who, to do. Neither of them: WHAT. That is, EP sounds like what, but what his is is only more methodology, in fact, simply, be political. Politics—not economics is him, And validly. For (1) politics is a context as wide as nature, and not only what we call 'politics'; and (2) its essence is will. What latter—will—is what EP cares abt. . . . And Bill's what, at heart, isn't any more than (no matter how much he damn well is) than, Bill—as much as he does make it possible for any man to breathe himself in like manner. That is, Bill's dispensation is a hell of a lot closer simply that he don't think it's stupid" (LO, p. 129). By the time the explanation has been added, the thought has been considerably mystified. But what remains clear throughout is that if Olson borrowed Pound's verb (doing) and Williams's noun (who), he will in his own epic provide the complement or object, the *what*; that is, Olson will adapt Pound's methodological verb to Williams's subject noun (the American local) and complete his metaphorical sentence with his own vital predicate complement (objective or nominative) missing from his predecessors.

The passage just quoted concludes with a cryptic reference that reveals a major source for Olson's *what*: "Lawrence, the / *real* one as one."[4] In his "Mayan period" Olson found himself confirming Laurentian principles of the primitive. His references to D. H. Lawrence during this period show that he ranked the British novelist with the American expatriate poet in modern literature: "Certainly Pound and Lawrence more and more stand up as the huge two of the 1st half of the 20th century" (*LO*, p. 63). Olson's *what*, then, will be supplied not only by his first-hand experience among the Maya of Yucatan (contemporary and ancient), but also by Lawrence's themes in novels written out of similar experience with ancient grounds and "primitive" peoples (as, for example, *The Plumed Serpent*). In tracing his own roots back to Pound, Williams, and Lawrence, Olson remained only one remove from their deeper source, the American barbarian Walt Whitman.[5]

Olson's sensitivity as to his own sources and predecessors, and his passion for pointing to his own original contribution, are no doubt related to the critical neglect he suffered during most of his career (he died in 1970, at age sixty). But his reputation probably suffered as much from his cult following, who hailed him as modern master and guru, as it did from his detractors, who tagged him a spin-off from Ezra Pound. Though he never won over the literary establishment, Olson (and many of his followers) received a lavish hearing in 1960 in the anthology entitled *The New American Poetry*, edited by Donald M. Allen.[6] Olson led off in the volume, and spread out over several pages in a rich sampling of his work; and his essay "Projective Verse" led off a series of "Statements on Poetics" for the "new poetry." This important volume was followed, a little over a decade later, by a companion entitled *The Poetics of the New American Poetry*, edited by Donald Allen and Warren Tallman. In this volume, Olson's poetic theory (including "Projective Verse") was amply represented, but the lead position was taken over by an older source of the new—Walt Whitman (his long letter to Emerson that Whitman included in the second, 1856, edition of *Leaves of Grass*). In their Preface the editors said: "We feel that the poets whose statements we include achieve spectacular fulfillments in our century of what Whitman was calling for in his. This isn't to suppose that their poetics stem directly from his since in a number of instances they obviously don't. But he is our great national poet because great national traits shine through and keep on shining."[7]

In their Preface, also, the editors set forth their conception of the history of twentieth-century American poetry: the first "wave...gathering effective force circa 1912," and the second "shortly after 1945." The first they name "Pound's generation," and the second, "Charles Olson's." This statement is, of course, as much political as critical, and was clearly meant to challenge many of the received truths and assumptions of the literary establishment. But if there is an element of braggadocio or even combativeness in the claims made, the claims nevertheless help to right an imbalance in the politics of modern poetry.

2

Even before he had launched his epic, Olson had in 1950 formulated a poetics entitled "Projective Verse," presumably from the patterns he traced in the work principally of Pound and Williams. But in retrospect his 1950 essay appears to be his preparation for launching his Maximus Poems and surely serves the same function as Whitman's 1855 Preface to *Leaves of Grass*. Both documents have been cited as marking basic historical shifts in conceptions of poetry, rejecting the old, delineating the new, and initiating movements that subsequently became the *way* of poetry. Both documents at first suffered neglect, as is often the case with the genuinely new, but then finally came into their own.

What has not been noticed about Olson's "Projective Verse" is that his purposes, like Whitman's before him, are clearly epic; in the essay he is in search of the kind of renewal of poetry that will enable the modern poet to once again encompass large themes. His "stance," he claims, is more than "technical," and may "lead to new poetics and to new concepts from which some sort of drama, say, or of epic, perhaps, may emerge" (SW, p. 15). If "projective verse is practiced long enough, is driven ahead hard enough along the course I think it dictates, verse again can carry much larger material than it has carried in our language since the Elizabethans" (SW, p. 26). Whitman's 1855 Preface, too, called for new concepts, a new poetics, that could embody not small subjects but a theme that is "creative and has vista" (CPSP, p. 413).[8]

Olson took his basic metaphor for "Projective Verse" from science (a borrowing that Whitman would have endorsed). He called for the poet to work in "open," or what he called "composition by field." The first principle of such a way of working is the "kinetics of the thing": "A poem is energy transferred from where the poet got it (he will have some several causations), by way of the poem itself to, all the way over to, the reader.... Then the poem itself must, at all points, be a high energy-construct and, at all points, an energy-discharge" (SW, p. 16). This passage is perhaps the most brilliant moment in Olson's essay, and provides a fresh vocabulary for talking about poetry's sources, nature, and effect. The vocabulary derives, however obliquely, from physics (the master science in the 1940s and 1950s, in the midst of the great developments in and expectations for atomic energy). In physics, a "field of force" is a space under the influence of some force, such as electricity or magnetism. "Field composition," in which the poet puts himself in the "open," must be composition under the influence of metaphorically similar forces— personal or political currents or pressures, perhaps, that bear down on the poet's immediate psychic environment. The overall image of a poet putting himself in the "open" is of a poet not controlling his intellectual and emotional environment, but opening himself instead to the lines of force (of whatever nature) that intersect with his being in the particular space he happens to occupy. From these lines he draws the energy for transmission to the reader via his poem (or "energy construct"). He and his poem function as a kind of electric dynamo. Whitman, of course, was not familiar with high-energy physics, but there is a passage in his 1855 Preface which presents an image of an "open field" poet very close in spirit to Olson's: the poet "places himself where the future becomes present. The greatest poet does not only dazzle his rays over character and scenes and passions . . . he finally ascends and finishes all . . . he exhibits the pinnacles that no man can tell what they are for or what is beyond . . . he glows a moment on the extremest verge" (CPSP, p. 417). In both Whitman and Olson, the poet positions himself in a vulnerable openness, transmitting energies or rays from cosmic sources to readers via poems.

For the other principles of "Projective Verse," Olson borrows language from his contemporaries. From Robert Creeley: "Form is never more than an extension of content." From Edward Dahlberg: "One perception must immediately and directly lead to a further perception" (SW, pp. 16–17). The statement on form appears simply a direct formulation of organic form, as, for example, Whitman set forth in his 1855 Preface: "The fluency and ornaments of the finest poems . . . are not independent but dependent. All beauty comes from beautiful blood and a beautiful brain." The statement on the flow of perceptions seems to echo a number of related statements in Whitman: "From the eyesight proceeds another eyesight and from the hearing proceeds another hearing and from the voice proceeds another voice eternally curious of the harmony of things with man" (CPSP, pp. 415, 416).

The latter half of "Projective Verse" turns from the "reality of a poem itself" to the "reality outside a poem," in a plea for "objectism": "Objectism is the getting rid of the lyrical interference of the individual as ego, of the 'subject' and his soul, that peculiar presumption by which western man has interposed himself between what he is as a creature of nature (with certain instructions to carry out) and those other creations of nature which we may, with no derogation, call objects" (*SW*, p. 24). The "real" was Whitman's concern also, and his challenge similar to Olson's—to transfer energy from "objects" to the reader with minimal ego-interference. Into the poet, he said, "enter the essences of the real things, and past and present events." Readers (or "folks") "expect of the poet to indicate more than the beauty and dignity which always attach to dumb real objects . . . they expect him to indicate the path between reality and their souls." But Whitman's poet, like Olson's, must get rid of the "lyrical interference of the individual as ego." Whitman wrote: "What I experience or portray shall go from my composition without a shred of my composition. You shall stand by my side and look in the mirror with me" (*CPSP*, pp. 413, 415, 418).

Although Olson points to the "reality outside a poem," he insists that the poet cannot apprehend that reality by "way of artificial forms outside himself": "But if he stays inside himself, if he is contained within his nature as he is participant in the larger force, he will be able to listen, and his hearing through himself will give him secrets objects share." Breath, sound, language—"when the poet rests in these as they are in himself . . . then he, if he chooses to speak from these roots, works in that area where nature has given him size, projective size" (*SW*, p. 25). (Olson might have added—"epic size"). Whitman spoke with a different vocabulary, but of similar concepts. The poet "is a seer . . . he is individual . . . he is complete in himself . . . the others are as good as he, only he sees it and they do not." The "attributes of the poets of the kosmos concentre in the real body and soul and in the pleasure of things they possess the superiority of genuineness over all fiction and romance." Such cosmic poets will (like Olson's projective poets) come to know the "secrets objects share": "The poets of the kosmos advance through all interpositions and coverings and turmoils and stratagems to first principles" (*CPSP*, pp. 415, 421). Both Whitman's and Olson's poet proceeds from the "roots" of the self to perception of the realities beneath and beyond the mere surface of the world.

If the appearance of "Projective Verse" in 1950 marked the beginning (and provided the poetics) for post-Modernist American poetry as has often been claimed, then it must be affirmed that that same post-Modernist poetry had its origins not only in Pound and Williams (as Olson confessed), but behind and beyond them in the first of American bards, Walt Whitman. "Projective Verse" is one of several recognizable descendants of that still-reverberating revolutionary document, Whitman's 1855 Preface.

3

Though not so well known as "Projective Verse," Olson's "Human Universe" (1951) rivals it in importance as it figures in the composition of the Maximus Poems. The essay grew directly out of a key experience of Olson's career—his stay in Mexico in 1950–51. He lived in Lerma, on the sea near the city of Campeche, on the Yucatan peninsula, from December 1950 to July 1951. And he was given a Wenner-Gren Foundation award to study Mayan hieroglyphs in the same area in 1952. Two volumes of Olson's letters covering this period have been issued: *Mayan Letters,* edited by Robert Creeley, published in 1953; and *Letters for Origin, 1950–1956 (Origin* was a little magazine edited by Cid Corman), edited by Albert Glover, published 1970. "Human Universe" was in a sense a distillation of the Mayan experience, and Olson considered it, as he was working on it in 1951, his "base": "i have, here, set my cultural position. . . . There is, here, the body, the substance, of my faith" (*LO,* p. 69). His continued belief in its importance is indicated by his entitling his collected essays *Human Universe and Other Essays* (1965).

At the beginning of his essay, Olson says that Western man has not discovered the laws of the human as separate from the "other" universe. Language, he believes, is "a prime of the matter." The Greeks, especially Aristotle, fastened "logic and classification" on the "habits of thought," and these "hugely intermit our participation in our experience." But Plato was also to blame, as is "idealism of any sort"— because it inevitably becomes an end rather than a means. Olson then formulates the basic law of the "human universe": "If there is any absolute, it is never more than this one, you, this instant, in action." We must find ways to "stay in the human universe, and not be led to partition reality at any point, in any way" (*SW,* pp. 53–56). And the contemporary Maya, though they have lost many of the secrets of their ancient counterparts (primarily through corrupting Western influences), still "carry their bodies with some of the savor and the flavor that the bodies of the Americans are as missing in as is their irrigated lettuce and their green picked refrigerator-ripened fruit. For the truth is, that the management of external nature so that none of its virtu is lost, in vegetables or in art, is as much a delicate juggling of her content as is the same juggling by any one of us of our own" (SW, p. 58).

If the only "absolute" is "you, this instant, in action," then "man at his peril breaks the full circuit of object, image, action at any point. The meeting edge of man and the world is also his cutting-edge. If man is active, it is exactly here where experience comes in that it is delivered back, and if he stays fresh at the coming in he will be fresh at his going out." Genuine art, therefore, cannot be description: "There is only one thing you can do about kinetic, reenact it. Which is why the man said, he who possesses rhythm possesses the universe. And why art is the only twin life has—its only valid metaphysic. Art does not seek to describe but to enact" (SW, pp. 61–62).

All of the language Olson introduces here is highly suggestive of one of his much admired predecessors, D. H. Lawrence. In the Preface to the American edition of New Poems (reprinted, appropriately if paradoxically, in The Poetics of the New American Poetry), Lawrence wrote, "Life, the ever-present, knows no finality, no finished crystallisation." It is this truth that gives rise to Lawrence's poetry—"the poetry of that which is at hand: the immediate present. In the immediate present there is no perfection, no consummation, nothing finished. The strands are all flying, quivering, intermingling into the web, the waters are shaking the moon." Such a poetry is "the unrestful, ungraspable poetry of the sheer present, poetry whose very permanency lies in its wind-like transit. Whitman's is the best poetry of this kind. Without beginning and without end, without any base and pediment, it sweeps past for ever, like a wind that is forever in passage, and unchainable. . . . The clue to all his utterance lies in the sheer appreciation of the instant moment, life surging itself into utterance at its very wellhead. . . . The quivering nimble hour of the present, this is the quick of Time. This is the immanence. The quick of the universe is the *pulsating, carnal self,* mysterious and palpable. . . . Because Whitman put this into his poetry, we fear him and respect him so profoundly."[9]

What Lawrence discovered in Whitman Olson discovered among the Maya: "If there is any absolute, it is never more than this one, you, this instant, in action." And Olson might well have absorbed the Whitmanian example in his early reading, and have observed the Maya through Whitmanian-Laurentian spectacles. It was Whitman, rooting his perceptions firmly in the self, who permitted "to speak at every hazard, / Nature without check with original energy." Whitman saw himself much as Olson saw the Maya: "Me imperturbe, standing at ease in Nature, / Master of all or mistress of all, aplomb in the midst of irrational things, / Imbued as they, passive, receptive, silent as they. . . . / Me wherever my life is lived, / to be self-balanced for contingencies, / To confront night, storms, hunger, ridicule, accidents, rebuffs, as the trees and animals do" (*CPSP*, pp. 11–12). But of course, this harmony with nature was also a basic component of Confucianism as portrayed in Ezra Pound's *Cantos* (see, for example, Canto 13)—still another shaping influence on Olson.

Although "Human Universe" is a distillation by Olson of his Mayan experiences, his published letters are useful in revealing sources of his perceptions so vital to his Maximus Poems. At the time Olson went to Mexico, he was in his early forties and it is more likely that he was seeking confirmation of views already formed than anticipating discovery of the genuinely new. Over and over again his letters reveal that he found in the Yucatan what he wanted to find. 22 March 1951: "What excites me, is, a whole series of scholarly deductions which widen out the rear of the Maya sufficiently for me to pick up confirmations to my imaginative thesis of the sea, that is, of migration." 28 March 1951: "no people i'm committed to [the ancient Maya] could be devoted to time as these loose-heads [professional anthropologists] say they were, but i knew no answer, and, surely they [the Maya] did spend a hell of a lot of time on time, surely. . . . but the first chance i get, and can get a copy of Copan D [a particular glyph from the Copan archeological site in Honduras] to send you, will, so that you can see, that time, in their minds, was *mass & weight!*" (*SW*, pp. 98, 110). Both the "imaginative thesis of the sea" and the view of time as other than chronology are recurring themes of the Maximus Poems.

In a 27 April 1951 letter, Olson can hardly contain his excitement on reading Tatiana Prouskouriakoff's *Classic Mayan Art* and discovering that every "example of inscription on sculpture in all, all the whole Mayan area . . . is built around . . . ONE central HUMAN figure! (no god, or abstract concept, no 'ideas', but ONE MAN!" And Olson adds significantly: "so, fr the good past, CONFIRMATION!" And in a letter of 10 June 1951 Olson devotes several pages to explaining why he is "beginning" to think that the slender, elaborately carved stelae of the Maya are like the Greek *Herms,* and thus derived from Priapus or phallic worship: "very early, the Maya *transposed* the phallus to the stela: it accounts for one thing no one has sd much about, that the stela were worshipped" (*LO*, pp. 46–47, 58). Perhaps. But more important than the truth of the theory is the revelation of themes that excited Olson at the moment his ideas about a long epic poem were taking shape. For Olson the Maya, both ancient and modern, became the important alternative—"another humanism"—to that consumer humanism in the civilization of the shoddy which was undermining Western culture (*SW*, p. 93).

4

The Maximus Poems open with "I, Maximus of Gloucester, to You":

> Off-shore, by islands hidden in the blood
> jewels & miracles, I, Maximus
> a metal hot from boiling water, tell you
> what is a lance, who obeys the figures of
> the present dance
>
> (1:1)[10]

Some two decades or so later, the Maximus Poems conclude with one line: "my wife   my car   my color   and   myself" (3: 229). These two passages bracket many obscurities that only many years of scholarly application will illuminate. Some problems are more or less readily solved, as for example, the person and the place. Scattered references to the ancient Greek seaport of Tyre identify Maximus for us. Maximus of Tyre (ca. A.D. 125–85) was an "itinerant lecturer" whose surviving work consists of forty-one lectures. The *Oxford Classical Dictionary* informs us: "His lectures show no philosophical originality, and are simply eloquent exhortations to virtue decked out with quotations, chiefly from Plato and Homer; he belongs to the same genus as the sophists, though his views have no affinity with theirs, being borrowed from Cynicism and Platonism."[11]

But of course, this American Maximus of Gloucester, Massachusetts, U.S.A., is as much Charles Olson as Maximus of Tyre. Or Maximus of Tyre is the mask or persona adopted by Olson for his epic.[12] All the biographical data in the poem fits Olson: he grew up in Gloucester and returned to Gloucester to visit the scenes of his boyhood; his father (a character in the poem) was in the postal service and was punished for his work in the postal union. These and many other such connections make it absurd to pretend that Maximus is not Olson. Moreover, it is possible that Maximus is meant to connote maximal or maximum, the most or the fullest or the biggest in the spiritual, imaginative experiential, or even physical sense (Olson often referred to his extraordinary height—he was six feet eight inches tall. The Gloucester of the poem is the Gloucester that Olson knew, street by street, house by house, its allied settlements (Dogtown, Stage Fort), its hills and valleys and coastal areas, Fishermans Field and Cressys Beach. Among other things, the Maximus Poems are a detailed map of Gloucester and environs, and the details and measurements are such that they invite absolute belief as real. This reality is reinforced by the history of Gloucester that accretes in the poem. By poem's end, the reader knows more about Gloucester than he ever expected to learn, and more, perhaps, than he is able consciously to assimilate to the larger patterns and movements of the poem.

Before ascertaining these larger movements, the reader must orient himself in the environment of the poem—no easy task. Even the titles of the various volumes can be confusing to the uninitiated reader. The Maximus Poems consist of three volumes: *The Maximus Poems* (1960), *Maximus Poems IV, V, VI* (1968), and *The Maximus Poems: Volume Three* (1975). But the reader who, noticing Parts IV, V, and VI of the second volume, expectantly searches the first volume for Parts I, II, and III is doomed to disappointment. He can know that Part I consists of Letters 1–10, Part II of Letters 11–22, and Part III of the remainder of the first volume, *The Maximus Poems*, only if he has read *Letters for Origin* (*LO*, p. 139), though he may note the publication history of the early poems (*Maximus Poems / 1–10*, 1953; *Maximus Poems / 11–22*, 1956) and may assume (and it would be only an assumption) that the parts coincide with the published groups. To add to the confusion, *The Maximus Poems: Volume Three* has no "Parts," at least as revealed within the text. And it is the only one of the three to carry a volume number.

Early in the first volume of the Maximus Poems, the individual poems begin to carry the title "Letter" followed by a number in sequence. But this scheme is carried through only Letter 23, and then the identification is dropped. The total number of "Letters" in this first volume may be thirty-seven or more, depending on how the reader counts the poems (often the first line of a new poem looks like the simple continuation of the preceding poem). In *Maximus Poems IV, V, VI*, the first poem is entitled "Letter #41 [broken off]" (2:1; Olson's brackets), but the reader is hard pressed to find the opening of Letter 41—unless he simply assumes that it is the last (unnumbered) letter of *The Maximus Poems* (1960). The next following poems in this second volume do carry letter designations, but soon the reader comes upon "Maximus to Gloucester, Letter 27 [withheld]" (2:14; Olson's brackets), which raises the possibility that more such "Letters" were withheld. And shortly thereafter, the reader turns to "Maximus Letter # whatever" (2:31)—suggesting that Olson has been playing a game and has become tired of the pretense. But such a suggestion is undermined by other letter titles—"Letter 72" (2:53), "A Later Note on Letter #15" (2:77), and, near the end of this second volume, "Maximus, to Gloucester, Letter 157" (2:175). No letter designations appear in *The Maximus Poems: Volume Three*, but poems are often dated (as occasionally in the second volume) and appear in chronological order of composition. To further disorient the reader (and particularly the critic), no pagination appears in the second volume, *Maximus Poems IV, V, VI* (pagination is also omitted in Olson's collected poems, *Archaeologist of Morning*, 1971).

In 1950, Olson wrote to Cid Corman, editor of *Origin*: "I had occasion to read I, Max here [Washington, D.C.] last week and it still moves me to the bottom of my feet that, such, is, to be, there, on yr pages, #1, for example: it is like an epistle of an apostle fr Rome to the Ephesians when it takes its place in yr pages!" (*LO*, p. 19). We may take this identification by Olson as suggestive of the meaning he attached to the title designation, Letter. There are biblical overtones, underlining the authoritative tone of voice, a voice coming from a fixed and affirmed moral position, decrying the wickedness, warning of retribution, offering moral guidance. The voice appears omniscient, and didactic, the voice of an apostle who has a fix on truth. Later on in the Maximus Poems, the voice varies, becomes pedestrian, mundane, fact-bearing. There seems little doubt that Olson found his unique voice for the Maximus Poems in the conception of the biblical letter or epistle. Why, then, did he not carry through with the designation?

The answer to this question may connect with the antipathy toward pagination. Obviously Olson had grave doubts about offering his readers clear and logically related sequential designations. In "Human Universe," Olson had cited "logic and classification" as the "habits of thought" interfering "absolutely" with action. With this point of view, it was inevitable that Olson would be extremely uncomfortable with any kind of neat sequentiality that made designation, reference, classification easy for the reader—inviting him to use those very "habits of thought" that were anathema to Olson and seducing the reader into a search for a structure in the Maximus Poems made up of recurring patterns, related passages and blocks. The entire thrust of the Maximus Poems is anti-logic, anti-classification, anti-structure.

But the omission of page numbers and sporadic use of letter numbers and occasional use of part numbers constitute only superficial signals to the reader of the anti-sequential nature of the Maximus Poems. Olson uses what might be designated the "open-parenthesis" style—a style in which parentheses seldom close. When pressed on the question of the parenthesis in 1950, Olson responded: "Opening, and then not closing a parenthesis, is merely to acknowledge that just that way is the way one does parenthesize, actually: true to feeling" (*LO,* p. 20). *Feeling*—not logic and classification. The justification for not closing a parenthesis (like the dropping of pagination and the omission of letter numbers lies in the reality of the way people actually talk and act mentally when free of the Western habit of logic—when they are committed solely (as Olson put it in "Human Universe") to "this one, you, this instant, in action."

But the "open-parenthesis" style is more than a matter of omitting close-parentheses. Olson's style, as any reader of the Maximus Poems knows, is made up of an endless series of metaphoric parentheses that neither open nor close—abrupt twists and turns, shifts in space, leaps in time, and most often a thought, idea, image, sentence, or phrase left dangling in incompletion. The "open-parenthesis" style, then, is a style meant to mirror the post-logical mind immersed in "this instant," and has some of the attributes of a fragmented "stream of consciousness" technique. Here is the whole of Song 1 of "The Songs of Maximus":

> colored pictures
> of all things to eat: dirty
> postcards
>   And words, words, words
> all over everything
>   No eyes or ears left
> to do their own doings (all
> invaded, appropriated, outraged, all senses
> including the mind, that worker on what is
>   And that other sense
> made to give even the most wretched, or any of us,
>   wretched,
> that consolation (greased
>   lulled
> even the street-cars
> song

                                                            (1:13)

In spite of the surface incoherence, the meaning comes through—
indignation at the way advertising and commercialism have appro-
priated the culture, the individual, all the senses. The reader who
attempts to extrapolate a totally coherent statement to which all the
words of the poem logically refer is bound for frustration. He must be
satisfied with hiatuses, lacunae, incompletenesses—and these are a
substantial part of the "meaning" of the poetry.

One of Olson's poems ("These Days") collected in *Archaeologist of
Morning* is useful for anyone encountering his style for the first time:

> whatever you have to say, leave
> the roots on, let them
> dangle
> And the dirt
>
>   just to make clear
>   where they came from
>   (*AM*, p. 13)

Throughout the Maximus Poems, the roots and the dirt (psychic,
mental, emotional, or spiritual origins and nutritive associations) are
left dangling from the words. And if they were pruned away, the
words would die: they are part of the essential vitality—and thus the
"meaning"—of the poem.

In addition to his anti-sequential technique and his open-
parenthesis style, Olson exploits typography for "meaning" in the
Maximus Poems. The arrangement of lines and line-clusters on a
page, although related to his notions about rhythm and breath, become important to meaning, especially with the frequent dropping of
conventional punctuation and capitalization. Typography seems to
have played an increasingly important role as the Maximus Poems
progressed. The last two volumes are of folio size, and the space of
the large pages and the arrangement of the lines (the spacing between
lines often varies from poem to poem) become an important part of
the effect. Sometimes a poem appears with only one or two lines.
Sometimes two facing pages are blank, forcing the reader to wonder
whether he has an imperfect copy. And sometimes the type is set
slantwise, or in a circle, or "counter clockwise" (see, for example, pp.
120–21, *The Maximus Poems: Volume Three*). All these techniques and
devices may be seen as related to the anti-sequential, anti-
conventional thrust of the Maximus Poems, visually forcing the
reader to break out of his habit of expecting logical progression and
reassuring recurrence. They succeed in evoking a spirit of rebellious-

ness and cheeky impertinence, a fundamental irreverence for the superficial orderliness that Western man has imposed on the bewildering chaos and threateningly jumbled nature of "this one, you, this instant, in action."

5

Although Olson has almost succeeded in making traditional critical discussion of the Maximus Poems impossible (surely he has rendered moot most conventional questions of structure), he has left his poem open—as any poet must—to a report from a diligent reader, one who has immersed himself in an experience of the poem on the poem's own terms where possible. What I shall attempt here is a brief report of this kind. The most intense energies I felt flowing from the poem as I read were those generated by a critical view of the contemporary world—the "pejorocracy" with its constant cacophony of "mu-sick" promoting and hawking and pushing and blaring a flood of consumer products for a society drowning in its huge over-abundance of goods and gadgets and possessions and belongings already acquired. Like Ezra Pound (whose all-inclusive term was "usura"), Olson cultivated a style of outrage at contemporary blunders and stupidities and cupidities that provided a basic frame on which to hang other ventures and themes. Outrage provides its own pleasures of a kind:

> It is not bad
> to be pissed off
> where there is *any*
> condition imposed, by whomever, no matter how close
> (2:158–59)

The opening Letter of the Maximus Poems provides a firm base for the recurrence of this theme throughout the work:

> But that which matters, that which insists, that which will last,
> that! o my people, where shall you find it, how, where, where shall you listen
> when all is become billboards, when, all, even silence, is spray-gunned?
> when even our bird, my roofs,
> cannot be heard
> when even you, when sound itself is neoned in?
> (1:2)

The abundance of modern civilization has not granted freedom but has provided clutter and diminished choice. The culture has been trivialized, submerged in irrelevance (Letter 15, "Maximus to Gloucester"):

> The American epos, 19–
> 02 (or when did Barton Barton Barton Barton and Barton?
>
>> To celebrate
>> how it can be, it is
>> padded or uncomforted, your lost, you
>> found, your
>> sneakers
>> (o Statue,
> o Republic, o
> Tell-A-Vision, the best
> is soap. The true troubadours
> are CBS. Melopoeia
>> > is for Cokes by Cokes out of
>> > Pause
>>> > (1:71)

The grand American "epos" has brought to the fore not a great cultural flowering but the age of advertising; the devices of song have been put in the service of the great American symbol, Coca-Cola and its "pause that refreshes."

Like Pound's *Cantos*, the Maximus Poems are filled with portraits of heroes and villains, or rather those who "know" and live by the knowledge and those who, with all their cunning, do not "know" and fail in the essentials of living, however much they succeed in life. The knowledge at stake is basically the knowledge outlined by Olson in "Human Universe," the knowledge in part of how to live in "this one, you, this instant, in action." But it is also an intuitive respect for nature and the cosmos. Among those cast in the role of the deficient are Miles Standish (figure of American history and folklore), James Conant (long-time contemporary president of Harvard), Vincent Ferrini (an editor of a little magazine, *Four Winds*, in Gloucester)[13]—and one Andrew Merry, a sailor of Dogtown who had seen bullfighting in Spain and Mexico, acquired a young bull on which to practice his prowess, and who decided one Sunday to fight the grown bull to display his "Handsome Sailor ism." But the Saturday night before the fight, he became drunk and decided to practice with the bull—and was killed:

> Not one mystery
> nor man
> possibly not even a bird
> heard Merry
> fight that bull by
> (was Jeremiah Millett's house
>
> Drunk
> to cover his shame
> blushing Merry
> in the bar
> walking up
>
> to Dogtown to try
> his strength
> the baby bull
> now full grown
>
>   (2:3–4)

Merry in his vanity violated his bonds with sea and earth, and sacrificed his life:

> Only the sun
> in the morning
> covered him
> with flies
>
> Then only
> after the grubs
> had done him
> did the earth
> let her robe
> uncover and her part
> take him in
>
>   (2:6)

Given the mythological significance of the bull, Merry's senseless fight takes on cosmic overtones in Olson's "Maximus from Dogtown–I,"[14] and his fate a lesson for those who would deliberately destroy man's harmony with nature. Like Sam Patch in Williams's *Paterson*, Merry becomes for Olson a point of reference in later poems, his legend a part of the epic's moral-ethical-cosmic vision.

When Olson opens his Maximus Poems, his home town of Gloucester symbolizes the possibility and hope that are lacking in America as a whole:

> (o Gloucester-man,
> weave
> your birds and fingers

> new, your roof-tops,
> clean shit upon racks
> sunned on
> American
> braid
> with others like you, such
> extricable surface
> as faun and oral,
> satyr lesbos vase
>
> o kill kill kill kill kill
> those
> who advertise you
> out)
>   (1:3–4)

If "Gloucester-man" can be cast in the role of hero battling the advertising culture, it is because Gloucester "can know polis" (the term for the Greek city-state, with its ideal of balance between individuality and community):

> As the people of the earth are now, Gloucester
> is heterogeneous, and so can know polis
> not as localism, not that mu-sick (the trick
> of corporations, newpapers, slick magazines, movie
>   houses,
> the ships, even the wharves, absentee-owned
>
> they whine to my people, these entertainers, sellers
>
> they play upon their bigotries (upon their fears
>   (1:10)

Polis, the community at harmony with nature composed of harmoniously organized individual human beings, is a live possibility in Gloucester when Olson begins the Maximus Poems.

But as the work progresses, a hesitant note tends to enter the poem's voice:

> An American
> is a complex of occasions,
> themselves a geometry
> of spatial nature
>   I have this sense,
> that I am one
> with my skin
>   Plus this-plus this:

that forever the geography
which leans in
on me I compell
backwards I compell Gloucester
to yield, to
change
          Polis
is this

                              (2:15)

If imaginative energy can accomplish the task, Olson will transfigure
("compell") Gloucester into "polis." And he senses, in this passage,
the American-ness of this ambitious task—the American "spatial nature" that has always been the basis for the American dreaming and
the dream.

But, ultimately, Gloucester proves unworthy of Olson's ambitions
for her. In a poem near the end of his epic, entitled "December 18th"
(written 1968), Olson observes that "the rosy red is gone":

          Oh Gloucester

has no longer a West
end. It is a
part of the
country now a mangled
mess of all parts swollen
& fallen
into
degradation, each bundle unbound and scattered
as so many
units of poor
sorts and strangulation   all hung up each one
like hanged
bodies

                              (3:202)

The heart of the town has capitulated: "what was Main / street are
now / fake gasoline station / and A & P supermarket" (3:203).

Olson concludes this anguished poem with the admission that
Gloucester has lost its identity and with it has lost its possibility:

          the fake
          which covers the emptiness
          is the loss
          in the 2nd instance of the

distraction. Gloucester too
>is out of her mind and
>is now indistinguishable from
>the USA.

>>>>(3:204)

After these despairing lines, Olson quotes Melville's *Redburn*: "We are not a narrow tribe of men . . . we are not a nation, so much as a world" (3:204). If we are the world, and we are lost, and even Gloucester has become one with the rest, where is there hope? To confront such a question Olson has traveled a long road, his epic as much a journey in self-education as a moral map for the reader. Olson does not let his work end in darkness, for a part of this "Archaeologist's" morning journey has been the discovery and exploration of various lodes of imaginative energy—and even affirmation.

6

From the very beginning, Olson's Maximus provides formulas for survival in the civilization of the shoddy:

>"In the midst of plenty, walk
>as close to
>bare
>>In the face of sweetness,
>piss
>>>In the time of goodness,
>go side, go
>smashing, beat them, go as
>(as near as you can
>tear
>In the land of plenty, have
>nothing to do with it
>>>>take the way of
>the lowest,
>including
>your legs, go
>contrary, go
>sing

>>>>(1:14–15)

Although written in the early 1950s, these lines might have been carried on the banners of the rebellious students during the 1960s, most of whom probably never heard of Olson. Even in the face of overpowering odds, Olson provided a way of coping, a strategy even for undermining.

Olson-Maximus was anxious to make it clear that his "value" or ideal did not rest in a romantically conceived past:

> I'd not urge anyone back. Back is no value as better. That
>   sentimentality
> has no place, least of all Gloucester,
> where polis
> still thrives
>
> Back is only for those who do not move (as future is,
> you in particular need to be warned,
> any of you who have the habit of
> "the people"—as though there were anything / the equal
>   of / the context of / now!
>
> (1:22)

The lines relate directly to Olson's essay, "Human Universe," and the value established there in "this one, you, this instant, in action." Elsewhere Olson writes, "Limits / are what any of us / are inside of" (1:17). It is within these limits imposed by this "now" that value must be pursued (compare Williams's search for Beautiful Thing in the common and even repugnant).

Though Olson would not "urge anyone back," still in his view there was a time in the beginning when America offered possibility and opportunity that were somehow betrayed. A poem central to the first volume of the Maximus Poems, "On first Looking out through Juan de la Cosa's Eyes" (de la Cosa was a Biscayan seaman who accompanied Columbus), is filled with the freshness of new beginnings ("But before La Cosa, nobody / could have / a mappemunde" [1:77]). The theme recurs, especially in a poem like "Capt Christopher Levett (of York)," an early explorer and settler, one of the New World's "first men." But the newness

> the first men knew was almost
> from the start dirtied
> by second comers. About seven years
> and you can carry cinders
> in your hand for what
>
> America was worth. May she be damned
> for what she did so soon
> to what was such a newing
>
> (1:134–35)

The theme was one that William Carlos Williams touched on in his

Columbus chapter ("The Discovery of the Indies") in *In the American Grain*, in which Columbus's impression of the New World is quoted—"the most beautiful thing which I had ever seen" (see chap. 7, sec. 6). Williams, of course, made Beautiful Thing a primary quest of Paterson in a world as grim as that Olson depicts in the Maximus Poems.

Olson presents a series of individuals who consciously or unconsciously embody the "value" he repeatedly attempts to define and inspire, as, for example, Juan de la Cosa and Christopher Levett. Often he presents pairs of persons to contrast, as in Letter 10, where he sets up as a model Roger Conant, a seventeenth-century Gloucester settler (and governor) who built a house so sound that it was later taken to Salem by Endecott for his mansion: and in contrast he presents James Conant, former president of Harvard (Harvard "owns too much," and Conant destroyed its "localism"). A similar contrast is developed between John Smith and Miles Standish.[15] But perhaps the most pervasive presence of an individual serving in some sense as model in the Maximus Poems is Olson's own father.

In a poem dealing with one William Stevens, a "primary Selectman" of Gloucester, 1642, who refused to sign an oath of allegiance to Charles the Second, Olson introduces his father not in contrast but in comparison. Like Stevens, Olson's father defied authority and was punished for it. Olson's father was a postman (his "now," the limits he was "inside of"), and he "was ground down / to death, taking night collections / joining Swedish fraternal / organizations, seeking to fight back / with the usual American political / means" (3:31).[16] A later poem provides more (but still scant) details of the persecution:

> the U.S. Post Office
> using his purpose to
> catch him
> in their trap   to bust him
> organizing
> Postal Workers
> benefits—Retirement age
> Widows pensions   a different
> leadership in Washington than
> Doherty   my father a Swedish
> wave of
> migration after
> Irish? like Negroes
> now like Leroy and Malcolm

            X the final wave
            of wash upon this
            desperate
            ugly
            cruel
            Land this nation
            which never
            lets anyone
            come to shore:
                    (3:118–19)

Olson's indignation transcends his explanation or clarification, but it
is amply clear that his father has been victimized by the government
for his union and other activities. In a farewell tribute to his father,
Olson writes a shaped poem, counterclockwise at the beginning, but
formed like a flower on the page. He writes in praise of his father as
he himself "goes forth to create Paradise" (a phrase written upside
down; Pound in the later *Cantos* developed a kind of refrain, "Le
Paradis n'est pas artificiel" [see chapter 5, sec. 5]). In the elegy, Olson
calls for an "end to Hell" and "even to Heaven," and for "a life
America shall yield / or we will leave her / and ask Gloucester / to sail
away / from this / Rising Shore" (3:121).

    Although Olson's "value" was grounded (in "Human Universe")
in his observations of Mayan culture, and although he sought and
found confirmation of the value in the actions of various personages,
historical and contemporary, he also found confirmation in
philosophy, as suggested in a poem in the second volume of the
Maximus Poems:

            In English the poetic became meubles—furniture—
            thereafter (after 1630
            & Descartes was the value
            until Whitehead, who cleared out the gunk
            by getting the universe in (as against man alone
                                                        (2:77)

Whitehead restored a "concept of history" which "makes any one's
acts a finding out for him or her / self, in other words restores the
traum." This concept is placed in contrast with "the objective" or
"any form of record on the spot / —live television or what—" which
"is a lie":

            as against what we know went on, the dream: the dream
                    being
            self-action with Whitehead's important corollary: that no
                    event

is not penetrated, in intersection or collision with, an
        eternal
event
            The poetics of such a situation
        are yet to be found out

                                                    (2:77)

The meaning shines through the murky syntax and the double negative: "this one, you, this instant, in action" does not stand isolated in
the universe but is intersected by, or collides with, "an eternal /
event." There are ever-expanding contexts for human acts that
reach out into the cosmic context and eternity. Olson's value, then,
his ultimate value, has something of the mystical reach or sweep to
it.[17] And his obsessive search in the Maximus Poems is to find the
poetics that will embody the full complexity of the value.

Although by the end of the Maximus Poems, Olson is outraged in
finding his beloved Gloucester "indistinguishable" from the rest of
the USA, his own ebullient spirit remains inextinguishable even if
more subdued. In a poem among the final pages of the work, entitled
"His health, his poetry, and his love all in one," he affirms
"happily, / among the dead there are a great many / who are still
alive. Well, like, some are / And in any case the few who are do
still, / in that sense, define the, like, possibility" (3:219–20). There is
still bitterness in his vision—

            One does only wish
        that these poor stuffed people,
        & their hopelessly untreated children
        —except to anything they want—
        cld either be removed
        to the cemetery
        or to the moon and

        it be less cluttered
        with obstacles to the
        still handsome & efficacious
        environment

                                (3:220)

The major images of the poem are not the curiously inhuman humans
(he envisions their banishment),[18] but the rocks of Settlement Cove
along the sea:

        And so I walked
        thinking as I did so, I come from the last walking period
            of man, homeward,
        happy and renewed, in that sense, by the sight of the

original cove of the City populated
megalithically. . . .

(3:220)

"Happy and renewed": the poem is dated 16 July 1969, the year
before Olson's death.

7

Any coherent discussion of the Maximus Poems is certain
to misrepresent the work's designed incoherence. The themes of ne-
gation and affirmation, of pejorocracy and value, by no means
exhaust the work's currents and cross-currents. Vital to the epic dimension of the work are the versions of history and geography, time
and space, that are interwoven in the poems' texture. With Olson,
geography seems to take precedence. On the cover of the second
volume of the Maximus Poems appears a simple map of Gondwana-
land, showing South America, Africa, and Australia connected, and
also above this land mass and linked to it, North America and Europe
interconnected: one world indeed. On one side is Oceanus, on the
other the Tethys sea (Tethys was the daughter of Uranus and Gaea
and the wife of Oceanus). There are innumerable references within
the Maximus Poems to this ancient (and mythical) united geography.
In one poem the origin of Gloucester is portrayed connected to it:

> Between Cruiser & Plato   sea mountains   and
> just south of Atlantis Gloucester
> tore her way West North West 1/2 West to arrive
> where she is   from her old union with Africa
> just where the Canaries lie off shore
>
> (3:205)

Throughout his epic, Olson has been pushing backward in space-
time in his exploration of Gloucester, until here he has reached those
mythical origins, showing Gloucester's geographical lineage that
links her with all the rest of the world (and universe).

Just as geography cannot be divorced from chronology, neither can
chronology be separated from geography. In a sequence of numbered
"Maximus, from Dogtown" poems in the second volume of the
Maximus Poems, Olson develops a mythological cosmology or
genesis, placing Gloucester again in the chronological lineage that
situates her in eternity:

> The sea was born of the earth without sweet union of love
>   Hesiod says
> But that then she lay for heaven and she bare the thing
>   which encloses
> every thing. Okeanos the one which all things are and by
>   which nothing
> is anything but itself, measured so
> screwing earth, in whom love lies which unnerves the
>   limbs and by its
> heat floods the mind and all gods and men into further
>   nature
>   Vast earth rejoices,
> deep-swirling Okeanos steers all things through all
>   things,
> everything issues from the one, the soul is led from
>   drunkenness
> to dryness, the sleeper lights up from the dead,
> the man awake lights up from the sleeping
>
>   (2:2)

From this opening of "Maximus, from Dogtown–I," Olson narrows down to Gloucester and Dogtown and its legends (particularly the story of the drunken "bullfighter," Andrew Merry), thus providing them a kind of cosmic resonance. "Maximus, from Dogtown–IV," which opens "a century or so before 2000 / BC," is perhaps the most elaborate embodiment in the Maximus Poems of a cosmology-theogony, borrowed from various mythologies, and placing contemporary Gloucester (or Dogtown) in a context of antiquity.

These themes of time and space, and many more, are developed in the Maximus Poems. Each reader will discover in this great ocean of a poem abundant themes fitting varied interests, enough to make arbitrary focus almost necessary. But there is no escaping Olson's presence in the poem. For a poem, however, that exploits the poet's life as much as does the Maximus Poems, there are curiously few genuinely revealing personal moments in the work. He does not stand revealed in the way, for example, that Whitman does in his "Calamus" poems, or that Pound does in the "Pisan Cantos," or that Ginsberg does in any of his poetry. As a result, there is (in addition to all the other difficulties of the poem) a certain dryness that could put off an eager reader, who might then connect all the ellipses, hiatuses, dangling parentheses and phrases to an evasiveness, a reticence in allowing anyone too near the poet's veiled self.

In an early poem, "Maximus, to himself," Olson appears on the

point of the confessional: "I have had to learn the simplest things /
last. Which made for difficulties." (1:52). A note of regret, far from
the voice's usual swagger, seems on the verge of entering the poem:

> The agilities
> they show daily
> who do the world's
> businesses
> And who do nature's
> as I have no sense
> I have done either

> I have made dialogues
> have discussed ancient texts,
> have thrown what light I could, offered
> what pleasures
> doceat allows
>   But the known?
> This, I have had to be given,
> a life, love, and from one man
> the world.

> Tokens
> But sitting here
> I look out as a wind
> and water man, testing
> And missing
> some proof

>   (1:52–53)

It is strange how the poem hovers on the edge of some revelation that
is never made, some regret that is never articulated. The poem concludes in melancholy: "It is undone business / I speak of, this
morning, / with the sea / stretching out / from my feet" (1:53).

In the last volume of the Maximus Poems, in a poem entitled
"Maximus of Gloucester" and dated 5 November 1965, Olson again
permits a plaintive note to enter his voice:

> Only my written word
> I've sacrificed every thing, including sex and woman
> —or lost them—to this attempt to acquire complete
> concentration. (The con-
> ventual.) "robe and bread"
> not worry or have to worry about
> either

>   (3:101)

Olson's at least momentary regret for the sacrifices that his poem has required seems nakedly genuine, especially that specification of loss, "sex and woman." And the latter half of his poem appears to confess a double vision of the self, an image of a Buddhistic self, and the real living-breathing self that is buried beneath the image (and that has escaped the poem):

> Half Moon beach ("the arms of her")
> my balls rich as Buddha's
> sitting in her like the Padma
> —and Gloucester, foreshortened
> in front of me. It is not I,
> even if the life appeared
> biographical. The Only interesting thing
> is if one can be
> an image
> of man, "The nobleness,   and the arete."
> (*Later*: myself (like my father, in the picture, a shadow)
> on the rock
>
> (3:101)

Olson seems to be saying that the Maximus Poems contains not the real Olson but only his created image, ennobled, devoted to "the arete" (virtue, humanliness): "It is not I, / even if the life appeared / biographical." There is ambiguity in the antecedent of that "It," but the reader will know by now that the reference is, however obscurely, to Olson's epic work, the Maximus Poems—where there is biography aplenty, and little of the self, and almost nothing of personal relationships; not the real Olson, but rather, perhaps (as in the poem's final image) his "shadow" on "the rock." It is surely significant that in this, one of his most nearly confessional poems, his final thoughts come to rest not on a woman in his life, nor a child, nor a friend—but on his father, who seems to have evoked the strongest private feelings experienced in the Maximus Poems.

Olson wrote in the second volume of the Maximus Poems: "I am making a mappemunde. It is to include my being" (2:85). Few readers will challenge the creation of the mappemunde. But more than a few will wonder, finally, at the depth of presence of Olson's "being" in that mappemunde.

A final word:
"Le Fou"
for Charles

Robert Creeley

who plots, then, the lines
talking, taking, always the beat from
the breath
            (moving slowly at first
the breath
            which is slow—
I mean, graces come slowly,
it is that way.

So slowly(they are waving
we are moving
                away from   (the trees
                        the usual   (go by
which is slower than this, is
                        (we are moving!
goodbye[19]

Ten

The idea was, sort of, the way Whitman puts his idea about "Leaves of Grass." The idea is to record a personality, to make him visible, put him through tests, see what the hell he's up to, and through him, the country—and to commit him to his country.

Berryman on his "Dream Songs"

John Berryman's "Dream Songs"

Walt Whitman makes direct appearances in John Berryman's *Dream Songs* in contexts that suggest that the contemporary poet was throwing out hints as to the model for his modern epic. Whitman appears first in Dream Song 78, entitled "Op. posth. no. 1," and thus stands at the beginning of the second volume of *The Dream Songs* as originally published (1968)—*His Toy, His Dream, His Rest* (which included Dream Songs 78–385, the last of the formal sequence). Whitman's role in this "transitional" poem is ambiguous: Henry is in process of disintegration and death (temporary, it turns out):

> Darkened his eye, his wild smile disappeared,
> inapprehensible his studies grew,
> nourished he less & less
> his subject body with good food & rest,
> something bizarre about Henry, slowly sheared
> off, unlike you & you,
>
> smaller & smaller, till in question stood
> his eyeteeth and one block of memories
> These were enough for him
> implying commands from upstairs & from down,

> Walt's 'orbic flex,' triads of Hegel would
> incorporate, if you please,
>
> into the know-how of the American bard
> embarrassed Henry heard himself a-being,
> and the younger Stephen Crane
> of a powerful memory, of pain,
> these stood the ancestors, relaxed & hard,
> whilst Henry's parts were fleeing.[1]

The disintegration and approaching death of Henry (or Berryman, a relationship discussed below) is intellectual or poetic. What is being sheared off from Henry are his previous poetic identities, and he is getting down to new essentials, stripped to his "eyeteeth" and "one block of memories": American poets Walt Whitman and Stephen Crane (the latter the subject of one of Berryman's books).

It would be a mistake to see this transfiguration as deliberate. Rather, it appears to be one that the poet did not consciously will; he is even "embarrassed" at his new identity of "American bard" that he hears "himself a-being." The "commands" that come from "upstairs & from down" appear to be influences (or currents) from both conscious and unconscious sources. But what of Hegel? Whitman included in *Leaves of Grass* a two-line poem entitled: "Roaming in Thought (*After reading Hegel*)": "Roaming in thought over the Universe, I saw the little that is Good steadily hastening towards immortality, / And the vast all that is call'd Evil I saw hastening to merge itself and become lost and dead."[2] It is Walt's "orbic flex" identified as the "triads of Hegel" that Henry will incorporate in his new (epic) poetry written in the role of the American bard.

Berryman's reference to "Walt's orbic flex" (which he will "incorporate" into the "know-how of the American bard" he feels himself becoming) is illuminated in the context of his essay, "'Song of Myself': Intention and Substance," written in 1957 but not published until 1976 (see discussion in chapter 1). As we have seen, the essay was Berryman's witness and confession, his witness to the impact of Whitman on him ("he operates with great power and beauty over a very wide range") and his confession to a shift in his own poetic allegiances. In this essay Berryman shows how he has Whitman's authority for not taking "Song of Myself" as a work of literature, but as a "work of *life*" (*FP*, pp. 227–28). In elaborating his meaning, Berryman discusses the *voice* of "Song of Myself," and notes: "it is . . . clear that the Johannine *Logos* (God's self-revelation, in Christ—whose name is Word, as His Father's is I AM or Being) influenced Whitman's thought even more than his passion for grand opera, which dominates section 26: 'The orbic flex of his mouth is pouring and filling me full'" (*FP*, p. 231). Some readers will be surprised at such a theological interpretation of this section of "Song of Myself," especially in view of the full context of the "orbic flex" passage: "A tenor large and fresh as the creation fills me, / The orbic flex of his mouth is pouring and filling me full." But Berryman is developing a thesis about voice in "Song of Myself" that places "orbic flex" at the heart of his understanding of Whitman. After quoting a number of "Song of Myself" passages which show Whitman taking in and then voicing *out*, filling up and then pouring forth, Berryman remarks: "The poet—one would say, a mere channel, but with its own ferocious difficulties—fills with experiences, a valve opens; he speaks them. I am obliged to remark that I prefer this theory of poetry to those that have ruled the critical quarterlies since I was an undergraduate twenty-five years ago. It is as humble as, and identical with, Keats's view of the poet as having no existence, but being 'forever in, for, and filling' other things" (*FP*, p. 232).

Thus Berryman associates "Walt's orbic flex" with a "theory of poetry" in conflict with the long dominant New Critical theories, and declares himself for Whitman's. The sharpness with which Berryman places these two "theories" in opposition may be seen in a long comment he makes after quoting Whitman's line, "A great poem is no finish to a man or woman but rather a beginning." Berryman says:

> It is this last quotation that brings him into conflict with current aesthetics, that of the artwork made, finished, autonomous. (Let us concede at once that *The Waste Land* winds up with various bogus instructions, and so might be thought to aim at a beginning; but except for the lines about "the awful daring of a moment's surrender," all this end of that poem is its weakest, most uneasy, crudest, least inventive, most willed part.) The conflict is absolute equally in Whitman's formulation of the fourth or *personal* intention [here Berryman is referring to the fourth of four purposes of Whitman he has identified earlier in the essay: national, religious, metaphysical, personal]. "'Leaves of Grass' . . ." he says, "has mainly been the outcroppings of my own emotional and personal nature—an attempt, from first to last, to put *a Person*, a human being (myself, in the latter part of the Nineteenth Century, in America,) freely, fully and truly on record." (*FP*, pp. 229–30)

Berryman thus places Whitman's role as "spiritual historian" in sharp contrast with Eliot's role as impersonal "maker."

At another critical juncture in *The Dream Songs* (Song 279) at the beginning of section VII (the last), Whitman appears once again:

> Leaving behind the country of the dead
> where he must then return & die himself
> he set his tired face due East
> where the sun rushes up the North Atlantic
> and where had paused a little the war for bread
> & the war for status had ceased
>
> forever, and he took with him five books,
> a Whitman & a Purgatorio,
> a one-volume dictionary,
> an Oxford Bible with all its bays & nooks
> & bafflements long familiar to Henry
> & one other new book-O.
>
> If ever he had crafted in the past—
> but only if—he swore now to craft better
> which lay in the Hands above.
> He said: I'll work on slow, O slow & fast,
> if a letter comes I will answer that letter
> & my whole year will be tense with love.

We may take the reading list here as significant for the form of the poem Henry-Berryman is writing. He has been awarded a Guggenheim and is headed for Ireland, secure financially (at least for the moment) and personally ("forever"), and ready to continue his epic in progress. The books he takes along are the dictionary, the Bible, a Dante, and a Whitman. The signals fly thick and fast that Berryman is committing his lot with the major poets. The Bible for reference (deep), perhaps; but Dante and Whitman for models, the latter homegrown, his immediate paradigm. And there is that additional volume—"one other new book-O"—surely his own *Dream Songs* now approaching their final section, and built on a scale with Dante and Whitman: a new American epic in the new mode—but in the old spirit.

In a 1971 interview with Joseph Haas, Berryman replied to a question about his "intention" in *The Dream Songs*: "It developed quite rapidly. The idea was, sort of, the way Whitman puts his idea about 'Leaves of Grass.' The idea is to record a personality, to make him visible, put him through tests, see what the hell he's up to, and through him, the country—and to commit him to his country." Berryman is clearly remembering the Whitman passage (putting a "personality . . . truly on record") that he quoted in his 1957 essay as central to Whitman's theory. But what does Berryman mean, "commit him to his country"? He immediately adds: "We have an atrocious government, very bad, and yet this country is magnificent. My people have been here since before the Revolution, except for one great-great-grandmother. So while I agree that our record as a nation is atrocious, it makes you sweat, still you have to be committed to this idea and its possibilities. I don't blame the kids, though, for waking up sweating."[3] *This idea and its possibilities*: Whitman tried to define it and them in *Democratic Vistas*. The Berryman commitment, then, is not to the America of reality, but (like Whitman's) to the America of possibilities, of *vistas*.

In another interview recorded in 1970, and published posthumously in the winter 1972 *Paris Review*, Berryman called attention to the Whitmanian model in a context suggesting the kind of radical shift in his work we have found adumbrated in Dream Song 78 (in which Henry disintegrates, stripped to Whitmanian and Cranean elements): "In *Homage to Mistress Bradstreet* [Berryman's first long poem] my model was *The Waste Land*, and *Homage to Mistress Bradstreet* is as unlike *The Waste Land* as it is possible for me to be. I think the model in *The Dream Songs* was the other greatest American poem—I am very ambitious—"Song of Myself"—a very long poem, about sixty pages."[4] In *Homage to Mistress Bradstreet* was published as a book in 1956. *The Dream Songs* was published in its entirety in 1968 (put in a single volume in 1969), representing a labor, Berryman says, of thirteen years. But when Berryman speaks of shifting his models, he certainly is not casting all accumulated freight overboard to take on new; rather he sees himself as shifting primarily his focus and vision.

2

Berryman's comparison of *The Dream Songs* with "Song of Myself" offers useful insights into his conception of his own work:

The poem [*The Dream Songs*] does not go as far as "Song of Myself." What I mean by that is this: Whitman denies that "Song of Myself" is a long poem. He has a passage saying that he had long thought that there was no such thing as a long poem and that when he read Poe he found that Poe summed up the problem for him. But there it is, sixty pages. What's the notion? He doesn't regard it as a literary work at all, in my opinion—he doesn't quite say so. It proposes a new religion—it is what is called in Old Testament criticism a wisdom work, a work on the meaning of life and how to conduct it. Now I don't go that far—*The Dream Songs* is a literary composition, it's a long poem—but I buy a little of it. I think Whitman is right with regard to "Song of Myself." I'm prepared to submit to his opinion. He was crazy, and I don't contradict madmen. When William Blake says something, I say thank you, even though he has uttered the most hopeless fallacy that you can imagine. I'm willing to be their loving audience. I'm just hoping to hear something marvelous from time to time, marvelous and true. Of course *The Dream Songs* does not propose a new system: that is not the point. In that way it is unlike "Song of Myself." It remains a literary work.[5]

When Berryman says ambiguously "Now I don't go that far . . . but I buy a little of it," he is obliquely characterizing *The Dream Songs* as, at least in a small way, a "wisdom work." In any event, the context here—the Bible, Whitman, Blake—suggests the kind of tradition with which Berryman expected *The Dream Songs* to link.

But if, as Berryman puts it, *The Dream Songs* differs from "Song of Myself" in not proposing a new religion, then how are they similar? Particularly in view of Berryman's repeated assertions that his "hero" Henry is not himself, John Berryman. Walter Whitman places a hero in "Song of Myself" (as in the rest of *Leaves of Grass*) and names him in the poem (section 24): "Walt Whitman, a kosmos, of Manhattan the son, / Turbulent, fleshy, sensual, eating, drinking, and breeding." And of course this Walt Whitman is linked to the "I" of the poem—"I speak the pass-word primeval, I give the sign of democracy." What does Berryman mean when he says he is not Henry? Does he mean anything more than that, with all the close links, there is a gap between the poetic personality Walt Whitman and the historical Walter Whitman, subject of biographies of the poet? In his 1957 essay on Whitman, Berryman observed that "a poet's first personal pronoun is nearly always ambiguous," but he accepted Whitman's assertion that the "I" of the poem was rooted in some sense in his own personality (*FP*, p. 230).

In a 1969 interview, Berryman, asked what the relationship between him and Henry was, replied: "I think I'll leave that one to the critics. Henry does resemble me, and I resemble Henry; but on the other hand I am not Henry. You know, I pay income tax; Henry pays no income tax. And bats come over and they stall in my hair—and fuck them, I'm not Henry; Henry doesn't have any bats." The disclaimer is tricky, and needs to be put in the context of another statement made in the same interview. Asked why he refers to *The Dream Songs* as one poem, he answers: "Ah—it's personality—it's Henry. He thought up all these things over all the years. The reason I call it one poem is the result of my strong disagreement with Eliot's line— the impersonality of poetry, an idea he got partly from Keats (a letter) and partly from Goethe (again a letter). I'm very much against that; it seems to me on the contrary that poetry comes out of personality."[6] Here Berryman is on the brink of identifying himself with Henry, because such an identity (in some sense) is the only element that would make *The Dream Songs* "personal"; otherwise they would exemplify Eliot's impersonal theory (divorced from authorial actuality).

Is, then, Berryman playing games when denying that he is Henry? Here he is on the same subject in his 1970 interview:

> Suppose I take this business of the relation of Henry to me, which has interested so many people, and which is categorically denied by me in one of the forewords. Henry both is and is not me, obviously. We touch at certain points. But I am an actual human being; he is nothing but a series of conceptions—my conceptions. I brush my teeth; unless I say so somewhere in the poem—I forget whether I do or not—he doesn't brush his teeth. He only does what I make him do. If I have succeeded in making him believable, he performs all kinds of other actions besides those named in the poem, but the reader has to make them up. That's the world.

Only a page or so after this explanation, Berryman is talking along about his "Bradstreet" poem and becomes temporarily confused. He is describing how, at the moment when he began the major writing of the "Bradstreet" poem, he had with one exception a good idea of the direction of the poem: "The great exception was this; it did not occur to me to have a dialogue between them—to insert bodily Henry into the poem . . . Me, to insert me, in my own person, John Berryman, I, into the poem." Asked by his interviewer, "Was that a Freudian slip?" Berryman answers: "I don't know. Probably. Nothing is accidental, except physics."[7]

All these statements, including his disclaimer in his prefatory Note to *The Dream Songs* (Henry is "not the poet, not me"), when reduced to their essence, and placed in the context of a careful reading of *The Dream Songs* itself, suggest a good deal less than meets the eye. When a poet (lyric or lyric-epic) puts himself in his work, that self immediately becomes in some sense *other* (while remaining closely linked), a being in a work of art, one self-conception (and therefore imaginative) among many that the poet will have on his way from birth to death. We may then, with this understanding, and using the usual precautions in talking about works of art, see Berryman as a presence in his work in the same way we see other poets of the lyric-epic present in theirs.

3

At the same time that Berryman has been ambivalent about the relationship of himself to Henry, he has been generally ambiguous about the structure of *The Dream Songs*. But he has not hesitated to apply the word "epic" to his work. Asked if he knew how long *The Dream Songs* would be when he began, he answered: "No, I didn't. But I was aware that I was embarked on an epic." And again: "When I finished *The Dream Songs*, two years ago, I was very tired. I didn't know whether I would ever write any more poems.... I saw myself only as an epic poet. The idea of writing any more short poems hadn't been in my mind for many years."[8] The casualness with which Berryman can refer to his poem as an epic suggests how firmly established the personal epic had become by the time he had finished his poem.

But the question of structure arose again and again. In his 1969 interview, Berryman was asked if there was "any ulterior structure to the *Dream Songs*." He replied playfully: "Ah—you mean, somebody can get to be an associate professor or an assistant professor by finding it out?... there is none.... There's not a trace of it. Some of the songs are in alphabetical order; but, mostly, they just belong to areas of hope and fear that Henry is going through at a given time. That's how I worked them out." Question from the interviewer: "In the last volume you said, the poem's ultimate structure is according to Henry's nature." And Berryman answers: "Now, that's right." The interviewer presses: "So, in fact, the book has no plot?" Berryman: "Those are fighting words. It has a plot. Its plot is the personality of Henry as he moves on in the world. Henry gains ten years. At one time his age is given as forty-one, 'Free, black, and forty-one,' and at a later point he's fifty-one. So the poem spans a large area, you see that."[9]

In his *Paris Review* interview, Berryman touched on the structure again, in effect implying a definition of the "open-ended" structure of the personal epic:

> The narrative such as it is developed as I went along, partly out of my gropings into and around Henry and his environment and associates, partly out of my readings in theology and that sort of thing, taking place during thirteen years—awful long time—and third, out of certain partly preconceived and partly developing as I went along, sometimes rigid and sometimes plastic, structural notions. That is why the work is divided into seven books, each book of which is rather well unified, as a matter of fact. Finally I left the poem open to the circumstances of my personal life. For example, obviously if I hadn't got a Guggenheim and decided to spend it in

Dublin, most of book VII wouldn't exist. I have a personality and a plan, a metrical plan—which is original.

Deflected momentarily in a discussion of his "metrical plan," Berryman comes back to his structure: "I had a personality and a plan and all kinds of philosophical and theological notions. . . . But at the same time I was what you might call open-ended. That is to say, Henry to some extent was in the situation that we are all in in actual life—namely, he didn't know and I didn't know what the bloody fucking hell was going to happen next. Whatever it was he had to confront it and get through. For example, he dies in book IV and is dead throughout the book, but at the end of the poem he is still alive, and in fairly good condition, after having died himself *again*."[10] Characteristically, as he clears up some enigmas, Berryman strews the path with new ones for the reader to puzzle over. But his description of the "open-ended" structure of *The Dream Songs* could be lifted virtually intact and applied,. with changes of dates and names and titles, to the structure of many other personal epics of the contemporary period.

4

The language of *The Dream Songs* is one of its most distinctive features, causing Berryman himself to call attention to it in his prefatory Note:

> Many opinions and errors in the Songs are to be referred not to the character Henry, still less to the author, but to the title of the work. It is idle to reply to critics, but some of the people who addressed themselves to 77 *Dream Songs* went so desperately astray (one apologized about it in print, but who ever sees apologies?) that I permit myself one word. The poem then, whatever its wide cast of characters, is essentially about an imaginary character (not the poet, not me) named Henry, a white American in early middle age sometimes in blackface, who has suffered an irreversible loss and talks about himself sometimes in the first person, sometimes in the third, sometimes even in the second; he has a friend, never named, who addresses him as Mr Bones and variants thereof. Requiescant in pace.

To plunge into *The Dream Songs* without preparation is to be confronted with a language that seems a mixture of drunken talk, black talk (or even pseudo-black talk), or (to take the clue of the title) dream talk verging at times on childish or baby talk. What justification can there be for such an ungrammatical, anti-English English? An English that at its roots is pure American?

The answer to the question is (as Berryman suggests) complex. But the nature of his cast of characters is basic. In his 1969 interview, asked why he had chosen to "employ the Negro dialect" in *The Dream Songs*, Berryman answered: "Well, that's a tough question. I'll tell you. I wrote a story once called 'The Imaginary Jew.' I was in Union Square in New York, waiting to see my girl, and I was taken for a Jew (I had a beard at the time). There was a tough Irishman who wanted to beat me up, and I got into the conversation, and I couldn't convince them that I wasn't a Jew. Well, the Negro business—the blackface—is related to that. That is, I feel extremely lucky to be white, let me put it that way, so that I don't have that problem. Friends of mine—Ralph Ellison, for example, in my opinion one of the best writers in the country—he has the problem. He's black, and he and Fanny, wherever they go, they are black."[11] Basic to the choice and nature of Berryman's language, then, is a political dimension: at least this comes through his instinctive response in answering questions about the language.

But there is a vaudeville form containing the Negro dialect that is important to *The Dream Songs*—a form that Berryman discovered to be unfamiliar to some readers. One of his young interviewers asked him in 1969—"Why is Henry called 'Mr Bones'?" Berryman answered: "There's a minstrel show thing of Mr Bones and the interlocutor. There's a wonderful remark, which I meant to use as an epigraph, but I never got around to it. 'We were all end-men' . . . that's what it says—'we were all end-men.'" Asked "who said that," Berryman replies: "One of the great minstrels. Isn't that adorable? 'We were all end-men, and interlocutors.' I wanted someone for Henry to talk to, so I took up another minstrel, the interlocutor, and made him a friend of my friend, Henry. He is never named; I know his name, but the critics haven't caught on yet. Sooner or later some assistant professor will become an associate professor by learning the name of Henry's friend."[12] Berryman's spoof cannot hide the seriousness with which he takes the dramatic structure he has invented for *The Dream Songs*, a structure taken over from an old American popular art form, the minstrel show.

Minstrel shows reached their peak of popularity in the mid-1800s, but, of course, survived into the twentieth century. One of the most popular was the Christy Minstrels, but all of them used the same format. They presented white men in black face lined up across the stage, with two end men and Mr. Interlocutor (in the center and remaining white). The end men were called Tambo and Mr. Bones, and they were always the butt of the jokes initiated by Mr. Interlocutor, but they invariably turned the tables and made him the butt, directly or indirectly. Berryman has taken two of these characters for his interior drama—the interlocutor and Mr. Bones. When in his prefatory Note Berryman says that Henry sometimes "talks about himself in the first person, sometimes in the third, sometimes even in the second," he is evading one of the problems the reader faces, particularly as he gets deeper and deeper in *The Dream Songs*: there is a voice that recurs that seems less and less like the voice of Henry, Bones, or the Interlocutor, and more and more like the voice of the poet himself (a confusion for the reader quite similar to that in *Paterson*, as Williams himself seems to take over the form of his invented Dr. Paterson in the poem). But the question is purely academic, because the secret of *The Dream Songs* is that all the characters of the poem are one—the poet himself: versions of the self, levels of consciousness. The "I" in its plainest form is closest to the poet's exterior life (a poet, a friend of Roethke, Jarrell, Williams, a man who wins Guggenheims); Henry is closer to the poet's interior life, the part that might escape the biographers because records of it seldom survive; the Interlocutor is the poet addressing this interior self; and when Henry becomes Mr. Bones, he is a version of the poet from the deepest levels of his consciousness, perhaps at the edge of the unconscious. The temptation is to label these versions of the self the superego, the ego, and the id, but this would be to force too rigid a structure on Berryman's easy-flowing forms. It is enough to know that *The Dream Songs* contains an intermingling of exterior and interior voices, all emanating from the same self—the poet's. Thus the poem is personal in the best sense of the word.

The title, after all, is *dream songs*. It is appropriate in dreams that we discover ourselves on various levels of consciousness, in touch somehow with the unconscious. Mr. Bones may be down there deep within the psyche, and we may be calling him from up above as Mr. Interlocutor. When Berryman said that his unused epigraph read, "We are all end-men, and interlocutors," he suggested the collapsed identities of his various characters. We are all both end-men and interlocutors, playing the one to the other, inside. And, too, Berryman touched on the universality of his meanings in this unused epigraph: we are all Henry, we are all interlocutors, we are all Mr. Bones; we discover within ourselves the various levels of response to experience that Berryman himself finds. In this sense, then, Henry is everyman, and Mr. Bones is everyman's alter ego.

Berryman makes a point of indicating that his "metrical plan" is his own, an original, and one which he started with and stuck to throughout: "I don't use other people as metrical models. I don't put down people who do—I just don't feel satisfied with them."[13] Berryman's verse form is surprisingly regular in its basic pattern—three stanzas of six lines each, with some, but not regular, rhymes. It is possible that there were so many variables in his "open-ended" form that Berryman felt more comfortable with some regularization of the metrics of his poem. The counted lines provide a steadying discipline within which to produce a poem that might strike out in any direction. Clearly it served him well—as the triadic, variable-foot line did Williams. Moreover, the free-swinging, ungrammatical, "undisciplined" language of The Dream Songs perhaps appears all the more striking in what looks like some kind of variation of the sonnet-form. In any case, the "metrical plan" served rather than hindered, and seems a part of the revolutionary nature of Berryman's whole poetic enterprise.

5

Berryman has said that it took him two years to get over the writing of his "Bradstreet" poem, first published in magazine version in 1953, as a book in 1956. He began work (or planning), then, in the mid-1950s and lived with the creation of The Dream Songs until publication of the last books in 1968—some thirteen years. The first three books were published in 1964 as 77 Dream Songs, the last four in 1968 as His Toy, His Dream, His Rest, and the two books joined as The Dream Songs in 1969.

The mid-1950s, then, was a critical moment in Berryman's career. It was at this time that he made the decision to remake himself as a poet, to give over the Eliotic kind of impersonal or "made" poetry that he had previously written and to launch a personal epic with an open-ended structure in the Whitmanian (or "orbic-flex") manner and tradition. His enthusiastic 1957 essay on "Song of Myself," with its extravagant praise of Whitman, provides an indirect account of his own poetic turmoil in change.

But it is The Dream Songs that provides the spiritual history of that remaking of the poetic self. The epic is in the broadest sense about Berryman's personal transfiguration from one kind of poet to another. As a newly committed personal poet, Berryman felt able for the first time in his poetry to confront the personal events of his life—as, for example, the earlier suicide of his father. The poetic remaking of the self, then, was in a sense a move to come to terms with the battering events of a difficult life.

Berryman's form, the interior "dream song," enables him to scramble chronology at will (as in a dream). But there is running throughout this work a recognizable "contemporary time" paralleling the time of the writing of the songs, roughly 1955–68, a period that provides the basic frame. But many poems break out of this frame into various levels of the past, treating those events that continue to haunt the poet.

Moreover, *The Dream Songs* has a symmetry of form in spite of its chaotic appearance. The first three books (*77 Dream Songs*) look back from the "contemporary time" frame to focus on the poet's life up through his first (or Eliotic) poetic identity. These books sketch in the long foreground of the poet before the radical change or remaking (death, resurrection) that comes in Book IV. They carry the poet not lineally but cyclically or spirally, to the point of publication of his poetry previous to writing of *The Dream Songs,* including *Homage to Mistress Bradstreet.* The short Book IV ("Op. posth. nos. 1–14"), the only book with a title, dramatizes the death of the old and the birth (or self-resurrection) of the new (or Whitmanian) poetic identity. When asked about Book IV in 1969, Berryman answered, "*Opus Posthumus* is just a recovery from the end of book three in the first volume of *Dream Songs.* The placement of the poems in *Dream Songs* is purely personal."[14] The new being that comes "back" to life in Book IV is clearly the poet who will embark on *The Dream Songs,* written in a style radically different from that of all his previous poetry. The last three books of the work, balancing the first three, focus on this new identity—and the problems of writing a long epic poem in the Whitman tradition. These last books carry the poet through significant stages of his later life to a deeper awareness of some of his most persistent personal problems (or recurring nightmares), to resolution of them or resignation to their endurance.

The "narrative" outlined above is embedded in a cyclic or spiral structure encrusted with a multitude of themes—those that enter the poet's consciousness over the years of the poem's writing (1955–68), carrying the poet from his forty-first year to his fifty-fourth; themes supplemented by memories and imaginative extensions, memories of past years (especially the poet's all-important boyhood) and imaginative re-creations of national or world events.

Berryman has said he thought each of the seven books of the poem "rather well unified." He may have offered a clue to this sequence of unities by the epigraphs he provides, three that stand at the beginning of *77 Dream Songs*, and four at the beginning of *His Toy, His Dream, His Rest*. These epigraphs appear to have thematic relevance to the particular books to which they attach. Reading *The Dream Songs*, then, might most usefully begin with a stroll through each of the seven books in order, remaining alert to the resonance of the various epigraphs and attentive to the clues relating to the unity of individual books, especially as the books embody structural elements from the poet's own life. Such a reading will help provide a sense of the work's overall movement, particularly as it embodies Berryman's development as a poet and dramatizes his ultimate, and crucial, self-transfiguration from an Eliotic *impersonal* poet into a Whitmanian *personal* poet, in the throes of launching, writing, and finishing a major personal epic, *The Dream Songs*:

77 Dream Songs

I. Dream Songs 1–26: "Go in, brack man, de day's yo' own." The epigraph is obviously an epigraph of beginnings, an exhortation to "go in" to life because the time—for the time being (a day)—is "yo' own." The Negro dialect of the epigraph is appropriate for introducing the black language of the poem (as derived from the tradition of the minstrel shows). The epigraph (Berryman does not cite the source) is a command from the fates (or God) to the poet to take what life has dealt (there is, after all, no other). The section then does indeed open with a childhood incident that the fates have dealt the poet, and that will haunt *The Dream Songs* to the end (the suicide of his father, discussed below).

Some of the poems of this section reveal dates through their subjects, as for example Song 18, "Strut for Roethke," occasioned by Theodore Roethke's death in 1963; or Song 23, "The Lay of Ike," which by its reference to Adlai Stevenson may date from the election of 1956. The placement of these two poems shows that Berryman was not simply placing poems in order of subject or writing. The last poem of this section, Song 26, suggests the movement of Henry from one stage of his life to another:

> The glories of the world struck me, made me aria, once.
> —What happen then, Mr Bones?
> if you cares to say.
> —Henry. Henry become interested in women's bodies,
> his loins were & were the   scene of stupendous achieve-
>   ment.
> Stupor. Knees, dear. Pray.

> All the knobs & softnesses of, my God,
> the ducking & trouble it swarm on Henry,
> at one time.
> —What happen then, Mr Bones?
> you seems excited-like.
> —Fell Henry back into   the original crime: art, rime
>
> besides a sense of others, my God, my God,
> and a jealousy for the honour (alive) of his country,
> what can get more odd?
> and discontent with the thriving gangs & pride.
> —What happen then, Mr Bones?
> —I had a most marvellous   piece of luck. I died.

We might guess that Henry-Berryman refers here to a youthful love affair (perhaps one like that which inspired the writing of the *Sonnets*, held back from publication until 1967). He thus turned to the "original crime" (original sin, sex): "art, rime." Because of this "glory" that made him "aria," the first Henry "died," and a new Henry—the poet—was born.

II. Dream Songs 27–51: "...I am their musick" (Lam. 3–63). The epigraph is appropriate for the incarnation of Henry as poet. There are several easy clues as to the dates of these poems. Later in Song 154 Henry reveals that he was in Asia in 1957; and Asia is the setting of Songs 27 and 31. And, too, there is an elegy for Robert Frost, who died in 1963, running through Songs 37–39. Song 40 makes specific mention of the poet's age:

> Wishin was dyin but I gotta make
> it all this way to that bed on these feet
> where peoples said to meet.
> Maybe but even if I see my son
> forever never, get back on the take,
> free, black & forty-one.

Whitman had announced at the beginning of "Song of Myself": "I, now thirty-seven years old in perfect health begin." Berryman, unlike Whitman, is "scared a lonely," but he is "free" (perhaps from a marriage), "black" (perhaps in the psychic-spiritual sense, from inner scarring), and "forty-one"; the year, then, 1955.

The closing poems of this section present glimpses of Henry in the role of poet. In the next-to-last (Song 50), his paranoia becomes the subject:

> In a motion of night they massed nearer my post.
> I hummed a short blues. When the stars went out

> I studied my weapons system.
> Grenades, the portable rack, the yellow spout
> of the anthrax-ray: in order. Yes, and most
> of my pencils were sharp.

And in Song 51 (the last of the section), there is something of an apology for Henry's poetry:

> Our wounds to time, from all the other times,
> sea-times slow, the times of galaxies
> fleeing, the dwarfs' dead times,
> lessen so little that if here in his crude rimes
> Henry them mentions, do not hold it, please,
> for a putting of man down.

Time has been so wounded by all the past time so severely that the wounding has not been "lessened" by Henry's time—and thus he writes about it in his poetry. His observation could apply both cosmically (as in the imagery here) and also personally (as in the case of his father's suicide). Berryman turns to "Ol' Marster" and asks for *his* confession:

> Ol' Marster, being bound you do your best
> versus we coons, spare now a cagey John
> a whilom bits that whip:
> who'll tell your fortune, when you have confessed
> whose & whose woundings—against the innocent stars
> & remorseless seas—
>
> —Are you radioactive, pal? —Pal, radioactive.
> —Has you the night sweats & the day sweats, pal?
> —Pal, I do.
> —Did your gal leave you? —What do *you* think, pal?
> —Is that thing on the front of your head what it seems to
>   be, pal?
> —Yes, pal.

Clearly another phase of Henry's life (as well as a love affair) has come to an end and he is in spiritual crisis ("radioactive"), anticipating—preparing for—a fundamental change, a new direction.

III. Dream Songs 52–77: "But there is another method" (Olive Schreiner). The epigraph, in the ambiguity of the word "method," suggests the ambiguity of the new phase of Henry's life: a new method of living, a new strategy for experience, a new way of art? Perhaps a bit of all. At the beginning of the section we find Henry in the hospital, recuperating: "Will Henry again ever be on the lookout for women & milk" (Song 52); "He lay in the middle of the world, and twitcht" (Song 53). Henry contemplates life: "I prop on the costly bed & dream of my wife, / my first wife, / and my second wife & son," and he observes, "They are shooting me full of sings" (Song 54). In Song 67, Henry describes an operation, self-performed, that suggests the transfiguration he is willing for himself:

> I am obliged to perform in complete darkness
> operations of great delicacy
> on my self.
> —Mr Bones, you terrifies me.
> No wonder they don't pay you. Will you die?
> —My
>   friend, I succeeded. Later.

This may well be a necessary prelude to the transition to be described in the death-resurrection poems of Book IV.

The songs in the latter part of Book III are filled with references to Henry's writing (Song 74):

> Henry hates the world. What the world to Henry
> did will not bear thought.
> Reeling no pain,
> Henry stabbed his arm and wrote a letter
> explaining how bad it had been
> in this world.

In Song 75, Henry publishes his writing:

> Turning it over, considering, like a madman
> Henry put forth a book.
> No harm resulted from this.
> Neither the menstruating   stars (nor man) was moved
> at once.
> Bare dogs drew closer for a second look
>
> and performed their friendly operations there.
> Refreshed, the bark rejoiced.
> Seasons went and came.
> Leaves fell, but only a few.

We might assume this book to be a composite of Berryman's early books of poetry, but it might be taken as *Homage to Mistress Bradstreet* (a kind of letter), published in 1956, which met a mixed critical reception. It clearly represented a culmination in Berryman's career of one kind of writing, what might be called the New Critical style (dense, hard, learned, difficult) of Eliot and his followers which prevailed from the time of *The Waste Land,* a poem which Berryman took as a model for his own.

The last poem of Book III, Song 77, portrays Henry ready for the change which he has throughout this section glimpsed in process:

> Seedy Henry rose up shy in de world
> & shaved & swung his barbells, duded Henry up
> and p.a.'d poor thousands of persons on topics of grand
> moment to Henry, ah to those less & none.
> Wif a book of his in either hand
> he is stript down to move on.
>
> —Come away, Mr Bones.
>
> —Henry is tired of the winter,
> & haircuts, & squeamish comfy   ruin-prone proud na-
>   tional
>   mind,   & Spring (in the city so called).
> Henry likes Fall.
> Hé would be prepared to live in a world of Fáll
> for ever, impenitent Henry.
> But the snows and summers grieve & dream;
>
> thése fierce & airy occupations, and love,
> raved away so many of Henry's years
> it is a wonder that, with in each hand
> one of his own mad books and all,
> ancient fires for eyes, his head full
> & his heart full, he's making ready to move on.

If one of his own books he has in his hands is *Homage to Mistress Bradstreet,* the other may well be his book on Stephen Crane (1950) or an earlier book of poems (*The Dispossessed,* 1948). In any case, the poem is full of references to the end of a major phase, chronological and creative, in Henry-Berryman's life, and the restless readiness, even eagerness, to "move on."

His Toy, His Dream, His Rest

IV. Dream Songs 78–91 (Op. posth. nos. 1–14): "No interesting project can be embarked on without fear. I shall be scared to death half the time" (Sir Francis Chichester in Sydney). The epigraph suggests explorations of unknown lands, confrontations of the strange and new. The key term is "scared to death"—not a real death; Henry's figurative death lasts for fourteen songs. In some of the most brilliant poetry in all *The Dream Songs*, Henry describes his dissolution and death, and then his self-resurrection. This passage in Henry's career might be described as his dark night of the soul, or the death of one self and the birth of another. We have already examined "Op. posth. no. 1," with Henry's reference to Whitman's "orbic flex" and to Stephen Crane, and to himself as the "American bard" ("embarrassed Henry heard himself a-being"). The suggestion is clear that the transfiguration Henry is undergoing is in large part literary, from lyric to bardic poet, from the Eliot "impersonal" tradition to the Whitman "personal" tradition.

Henry imagines (Song 79) his obituary in the *New York Times*, imagines that "Statues & rhymes / signal his fiery Passage," and cries out a warning: "let this day be his, throughout the town, / region & cosmos, lest he freeze our blood / with terrible returns." And he discovers (in Song 81) that in the grave "they will take off your hands, / both hands; as well as your both feet, & likewise / both eyes, / might be discouraging to a bloody hero / Also you stifle, like you can't draw breath. / But this is death—" And then he considers, "It wasn't so much after all to lose . . . / A body." Henry sends forth a message (Song 82): "Herewith ill-wishes. From a cozy grave / rainbow I scornful laughings." But his "cozy grave" has its discomforts (Song 85): "Flak. An eventful thought came to me, / who squirm in my hole. How will the matter end? . . . / My wood or word seems to be rotting." Moreover, "The cold is ultimating. The cold is cold," and Henry feels himself breaking up: "and Henry now has come to a full stop— / vanisht his vision, if there was, & fold / him over himself quietly."

There are many references to poetry and writing throughout these dark songs (as in "wood or word" above), and Song 83 indicates that the experience the poet is undergoing has bestowed on him a new knowledge he is ready to impart:

> I recall a boil, whereupon as I had to sit,
> just where, and when I had to, for deadlines.
> O I could learn to type standing,
> but isn't it slim to be slumped off from that,
> problems undignified, fiery dig salt mines?—
> Content on one's back flat:
>
> coming no deadline—is all ancient nonsense—
> no typewriters—ha! ha!—no typewriters—
> alas!
> for I have much to open, I know immense
> troubles & wonders to their secret curse.
> Yet when erect on my ass,

> pissed off, I sat two-square, I kept shut my mouth
> and stilled my nimble fingers across keys.
> That is I stood up.
> Now since down I lay, void of love & ruth,
> I'd howl my knowings, only there's the earth
> overhead. Plop!

Here perhaps is an almost direct statement of the poetic change the poet is undergoing. The poet knows "immense / troubles & wonders to their secret curse," but before (before this "death"), he had "kept shut his mouth / and stilled my nimble fingers across keys." That is, before, the poet had written the kind of "impersonal" poetry approved by the poetic establishment. But now, in what he has learned from this low level to which his life has been hurled, "void of love & ruth," he is ready (like Allen Ginsberg) to "howl" his "knowings." But alas, "there's the earth / overhead." Real death would, of course, still the poet's howl. But in this death, the poet can will his life, and dig his own self up.

In the concluding poem of Book IV (Song 91), Henry is saved:

> Noises from underground made gibber some
> others collected & dug Henry up
> saying 'you *are* a sight.'
> Chilly, he muttered for a double rum
> waving the mikes away, putting a stop
> to rumours, pushing his fright
>
> off with the now accumulated taxes
> accustomed in his way to solitude
> and no bills.
> Wives came forward, claiming a new Axis,
> fearful for their insurance, though, now, glued
> to disencumbered Henry's many ills.
>
> A fortnight later, sense a single man
> upon the trampled scene at 2 a.m.
> insomnia-plagued, with a shovel
> digging like mad, Lazarus with a plan
> to get his own back, a plan, a stratagem
> no newsman will unravel.

The digging up of the body is performed by others; but the resurrection of the new self is done in secret by Henry-poet—the only one who knows that there has been a new identity born in the grave of the old.

V. Dream Songs 92–145: "For my part I am always frightened, and very much so. I fear the future of all engagements" (Gordon in Khartoum). The new life is fearful: Book V represents the recovery from death and the emergence into the new life—but with "fear of the future" endemic. The opening Song 92 finds Henry in the hospital, "Something black somewhere   in the vistas of his heart." In Song 94: "Ill lay he long, upon this last return, / unvisited. The doctors put everything in the hospital / into reluctant Henry / and the nurses took it out & put it back, / smiling like fiends, with their eternal 'we.' / Henry did a slow burn."

In one poem (Song 104), Henry celebrates his birthday: "Welcome, grinned Henry, welcome, fifty-one! / I never cared for fifty, when nothing got done / The hospitals were fun / in certain ways, and an honour or so, / but on the whole fifty was a mess as though / heavy clubs from below / and from—God save the bloody mark—above / were loosed upon his skull & soles." Berryman would have been fifty-one years old in 1965, a year signaled again by several references to Randall Jarrell's death, as in Songs 121 and 127 (a death mourned also in Book IV, Song 90). In Song 133, Berryman questions some of the side benefits of his new identity (recognition that has come with the publication of *77 Dream Songs*, including a Pulitzer Prize):

> As he grew famous—ah, but what is fame?—
> he lost his old obsession with his name,
> things seemed to matter less,
> including the fame—a television team came
> from another country to make a film of him
> which did not him distress:
>
> he enjoyed the hard work & he was good at that,
> so they all said—the charming Englishmen
> among the camera & the lights
> mathematically wandered in his pub & livingroom
> doing their duty, as too he did it,
> but where are the delights
>
> of long-for fame, unless fame makes him feel easy?
> I am cold & weary, said Henry, fame makes me feel lazy,
> yet I must do my best.
> It doesn't matter, truly. It doesn't matter truly.
> It seems to be solely a matter of continuing Henry
> voicing & obsessed.

The fame is empty, and doesn't indeed matter. What does matter to the new Berryman is "continuing Henry / voicing & obsessed"—that is, the continuation of his epic in his new poetic style.

And that continuation is the battle, the outcome never certain.

Song 140: "Henry is vanishing. In the first of dawn / he fails a little, which he figured on. / Henry broods & recedes. / Like the great Walt, come find him on his way / somewhere. I hear thunder in stillness." And later: "It's a race with Time & that is all it is." That is all—but it is *all*. Henry sees himself (like Whitman) on the open road, on his way—"somewhere." But where? The destination remains hidden from view. The last three songs of Book V are devoted to the father's suicide—an attempt to come to final terms with the terrible fact of it, thus signaling a new stage in the poet's journey in his new identity.

VI. Dream Songs 146–278: "I am pickt up and sorted to a pip. My imagination is a monastery and I am its monk" (Keats to Shelley). If *The Dream Songs* may be called a death-haunted poem, Book VI is the most death-obsessed of all the poem's books. Allen Ginsberg, in describing one of his early "visions," has described "the complete death awareness that everybody has continuously with them all the time."[15] Here that "death awareness" has expanded so as to absorb almost the whole of consciousness. Like Pound in the "Pisan Cantos," or Ginsberg in the later sections of *The Fall of America*, Berryman mourns the dead, and counts them over and over again, compulsively. We have already noted his elegies for the various dead poets (Roethke, Frost, Jarrell). Book VI (Song 146) opens with the poet sensing the presence of the dead—"round me the dead / lie in their limp postures"—and brooding on himself: "Their deaths were theirs. I wait on for my own, / I dare say it won't be long. / I have tried to be them, god knows I have tried, / but they are past it all, I have not done." The death of Delmore Schwartz (in 1966) has called forth this lament, and Henry seems unable to lay the subject to rest (Song 147): "Henry's mind grew blacker the more he thought." In song after song, the elegy continues in growing bitterness (Song 153): "I'm cross with god who has wrecked this generation. / First he seized Ted, then Richard, Randall, and now Delmore. / In between he gorged on Sylvia Plath." But somehow the writing does not exorcise the pain of memory. Song 155: "I can't get him out of my mind, out of my mind"; Song 156: "I give in. I must not leave the scene of this same death"; Song 157: "Ten Songs, one solid block of agony."

In Book VI (the longest of all the sections) there are other deaths to mourn: Song 173, Richard Blackmur (died 1965); Song 193, Yvor Winters (died 1968); and other deaths to recall: Song 219, Wallace Stevens (died 1955). And in Song 224 Berryman presents a portrait of the eighty-year-old Pound at T. S. Eliot's burial ceremony in Westminster Abbey (1965). Delmore Schwartz's death, and those that followed, are no doubt reflected by the Keats epigraph to this book. The pursuing fates have indeed picked Henry up and sorted him to a "pip" (like a discarded seed); and in his loneliness he has become a monk in retreat in the monastery of his imagination.

But this retreat within is paralleled by increasing activity without, almost a frenzy of travel, lecturing, reading in the new (and really empty) fame that has come to the poet: Song 249: "I was off to spit a double lecture . . . wise with notes"; Song 250: "Let's put the road on the show." In Songs 251–53, entitled "Walking, Flying," the poet conveys some sense of the frenzied activities of these years:

> Henry wandered: west, south, north, and East,
> sometimes for money, sometimes for relief,
> sometimes of pure fatigue,
> sometimes a stroller through the mental feast
> found him at Schwetzingen or Avila
> or the Black Hills in Dakota,
>
> found him in bizarre Tangier or outside Dublin
> or inside the Palais des Papes at Avignon
> where the guide suddenly sang
> to show off the acoustics or in the Lakes to relax.

The place names continue to fly—Hong Kong, Bangkok—but their recital is curiously meaningless. Henry confesses: "but mostly travel is missing, by a narrow margin / things desired."

More and more as this book progresses, the subject becomes the writing of the poem being written. We learn in Song 267: "Book V is done." And as Book VI draws to a close, we learn that the poet is preparing, with Guggenheim fellowship in hand, to leave America for Ireland, there to continue his work away from all the distractions he has recounted in this seemingly endless Book VI. In Song 274, the poet's thoughts are already on his imminent trip: "I've booked our passage to a greener scene / and there my soul is earning. My insulted body / though still is earning here. / My o'ertaxed brain, in its units, hangs on between." Among the preparations made are the rugs rolled up, but more important—"my manuscripts are ready / for transport." Book VI ends with a sequence of farewells, which suggests that more than a voyage is in the offing, rather, the end of another phase, the beginning of a new, in Henry's long sojourn.

VII. Dream Songs 279–385: "He went away and never said goodbye. / I could read his letters but I sure can't read his mind. / I thought he's lovin me but he was leavin all the time. / Now I know that my true love was blind" (*Victoria Spivey?*) Berryman explained in his *Paris Review* interview: "if I hadn't got a Guggenheim and decided

to spend it in Dublin, most of book VII wouldn't exist.''[16] Clearly the
unity of this segment of Berryman's career gives a single focus to this
last book of his epic. Song 301 reveals the poet's age as fifty (1964) on
this trip to Ireland. And Song 341, set in Ireland, is entitled "The
Dialogue, aet. 51" (1965). More and more the finishing of the poem
becomes the subject of the poem. But, as the epigraph suggests,
separation is an important theme. Henry does review his old loves in
this book, but the epigraph might well apply to his father's suicide,
the departure of death—that veiled center of the poem's structure.

Book VII opens with Song 279 (discussed above) listing the five
books that the poet carries with him on his journey, including a
Whitman, a Dante, and his own "new book-O." In Song 293, Berryman considers the structure of his last book:

> What gall had he in him, so to begin Book VII
> or to design, out of its hotspur materials,
> its ultimate structure
> whereon will critics browse at large, at Heaven Eleven
> finding it was not cliffhangers or old serials
> but according to his nature

He is self-conscious about his "hotspur materials" (Hotspur is a var-
iant name for Henry–Prince Hal)—materials that arise out of spur-of-
the-moment experience but which must provide him the structure of
his concluding book as he submits it to the determining element of
the structure—his own "nature." He announces in Song 305 that he
has at last identified his theme:

> Like the sunburst up the white breast of a black-footed
>   penguin
> amid infinite quantities of gin
> Henry perceived his subject.
>
> It came nearer, like a guilty bystander,
> stood close, leaving no room to ponder,
> Mickey Mouse & The Tiger on the table.
>
> Leaving the ends aft open, touch the means,
> whereby we ripen. Touch by all means the means
> whereby we come to life,
> enduring the manner for the matter, ay
> I sing quickly, offered Henry, I
> sing more quickly.
>
> I sing with infinite slowness finite pain
> I have reached into the corner of my brain
> to have it out.

> I sat by fires when I was young, & now
> I'm not I sit by fires again, although
> I do it more slowly.

The means "whereby we ripen," "whereby we come to life": this is the subject he has pursued all along, only now fully realized. And the burden becomes weightier as he grows older. In Song 354, Henry cries out: "The only happy people in the world / are those who do not have to write long poems." And he knows the title of his next essay (which "will come out when / he wants it to"): "The Care & Feeding of Long Poems."

In Song 308, Berryman provides a set of "Instructions to Critics": "I feel the end is near / & strong of my large work, which will appear, and baffle everybody. / They'll seek the strange soul, in rain & mist, / whereas they should recall the pretty cousins they kissed, and stick with the sweet switch of the body." In Song 366, Berryman announces: "These Songs are not meant to be understood, you understand. / They are only meant to terrify & comfort." Whitman had written of *Leaves of Grass* (in "Shut Not Your Doors"): "The words of my book nothing, the drift of it everything."

As we read our way, with all these warnings, toward the end of *The Dream Songs,* we begin to sense a winding up (or at least a winding down) of a number of themes and obsessions. In Song 357, we learn that Henry's "leaving for America & things, / things." And we discover an entire sequence of determinations, transitions, conclusions in Song 359:

> In sleep, of a heart attack, let Henry go.
> The end of tennis. The beginning of the dark.
> The beginning of the wagon.
> It is the onward coming terrifies.
> Now at last the effort to make him kill himself
> has failed.
>
> Take down the thing then to which he was nailed.
> I am a boat was moored on the wrong shelf.
> Love has wings & flies.
> Amazed it could engineer such agony,
> Henry tried the world again   & again, falling short of the
>   mark.
> Unblock! let all griefs flow.
>
> There are more over there than over here,
> for welcome eerie. The whole city turned out
> to rustle Henry home.

He'd made his peace & would no further roam.
He wondered only what it was about.
He felt the news was near.

This song in which Henry has made his peace might have concluded the whole poem, but there are twenty-six more songs, most of them untangling some thread, or marveling at the nature of the tangle. There are terminations if not conclusions to the poet's (Henry's) questings—for knowledge (Song 370), for the secret of death (Songs 380, 382), for understanding of his father's suicide (Song 384). These, however, are better dealt with in the context of these developing themes (below). The very last song (385) of the book finds Henry noting that his "daughter's heavier," and that "Light leaves are flying"; "Fall comes to us as a prize / to rouse us toward our fate." And what is the fate? The poet can only remark the absolute gulf between the physical and the spiritual, as he watches (and "scolds") his daughter: "If there were a middle ground between things and the soul / or if the sky resembled more the sea, / I wouldn't have to scold / my heavy daughter." But there is no "middle ground," and his daughter will have to learn, like the poet, that she must live in this physical world with all its pain.

6

The most vital event of *The Dream Songs* is one which occurred long before the time of the loose "narrative frame" of the poem, but which haunts it throughout and provides its most deeply obsessive theme. Berryman was no doubt referring to it when he mentioned in his prefatory Note that Henry had "suffered an irreversible loss": the suicide of his father when the poet was only twelve years old. In his interview, Berryman recalls that he lost his childhood faith in Catholicism on that occasion: "Then all that went to pieces at my father's death, when I was twelve." Shortly after this comment in the interview, Berryman is describing his theory of what is necessary for great achievement: "Mostly you need ordeal. My idea is this: the artist is extremely lucky who is presented with the worst possible ordeal which will not actually kill him. At that point, he's in business. Beethoven's deafness, Goya's deafness, Milton's blindness, that kind of thing." His own future work, he says, will depend on his "being knocked in the face, and thrown flat, and given cancer, and all kinds of other things short of senile dementia. . . . I hope to be nearly crucified."[17] His ordeal for *The Dream Songs* clearly was his father's suicide. For it he almost suffered crucifixion, but after writing his long poem, he could say in Song 359: "Take down the thing then to which he was nailed."

Dream Song 1 is an oblique dramatization of the event that was to become the ordeal of Berryman's life:

> Huffy Henry hid   the day,
> unappeasable Henry sulked.
> I see his point,—a trying to put things over.
> It was the thought that they thought
> they could *do* it made Henry wicked & away.
> But he should have come out and talked.
>
> All the world like a woolen lover
> once did seem on Henry's side.
> Then came a departure.
> Thereafter nothing fell out as it might or ought.
> I don't see how Henry, pried
> open for all the world to see, survived.
>
> What he has now to say is a long
> wonder the world can bear & be.
> Once in a sycamore I was glad
> all at the top, and I sang.
> Hard on the land wears the strong sea
> and empty grows every bed.

The "departure" is his father's death; the adults, as they will, tried to mislead the boy about the death, or perhaps to tell him his father had gone to heaven. But he saw through their deceptions. From that moment he lost his faith and acquired the death consciousness that would haunt his entire life. Before, the world was like a "woolen lover," and he had sung "all at the top" in a "sycamore." But after, he is filled with a "long / wonder that the world can bear & be," living with the hard and bitter fact of transience (on "the land wears the strong sea") and death ("empty grows every bed").

It is perhaps impossible to ferret out the entire presence of this event in *The Dream Songs*. But it is easy to guess that it exists behind the guilt so brilliantly dramatized in Song 29: "There sat down, once, a thing on Henry's heart / so heavy, if he had a hundred years / & more, & weeping, sleepless, in all them time / Henry could not make good. / Starts again always in Henry's ears / the little cough somewhere, an odour, a chime." And the lost father is clearly the "journeyer" in Song 42: "O journeyer, deaf in the mould, insane / with violent travel & death: consider me / in my cast, your first son." Song 76 ("Henry's Confession"), coming near the end of *77 Dream Songs*, is a more direct confrontation of the event than was Song 1:

Nothing very bad happen to me lately.
How you explain that?—I explain that, Mr Bones,
terms o' your bafflin odd sobriety.
Sober as man can get, no girls, no telephones,
what could happen bad to Mr Bones?
—*If* life is a handkerchief sandwich,

in a modesty of death I join my father
who dared so long agone leave me.
A bullet on a concrete stoop
close by a smothering southern sea
spreadeagled on an island, by my knee.
—You is from hunger, Mr Bones,

I offers you this handkerchief, now set
your left foot by my right foot,
shoulder to shoulder, all that jazz,
arm in arm, by the beautiful sea,
hum a little, Mr Bones.
—I saw nobody coming, so I went instead.

If life is an empty joke—like a "handkerchief sandwich" (no nourishment, only grief there)—then Henry might as well join his father, who "dared so long agone leave me." The resentment is still strong, the details true: the suicide occurred in Florida, near Berryman's room (and presence). The courage urged on Henry by Mr. Interlocutor—"by the beautiful sea, / hum a little"—is ironic, even bitter, and ultimately meaningless. The ambiguity of the last line suggests the weight of the knowledge Henry has had to bear alone.

In the light of this theme in *The Dream Songs*, Henry's own "death" in Book IV takes on new meaning. Songs 86 and 87 represent a plea of "Not Guilty by reason of death": the guilt linking, no doubt, with that of Song 29, and that can be traced back to the deep resentment, even hatred, of the father for committing suicide. In Book V, the last three poems (Songs 143–45) come back once again directly to the father's suicide. Song 143 is most interesting in letting Mr. Interlocutor (not Henry as Mr. Bones) give the fullest account of the suicide, revealing details that were indeed threatening for a twelve-year-old boy:

—That's enough of that, Mr. Bones. *Some* lady you make.
Honour the burnt cork, be a vaudeville man,
I'll sing you now a song
the like of which may bring your heart to break:
he's gone! and we don't know where. When he began
taking the pistol out & along,

you was just a little; but gross fears
accompanied us along the beaches, pal.
My mother was scared almost to death.
He was going to swim out, with me, forevers,
and a swimmer strong he was in the phosphorescent
    Gulf,
but he decided on lead.

That mad drive wiped out my childhood. I put him down
while all the same on forty years I love him
stashed in Oklahoma
besides his brother Will. Bite the nerve of the town
for anyone so desperate. I repeat: I love him
until *I* fall into coma.

Berryman was born in Oklahoma, his father's place; and his father
used a gun for his suicide. The threat to take the boy with him in his
going no doubt accounts for the deep fear, resentment, guilt, hatred,
love—all in a tangled web—that endures in Berryman (Henry's, or
Mr. Interlocutor's) memory. Song 144 records the impact on Henry:
"this convert lost his faith." And the undermining was total:

Henry was almost clear on this subject, dying
as all we all are dying: death grew tall
up Henry as a child:
the truths that are revealed he is not buying:
he feels his death tugging within him, wild
to slide loose & to fall:

Henry's father's death—unforgiveable—revealed to him his own
death. The "death-consciousness" came early to him and "grew"
him up "tall"—replaced the father as the constant presence in
Henry's life.

Song 145 presents Henry's struggle to forgive his father:

Also I love him: me he's done no wrong
for going on forty years—forgiveness time—
I touch now his despair.
he felt as bad as Whitman on his tower
but he did not swim out with me or my brother
as he threatened—

a powerful swimmer, to   take one of us along
as company in the defeat sublime,
freezing my helpless mother:
he only, very early in the morning,

> rose with his gun and went outdoors by my window
> and did what was needed.
>
> I cannot read that wretched mind, so strong
> & so undone. I've always tried. I—I'm
> trying to forgive
> whose frantic passage, when he could not live
> an instant longer, in the summer dawn
> left Henry to live on.

The Whitman "on his tower" is the demented individual who climbed to the top of the "tower" on the campus of the University of Texas (Austin) in 1966 and killed and wounded at random until killed himself. The poem appears to be a confrontation that the poet had been unable to experience heretofore: that his father could indeed have taken him or his brother with him in a suicide in the sea, but he didn't. The resentment is deep—that Henry "cannot read that wretched mind"; and the forgiveness is not the thing itself, only the attempt—"trying to forgive."

In Book VI, Song 235, ostensibly on Hemingway's suicide, turns into another poem on Henry's father's suicide (perhaps merging in imagination with Hemingway's father's suicide), concluding: "Mercy! my father; do not pull the trigger / or all my life I'll suffer from your anger / killing what you began." And Song 241 begins: "Father being the loneliest word in the one language." Song 242, portraying a female student coming into Henry's office and crying uncontrollably after a lecture, insisting that nothing was the matter and leaving, concludes: "I am her." Henry's motiveless, uncontrollable grief is buried deep in the psyche, like the girl's, and has here become generalized to the human fate—beyond the father, beyond the self, a grief for the death of all mankind.

In Song 292, in Book VII, Henry makes a bad pun—"past puberty & into pub-erty"—but one that perhaps makes a link between Henry's long-agone grief and his adult drinking to near self-destruction. In this same poem, after the pun, Henry recalls the pain of his father's absence (his "irreversible loss"): "whose father will not swim back / ruined in a grave in Oklahoma / loveless except for Henry steept in Homer / & *Timon* & livid." And in Song 384, the next-to-last song of the entire poem, Henry makes one last attempt to exorcise his father's terrible presence in his life by digging him up for confrontation:

> The marker slants, flowerless, day's almost done,
> I stand above my father's grave with rage,
> often, often before

I've made this awful pilgrimage to one
who cannot visit me, who tore his page
out: I come back for more,

I spit upon this dreadful banker's grave
who shot his heart out in a Florida dawn
O ho alas alas
When will indifference come, I moan & rave
I'd like to scrabble till I got right down
away down under the grass

and ax the casket open ha to see
just how he's taking it, which he sought so hard
we'll tear apart
the mouldering grave clothes he & then Henry
will heft the axe once more, his final card,
and fell it on the start.

He will murder this father who had the audacity to commit suicide—
and die—leaving his twelve-year-old son fatherless. Where is the
love? All the resentment floods out, and the will to kill, there all the
time, and the cause of all that guilt (as in Song 29, where Henry is
surprised to discover that he never did "end anyone and hacks her
body up," because then "Nobody is ever missing"). Maybe this symbolic enactment will bring the peace the poet has sought. But the
question hangs heavy at the end of *The Dream Songs*: "When will
indifference come." (And we might speculate, in the light of Berryman's own suicide in 1972, that it never actually came.)

7

    If we consider the father's suicide the central theme of *The
Dream Songs*, we may imagine the other themes as radiating out from
this core and shaped by it. Song 1 ended with an image of continuous,
universal death—"Hard on the land wears the strong sea / and empty
grows every bed." In our view of the poem's structure above, we noted
the many elegies that Henry-Berryman wrote for various poets as they
died—an attention (as in the case with Delmore Schwartz) that becomes almost obsessive. There is, of course, all of Book IV envisioning
Henry's death and burial—and ultimate resurrection. There are many
many other songs that touch on death—friends, acquaintances, often
unnamed; and there are many poems that touch on death in a general
way, often with a personal twist. Henry begins Song 335, "In his
complex investigation of death / he called for a locksmith, to burst the
topic open." Song 129 portrays an early experience with death,

frightening and puzzling. In this song the poet remembers the death of an older boyhood playmate "who died by the cottonwood," who "was good beyond his years," and "never did / one extreme thing wrong." Henry-Berryman was a pallbearer and the first to enter the parlor, and, on a dare with himself, touched his dead friend's hand: "but tender his cold hand, latent with Henry's fears / to Henry's shocking touch, whereat he fled / and woke screaming, young & strong."

More often than not, death is the inescapable horror in *The Dream Songs*, and most frequently the poet draws a personal connection—even envisioning his own death, sometimes even seeming to hope for it, sometimes trying to evade it. Song 172, for example, opens: "Your face broods from my table, Suicide"; the poem is on Sylvia Plath, but turns inward at the end as Henry wonders why he "alone breasts the wronging tide." Two songs near the end of *The Dream Songs* seem to bring this pervasive theme into final focus. The haunting question of death is succinctly presented (in personal terms) in Song 380 (entitled "From the French Hospital in New York, 901"):

> Wordsworth, thou form almost divine, cried Henry,
> 'the egotistical sublime' said Keats,
> O ho, you lovely man!
> make from the rafter some mere sign to me
> whether when after this raving heart which beats
> & which to beat began
>
> Long so years since   stops   I may (ah) expect
> a fresh version of living or if I stop
> wholly.
> Oblongs attend my convalescence, wreckt
> and now again, by many full propt up,
> not irreversible Henry.
>
> Punctured Henry wondered would he die
> forever, all his fine body forever lost
> and his very useful mind?
> Hopeless & violent the man will lie,
> on decades' questing, whose crazed hopes have crossed
> to wind up here blind.

This poem seems, indeed, a farewell to this theme, an admission that all the "decades' questing" (no doubt since the age of twelve) has ended up without illumination, "blind." The poet begins in this song with the fellow poets of the past who wrote on death, and he puts the question in such simple, childlike terms that it tends to refute whatever sophisticated affirmation might be offered, from book or friends. Would he—his body, his "very useful mind"—"die forever"?

After Song 380 there is one more return to this theme, in Song 382. But this song is not a questing or a questioning; it is rather a set of directions for Henry's funeral as Henry hands them down in an accepting and gay mood:

> At Henry's bier let some thing fall out well:
> enter there none who somewhat has to sell,
> the music ancient & gradual,
> the voices solemn but the grief subdued,
> no hairy jokes but everybody's mood
> subdued, subdued,
>
> until the Dancer comes, in a short short dress
> hair black & long & loose, dark dark glasses,
> uptilted face,
> pallor & strangeness, the music changes
> to 'Give!' and 'Ow!' and how! the music changes,
> she kicks a backward limb
>
> on tiptoe, pirouettes, & she is free
> to the knocking music, sails, dips, & suddenly
> returns to the terrible gay
> occasion hopeless & mad, she weaves, it's hell,
> she flings to her head a leg, bobs, all is well,
> she dances Henry away.

Yes, what a way to go; and why not? The questing of decades had ended in blindness. Then why not construct an end in the imagination—danced away by the Dancer, with her "short short dress." Death as a semi-sexual event, a flinging of the leg to the head —and "all is well." This poem does not contain the answer (the poet has already indicated that there is no answer), but it presents a way— Henry's way—to arrange the event. Can imagination do better?

8

In Song 4, the sex-love theme is introduced in *The Dream Songs*—a theme that seems omnipresent but seldom emotionally dominant. In its context of death, sex seems to get short shrift from Henry, like a passionate spasm followed abruptly by the old familiar agony. It is perhaps significant that in Song 4, as this theme enters the book, Henry's "passion" is directed to a "body" that is visible but unattainable; the woman is with her husband, in a party, glimpsed at a distance by Henry:

Filling her compact & delicious body
with chicken páprika, she glanced at me
twice.
Fainting with interest, I hungered back
and only the fact of her husband & four other people
kept me from springing on her
or falling at her little feet and crying
'You are the hottest one for years of night
Henry's dazed eyes
have enjoyed, Brilliance.'

The scene is purely imaginary, Henry's feelings perhaps intensified by the impossibility of attainment. The elusiveness one feels in
this poem is perhaps characteristic of the theme of passion in *The Dream
Songs*. There are love poems, sex poems, body poems—but they tend
to begin with intensity and end in ambiguity. Women come and
women go, almost as though in an alcoholic haze, but rarely is a
relationship sustained poetically long enough for interest to come into
focus.

But, we may ask, given Henry's grief, could it have been any other
way? Henry's severely wounded spirit is disabling in all the vital areas
of life, including love and procreation. But Henry must be given marks
for trying, and for accumulating a large number of girls, women,
mistresses, and wives. And casual acquaintances, who inspire some of
the most intense lines, as in Song 69:

Love her he doesn't but the thoughts he puts
into that young woman
would launch a national product
complete with TV spots & skywriting
outlets in Bonn & Tokyo
I mean it

Let it be known that nine words have not passed
between herself and Henry;
looks, smiles.
God help Henry, who deserves it all
every least part of that infernal & unconscious
woman, and the pain.

Surprise? hardly. She who is admired from afar can become no
challenge to virility. Henry ends this poem with a prayer: "Vouchsafe
me, Sleepless One, / a personal experience of the body of Mrs
Boogry / before I pass from lust!" Real lust, or lust of the imagination?
Only Henry knows.

There is a wide range of treatment of the sex-love theme in *The Dream*

Songs. In poems like Song 142, the poet records an "animal moment," in this instance Henry's drunken proposition to his "vivid hostess" and her refusal. These poems verging on the ludicrous and sordid are balanced by more sensitive and tender poems, like Song 171, which begins: "Go, ill-sped book, and whisper to her." This poem's variation on Pound's "Mauberly" variations on the Henry Lawes original give it a literary context that deepens its resonance and enhances its charm. This theme is, in a way, put in its place in *The Dream Songs* in Song 311, in which Henry makes an inventory of his desires and needs:

> Famisht Henry ate everything in sight
> after his ancient fast. His fasting was voluntary,
> self-imposed.
> He specially liked hunks of decent bread
> sopped in olive-oil & cut raw onion,
> specially.
>
> Hunger was constitutional with him,
> women, cigarettes, liquor, need need need
> until he went to pieces.
> The pieces sat up & wrote. They did not heed
> their piecedom but kept very quietly on
> among the chaos.

A list of needs, and on the list: women. Before them, hunks of bread and raw onion. Well! But the point is made: the poem above all. When the poet goes to pieces, even the pieces will sit up—and write. The poet's creative vitality is to be conserved, not for love, but for the making of poetry.

9

The personal dimension is so all-consuming in *The Dream Songs* that it is sometimes forgotten that the poem was written in a historical context with a great many historical-political references. The period of 1955–68 was a period of great moment in American and world history, and Berryman includes many songs on topics of the day. The political theme begins early and enters the book with real force in Song 23, "The Lay of Ike":

> This is the lay of Ike.
> Here's to the glory of the Great White—awk—
> who has been running—er—er—things in recent—ech—
> in the United—If your screen is black,
> ladies & gentlemen, we—I like—
> at the Point he was already terrific—sick

> to a second term, having done no wrong—
> no right—no right—having let the Army—bang—
> defend itself from Joe, let venom' Strauss
> bile Oppenheimer out of use—use Robb,
> who'll later fend for Goldfine—Breaking no laws,
> he lay in the White House—sob!!—

The poem does satirize, in an impressive way, Eisenhower's inarticulateness. But rather like a shot-gun blast, the topical references fly so thick and fast as to render the poem virtually meaningless to those uninitiated in the period.

Less scattered in its presentation is Song 60, touching on the Civil Rights movement of this period—a must, we presume, in a poem using black dialect. The poem takes its inspiration from, of all things, statistics: the low percentage of school integration achieved in the eight years since the Supreme Court ruling of 1954. Unpromising material for poetry? Listen:

> After eight years, be less dan eight percent,
> distinguish' friend, of coloured wif de whites
> in de School, in de Souf.
> —Is coloured gobs, is coloured officers,
> Mr Bones. Dat's nuffin? —Uncle Tom,
> sweep shut yo mouf,
>
> is million blocking from de proper job,
> de fairest houses & de churches eben.

It perhaps strikes the reader as an authentic conversation scrap from the period—perhaps even white liberal conversation that has been translated by the poet into black dialect. But however authentic, the poem manifests a curious remoteness from vital issues—a remoteness as marked as that between statistics and the human anguish statistics blur.

Song 162, "Vietnam," refers to its source, the "front page":

> Henry shuddered: a war which was no war,
> the enemy was not our enemy
> but theirs whoever they are
> and the treaty-end that might conclude it more
> unimaginable than *Alice's* third volume-eee—
> and somehow our policy bare
>
> in eighteen costumes kept us unaware
> that we were killing Asiatics, daily,
> with the disgusting numbers given
> on my front page, at which, my love, I stare.

> Better would be a definite war with the dragon,
> taught to hate us wholly.
>
> Better than the Buddhists self-incinerated
> a colossal strike: on military targets
> near eighteen Chinese cities.
> That would make them think: as we have stated,
> an end to aggression will open up new markets
> and other quarter-lies.

The frustration of the period comes through in this domestic poem: One can imagine a man sitting comfortably at breakfast, scanning the front page, noting the number of "enemy killed," and knowing that the figures were games the U.S. was playing with human (men's—women's—children's) lives, "Asiatics." And the frustration explodes in its own violent images, insanity. And then the poem ends.

And then the poem ends. Nowhere do we feel the passion of political outrage sustained, as, for example, in Ezra Pound or Allen Ginsberg. It seems clear that Berryman felt uneasy in writing these "political" poems. He was asked in the 1969 interview, "What do you see as the present relationship between politics and poetry in terms of your own work?" He answered:

> Oh, I don't think I can answer that question, but I'll try. Robert
> Bly makes a living out of the war, and I'm against this. He uses
> my name in different cities; and he finally rang me up once and
> asked me to read in a given city at a given time, and I told him
> to go fuck himself. And he said, "Do you mean you're not
> willing to read against the war?" And I said, "No." And he
> said, "Well, I'm appalled." And I said, "Well, be appalled!"
> and hung up. I'm completely against the war—I hate everything
> about it. But I don't believe in works of art being used as
> examples. I would like to write political poems, but aside from
> *Formal Elegy*, I've never been moved to do so."[18]

("Formal Elegy" was written on the occasion of Jack Kennedy's assassination.)[19] The opinions Berryman expressed here, obviously deeply felt, surely lie behind the paleness of the political theme in *The Dream Songs*.

10

The sex-lust-love theme and the political (or topical) themes in *The Dream Songs* by no means go against the grain of the poem; on the contrary, they fill out the "record of a personality" (in the way the various themes in *Leaves of Grass*, Berryman's acknowledged model, put a personality on record). When Berryman described his model as "Song of Myself," he pointed out that Whitman's poem proposed "a new religion," that it was a "wisdom work, a work on the meaning of life and how to conduct it." Berryman said, "Now I don't go that far . . . [in *The Dream Songs*] but I buy a little of it."[20] In short, Berryman believed that, although *The Dream Songs* did not propose a new religion, they were—in some measure—a wisdom work.

And indeed, the poem conveys a strong sense of "questing" throughout, a search for (to use Berryman's words for Whitman) "the meaning of life and how to conduct it." Although this motive appears to lie implicitly behind and within every poem in the book, there are many poems in which it becomes explicit. For example, in Song 73, Henry turns up in Kyoto, Japan, to visit one of the ancient Zen temples with a rock garden containing fifteen rocks irregularly placed in meticulously raked gravel:

> The taxi makes the vegetables fly.
> 'Dozo kudasai,' I have him wait.
> Past the bright lake up into the temple,
> shoes off, and
> my right leg swings me left.
> I do survive beside the garden I
>
> came seven thousand mile the other way
> supplied of engines all to see, to see.
> Differ them photographs, plans lie:
> how big it is!
> austere a sea rectangular   of sand by the piled mud wall,
> and the sand is not quite white: granite sand, grey,
> —from nowhere can one see *all* the stones—
> but helicopters or a Brooklyn reproduction
> will fix that—
>
> and the fifteen changeless stones in their five worlds
> with a shelving of moving moss
> stand me the thought of the ancient maker priest.
> Elsewhere occurs—I remembers—loss.
> Through awes & weathers neither it increased
> nor did one blow of all his stone & sand thought die.

The quest has brought him seven thousand miles (around the world "the other way") to look on this famous holy place, where there is neither increase nor decrease, but an eternity like a sea of "stone and sand." "Elsewhere occurs—I remembers—loss." Is this then the answer to the enigma of loss, to the horror of death? The "ancient maker priest" may suggest the artist to Henry—the artist whose "strong & sand thought" does not die. Thus the communion on the temple portico is deep, and drives Henry on with his own art, his poem.

In Song 74, Henry presents a brief summation of his search: "Kyoto, Toledo, / Benares—the holy cities— / and Cambridge shimmering do not make up / for, well, the horror of unlove, / nor south from Paris driving in the Spring / to Siena and on." Henry is a driven man, but all his searching seems not to suffice for that "horror of unlove" Henry experienced forever at the age of twelve. Through cities Henry continues, and through books, too, becoming, in Song 136, a rabbi: "While his wife earned the living, Rabbi Henry / studied the Torah, writing commentaries / more likely to be burnt than printed." He is persistent: "like a dog with a bone he worried the Sacred Book." At the end of the poem, Henry ambiguously reveals: "It all centered in the end on the suicide / in which I am an expert, deep & wide." In the throes of his grief for Delmore Schwartz's death, Henry sees himself in Song 159 as a "half-closed book": "Maybe it's time / to throw in my own hand. / But there are secrets, secrets, I may yet— / hidden in history & theology, hidden in rhyme— / come on to understand." The quest is in some obscure sense a race with death. It is what makes Henry run and read, and write as he goes. And the secrets continue to elude, and elude . . .

In Song 201, Henry presents a kind of summing up, and the tally is not totally minus:

> Hung by a thread more moments instant Henry's mind
> super-subtle, which he knew blunt & empty & incurious
> but when he compared it with his fellows'
> finding it keen & full, he didn't know what to think
> apart from typewriters & print & ink.
> On the philosophical side
>
> plus religious, he lay at a loss.
> Mostly he knew the ones he would not follow
> into their burning systems
> or polar systems, Wittgenstein being boss,
> Augustine general manager. A universal hollow
> most of the other seems;
>
> so Henry in twilight is on his own:
> marrying, childing, slogging, shelling taxes,
> pondering, making.
> It's rained all day. His wife has been away
> with genuine difficulty he fought madness
> whose breast came close to breaking.

Wittgenstein? Augustine? A pared list, indeed austere. And all the rest, "a universal hollow." So much for philosophy and religion! And Henry, then, is left after much of his search, traveling, reading, "in twilight," "on his own." Alone. And still questing. In Song 238, in "Henry's Programme for God," Henry speculates: "Perhaps God ought to be curbed." The resources left are small, bleak: "*Our* only resource is bleak denial or / anti-potent rage, / both have been tried by our wisest." And will be tried by Henry, continuing his quest.

Many of the poems in the last sections of *The Dream Songs* touch on the continuing quest, and near the end of the journey, in Song 370, Henry seems to present a final appraisal:

> Henry saw with Tolstoyan clarity
> his muffled purpose. He described the folds—
> not a symbol in the place.
> Naked the man came forth in his mask, to be.
> Illnesses from encephalitis to colds
> shook his depths & his surface.
>
> When he dressed up & up, his costumes varied
> with the southeast wind, but he remained aware.
> Awareness was most of what he had.
> The terrible chagrin to which he was married—
> derelict Henry's siege mentality—
> stability, I will stay
>
> in my monastery until my death
> & the fate my actions have so hardly earned.
> The horizon is all cloud.
> Leaves on leaves on leaves of books I've turned
> and I know nothing, Henry said aloud,
> with his ultimate breath.

"My imagination is a monastery and I am its monk," Keats had written (and Berryman quoted as epigraph). Henry's imagination—the source of his poetry, the place of his quest—will be his house until his death. The quest has not revealed the secret, but the quest must go on: in the questing itself is life. In a sense, then, Henry is wrapped in the secret he cannot find. To quest is to live, to know, to be. With the "ultimate breath": "I know nothing." Is this end, perhaps, the beginning—the beginning of wisdom—the "awareness" that was "most of what" Henry had? In the final song (385), Henry notes that his daughter is "heavier," heavier, perhaps, in the light of the life-death awareness that Henry has come to in his endless—but not fruitless—quest.

A final word:
"For John Berryman
(January, after his death)"

Robert Lowell

Your Northwest and my New England are hay and ice;
winter in England's still green out of season,
here the night comes by four. *When will I see you,*
John? You flash back brightly to my mind,
a net too grandly woven to catch the fry.
Brushbeard, the Victorians waking looked like you . . .
last Christmas at the Chelsea where Dylan Thomas died—
uninterruptible, high without assurance,
of the gayest cloth and toughly twisted.
"I was thinking through dinner, I'll never see you again."
One year of wild not drinking, three or four books. . . .
Student in essence, once razor-cheeked like Joyce,
jamming your seat in the crew race, bleeding your ass—
suicide, the inalienable right of man.[21]

Eleven

. . . this kind of Bardic frankness prophecy is what Whitman
called for in American poets—them to take over from
Priests—lest materialism & mass-production of emotion
drown america (which it has) & we become what he called
the Fabled Damned among nations which we have—and
it's been the cowardice and treason & abandonment of the
poetic natural democratic soul by the poets themselves that's
caused the downfall & doom of the rest of the world too—
an awful responsibility.

Ginsberg, 1958

Allen Ginsberg's "Fall of America"

In 1956, some one hundred years after the appearance of the first edition of *Leaves of Grass*, there appeared a book that was to have (though in different ways) just as startling an impact on the history of American poetry: Allen Ginsberg's *Howl*. Indeed, the book might have been called *Yawp!* after that famous line in "Song of Myself": "I sound my barbaric yawp over the roofs of the world" (*CPSP*, p. 68).[1] But in retrospect, *Howl* was the better title— and a word that might be used to characterize the whole body of Ginsberg's work. That work by now constitutes a considerable body, but Ginsberg continues to be (as did Whitman) a highly controversial writer. By 1972 when *The Fall of America* appeared, Ginsberg had published several volumes systematically collecting the work of over two decades, including even his early poems of the late 1940s (*Empty Mirror*, 1961, and *The Gates of Wrath: Rhymed Poems, 1948–1952*, 1972). My own feeling toward Ginsberg since my first reading of *Howl* in the late 1950s has gone through several changes. Having just now read through the successive volumes of his poetry, I am convinced that he is an important poet knowledgeable in his craft, a serious seeker in the American epic tradition.

1

It is difficult to assess Ginsberg's relation to Whitman, primarily because Whitman seems such a constant and continuous presence in his work, almost an alter ego. To cite a few of Ginsberg's references to Whitman is to distort, because they suggest only in a superficial way the impact of Whitman on Ginsberg. But some of Ginsberg's direct uses of the Whitman figure are worthy of attention because they reveal Ginsberg's profound imaginative attachment. The best known of these is "A Supermarket in California," which appeared as the first poem to follow "Howl" in Ginsberg's first book in 1956: "What thoughts I have of you tonight, Walt Whitman, for I walked down the sidestreets under the trees with a headache self-conscious looking at the full moon." In a "neon fruit supermarket," the poet found Walt, "childless, lonely old grubber, poking among the meats in the refrigerator and eyeing the grocery boys." Together the poet and Walt wander through the supermarket, and then out into the night: "Where are we going, Walt Whitman?" The poet adds parenthetically, "I touch your book and dream of our odyssey in the supermarket and feel absurd." ("Camerado, this is no book, / Who touches this touches a man"[*CPSP,* p. 349]). The night that the poet and Walt wander out into is suggestive of Ginsberg's world, the beginning of Ginsberg's poetic life or journey (odyssey). Walt will wander with him in spirit, a kind of male muse evoked for support: "Will we walk all night through solitary streets? The trees add shade to shade, lights out in the houses, we'll both be lonely. / Will we stroll dreaming of the lost America of love past blue automobiles in driveways, home to our silent cottage?" (*H*, pp. 23–24).[2] After the madness and rage of the opening poem in the volume ("Howl"), the Whitman evoked as "dear father, graybeard, lonely old courage-teacher" assumes an even profounder mythological role in Ginsberg's poetic universe: an imaginative center or base for supporting, measuring, testing, loving.

What is the nature of the Whitman evoked by Ginsberg? There are many Walts that have been both celebrated and rejected by poets and critics. Ginsberg suggested something of the nature of *his* Walt in his "Supermarket" poem ("dreaming of the lost America of love"). He suggested more in a 1965 interview, when he was trying to explain the self-censorship he had to overcome to write about himself as he really was: "It's also like in Whitman, 'I find no fat sweeter than that which sticks to my own bones'—that is to say the self-confidence of someone who knows that he's really alive, and that his existence is just as good as any other subject matter."[3] The Whitman line Ginsberg quotes comes from section 20 of "Song of Myself," from the middle of a remarkable sequence of sections in which Whitman insists on being "poet of the Body" as well as "poet of the Soul." Some lines from section 24 might be printed as the epigraph to Ginsberg's collected poems when they are published:

> Through me forbidden voices,
> Voices of sexes and lusts, voices veil'd and I remove the
>   veil,
> Voices indecent by me clarified and transfigur'd.
>
> I do not press my fingers across my mouth,
> I keep as delicate around the bowels as around the head
>   and heart,
> Copulation is no more rank to me than death is.
>
> I believe in the flesh and the appetites,
> Seeing, hearing, feeling, are miracles, and each part and
>   tag of me is a miracle.
>
> Divine am I inside and out, and I make holy whatever I
>   touch or am touch'd from,
> The scent of these arm-pits aroma finer than prayer,
> This head more than churches, bibles, and all the creeds.
>
>   (*CPSP*, p. 42)

The astonishing thing is not, perhaps, that Ginsberg represents a fulfillment of these lines, but rather that the lines stood for over one hundred years before someone appeared with the courage to take them for what they really appear to say: "sexes and lusts ... clarified and transfigur'd."

But what of the optimistic, materialistic, technologically slap-happy Whitman that Allen Tate and Yvor Winters accused Hart Crane of ignoring? They could certainly not accuse Ginsberg of ignoring the materialism and scientific-technological-industrial madness of America. Unlike Tate and Winters, Ginsberg had read Whitman deeply, and especially that work that Crane had accused Tate of not reading at all, *Democratic Vistas*. In an endless letter Ginsberg sent to John Hollander in 1958, he wrote in defense of his own poetic subject matter, and of the "area of reality" that should be open to genuine poetry:

> ... expanding the area you can deal with directly, especially to
> include all the irrational of subjective mystic experience & queer-
> ness & pants—in other words individuality—means again (as it
> did for Whitman) the possibility in a totally brain-washed age
> where all communication is subject to mass control (including

especially including off-beat type talks in universities & places like Partisan)—means again at last the possibility of Prophetic poetry—it's no miracle—all you have to know is what you actually think & feel & every sentence will be a revelation—everybody else is so afraid to talk even if they have any feelings left. & this kind of Bardic frankness prophecy is what Whitman called for in American poets—them to take over from Priests—lest materialism & mass-production of emotion drown america (which it has) & we become what he called the Fabled Damned among nations which we have—and it's been the cowardice and treason & abandonment of the poetic natural democratic soul by the poets themselves that's caused the downfall & doom of the rest of the world too—an awful responsibility.[4]

In *Democratic Vistas,* Whitman had prophesied:

> I say of all this tremendous and dominant play of solely materialistic bearings upon current life in the United States, with the results as already seen accumulating, and reaching far into the future, that they must either be confronted and met by at least an equally and tremendous force-infusion for purposes of spiritualization, for the pure conscience, for genuine esthetics, and for absolute and primal manliness and womanliness—or else our modern civilization, with all its improvements, is in vain, and we are on the road to a destiny, a status, equivalent, in its real world, to that of the fabled damned. (*CPSP*, p. 500)

"Fabled damned" would recur in Allen Ginsberg's poetry, especially in "Wichita Vortex Sutra" (part of *The Fall of America*), as would many other Whitman allusions and references and citations. "America" (in *Howl,* 1956) appears to be a direct and intended imitation and evocation ("America when will you be angelic? / When will you take off your clothes?" [*H,* p. 31]). In *Kaddish and Other Poems* (1961) Whitman appears briefly in "Ignu" and in "Death to Van Gogh's Ear!" ("Whitman warned against this 'fabled Damned of nations'" [*K,* p. 64]); and in "The End" ("I am I, old Father Fisheye that begat the ocean, the worm at my own ear, the serpent turning around a tree" [*K,* p. 99]), Ginsberg seems to become the Whitmanian night-voyager of "The Sleepers." In *Reality Sandwiches* (1963) we find "Love Poem on Theme by Whitman" ("I'll go into the bedroom silently and lie down between the bridegroom and the bride" [*RS,* p. 41]), inspired by Whitman's sexual omnipresence in his catalogs, as in "Song of Myself" or "The Sleepers." In *Planet News* (1968) Ginsberg wrote a Whitmanian answer to "Why Is God Love, Jack?": "Not refusing this / 38 yr. 145 lb. head / arms & feet of meat / Nor one single

Whitmanic / toenail contemn / nor hair prophetic banish / to re-
morseless Hell, / Because wrapped with machinery / I confess my
ashamed desire" (*PN*, p. 65). Ginsberg's epic, *The Fall of America*
(1972), is dedicated to Whitman, and contains innumerable allusions,
direct and indirect. It would be a mistake, however, to take this listing
as definitive; the Whitman presence in Ginsberg is ultimately so deep
as to be beyond measure—in his physical-spiritual roots themselves.

2

It would be a mistake, too, of course, to discount all influences other than Whitman's. We have already seen Allen Ginsberg
enter William Carlos Williams's epic *Paterson* through his letters as a
young poet sharing the same locale (and aspiration) as the older poet.
And it was Williams who wrote the important Introduction for *Howl*
("Hold back the edges of your gowns, Ladies, we are going through
hell" [*H*, p. 8]). And Ginsberg himself has talked about the impact on
him and his poetics of Jack Kerouac and William Burroughs (both of
whom were close personal friends during his student days at
Columbia), as well as Charles Olson and William Blake. And it is
clear that Hart Crane was much in the poet's mind during the writing
of many of his poems (especially in a poem like "Kansas City to St.
Louis," in *The Fall of America*). These names (along with Whitman's)
must be conjured with in seeking the origins of Ginsberg's notions on
poetics, particularly form.

First of all, naturally, there is Ginsberg shaping Ginsberg. Like Hart
Crane, and also perhaps Whitman, Ginsberg experienced a vision (or
two) that figured importantly in his thinking about poetry. Ginsberg
has described his visionary experience several times, but perhaps the
most detailed description appears in his 1965 *Paris Review* interview.
The most extraordinary aspect of the key experience is its connection
with auto-sexuality or masturbation (which Ginsberg used as subject
matter for poetry—as did Whitman ["Spontaneous Me"] and Dylan
Thomas ["My Hero Bares His Nerve"] before him). He tells the interviewer: "There I was in my bed in Harlem [in 1948] . . .jacking off. With
my pants open, lying around on a bed by the window sill, looking out
into the cornices of Harlem and the sky above. And I had just
come. . . . As I often do, I had been jacking off while reading." He had
been, he said, in "a very lonely solitary state, dark night of the soul sort
of," as described in St. John of the Cross (with which he was familiar),
and the book in his lap was Blake, turned to "Ah, Sun-Flower." "Now,
I began understanding it, the poem while looking at it, and suddenly,

simultaneously with understanding it, heard a very deep earthen grave voice in the room, which I immediately assumed, I didn't think twice, was Blake's voice. . . . it was like God had a human voice." Ginsberg then looked out the window: "Suddenly it seemed that I saw into the depths of the universe, by looking simply into the ancient sky. The sky suddenly seemed very *ancient*. And this was the very ancient place that he was talking about, the sweet golden clime, I suddenly realized that *this* existence was *it*! And, that I was born in order to experience up to this very moment that I was having this experience, to realize what this was all about—in other words that this was the moment that I was born for. This initiation. Or this vision or this consciousness, of being alive unto myself, alive myself unto the Creator."[5]

A minor experience, related to this Blakean experience, occurred soon after, when Ginsberg entered a bookstore that he had been in many times before, and suddenly felt that he was in "the eternal place *once more*": "I looked around at everybody's faces, and I saw all these wild animals!" A clerk that he had never really noticed much before suddenly looked "like a great tormented soul": "All of a sudden I realized that *he* knew also, just like I knew. And that everybody in the bookstore knew, and that they were all hiding it! They all had the consciousness . . ." Of what? Ginsberg first describes some of the "millions of thoughts" people were "worrying about" (getting laid, mothers dying of cancer), and then he sums up: "The complete death awareness that everybody has continuously with them all the time" was "all of a sudden revealed" to him "in the faces of the people, and they all looked like horrible grotesque masks, grotesque because *hiding* the knowledge from each other."[6]

The impact of these experiences can be estimated when it is realized that Ginsberg's impassioned description of them comes almost twenty years after their occurrence. He embodied the Blakean experience, he said, in "The Lion for Real" (in *Kaddish*), but it is clear that this early visionary experience had a shaping effect on all his poetry, as well as his life—the two almost inseparable, as a matter of fact, his poetry being a distillation of his life, his life being lived poetry.

It usually comes as a surprise to readers of Ginsberg, in view of the visionary or mystic thrust of his poems, that he has a genuine interest in poetic theory, and particularly technique. But he has demonstrated over and over again a lively interest in the technical aspects of his craft. He early learned from his fellow poet in New Jersey, William Carlos Williams, to give up slavish imitation of predecessor poets, to write out of immediate, sensuous experience—"no ideas but in things" (a maxim he has continued to quote throughout his career). But his line for *Howl* he developed not out of Williams ("I've gone forward from Williams because I literally measure each line by the physical breath—each one breath statement") but Whitman (his long line "perhaps carries on from where Whitman in US left off with his long lines";[7] "So these poems are a series of experiments with the formal organization of the long line. . . . I realized at the time that Whitman's form had rarely been explored [improved on even] in the U.S.—Whitman always a mountain too vast to be seen").[8]

In going back to Whitman for his model, Ginsberg jumped over a number of more recent possibilities, including Ezra Pound and Charles Olson. It is perhaps impossible to disentangle the poetics of the Whitman-Pound-Williams-Olson tradition, but there are some major elements which this tradition emphasized in theory or practice. The first and perhaps most important was the break with traditional English meter, particularly iambic pentameter. As Pound put it in *The Cantos* (Canto 81), "To break the pentameter, that was the first heave."[9] And, of course, it was Whitman who "broke the new wood," whose very rhythms the young Pound found himself following ("when I write of certain things I find myself using his rhythms").[10] William Carlos Williams called this "new" measure the "variable foot" (the "reply" to the "fixed foot" of the traditional British poetry is "the variable foot which we are beginning to discover after Whitman's advent").[11] Charles Olson codified many of these developing ideas in an influential essay published in 1950, "Projective Verse," in which he declared that the basic poetic units were the syllable (the head) and the line (the "threshing floor for the dance"). And it was breath (not accent) that was the basic determinant of the new "line" rhythm.[12]

Ginsberg was the heir of this developing body of revolutionary theory and practice, but he intuitively sensed that he could take from the primal source itself: Whitman. Thus he broke out of the somewhat narrow bounds that some of his fellow poets tried to draw. But there is another important aspect of Ginsberg's technique—his somewhat surrealistic patterning of language—that has more affinity with (of all people) Hart Crane than with Olson or Whitman. In his interview of 1965, Ginsberg tried to explain his use of "hydrogen jukebox" in *Howl* in relation to Cézanne's use of space:

> Cézanne is reconstituting by means of triangles, cubes, and colors
> —I have to reconstitute by means of words, rhythms of course,
> and all that—but say it's words, phrasings. So. The problem is
> then to reach the different parts of the mind, which are existing
> simultaneously, the different associations which are going on

simultaneously, choosing elements from both, like: jazz,
jukebox, and all that, and we have the jukebox from that:
politics, hydrogen bomb, and we have the hydrogen of that, you
see 'hydrogen jukebox.' And that actually compresses in one
instant like a whole series of things.[13]

Although Ginsberg evokes Cézanne in elaborate explanation for his
method, he might have mentioned Hart Crane's well-known 1926
letter to Harriet Monroe (or his essay "General Aims and Theories")
describing similar combinations in his own poetry, and explaining
patiently what he called the "logic of metaphor."[14]

In a cryptic note in his *Indian Journals,* Ginsberg touches on still
another aspect of his technique: "Revision of the *Names,* the trick of
superimposition of key words by cutting out the fat participles [parti-
cles?] & getting deeper images: Example: 'His dream, a mouthful of
white prick trembling in his head' to: 'His dream mouthful of white
prick trembling in his head.'" The wrenching of the syntax is deliberate, and perhaps does through temporary syntactic confusion force
connections the reader otherwise wouldn't make, providing "deeper"
(or surrealistic) images. In this same book, Ginsberg provides the notes
for a lecture on "New US Prosody," dated December 1962. The reasons
for change in prosody Ginsberg finds in "increased depth of perception of nonverbal-nonconceptual level." This depth comes about by
"spontaneous natural visionary," or "organized experiment in consciousness," that is—drugs, electronic machinery, Zen, etc. Thus the
new prosody is designed to "include more simultaneous perceptions
and relate previously unrelated . . . occurrences." The means: "Re-
liance on spontaneous writing to capture the whole mind of the
Poet—not just what he thinks he should think with his front brain";
"Interest in the awkwardness / accidents / rhythm," providing a jump
of perception from one thing to another breaking / syntactical order /
punctuation order / logical orders / old narrative order / meaning
order." The search is for a "relative natural process" of the mind
"uncensored by / grammar / syntax / order": because these "Conventions / we find not a / rational, ordering of / experience / but an
attempt to censor experience / & keep out certain / facts which embar-
rass / & throw doubt on / whole of previously / accepted / Human /
Humanistic / rational / Reality—."[15] Though these notes are cryptic,
they do throw a good deal of light on Ginsberg's poetry, particularly
that of the later period including his epic, *The Fall of America.*

3

Ginsberg himself has tended to see a series of stages
in his development as both person and poet. There is first of

all the early Ginsberg who was vaguely romantic and conventional, in the process of discovering the secrets of the poetry of William Carlos Williams—the poet of the more or less imitative poems of *Empty Mirror* and *Gates of Wrath*. Then there is the familiar Ginsberg of *Howl* (1956) and *Kaddish* (1961), the prophetic vision-seeker, a mystic in search of cosmic consciousness; during this period Ginsberg's early Blakean and visionary experiences serve as models for replication through whatever means, including drugs. But a change comes which Ginsberg dates from 1960–61, described in his poem, "The Change: Kyoto-Tokyo Express" (dated 1963, in *Planet News*), as well as in his 1965 interview, and referred to elsewhere in his work. The change grew out of some frightening trips ("monster vibrations") Ginsberg experienced with exotic drugs in Peru in 1960, followed by advice he received from various sages, including Martin Buber and various Indian gurus in his world travels in 1961: "The Asian experience kind of got me out of the corner. I painted myself in with drugs. That corner being an inhuman corner in the sense that I figured I was expanding my consciousness and I had to go through with it but at the same time was confronting this serpent monster." Ginsberg suddenly felt free to love himself again: "And love myself in my own form as I am. . . . Fortunately I was able to write then, too, 'So that I do live I will die'—rather than be cosmic consciousness, immortality, Ancient of Days, perpetual consciousness existing forever."[16] In 1971, Ginsberg would remember his "change" this way: "I spent about fifteen-twenty years trying to recreate the Blake experience in my head, and so wasted time. It's just like somebody taking acid and wanting to have a God trip and straining to see God, and instead, naturally, seeing all sorts of diabolical machines coming up around him, seeing hells instead of heavens."[17] The principal work of poetry during this third or last period of Ginsberg's development is his epic, *The Fall of America: Poems of These States, 1965–1971* (1972).

During this third period, Ginsberg moves away from the organized or intellectually shaped poems of his earlier books in the direction of the spontaneous language of Jack Kerouac, his long-time friend whose work he always admired. He recalls in his 1965 interview: "There was a time that I was absolutely astounded because Kerouac told me that in the future literature would consist of what people actually wrote rather than what they tried to deceive other people into thinking they wrote, when they revised it later on. And I saw opening up this whole universe where people wouldn't be able to lie any more!"[18] Kerouac's influence on the notes for a lecture on prosody (above) is clear. But it would be a mistake to believe that Ginsberg's later work simply became another dreary example of experiments in automatic writing. In reality, as he shows in his remarks in *Allen Verbatim* (1974), Ginsberg is fairly sophisticated in his notions about language. He wrote, for example, in the chapter "Words and Consciousness": "Most public speech is pseudo-event in the sense that it is not the product of a literal human being; it's literally non-human. It's passed through so many hands and so many machines that it no longer represents a human organism inspiring and expiring, inhaling and exhaling, rhythmically." In this context, Ginsberg sees Gertrude Stein's work as significant: her work was "a form of meditation or examination of language itself by means of repeating it over and over again in different combinations to see if it could be removed from conditioned associations, as if associations could be cleaned off the words so that they were just mantric sounds."[19] These and other related ideas about and attitudes toward language have contributed significantly to Ginsberg's developing poetic style.

In his 1965 interview, Ginsberg described "Howl" as a lyric, "Kaddish" as basically a narrative poem, and spoke of his desire to write an epic:

> The epic would be a poem including history, as it's defined [by Pound]. So that would be one about present-day politics, using the methods of the Blake French Revolution. I got a lot written. Narrative was "Kaddish." Epic—there has to be totally different organization, it might be simple free association on political themes—in fact I think an epic poem including history, at this stage. I've got a lot of it written, but it would have to be Burrough's sort of epic—in other words, it would have to be *dis*-sociated thought stream which includes politics and history. I don't think you could do it in narrative form, I mean what would you be narrating, the history of the Korean War or something?

At this point in the discussion, the interviewer asked: "Something like Pound's epic?" And Ginsberg replied:

> No, because Pound seems to me to be over a course of years fabricating out of his reading and out of the museum of literature; whereas the thing would be to take all of contemporary history, newspaper headlines and all the pop art of Stalinism and Hitler and Johnson and Kennedy and Viet Nam and Congo and Lumumba and the South and Sacco and Vanzetti—whatever floated into one's personal field of consciousness and contact. And then to compose like a basket—like weave a basket, basketweaving out of those materials. Since obviously nobody has any idea where it's all going or how it's going to end unless you have some vision to deal with. It would have to be done by a process of association, I guess.[20]

Whatever floated into one's personal field of consciousness and contact: to compose like a basket. Not very different, really, from Pound's early conception of *The Cantos*: "the modern world / Needs such a rag-bag to stuff all its thoughts in; / Say that I dump my catch, shiny and silvery / As fresh sardines slapping and slipping on the marginal cobbles?"[21] But Ginsberg specifically disavows the Poundean fabrication from reading and "the museum of literature." Unlike Pound, but like Pound too—at least perhaps Ginsberg's conception of Pound. When, in 1972, informed of Pound's death, Ginsberg remembered telling him in 1967 (at a time when he was writing his own epic) that the "Cantos were for the first time a single person registering over the course of a lifetime all of his major obsessions and thoughts and the entire rainbow arc of his images and clingings and attachments and discoveries and perceptions, that they were an accurate representation of his mind." Thus, Ginsberg said, Pound had "built a model of his consciousness over a fifty-year time span...a great human achievement." A questioner asked (or reminded) Ginsberg: "Like *Leaves of Grass*, again, isn't it. Like Whitman again, where he did that in making *Leaves of Grass*." Ginsberg answered: "Yes, he did."[22]

For his epic, then, Ginsberg had his models to follow, his differences to work out. He knew very well the American tradition within which he was working, and he knew the changes he wanted to forge for himself. His epic of six years labor (more, counting the long "foreground") was published in 1972, with the prophetic title, *The Fall of America*.

4

The Fall of America: poems of these states, 1965–1971 announces its epic (maybe apocalyptic) purpose in the title itself. It reveals its point of view in the ambiguous word *fall*: season? yes, before death; decline? yes, imminent. Not a poem of pretty colored fall leaves, but a poem of decline and death. The title also reveals, through the prominence of the dates attached to "these states," 1965–71, a focus that will wrench most readers: dates of America's most excruciating agony of spirit. Other American epic writers had critical historical periods to live through and embrace—Whitman had the Civil War, realized in "Drum-Taps," Pound, Eliot, and Crane had World War I, and Pound in addition had World War II, realized ambivalently in the "Pisan Cantos." In comparison with these wars, the period of 1965–71 appears, from one perspective, empty of cataclysmic significance. Yet a glance beyond the superficial will reveal the most scarring years perhaps of American history. There was the

Vietnam war—a minor war fought in an insignificant country halfway around the world, with large, but not staggering casualties for American soldiers. But the battlefield casualties were only a minor part of the cost of the war: the American dream collapsed and died, interred so deeply within the soul-sick psyche of a shattered nation that resurrection seemed beyond hope. Something died more than soldiers during 1965–71, and the country has not yet figured out just what. It is the challenge of Ginsberg's book to help in the exploration—and perhaps a rediscovery of a lost America of love.

Conjured by Ginsberg's title, too, is the Virgil to his Dante: "these states" is Whitman's phrase, scattered through his book like leaves of grass: "America isolated yet embodying all, what is it finally except myself? / These States, what are they except myself?" ("By Blue Ontario's Shore" [*CPSP*, p. 251]); "I fain confront the fact, the need of powerful native philosophs and orators and bards, these States, as rallying points to come, in times of danger, and to fend off ruin and defection" (*Democratic Vistas* [*CPSP*, p. 498]). Ginsberg's poem is a search through what "these States" of Whitman have become, a century after he embodied his hope and faith in the vistas that lay ahead. And appropriately, Ginsberg dedicates his book to Whitman on a page containing a long quote from *Democratic Vistas*: "Intense and loving comradeship, the personal and passionate attachment of man to man—which, hard to define, underlies the lessons and ideals of the profound saviors of every land and age, and which seems to promise, when thoroughly develop'd, cultivated and recognised in manners and literature, the most substantial hope and safety of the future of these States, will then be fully express'd." This "fervid comradeship," this "adhesive love," will be the "counterbalance and offset of our materialistic and vulgar American democracy.... I say democracy infers such loving comradeship, as its most inevitable twin or counterpart, without which it will be incomplete, in vain, and incapable of perpetuating itself" (*FA*, p. i). What irony is this? Or is it another poet, like Hart Crane, whistling in the dark, shouting through the roar of the wind to the Meistersinger—"thy vision [of 'living brotherhood'] is reclaimed!"[23] Or does Ginsberg really believe that Whitman's "Calamus" message does indeed, as Whitman claimed, underlie the "lessons and ideals of the profound saviors of every land and age." Is there, perhaps, some deep truth to be probed in the "Calamus" vision, light against dark, peace against war, joy against pain, love against hate, life against death?

Whatever the case, Ginsberg presents at the outset, before his first page of poetry, his two themes to be inextricably intertwined: national nightmare, personal ecstasy: themes which merge, cross, intermingle in pools of agony-ecstasy that are as complex as life itself; political vision and sexual vision merged in a modern, an American hallucination; a bad trip with only a few good moments to remember.

At the outset, a comment on structure. Ginsberg has alerted the reader that two poems must be added to the published volume of *The Fall of America* to make it complete: "Wichita Vortex Sutra," which appeared in *Planet News* (1968), is to be fitted in after the fourth poem in section I; and "Iron Horse," published separately in 1973, is to be inserted as the beginning poem in section II. The advice is well taken, maybe even discoverable without warning: the poems' dates reveal their places in the sequence. Thus the structure of *The Fall of America* is a simple one: chronology. The parts are titled to tell us:

> I. Thru the Vortex West Coast to East 1965–1966
> II. Zigzag Back Thru These States 1966–1967
> III. Elegies for Neal Cassady 1968
> IV. Ecologues of These States 1969–71
> V. Bixby Canyon to Jessore Road

In addition to these dates in the subtitles, each poem has lurking somewhere about it its own date. If we found the poems scrambled, we would be able to put them in order again.

But is this all? A book of poems in the order in which written? hardly. There are other elements in the structure. Perhaps the most important of these is the geography, manifest in the section titles and in the titles of most of the poems: American place names, American sacred sites, American landscapes, lakes, forests, fields, and towns. The coverage is comprehensive, exhaustive, exhausting; Ginsberg in car, train, and plane, on the open road of America, even on foot, on path and sidewalk. "These states" of the title, then, is to be taken literally; the book is a report through, from, on these states, in search of the still center of the hurricane, in quest of the secret source of the modern American mania and madness.

This language—search, quest—suggests still another dimension of the structure: in the sensibility of the poet, his panic in search, his outrage at a country committed to its lostness, his deepening of despair. The poems do not end where they begin, and they are not interchangeable. This American spokesman lives through the critical years, permanently scarred by them, changed as the country itself, feeling the lostness of his country and his life with an intensity at the end that could not have been anticipated at the beginning. For the poems, at the same time that they are relentlessly national or political, are intensely and determinedly personal. The two threads are not kept separate: the political report comes in the form of a personal vision or nightmare; the personal report is placed in the context of the national hallucination.

This strange but effective (certainly intentional) mixture is perhaps best exemplified by section III, "Elegies for Neal Cassady 1968." What, we might ask, has Neal Cassady to do with the fate of these states? He has much to do with Ginsberg, a brief and early lover, and named in *Howl* as the "secret hero of these poems," and the subject of a nostalgic poem in *Reality Sandwiches*, "The Green Automobile." He had been the model for the Kerouac hero in *On the Road*, had married, gone to Mexico, and had died there on a drug trip in 1968—a son of "these states," lost like them. The "elegies" of section III turn out to be as much political as personal, the political agony deepened by the personal weight of loss—as in life, Ginsberg's life. Ginsberg's epic is to contain, as he said, "whatever floated into one's personal field of consciousness and contact." Cassady's death might have been re-flected indirectly, by some "objective correlative," in a wasteland vision. But Ginsberg's commitment to honesty and total revelation causes him to venture many risks of sentimentality, even triviality. And the astonishing thing is the frequency with which he rises above these seductive entrapments.

A good preparation for the effects Ginsberg seeks in his epic, as well as an introduction to his style of syntactic wrenching, is a reading of his "After Words" (*FA*, p. 190), a kind of surrealistic summary of his book and a poem in its own right. It might be divided in accord with the book's sections:

> Overall: "Beginning with 'long poem of these states,' *The Fall of America* continues *Planet News* chronical taperecorded scribed by hand or sung condensed, the flux of car bus airplane dream con-sciousness Person during Automated Electronic War years, news-paper headline radio brain auto poesy silent desk musings, headlights flashing on road through these States of consciousness. Texts here dedicated to Whitman Good Grey Poet complement otherwhere published *Wichita Vortex Sutra* and Iron Horse."
> I. Thru the Vortex West Coast to East 1965–1966: "The book enters Northwest border thence down California Coast Xmas 1965 and wanders East to include history epic in Kansas & Bayonne,"
> II. Zigzag Back Thru These States 1966–1967: "mantra chanting in Cleveland smoke flats, Great Lake hotel room midnight sol-iloquies, defeatest prophetics Nebraskan, sociable kissass in Hous-ton, sexist gay rhapsodies"

III. Elegies for Neal Cassady 1968: "elegy for love friend poet heroes threaded through American silver years, pacifist-vowelled changes of self in robot city, wavecrash babbling & prayers airbourne, reportage Presidentiad Chicago police-state teargas eye, car crash body consciousness"

IV. Ecologues of These States 1969–1971: "ecologue inventory over Atlantic seabord's iron Megalopolis & west desert's smog-tinged Vast. Back home, Mannahatta's garbaged loves survive, farm country without electricity falltime harvest's the illegal Indochina bomb paranoia guilt. Guru Om meditation breaks through onto empty petrochemical wonderland, & so adieu to empty-lov'd America."

V. Bixby Canyon to Jessore Road: "Book returns to Pacific flowered seashore with antibomb call, then across ocean great suffering starvation's visible, bony human *September on Jessore Road* ends as mantric lamentation rhymed for vocal chant to western chords F minor B flat E flat F minor."

Ginsberg is his own epic hero, and you can take him or leave him in all his startling confessional honesty. In an America with its Midwest cult of masculinity, he presents himself as the country's gay epic poet. But there is nothing falsetto about his gayness. He knows its spiritual depths for himself, and he believes fervently (like Whitman) in the spiritual possibilities of his vision. But gayness is not his message; commitment to the self's being is. He would, like Whitman, celebrate phallicism, "cockjoys," sexuality in all its complexity—as the beginning point for return of these states from their self-righteous, hallucinatory nightmare: *being* in the flesh, in all its physical and mystical joys. From this return and commitment to the person can spring the vision of human brotherhood, rooted in sexuality, but dedicated exclusively to neither the auto-, homo-, or hetero- variety. Whitman said: "That I was I knew was of my body, and what I should be I knew I should be of my body" (*CPSP*, p. 118). Ginsberg reaffirmed: "Live in the body: this is the form that you're born for."[24] Both poets might have subscribed to the declaration: "In the beginning is the body: live there first."

5

I. Thru the Vortex West Coast to East 1965–1966

The opening lines of *The Fall of America* hum with a familiar frontier innocence evoked by the great sweep of the western landscape:

> Under the bluffs of Oroville, blue cloud September
> skies, entering U.S. border, red red apples bend their tree
> boughs propt with sticks—
>   At Omak a fat girl in dungarees leads her big grown
> horse by asphalt highway.
>   Thru lodgepole pine hills Coleville near Moses'
> Mountain—a white horse standing back of a 2 ton truck
> moving forward between trees.
>   At Nespelem, in the yellow sun, a marker for Chief
> Joseph's grave under rilled brown hills—white cross over
> highway.
>   At Grand Coulee under leaden sky, giant red
> generators humm thru granite & concrete to materialize
> onions—
>   And grey water laps against the grey sides of steamboat
> Mesa.
>
>   (FA, p. 1)

The lines are deceptively low-key in their concern for minor details,
their listing of the small towns and landmarks of the American Northwest, their focus on color, even beauty. Weak Whitman? Far Western Sandburg? But gradually, off-key notes begin to sound:

> On plains toward Pasco, Oregon hills at horizon, Bob
> Dylan's voice on airways, mass machine-made folksong
> of one soul—*Please crawl out your window*—first time
> heard.
>   Speeding thru space, Radio the soul of the nation. The
> Eve of Destruction and the Universal Soldier.
>   And tasted the Snake: water from Yellowstone under a
> green bridge; darshan with the Columbia, oilslick & small
> bird feathers on mud shore. Across the river, silver bub-
> bles of refineries.
>   There Lewis and Clark floated down in a raft: the
> brown-mesa'd gorge of Lake Wallula smelling of rain in
> the sage, Greyhound buses speeding by.
>
>   (FA, pp. 1–2)

The images emerge and subside naturally in the flow of mind as it
absorbs the total environment (including radio) and as memory pours
in and out:

> Up hills following trailer dust clouds, green shotgun
> shells & beer-bottles on road, mashed jackrabbits—
> through a crack in the Granite Range, an alkali sea—
> Chinese armies massed at the borders of India.
>   Mud plate of Black Rock Desert passing, Frank Sinatra

lamenting distant years, old sad voic'd September'd re-
cordings, and Beatles crying Help! their voices woodling
for tenderness.
    All memory at once present time returning, vast dry
forests afire in California, U.S. paratroopers attacking
guerrillas in Vietnam mountains, over porcelain-white
road hump the tranquil azure of a vast lake.

                                                    (*FA*, p. 4)

The poem works its way to its geographical close, with arrival in San
Francisco ("here is the city, here is the face of war"), but by the time
we arrive there with the poet, we have found ourselves (if we have
yielded) participating fully in a modern consciousness as it assimilates
the beautiful with the ugly, the immense with the trivial, the euphoric
with the horrible, through all the attuned senses and an alert memory. This is the way it is, this is the way it was, this is the way we
apprehend reality, we say—if the poet pulls us into his consciousness. And we might even say, yes, yes, this is the way the epic of
modern consciousness has to be: to tell it the way it really was, is.
Though the poem may look like a jumble of images, there is art and
craft aplenty, a studied sequence of images and details within the
given or fixed structure of the journey.
    This electronically attuned consciousness we find throughout *The
Fall of America*. The poet seldom appears in isolation, but nearly always, as he moves on car or bus, train or plane, the outer world
through radio, newspaper headlines, or memory, presses in, demanding attention, commanding care and concern. This technique
makes for a shrill poetry usually, but one that re-creates the experience of being alive and exposed to the flow of the world. Awareness
brings sharp pangs of consciousness that erupt into language, then
subside—and then immediate reality presses in again. The technique
is a variation, perhaps, of the meditative technique used by Pound in
the "Pisan Cantos," but with Pound relying more on levels of memory, and Ginsberg more on the contemporary world as it pours into
his consciousness through all the modern means of travel and communication.
    The centerpiece poem of section I of *The Fall of America* is "Wichita
Vortex Sutra" (which must be picked up from *Planet News*). The poet
in this poem seems to be in a constant state of movement, like the
vortex of the title. Whitman is evoked early in the poem ("Blue eyed
children dance and hold thy Hand O aged Walt"[*PN*, p. 110]), and the
strange title explained: "Vortex / of telephone radio aircraft assembly
frame ammunition / petroleum nightclub Newspaper streets illumi-

nated by Bright / EMPTINESS" (PN, p. 111). Wichita in the great heart-
land of America is the vortex, with all its innocence, of the American
feelings and sentiments and industry and manufacturing for the Vietnam war, for production and use of American power. As the poem
moves with a strange nervous energy, almost jumping, from place to
place on the page (the breath of wonder, of rage, of pleading), it
begins to develop two themes: the bankruptcy and betrayal of language (reminding us of Williams's *Paterson*); and the loss and betrayal
of young flesh-joys. Over the radio or by newspapers, the poet has
learned that the bombing of North Vietnam was begun because a
general made "a bad guess" (the "bad guess" that bombing the North
would stop the North infiltrating the South). He picks up the phrase
and repeats it as a refrain, enraged at the way horrors have been
brushed aside as minor matters, with corrupt language:

> Headline language poetry, nine decades after Democratic
> Vistas
> and the Prophecy of the Good Grey Poet
> Our nation "of the fabled damned"
> or else . . .
> Language, language
> Ezra Pound the Chinese Written Character for truth
> defined as man standing by his word
> Word picture: forked creature
> Man
> standing by box, birds flying out
> representing mouth speech
> Ham Steak please waitress, in the warm cafe.
> Different from a bad guess.
> The war is language,
> language abused
> for Advertisement,
> language used
> like magic for power on the planet:
> Black Magic language,
> formulas for reality—
>
> (PN, p. 119)

The poet's horror at the deceptions of official language is intensified
because of his feelings of powerlessness. "I'm an old man now, and a
lonesome man in Kansas," he says, almost wistfully, and adds, "but
not afraid / to speak my lonesomeness in a car, / because not only
my lonesomeness / it's Ours, all over America, / O tender fellows."
His vision is a vision of fulfilled love:

It's not the vast plains mute our mouths
> that fill at midnight with ecstatic language
> when our trembling bodies hold each other
> breast to breast on a mattress—
Not the empty sky that hides
> the feeling from our faces
nor our skirts and trousers that conceal
> the bodylove emanating in a glow of beloved
>> skin,
> white smooth abdomen down to the
>> hair
> between our legs,
It's not a God that bore us that forbid
> our Being, like a sunny rose
> all red with naked joy
>> (PN, pp. 124–25)

The poet pleads—"how to speak the right language," and again: "I search for the language." And out of his desperation, he makes his own declaration—not of war, but of an end to war:

I lift my voice aloud,
> make Mantra of American language now,
>> pronounce the words beginning my own millen-
>>> nium,
> I here declare the end of the War!
>> (PN, p. 127)

His declaration will have consequences: "Let the States tremble, / let the Nation weep, / let Congress legislate its own delight / let the President execute his own desire— / this Act done by my own voice, / nameless Mystery" (PN, p. 128).

Near the end of "Wichita Vortex Sutra," Ginsberg hits upon an unlikely Kansas target: "Carrie Nation began the war on Vietnam here / with an angry smashing axe / attacking Wine— / Here fifty years ago, by her violence / began a vortex of hatred that defoliated the Mekong Delta" (PN, pp. 131–32). But Carrie Nation is merely a symbol of that strange and ugly hatred in the heart of the American vortex, a hatred that can be countered by its opposite—trembling, tender love. Ginsberg concludes his poem: "The war is over now— / except for the souls / held prisoner in Niggertown / still pining for love of your tender white bodies O children of / Wichita!" (PN, p. 132). Can a vortex of hate be transfigured into a vortex of love, through language, a magic spell? Perhaps not. But perhaps honest language can be the beginning of a beginning for change.

In another poem of this first section of *The Fall of America*, "Kansas to Saint Louis," Ginsberg presents much the same conflicting themes as in the "Wichita" poem, but the poem turns out to be a kind of ode to Hart Crane (using Crane much as Crane used Whitman). Early in the poem a line from Crane's *The Bridge* ("The River") appears—a scrap of recorded conversation: "No place like Booneville though, buddy." We are thus reminded that Ginsberg is moving across the American mid-continent much as Crane's protagonist moved out across America in "Powhatan's Daughter." The poem concludes with a number of Cranean puns and rhymes:

> Crane all's well, the wanderer returns
> from the west with his Powers,
> the Shaman with his beard
> in full strength,
> the longhaired Crank with subtle humorous voice
> enters city after city
> to kiss the eyes of your high school sailors
> and make laughing Blessing
> for a new Age in America
> spaced with concrete but Souled by yourself
> with Desire,
> or like yourself of perfect Heart adorable
> and adoring its own millioned population
> one by one self-wakened
> under the radiant signs
> of Power stations stacked above the river
> highway spanning highway,
> bridged from suburb to suburb.
>
> (FA, p. 34)

Like Whitman, Crane is evoked and canonized—a saint of love with whom Ginsberg can vibrate in perfect sympathy. As Crane reclaimed Whitman's vision, Ginsberg reclaims Crane's—one more counter to the terror of the hatred unleashed in modern America.

In the last poem of section I of *The Fall of America*, "Bayonne Entering NYC," Ginsberg reminds us once again of the clashing themes of his poem as he rolls into his home town:

> Evening lights reflected across Hudson water—
> brilliant diamond-lantern'd Tunnel
> Whizz of bus-trucks shimmer in Ear
> over red brick
> under Whitmanic Yawp Harbor here
> roll into Man city, my city, Mannahatta
> Lower East Side ghosted &

> grimed with Heroin, shit-black from Edison towers
> on East River's rib—
>
> (FA, p. 37)

Whitman is evoked, but in an ironic context, the details of the scene deliberately mocking Whitman's vision and faith.

II. Zigzag Back Thru These States 1966–1967

Section II of Ginsberg's epic opens with a poem separately published, "Iron Horse," which must be inserted by the reader. It is perhaps the most impressive poem of the group, covering the entire country from California to New York, first by train (of the title) and then by bus. It is a remarkable poem almost calculated to turn off readers at the beginning, where we find the poet lying in his roomette on the Santa Fe—masturbating:

> This is the creature I am!
> > Sitten in little roomette Santa Fe train
> > naked abed, bright afternoon sun light
> > > leading below closed window-blind
> White hair at chest, ridge
> > > where curls old Jewish lock
> > Belly bulged outward, breathing as a baby
> > > old appendix scar
> > creased where the belt went
> detumescent cannon on two balls soft pillowed
> Soft stirring shoots thru breast to belly—
>
> (IH, p. 7)

We have the full description, including the poet waving his "baton" at a passing truck driver, lying back enjoying the sun on his "flagpole," then reaching climax ("Awk—if you jerk—oh it feels so good" [IH, p. 8]).

What purpose can this embarrassing exposure serve? In the first place, we should note that the episode covers only the first few opening lines. After the event we become party to more complex feelings in a more complicated context:

> Felt good for a minute, flesh came thru body
> And the Sphincter-spasm spoke
> > backward to the soldiers in the observation car
> > > I'd hated their Cambodia gossip!
> > > but longed for in moment truth
> > > > to punish my 40 lies—
> Oh what a wretch I am! What

> monster naked in this metal box—
> Hart Crane,
> > Laughing Gas in the Dentist's Chair 1922 saw
> > > Seventh Heaven
> > said Nebraska scholar
> On thy train O Crane I had small death too.
> > > > > > (*IH*, pp. 9–10)

What looked at first like self-indulgence turns out to be poetic strategy. "Masturbation in America" (*IH*, p. 7) is, in all its loneliness, Ginsberg's secret—and absurd—weapon against the war. The figures in which he sees his cock—a baton, a flagpole, a "detumescent cannon on two balls soft pillowed"—are military, and the orgasm, or "Sphincter-spasm," is aimed back ("spoke / backward to") the soldiers in the observation car that he had fled in horror and despair. The momentary spasm of ecstasy has provided a minor "in moment truth" (*IH*, p. 9), a "small death" (*IH*, p. 10) to counter not only the lies lived by the soldiers but the lies also lived by the poet ("wretch," "monster naked"). The masturbation is unsatisfactory, as we learn even as we witness the poet's longing unfulfilled, but it serves the need of the desperate moment: to counter psychically the overwhelming image of the war machine embodied in the soldiers turned into automatons.

The body of the poem consists of contemporary horror crowding in from newspapers and radio together with memory and desire, memory and desire. Immediate happenings are incorporated, integrated:

> Lightning's blue glare fills Oklahoma plains,
> the train rolls east
> > casting yellow shadow on grass
> > > > Twenty years ago
> approaching Texas
> > > I saw
> > > > sheet lightning
> > > > cover Heaven's corners
> > Feed Storage Elevators in grey rain mist,
> > > checkerboard light over sky-roof
> same electric lightning South
> > follows this train
> > > Apocalypse prophesied—
> > the Fall of America
> > > signalled from Heaven—
> Ninety nine soldiers in uniform paid by the Government
> > > > > > to Believe—
> ninety nine soldiers escaping the draft for an Army job,

> ninety nine soldiers shaved
>> with nowhere to go but where told,
> ninety nine soldiers seeing lightning flash
>> a thousand years ago
>>> (*IH*, pp. 29–30)

These are the conformist soldiers that the poet has fled in despair, embodied in the poem in repeated phrases that evoke their chosen anonymity.

The poet asks: "And Hart Crane's myth and Whitman's— / What'll happen to that?" (*IH*, p. 43). The answer is terror and destruction; fate will work its will:

> The Karma
> accumulated bombing Vietnam
>> The Karma bodies napalm-burned
>> Karma suspicion
>> where machinery's smelt the heat of bodies trembling
>>> in the jungle
> The Karma of bullets in the back of the head by thatched
>> walls
>> The Karma of babies in their mothers' arms
>>> bawling destroyed
> The Karma of populations moved from center to center of
>> Detention
> Karma bribery, Karma blood-money
>> Must come home to America,
>> There must be a war
>>> America has builded herself a new body.
>>>> (*IH*, p. 43)

This vision of America, of 22–23 July 1966, appears in retrospect highly prophetic: *Must come home to America.* What indeed has happened to the Whitman-Crane myth? What, indeed, has happened to America? The poet seems as wide-eyed in his startled reaction as he is steady-eyed in his assurance that the Karma will "come home." His advice: "Peaceful young men in America get out of the Cities & go to the countryside & the trees— / Bearded young men in America hide your hair & shave your beards & disappear / The destroyers are out to destroy" (*IH*, p. 43). This train-bus ride across America has brought an intensified vision of horror, destruction, and retribution that almost drowns out the personal dimension of the poem. That frail little masturbation at the beginning fades from memory, a weak gesture of defiant "cock-joy" lost in the gathering of the immense hate of the nation.

The remaining poems of section II of *The Fall of America* are, in large part, poems of despairing movement across the lonely landscape of America. Isolated lines flash out: "Vast hoards of men Negro'd in the gloom, / gnashing their teeth for miles" (*FA*, p. 42); "Auto exhaust— / Civilization shit littering the streets" (*FA*, p. 43); "Like an organpipe that smokestack / Hart Crane died under" (*FA*, p. 44); "the money munching / war machine, bright lit industry / everywhere digesting forests & excreting pyramids / of newsprint" (*FA*, p. 46); "Trees scream & drop bright leaves" (*FA*, p. 49). In "An Open Window on Chicago," Ginsberg has a Whitmanian vision of self and the world fused, one—but updated with horror:

> Elbow on windowsill,
>> I lean and muse, taller than any building here
> Steam from my head
>> wafting into the smog
>> Elevators running up & down my leg
> Couples copulating in hotelroom beds in my belly
>> & bearing children in my heart,
>> Eyes shining like warning-tower Lights,
>> Hair hanging down like a black cloud—
> Close your eyes on Chicago and be God,
>> all Chicago is, is what you see—
> That row of lights Finance Building
>> sleeping on its bottom floors,
>> Watchman stirring
>> paper cups of coffee by great Bronzed glass doors—
> and under the bridge, brown water
>> floats great turds of ice beside buildings' feet
> in windy metropolis
>> waiting for a Bomb.
>
> (*FA*, p. 63)

The scene is surrealistic, the poet hallucinatory, the city mundane in its detail—but expectant, awash, waiting.

In "A Vow," the poet dedicates himself to a stern public role:

> I'll haunt these States all year—
>> gazing bleakly out train windows, blue airfield
>> red TV network on evening plains,
>> decoding radar Provincial editorial paper message,
>> deciphering Iron Pipe laborers' curses as
>> clanging hammers they raise steamshovel claws
>> over Puerto Rican agony lawyers' screams in slums.
>
> (*FA*, p. 47)

The tone here is angry, certain, determined, as the tone of most avenging "vows" perhaps tend to be. But such a tone is by no means sustained throughout the section, as the poet shows signs of uncertainty, weariness, indecision. This personal ambivalence is quite persuasive in its presentation:

> The body's a big beast,
>   The mind gets confused:
>   I thought I was my body the last 4 years,
> and everytime I had a headache, God dealt me
>   Ace of Spades—
> I thought I was mind-consciousness 10 yrs before that,
>   and everytime I went to the Dentist the Kosmos
>   disappeared,
> Now I don't know who I am—
>   I wake up in the morning surrounded
>   by meat and wires,
>   pile drivers crashing thru the bedroom floor,
> War images rayed thru Television apartments,
> Machine chaos on Earth,
>   Too many bodies, mouths bleeding on every
>   Continent,
>   my own wall plaster cracked,
>   What kind of prophecy
>   for this Nation
> Of Autumn leaves
>
>   (*FA*, pp. 50–51)

The poet is genuinely troubled by his own ultimate sense of identity in the new nightmare world of America: a part of the agonizing change going on in the country before his very eyes. What kind of prophecy, what kind of prophecy indeed? What would Whitman, what would Crane, have been, done, written, prophesied? The burden is great—and the "body's a big beast, / The mind gets confused." Here Ginsberg by his very doubts, his troubled uncertainties, becomes the representative man of his country's crisis: his epic's own true hero.

III. Elegies for Neal Cassady 1968

In section III of *The Fall of America*, there is what might almost be called an eruption of the personal, crowding out the national-political. But not entirely: the 1968 Democratic Convention in Chicago, among other events, receives attention. But the section begins and ends in a dark mood, with thoughts on love and death, on the body and its vulnerability: from the death of a friend to the near death of the self in a car crash. The open celebration of homosexual love in this section is, in the context of the surrounding sections of *The Fall of America*, a kind of brave defiance of the world and all its conventions—a conventionally moral world whose values support such horrors as the Vietnam war. Like the opening masturbation in section II, the celebration of ecstasy of the body, of male bodies in orgasmic climax together, is offered as a counter to the maiming and mutilation and destruction of bodies in the war. As the war becomes more violent, more demanding of more and more bodies, Ginsberg's poem becomes more counter-ecstatic in its description of homosexual love. But this movement comes to a kind of stasis in the crack-up the poet suffers in an automobile accident at the end of the year, leaving him hospital-bound and acutely body-conscious—and alone with his memories—on New Year's Day, 1969.

In a way, this section of elegies is a dark night of the soul for the poet. He is thrust back on his memories more and more, until at the end of the year he is completely alone and wounded in body and spirit. His mind wanders often from the contemporary reports of horror in Vietnam to the absence of friends, mostly dead. In character and tone these poems resemble Pound's "Pisan Cantos," in which Pound too is thrown back on his memories. But at the end, the bitterness persists, even deepens, in *The Fall of America*; the poet does not reconcile himself with the Poundean refrain—"What thou lovest well remains."[25]

Although the section is called "elegies" for Neal Cassady, only two poems are devoted to him—although the others are haunted by his death. In the opening "Elegy," Ginsberg risks and perhaps does not evade sentimentality:

> Tender Spirit, thank you for touching me with tender
>   hands
> When you were young, in a beautiful body,
>   Such a pure touch it was Hope beyond Maya-meat,
>   What you are now,
>   Impersonal, tender—
> you showed me your muscle / warmth / over twenty
>   years ago
> when I lay trembling at your breast
>   put your arm around my neck,
> —we stood together in a bare room on 103'd St.

> Listening to a wooden Radio,
>   with our eyes closed
>   (*FA*, pp. 75–76)

Whether this is moving or merely embarrassing will depend to a great extent on the predisposition of the reader. I am dubious that the passage requires a homosexual sensibility in the reader to respond, and I feel the intensity of the passage at the same time I find some of the language jarring ("Maya-meat"). It is possible that Ginsberg wished to thrust his heterosexual reader into the position of uncomfortable voyeur, fascinated even when repelled. Whatever the case, there are no doubt similar ambivalences evoked by "On Neal's Ashes," the other poem devoted to Cassady:

> Delicate eyes that blinked blue Rockies all ash
> nipples, Ribs I touched w/ my thumb of ash
> mouth my tongue touched once or twice all ash
> bony cheeks soft on my belly are cinder, ash
> earlobes & eyelids, youthful cock tip, curly pubis
> breast warmth, man palm, high school thigh,
> baseball bicept arm, asshole anneal'd to silken skin
>   all ashes, all ashes again.
>   (*FA*, p. 99)

Perhaps this more open celebration of the body in a Whitmanian catalog is less risky in sentiment than the opening elegy.

What reconciliation is there in these elegies? There is certainly no easy coming to terms with death in the traditional elegiac or religious sense. In a poetry so body-conscious as *The Fall of America*, it would be surprising to find the letting go of the physical an easy matter. But there is some sense of peace:

> My body breathes easy,
>   I lie alone,
>   living
> After friendship fades from flesh forms–
> heavy happiness hangs in heart
>   (*FA*, p. 77)

The close of the opening elegy is difficult to judge in tone:

> Sir Spirit in Heaven, What difference was yr mortal form.
>   What further this great show of Space?
>   Speedy passions generations of
>   Question? agonic Texas Nightrides?
>   psychedelic bus hejira-jazz,

> Green auto poetries, inspired roads?
> Sad, Jack in Lowell saw the phantom most—
>   lonelier than all, except your noble self.
> Sir Spirit, an' I drift alone:
>   Oh deep sigh.
>
>   (FA, p. 78)

That closing "deep sigh" seems inevitably ironic in its phrasing. It is almost as though the poet is letting the reader know that the childlike questions about what it is like in Heaven (how much like life on earth) are a part of a game that he is playing with himself and the reader, a game that both know is a creation of the imagination.

The personal sense of loss in Neal Cassady's death intensifies the bitterness at the national mania for war. The following passage from "Crossing Nation" is typical (and also in its way elegiac—for other dead or lost, and for the nation in its fall):

> Jerry Rubin arrested! Beaten, jailed,
>   coccyx broken—
> Leary out of action—"a public menace . . .
>   persons of tender years . . . immature
>   judgment . . . psychiatric examination . . ."
> i.e. Shut up or Else   Loonybin or Slam
> Leroi on bum gun rap, $7,000
>   lawyer fees, years' negotiations—
> SPOCK GUILTY headlined temporary, Joan Baez'
>   paramour husband Dave Harris to Gaol
> Dylan silent on politics, & safe—
>   having a baby, a man—
> Cleaver shot at, jail'd, maddened, parole revoked,
> Vietnam War flesh-heap grows higher,
>   blood splashing down the mountains of bodies
>   on to Cholon's sidewalks—
> Blond boys in airplane seats fed technicolor
>   Murderers advance w/ Death-chords
>   thru photo basement,
>   Earplugs in, steak on plastic
>   served—Eyes up to the Image—
> What do I have to lose if America falls?
>   my body? my neck? my personality?
>
>   (FA, pp. 90–91)

Ezra Pound could have written these lines, under other circumstances; the litany of the lost here is quite similar to such litanies in the "Pisan Cantos." And the bitterness about the world—and the self—is deep.

In view of the bitterness, it is a little surprising to find so little outrage in this section about the events of the 1968 Democratic Convention in Chicago. Perhaps the juices of anger have run thin. From "Grant Park: August 28, 1968":

> Miserable picnic, Police State or Garden of Eden?
> in the building walled against the sky
> magicians exchange images, Money vote
>   and handshakes—
> The teargas drifted up to the Vice
>   President naked in the bathroom
> —naked on the toilet taking a shit weeping?
> Who wants to be President of the
>   Garden of Eden?
>
>   (*FA*, p. 101)

It is almost as though all this was foreseen, all the prophecies long since made, and now come true. And there must at some time come an end to outrage, an end to horror. The Garden of Eden America has already fallen into the American Police State. What next?

The following poem (after the Democratic Convention poems) is "Car Crash," the last of the section; the poetic subject turns inward:

> Cigarettes burned my tastebuds' youth,
> I smelled my lover's behind,
> This autocrash broke my hip and ribs,
> Ugh, Thud, nausea-breath at solar plexus
> paralysed my bowels four days—
> Eyeglasses broke, eyeballs still intact—
> Thank God! alas, still alive but talk words
> died in my body, thoughts died in pain.
>   (*FA*, p. 103)

There is the startling reality of flesh-pain, the dark underside of cock-joys. The poem is full of awe at the pain, the casualness of death: "And who's left watching, or even / remembers the car crash that severed / the skull from the spinal column?" (*FA*, pp. 103–4). The poem closes some days after the hospitalization, on New Year's Day, 1:30 A.M. The poet's bitterness is contained in his self-advice that appears to be advice to give up poetry (but it appears in a poem!): "Growing old, growing old, forget the words, / mind jumps to the grave, forget words, / Love's an old word, forget words" (*FA*, pp. 104–5). It is a lonely hour for the soul:

> Neal almost a year turned to ash, angel
> in his own midnight without a phonecall,

> Jack drunk in my mind or his Florida.
> Forget old friends, old words, old loves,
> old bodies. Bhaktivedanta advises Christ.
> The body lies in bed in '69 alone,
> a gnostic book fills the lap, Aeons
> revolve 'round the household, Rimbaud
> age 16 adolescent sneers tight lipt
> green-eyed oval in old time gravure
> —1869 his velvet tie askew, hair
> mussed & ruffled by policeman's rape.
>
> (*FA*, p. 105)

It is a dark and dismal hour, but the poet, with the century-old picture of Rimbaud on his lap, is clearly plotting his survival, his endurance, his return. And there are pages to go before he can come to the end of his epic!

IV. Ecologues of These States 1969–1971

If the first two sections of *The Fall of America* are engagement and outrage, "Elegies" and "Ecologues" are despair and withdrawal. In what sense are the poems of section IV eclogues? In the first place, Ginsberg inserts an unusual *o* in the word—ecologues. The eclogue was traditionally a pastoral. Ginsberg's ecologues connect with the pastoral tradition ironically, and they also connect with the modern concern for ecology. They are ecologues in the modern sense of expressing concern for the relationship of modern man and his modern environment: earth pollution, mind pollution, soul pollution. As in the previous section ("Elegies"), the personal element seems to dominate, but it is a personal despair: despair at a life diminished by loss of vital human connections through deaths, absences, imprisonments, wanderings; and despair at the mad course of "these States" toward destruction, torment, torture, not only of "enemies" but of its own children.

Many of the poems of this section are little vignettes of modern horror. In "Imaginary Universes" a returned soldier, nineteen years old, tells proudly how he killed two Vietcong "Gooks" rather than take them prisoners (*FA*, p. 108). In "To Poe: Over the Planet, Air Albany-Baltimore": "Poe! d'ja know yr prophecies' RED DEATH / would pour thru Philly's sky like Sulfurous Dreams? / Walled into Amontillado's Basement! Man / kind led weeping drunk into the Bomb / Shelter by Mad Secretaries of Defense!" (*FA*, p. 111). In "In a Moonlit Hermit's Cabin," written to commemorate "July Mood

Day '69": "What Comedy's this Epic! The lamb lands on the Alcohol Sea—Deep voices / 'A Good batch of Data'—The hours of Man's first landing on the moon— / One and a Half Million starv'd in Biafra— Football players broadcast cornflakes" (*FA*, p. 127). The bitterness runs deep, and the flesh-joys seem almost nonexistent.

Indeed, the elegiac mood prevails here as in section III. Memories crowd in: "Desires already forgotten, tender persons used and kissed goodbye / and all the times I came to myself alone in the dark dreaming of Neal or Billy Budd / —nameless angels of half-life—heart beating & eyes weeping for lovely phantoms" (*FA*, p. 130). In fact, the poet's flesh has grown weary, and the mirror returns no image of fresh joy, the dawn no hope of awakened dreams:

> I wake before dawn, dreading my wooden possessions,
> my gnostic books, my loud mouth, old loves silent,
>   charms
> turned to image money, my body sexless fat, Father
>   dying,
> Earth Cities poisoned at war, my art hopeless
> Mind fragmented—and still abstract—Pain in
> left temple living death—
>
> (FA, p. 131)

And in the midst of all this, another friend, Jack Kerouac, dead—and another elegy to write: "Memory Gardens." Opening: "covered with yellow leaves / in morning rain / —Quel Deluge / he threw up his hands / & wrote the Universe dont exist / & died to prove it" (*FA*, p. 132). There is a gathering for the ceremony, the ritual to lay the body to rest:

> Now taken utterly, soul upward,
>   & body down in wood coffin
>   & concrete slab-box.
> I threw a kissed handful of damp earth
>   down on the stone lid
>   & sighed
>   looking in Creeley's one eye,
> Peter sweet holding a flower
>   Gregory toothless bending his
>   knuckle to Cinema machine—
> and that's the end of the drabble tongued
>   Poet who sounded his Kock-rup
>   throughout the Northwest Passage
> (FA, p. 135)

Close of elegy? No. The poet—like Milton, Whitman—must find renewal for himself. Ginsberg's renewal is fatalism, a mix of despair and determination: "Well, while I'm here I'll / do the work— / and what's the Work? / To ease the pain of living. / Everything else, drunken / dumbshow" (*FA*, p. 135).

In this dark mood, Ginsberg produced some of his most impressive apocalyptic poetry, broadcasting to the planet Earth the latest bad news, fitting it into the pattern of continuous modern catastrophe. "Friday the Thirteenth" tells us:

> Earth pollution identical with Mind pollution, conscious-
> ness Pollution identical with filthy sky,
> dirty-thoughted Usury simultaneous with metal dust in
> water course
> murder of great & little fish same as self besmirchment
> short hair thought control,
> mace-repression of gnostic street boys identical with DDT
> extinction of Bald Eagle—
> Mother's milk poisoned as fathers' thoughts, all greed-
> stained over the automobile-body designing table—
>
> (*FA*, p. 142)

What man remains innocent in a society woven of such intricately interconnected suicidal patterns? What can one man, any man, do in face of the overwhelming commitment of the society to its own annihilation?

> What can Poetry do, how flowers survive, how man see
> right mind multitude, hear his heart's music, feel
> cockjoys, taste
> ancient natural grain-bread and sweet vegetables, smell
> his own baby body's tender neck skin
> when 60% State Money goes to heave on gas clouds
> burning off War Machine Smokestacks?
>
> (*FA*, pp. 142–43)

Although Pound's "usury-rage" presence can be felt in this passage (and even Pound's use of Anglo-Saxon rhythms), Ginsberg has made the outraged despair his own for his own bitter time. He asks: "Who can prophesy Peace, or vow Futurity for any but armed insects, / steeltip Antennaed metal soldiers porting white eggbombs where genitals were?" (*FA*, p. 143). What is a poet to do—but endure? At the end of "Friday the Thirteenth," Ginsberg addresses his dead friend: "O Jack thou'st scaped true deluge. / Smart cock, to turn to shade, I drag hairy meat loss thru blood-red sky / down thru cloud-floor to Chicago, sunset fire obliterate in black gas" (*FA*, p. 145).

The principal poem of this section, and one of the best of *The Fall of America*, is the one entitled "Ecologue." After all this dreary news of a lost and dying planet, a pastoral? Hardly. Perhaps an apocalyptic pastoral. In the midst of what looks more and more like a futile attempt to create a still center of peace within the hurricane of modern madness, the poet shouts out: "The Farm's a lie!" And he recalls: "Marie Antoinette had milkmaid costumes ready, / Robespierre's eyeball hung on his cheek / in the tumbril to guillotine" (*FA*, p. 154). We might have guessed before this outburst, by the sheer tensions building in the poem between outer fierceness and inner frailty, that the withdrawal into nature is not working. The poem opens with some of its most bitter lines:

> In a thousand years, if there's History
> America'll be remembered as a nasty little
>   Country
> full of Pricks, thorny hothouse rose
> Cultivated by the Yellow Gardeners.
> "Chairman Mao" for all his politics, head of a Billion
>   folk, important old & huge
>   Nixon a dude, specialized on his industrial
>   Island, a clean paranoiac Mechanic—
> Earth rolling round, epics on archaic tongues
>   fishermen telling island tales—
> all autos rusted away,
>   trees everywhere.
>
>   (*FA*, p. 147)

There then follow some stanzas with pastoral images—"Bessie Cow's loose near the Corn!" (*FA*, p. 147). "Smell of apples & tomatoes bubbling on the stove" (*FA*, p. 147). "Chickens bathe in dust at house wall, / rabbit at fence bends his nose to a handful of Cornsilk" (*FA*, p. 148); "Horse by barbed wire licking salt" (*FA*, p. 149); "The well's filled up" (*FA*, p. 149); "little apples in old trees red, / tomatoes red & green on vines, / green squash huge under leafspread, / corn thick in light green husks, / sleepingbag wet with dawn dews / & that one tree red at woods' edge!" (*FA*, p. 149).

But the pastoral detail cannot be sustained. Before long outer reality breaks through the frail shield of nature—through memory, through simply the daily news:

> Eldridge Cleaver exiled w/ bodyguards in Algiers
> Leary sleeping in an iron cell,
>   John Sinclair a year jailed in Marquette
> Each day's paper more violent—

> War outright shameless bombs
> Indochina to Minneapolis—
> a knot in my belly to read between lines,
> lies, beatings in jail—
>
> (*FA,* p. 150)

The poet is self-conscious about his attempt to escape, and invokes his ancient models: "Bucolics & Eclogues! / Hesiod the beginning of the World, / Virgil the end of his World" (*FA,* p. 151). And he draws analogies between the modern and the ancient examples: "Empire got too big, cities too crazy, garbage-filled Rome / full of drunken soldiers, fat politicians, / circus businessmen— / Safer, healthier life on a farm, make yr own wine / in Italy, smoke yr own grass in America" (*FA,* p. 151). But more and more memory intrudes—"Phil Whalen in Japan"; "Jack in Lowell farming worms"; "Neal's ashes sitting under a table piled with books" (*FA,* p. 152). As the poem moves along, the poet's anguish deepens, nature does not heal his soul, and his awareness of the paradox of his withdrawal (which is not a withdrawal but an inner confrontation) sharpens: "Broken legs in Vietnam! / Eyes staring at heaven, / Eyes weeping at earth. / Millions of bodies in pain! / Who can live with this Consciousness / and not wake frightened at sunrise?" (*FA,* p. 154). And he cries out to a picture of Earth taken from the moon—"globe in a black sky / living eyeball bathed in cloud swirls— / Is Earth herself frightened? / Does she know?" (*FA,* p. 155).

Ginsberg's "Ecologue" threads its way through nature's blessings and the world's increasing horrors, from apples to bombs, from cows to burning human flesh. Near the end, there is an awakened moment of possible surcease, an upbeat going against the poem's downward drag:

> Eclogues! the town laundry's detergent phosphate
> glut's foul'd clear Snyders Creek—
> I have a beautiful boy in the house,
> learn keyboard notation, chords, & improvise
> freely on Blake's mantras at midnite.
> Hesiod annaled Beginnings
> I annal ends for No man.
> Hail to the Gods, who are given Consciousness.
> Hail to Men Conscious of the Gods!
>
> (*FA,* p. 160)

The poet's line—"I annal ends for No man"—is ambiguous: is his annal a record (prophecy) of the earth without man? The capitalized *No* gives the phrase an eerie emphasis. He has his "beautiful boy"—

but for how long: in the bunker while the bombs fall? The poem moves next into an "electric tempest": "Entire hillsides turned wet gold, / Leaf death's begun, universal September" (*FA*, p. 160). The fall is the season of death; is this fall the fall of America? The poem ends not in bucolics, but in dissonance:

> Civilization's breaking down! Freezertrays
>   lukewarm, who knows why?
> The year-old Toilet's leaking at the heel—Wind
>   Charger's so feeble batteries are almost down—
> Hundreds of black spotted tomatoes
>   waiting near the kitchen wood stove
> "Useless! useless! the heavy ruin driving into the sea!"
> Kerouac, Cassady, Olson ash & earth, Leary the Irish
>   coach on the lam,
> Black Magicians screaming in anger Newark to Algiers,
> How many bottles & cans piled up in our garbagepail?
>   (*FA*, pp. 160–61)

These are not the words of a man who has escaped into nature; rather, they are the words of a confession that escape is impossible: only retreat and waiting—waiting for the end. . . .

V. Bixby Canyon to Jessore Road

The last section of *The Fall of America* is the only one without a date in the title. Its brevity (only three poems) suggests something in the nature of a conclusion—or capitulation. It is a strange experience to move from the long screaming lines of section IV ("Sing thy Kingdom to Language deaf America! Scream thy black Cry thru Radio electric Aether— / Scream in Death America! Or did Captain Ahab not scream Curses as he hurled harpoon / into the body of the mother, great White Whale Nature Herself" [*FA*, p. 166]) to the short quiet lines opening section V, with their almost trembling but determined concentration on details of the nonhuman world of nature at ease with itself:

> Tiny orange-wing-tipped butterfly
> fluttering sunlit
> from violet
> blossom to violet
> blossom
>
> Ocean is private
> you have to visit
> her to see her

>   Garden undercliff
>   Dewey Pinks,
>   bitter Mint,
>   Sea Sage,
>   Orange flaming
>   Paintbrush
>   greenspiked fleurs,
>   Thick dainty stalked
>   Cow Parsley,
>   Starleaf'd violet bushes,
>   yelloweyed blue
>   Daisy clump—
>   red brambled mature sour
>   blackberry briars
>
>   (FA, p. 171)

The poem is entitled "Bixby Canyon Ocean Path Word Breeze"; the form, a "word breeze"? The poem is like a breath of fresh air in a book that has, in the last pages, been verging on the hysterical. Here are the accents of restraint, an enforced restraint that holds onto sanity by carefully focusing the mind away from the burning world, away from the decaying self, and on the minute details of neutral, restoring nature.

But nature inevitably reflects the beholder, becomes subtly emblematic of the human possibility. The poet's sexual vision is dramatized by creatures of the natural world:

>   Ah fluted morning
>   glory bud
>   oped
>   & tickled to yellow
>   tubed stamen root
>   by a six legged
>   armed mite
>   deeping his head
>   into sweet pollened
>   crotches,
>   Crawls up yr veined
>   blossom wall
>   to petal lip in
>   sunshine clear
>   and dives again
>   to your tongue-stamen's
>   foot-pipe, your
>   bloom unfolded
>   to light—
>
>   (FA, p. 172)

Nature on the side of life, flesh-joys, like the poet: openly celebrating
to the sun the sheer physical ecstasy of being.

This nature is also gently embracing the discards of man's
world—TV, automobile, telephone pole: the modern world's
phenomena of communication, transportation—and soul pollution:

> Shrowded
>   under the
> Ash spread, on
>   damp leafwither,
> shield tubes
>   & condensers
>   of small Sony
>   TV machine enwired
>   rusty w/ resistences
>   (*FA*, p. 175)

The telephone pole is obviously in process of being reclaimed by
nature:

> Telephone
>   pole trunk
> stuck
>   out of old
>   landslide head
>   covered with iceplant
>   green lobsterclaw
>   trefoil solid
>   edged,
>   pinked with
>   hundredfingerpetaled
>   Sea vine blossoms
>   (*FA*, p. 177)

And the automobile is being drawn into the ocean with an almost
sexual caress:

> Ocean wavelet's
>   salt tongue
>   touching
>   forward thru
>   sand throated
>   streambed
>   to lave foam &
>   pull back bubbles
>   from the iron
>   Car's rusty
>   under carriage
>   kelp pipes

           & brown chassis,
          one rubber wheel
             black poked from
                Sand mattresses
                    rock wash
              (*FA*, pp. 178–79)

Here on ocean's edge the poet has found some healing for his many wounds. There is something elemental, primal, in the nature the poet has evoked, and the sea itself seems to signal a message:

Oh father
    Welcome!
The seal's
   head lifted
above the wave,
eyes watching
  from black
      face
in waterfroth
    floating!
Come back again!
        (*FA*, p. 180)

We are reminded, perhaps, of the Williams refrain at the end of Book IV of *Paterson*: "The sea is not our home." Or of Thomas Wolfe's cry in *Look Homeward, Angel!*: "O lost, and by the wind grieved, ghost, come back again!"[26]

Or perhaps we are reminded of Whitman's boy-bard sitting by the sea in "Out of the Cradle Endlessly Rocking." Ginsberg's poem concludes:

Huge white
waves rolling
in grey mist
birds flocking
    rocks foamed
    floating above
    the
        horizon's
          watery
            wrinkled
              skin
    grandmother
    oceanskirt
      rumbling
        pebbles
silver hair ear to ear.
        (*FA*, p. 180)

In Whitman's poem, the sea whispers the word "death,"—"like some old crone rocking the cradle, swathed in sweet garments, bending aside" (*CPSP*, p. 184). In both poems, the sea presents an overpowering image—but one ultimately reassuring, reconciling, renewing.

It is something of a shock to move from this quietly restrained poem to the next following poem, "Hūm Bom!" opening:

> Whom bomb?
> We bomb them!
> Whom bomb?
> We bomb them!
> Whom bomb?
> We bomb them!
> Whom bomb?
> We bomb them!
>
> (*FA*, p. 181)

The poem appears to have all the subtlety and grace of a football yell, mindless in its exaltation of power, superiority, dominance, and destruction. But what appears at first glance to be tedious repetition turns out on examination to contain interesting variation: "Whom bomb? / You bomb you." *You* bomb *you*. The pronouns shift so quietly as to veil for a time the savage self-destruction that the poem invokes. Our bombing of *them* has imperceptibly become our bombing of *ourselves*.

And the last poem of the section (and of the book), "September on Jessore Road," offers a similar shock. The scene shifts to Pakistan, and holocaust—a scene of suffering that is something like the Last Judgment paintings of the Old Masters:

> Millions of babies watching the skies
> Bellies swollen, with big round eyes
> On Jessore Road—long bamboo huts
> No place to shit but sand channel ruts
> Millions of fathers in rain
> Millions of mothers in pain
> Millions of brothers in woe
> Millions of sisters nowhere to go
>
> (*FA*, p. 183)

The poem seems made for chanting, almost mindlessly, uttering images of misery endlessly. The ballad form, with the insistent rhyme scheme, forces attention on itself by its strong contrast with the experimental poetic forms that have been used in the preceding pages of *The Fall of America*. The form seems to signal a last desperate attempt to get the book's message across—

Ring O ye tongues of the world for their woe
Ring out ye voices for Love we dont know
Ring out ye bells of electrical pain
Ring in the conscious American brain

(*FA*, p. 186)

Heretofore the poet has presented a record of his consciousness in its totality, merging and fusing images of personal life with the national life, personal joys and defeats with national madness and destruction, resulting in a sometimes surrealistic sequence both complex and powerful. But here, at the end, his poem seems to have become almost schizophrenic—the personal search for renewal embodied in the quiet, fragile lines of "Bixby Canyon Ocean Path Word Breeze," and the global insanity hurled out in rhymed verses of "September on Jessore Road." The end in 1971, when the last of *The Fall of America* was written, seemed to be: hold on to sanity by renewal with nature, flowers, grass, ocean; hurl the truth at the world as it sinks—bombs bursting in air, floods, famine, fire everywhere.

A final word:
from
"Lyric for Ginsberg"

James Magner

O Angel of the Sunflower
and, through you, all manshaped forms of hope,
erotic and agapic,
save us from the what-end, hung-over, dry-heave
nada-dawn of our morns
and the shivered ditches of the night.
River your lines and reservoir of love
and through all misshapen forms
spring sunflowers from the earth.[27]

Twelve

Where are Whitman's wild children?
Lawrence Ferlinghetti, 1975

1 Over and over again in *Leaves of Grass*, Whitman looked for his appreciation and justification from future poets: "Poets to come! orators, singers, musicians to come! / Not to-day is to justify me and answer what I am for, / But you, a new brood, native, athletic, continental, greater than before known, / Arouse! for you must justify me" (*CPSP*, p. 13).[1] And over and over again, Whitman outlined the stern demands to be made for the poets of the future (as in "By Blue Ontario's Shore," that poetic version of the 1855 Preface):

> Who are you indeed who would talk or sing to America?
> Have you studied out the land, its idioms and men?
> Have you learn'd the physiology, phrenology, politics,
>   geography, pride, freedom, friendship of the land?
>   its substratums and objects?
> Have you consider'd the organic compact of the first day
>   of the first year of Independence, sign'd by the
>   Commissioners, ratified by the States, and read by
>   Washington at the head of the army?
> Have you possess'd yourself of the Federal Constitution?
> Do you see who have left all feudal processes and poems

> behind them, and assumed the poems and processes
> of Democracy?
>
> (*CPSP*, p. 247)

Whitman's list of demands is long, and there are indeed few who could measure up. But like most of Whitman's seemingly endless lists, the catalog of attributes for future poets resolves ultimately into simple human principles: "Underneath all is the Expression of love for men and women, / (I swear I have seen enough of mean and impotent modes of expressing love for men and women, / After this day I take my own modes of expressing love for men and women)" (*CPSP*, p. 250).

At the end of "By Blue Ontario's Shore," Whitman calls forth the poets of the future: "Bards for my own land only I invoke / . . . . Bards of the great Idea!" (*CPSP*, p. 252). That American poets continue to harken to this invocation may be demonstrated by a glance at A. R. Ammons's *Sphere: The Form of a Motion,* published in 1974:

> I want, like Whitman, to found
>
> a federation of loveship, not of queers but of poets, where
> there's a difference: that is, come on and be a poet, queer
> or straight, adman or cowboy, librarian or dope fiend,
>
> housewife or hussy: (I see in one of the monthlies an as-
> tronaut
> is writing poems—that's what I mean, guys): now, first of
> all, the way to write poems is just to start: it's like
>
> learning to walk or swim or ride the bicycle, you just go
> after it: it is a matter of learning how to move with
> balance among forces greater than your own, gravity, wa-
> ter's
>
> buoyance, psychic tides: you lean in or with or against the
> ongoing so as not to be drowned but to be swept ef-
> fortlessly
> up upon the universal possibilities: you can sit around
>
> and talk about it all day but you will never walk the
> tightwire
> till you start walking: once you walk, you'll find there's
> no explaining it

Ammons's language marks him as a twentieth-century American, but his notions clearly connect with Whitman's, transparently so. He continues:

> O compatriotos,
>
> sing your hangups and humiliations loose into song's
> disengagements (which, by the way, connect, you know,
>   when
> they come back round the other way): O comrades! of the
>
> seemly seeming—soon it will all be real! soon we will
>   know
> idle raptures (after work) leaning into love: soon all our
> hearts will be quopping in concert[2]

The language here even appears to be a friendly parody of Whitman's, but the sense is clearly serious in intention, and connects in interesting ways with the bards who followed (in some sense, to some degree) in Whitman's footsteps, the bards we have been examining in the foregoing pages.

Whitman revealed his determination to "articulate and faithfully express . . . uncompromisingly . . . [his] own physical, emotional, moral, intellectual, and aesthetic Personality," at the same time that he "tallied" current America, in *Leaves of Grass* (*CPSP*, p. 444). Ammons calls for poets to "sing" their "hangups and humiliations," which, he asserts, "connect . . . when they come back round the other way." Whitman dared (as Emerson said of Dante) to "write his autobiography in colossal cipher, or into universality." All the poets that we have dealt with have attempted much the same thing, beginning with their lives, and connecting ("when they come back round the other way") with America, politics, the universal. Pound's colossal ego enabled him to move at ease between the eccentric self and universal politics, and as his work progressed, it seemed to become more and more bogged down in details of economics and sociology—until, that is, he was thrown forcefully back on the personal in the agony of his imprisonment described in the "Pisan Cantos." Whereas we used to believe that Eliot's *Waste Land* was the modernist Impersonal Poem par excellence, we now see that it was rooted in the most personal of involvements—*hangup* or *humiliation*—that could be imagined, and we realize that he did indeed write his "autobiography in colossal cipher," into a "universality" so persuasive that the readers recreated it *their* poem.

William Carlos Williams came more and more to dominate *Paterson* as the poem moved through its various phases, until, in Book V, the personal clearly moved to the fore, the poet's concerns becoming the poem's and thus the reader's. In digging deep in one place, his place, Williams came to terms with his—and America's—roots. Hart Crane's

The Bridge might be taken as the paradigm poem that is the "colossal cipher" shaped by the poet's autobiography. The poet's "hangups and humiliations" are obliquely there, giving intensity to some of the poem's most deeply moving moments. By the time we reach the post–World War II period, the "hangups and humiliations" no longer need be written in "cipher" (as in Eliot and Crane), but may be worn like badges of honor, admitting the bearer into the brotherhood of the poetic wounded. Like Williams in *Paterson,* Charles Olson in the Maximus Poems gradually displaces his persona-protagonist and speaks with his own voice, as when he recollects in rage the official persecution of his father for his activities in support of his fellow postal workers. Berryman's *Dream Songs* has as its not very well kept secret the suicide of the poet's father when the poet was a boy; this is a "hangup" with a vengeance, and out of this terrifying incident pours the psychic energy that creates the poem. Allen Ginsberg's "wound" is clearly his homosexuality, from which derives much of the visionary intensity of his poetry. But unlike Whitman's shy confessional tone in "Calamus," Ginsberg's proclamation of his "hangup" (if it may be so termed) becomes at times almost shrill, and is elevated in *The Fall of America* into a principal theme: mystical and visionary "cockjoys" are a mainstay against the coming of the night.

All of these poets, at the same time that they grappled poetically with their own self-conceptions, attempted to "tally" their "immediate days" and "current America." That their tallies differ and their reports diverge merely indicates the infinite variety that the Whitmanian form may hold—a diversity as wide as humanity itself. In attempting to create a "Supreme Fiction" for America, for the modern age, each of these poets took a view darker than Whitman's. Some, like Pound and Williams, became at times poetically mired in visionary economics. Pound found at the base of all the multitude of iniquities running through history one comprehensive evil—*usury*, a word he exchanged in his old age for *avarice.* Williams set out in search of a redeeming language for an America that seemed inundated in a language of chaos. Eliot found the spiritual desiccation of the modern age best characterized by the image of a vast wasteland (close in resemblance to the American desert of the west and southwest), while Crane turned the New York subway into a tunnel modeled on Dante's *Inferno.* From a period a few decades later, Olson, Berryman, and Ginsberg had other grievances to bring in their tally, other wars to decry, other leaders to expose and denounce. Pound, later echoed by Ginsberg, had once casually defined an epic as a poem that contained history, a definition that is simply another way of putting Whitman's *tallying* the "momentous spirit and facts of" the poet's "immediate days, and of current America."

All these epic poems contain history in this sense. And although all are, to a greater or lesser degree, dark in their outlook on the world, implicit in their darkness and denial, pessimism and despair, is the Whitmanian vision of *Democratic Vistas*, the future possibility of an unfulfilled dream; any perception of chaos must be grounded in a sense of order; any view of a wasteland must be based on a vision of spiritual fertility. Pound moved to affirm in the later fragmentary Cantos that Paradise was not artificial, was attainable. At the end of *The Waste Land*, the Thunder sounds and the showers come. Williams attained glimpses throughout *Paterson* of Beautiful Thing, and found in the poem's last book a hole through the bottom of death. At the end of *The Bridge* soars the vision of Atlantis. Olson found in the Maximus Poems that, though Gloucester came to be indistinguishable from the rest of the U.S.A., there remained the possibility of *Polis* as long as a faithful band of intimates went on dreaming and believing. Berryman's *Dream Songs* work their weary way to a resolution (of sorts) of the despair at the father's suicide, and conclude in tentative hope. And Ginsberg's *Fall of America* embraces in its "Ecologues" the possibility of resurrection after the fall.

At the beginning of this book we noted Donald Davie's observation (in 1976) that there was an "inescapable figure in every American poet's heritage, Walt Whitman." And we have examined the complexity of the Whitman relationship in the case of each of these epic poets. What is remarkable is the extent to which each of them felt the need to drop tokens—in public view in their work—of the Whitman connection.

For Pound we find Whitman and his "Out of the Cradle Endlessly Rocking" enter *The Cantos* directly, in Canto 82 of the "Pisan Cantos," at a critical moment when the poet is struggling with a vision of death: "O troubled reflection / O Throat, O throbbing heart. . . . three solemn half notes."[3] For Eliot, at an equally critical moment of *The Waste Land*, Part V, "What the Thunder Said," we find an evocation of Whitman's "When Lilacs Last in the Dooryard Bloom'd" in the line—"Where the hermit-thrush sings in the pine trees."[4] Williams reveals in his *Autobiography* that the figure rising from the sea at the end of Book IV (then the last book) of *Paterson* "turns inland toward Camden where Walt Whitman, much traduced, lived the latter years of his life and died."[5] Hart Crane took Whitman as his mythic hero, his American Muse, for *The Bridge*, addressed him as "Our Meistersinger," and joined hands with him on the continuing Whitmanian journey on the open road—"Afoot again, and onward without halt."[6] Charles Olson's advice in the Maximus Poems—"go / contrary, go / sing"[7]—is advice in essence to sing the Whitmanian song of oneself (yet uttering the word *Polis* [or En-Masse]). In John Berryman's *Dream Songs*, Whitman appears a number of times in key poems, as for example in Song 78, opening Book IV: "Walt's 'orbic flex,' triads of Hegel would / incorporate, if you please, / into the know-how of the American bard / embarrassed Henry heard himself a-being."[8] The Whitman spirit pervades Allen Ginsberg's *Fall of America*: the epic is passionately dedicated to Walt Whitman, he is evoked again in "After Words" as the "Good Grey Poet," and the "Whitmanic Yawp" sounds from every page.[9]

The compulsion to confess the Whitman connection is strong and irresistible, even in poets often considered most antithetical. It is as though they understood, in at least some obscure sense, that their history had its beginning with Whitman—an understanding that Ezra Pound made explicit in that remarkable early essay of his, "What I Feel about Walt Whitman": "Yet I am but one of his 'ages and ages' encrustations' or to be exact an encrustation of the next age."[10] The range of overt reactions to Whitman, from the revulsion of Eliot to the embrace of Ginsberg, seems to bear out Davie's astute remark—that Whitman remains, even for the hostile and rebellious poet, that "inescapable figure" in his heritage.

Davie's statement is close in meaning and spirit to a statement made by Roy Harvey Pearce in *The Continuity of American Poetry* (1961): "All American poetry since [Whitman] is, in essence if not in substance, a series of arguments with Whitman. In the twentieth century, when poets would set themselves so powerfully against what they felt to be the exhausted 'Romanticism' of American poetry thus far, it was above all Whitman whom they chose to oppose; they could forget him only at their great peril. If they battled against Whitman and Whitmanism, the battle—whether or not they could bring themselves to admit it—was on his terms and on his grounds."[11] Picking up on this insight, Ronald Hayman published (in 1971) *Arguing with Walt Whitman*, a booklet exploring Whitman's relation to a number of the poets we have been discussing. The thesis of this work is that the "20th century flowering" of American poetry may be traced back to "19th century roots"—basically Whitmanian.[12]

But neither Davie nor Pearce nor Hayman—nor I—would maintain that the history of modern American poetry is merely the history of the modern poets borrowing from and imitating Whitman. William

Carlos Williams's remark, cited in the Preface, is relevant for most modern poets: "The only way to be like Whitman is to write *unlike* Whitman. Do I expect to be a companion to Whitman by mimicking his manners?"[13] The mere presence of Whitman, looming as hugely out of the past as he does, has inevitably affected the way later poets have thought about poetry and have gone about making themselves into poets.

No critic has made more extravagant claims for Whitman's influence in recent criticism than Harold Bloom, as, for example, in his book on Wallace Stevens, *The Poems of Our Climate* ("a pervasive and of course wholly unacknowledged influence upon all of Stevens' major poetry").[14] Bloom's definition of "influence" is close in spirit and meaning to that implicit in this discussion. Bloom writes in *The Anxiety of Influence*: "By 'poetic influence' I do not mean the transmission of ideas and images from earlier to later poets. This is indeed just 'something that happens,' and whether such transmission causes anxiety in the later poets is merely a matter of temperament and circumstances. These are fair materials for source-hunters and biographers, and have little to do with my concern. Ideas and images belong to discursiveness and to history, and are scarcely unique to poetry. Yet a poet's stance, his Word, his imaginative identity, his whole being, *must* be unique, or he will perish, as a poet, if ever even he has managed his re-birth into poetic incarnation. But this fundamental stance is as much also his precursor's as any man's fundamental nature is also his father's, however transformed."[15]

The poet's *stance*, his *poetic identity*—unique, yet shared with an ancestry: it is some such complex, even paradoxical, concept of "influence" as this that rescues a study of influence from mere pedantry, a shuffling of parallel passages. As an example of Bloom's conception we might turn to a passage from Robert Duncan's "Changing Perspectives in Reading Whitman":

> Setting out in 1855, Whitman had to go on faith. He had the courage of a grand fidelity. But he had no alternative. The poem commanded him. Its reality and truth were imperative. It commands me reading today—the vision of what the Poem is, and within that, *Leaves of Grass* as it has been for me in my own creative life an incarnation of that Presence of a Poetry. This body of words the medium of this spirit. Writing or reading, where words pass into this commanding music, I found a presence of person more commandingly real than what I thought to be my person before; Whitman or Shakespeare presenting more of what I was

than I was. And in the course of my own poetry what has drawn me into its depths is this experience of a more intense presence of world and self than I know in myself.[16]

Like Bloom, Duncan's concern is with stance, or identity, or *Presence*. Whitman's achievement—an intense Presence in the Poem—cannot be matched (can only be parodied) by mere imitation and copying. The power of such a Presence is that it throws the successor poet back on his own resources, his own *presence*, his own identity, his unique being. Whitman is there in the path, all right, as an "inescapable figure"; in the unavoidable encounters with him, genuine poetic talents do not become pale and washed-out Whitmans but unique poetic (or imaginative) identities bearing even in their uniqueness some family resemblance to Whitman's "fundamental stance."

2

Whitman once wrote a note to himself: *"Tell the American people their faults*—the departments of their character where they are most liable to break down—speak to them with unsparing tongue—carefully systematize beforehand their faults."[17] Whitman probably fulfilled this self-command most fully in that work, *Democratic Vistas*, which of all his prose works comes closest to a literal embodiment (or mythic creation) of what may be called a "Supreme Fiction." Two passages, cited in chapter 3, should remind us that Whitman could probably win the assent of all the diverse poets drawn together here. And these passages might be taken by "poets to come," to nail above their study tables, as reminders that an American poet before them had also been troubled by visions of disaster:

> Shift and turn the combinations of the statement as we may, the problem of the future of America is in certain respects as dark as it is vast. Pride, competition, segregation, vicious wilfulness, and license beyond example, brood already upon us. Unwieldy and immense, who shall hold in behemoth? who bridle leviathan? Flaunt it as we choose, athwart and over the roads of our progress loom huge uncertainty, and dreadful, threatening gloom. It is useless to deny it: Democracy grows rankly up the thickest, noxious, deadliest plants and fruits of all—brings worse and worse invaders—needs newer, larger, stronger, keener compensations and compellers. (*CPSP*, p. 498)

The poet who can read this passage and not feel himself inspired to join the ranks of those "compellers" may safely assume that he will not become (as Pound and others) one of Whitman's "encrustations."

But he must test himself also on the following passage, with its identification of the vital element needed:

> I say of all this tremendous and dominant play of solely materialistic bearing upon current life in the United States, with the results as already seen, accumulating, and reaching far into the future, that they must either be confronted and met by at least an equally subtle and tremendous force-infusion for purposes of spiritualization, for the pure conscience, for genuine aesthetics, and for absolute and primal manliness and womanliness—or else our modern civilization, with all its improvements, is in vain, and we are on the road to a destiny, a status, equivalent, in its real world, to that of the fabled damned. (*CPSP,* p. 500)

There seems little in this passage, one of Allen Ginsberg's favorites, to which T. S. Eliot himself would refuse his assent. And indeed, the passage might be taken as a foreshadowing of the themes that were to become embodied in Eliot's own "Supreme Fiction," *The Waste Land.*

There is one other passage from *Democratic Vistas* that bears a close look by anyone interested in the history of modern American poetry, a passage that seems in retrospect remarkably prophetic. The reader must have patience with Whitman's tangled prose—a patience that will be rewarded with unusual insight:

> Prospecting thus the coming unsped days, and that new order in them—marking the endless train of exercise, development, unwind, in nation as in man, which life is for—we see, foreindicated, amid these prospects and hopes, new law-forces of spoken and written language—not merely the pedagogue-forms, correct, regular, familiar with precedents, made for matters of outside propriety, fine words, thoughts definitely told out—but a language fann'd by the breath of Nature, which leaps overhead, cares mostly for impetus and effects, and for what it plants and invigorates to grow—tallies life and character, and seldomer tells a thing than suggests or necessitates it. In fact, a new theory of literary composition for imaginative works of the very first class, and especially for highest poems, is the sole course open to these States. (*CPSP,* p. 500)

This "new theory" will be possible because, Whitman predicts, a new kind of reader will develop demanding a new kind of literature:

> Books are to be call'd for, and supplied, on the assumption that the process of reading is not a half-sleep, but, in the highest sense, an exercise, a gymnast's struggle; that the reader is to do something for himself, must be on the alert, must himself or herself construct indeed the poem, argument, history, metaphysical

essay—the text furnishing the hints, the clue, the start or framework. Not the book needs so much to be the complete thing, but the reader of the book does. That were to make a nation of supple and athletic minds, well-train'd, intuitive, used to depend on themselves, and not on a few coteries of writers. (*CPSP*, pp. 500–501)

First, as to the new theory: Whitman himself was one of the literary innovators of the nineteenth century, setting a pattern for poets to follow. The battle cry of Ezra Pound was "Make It New!" And he seized upon a series of "-isms" for rallying the forces of modernism—Imagism, Vorticism—as well as new techniques, such as the much touted "ideogrammic" method he adapted from the oriental materials he inherited from Fenollosa. Eliot, too, spun new theories of poetic technique, as in his "Impersonal theory" and his "objective correlative." Williams took as his battle cry "no ideas but in things," and moved with imagism into objectivism in search of a new poetry, toward discovery of his "variable foot" and "triadic line." Hart Crane developed his theory of the "logic of metaphor" to support his innovative obscurities. Although neither Berryman nor Ginsberg became closely identified with individual theoretical terms, it is clear that both sought throughout their careers those methods and techniques and styles that would render their voices as identifiably theirs, and in the process broke away from prevailing orthodoxies to cut new paths. Charles Olson's celebrated essay, "Projective Verse" (1950), although distilled in essence from the theory and practice of Pound and Williams, appears to be the embodiment of the "new theory" that Whitman himself delineated in the scattered comments in both his poetry and prose. An avowed disciple of Olson, Robert Duncan, found his reading of Pound and Williams leading him back to Whitman: "Once I returned to Whitman, in the course of writing *The Opening of the Field* when *Leaves of Grass* was kept as a bedside book, Williams' language of objects and Pound's ideogrammatic [*sic*] method were transformed in the light of Whitman's hieroglyphic of the ensemble."[18] When an astute critic of modern poetry like M. L. Rosenthal surveys the modern long poem (especially its open structure, as in "Dynamics of Form and Motive in Some Representative Twentieth-Century Lyric Poems"),[19] he turns often to Whitman as the inescapable predecessor shadowing forth embryonically much of modern innovation.

It is important to note that Whitman's comment on the need for a "new theory" is introduced by some acute remarks on the "new law-forces of spoken and written language," and it is significant that he immediately indicates he does not mean mere correctness, or propriety, or "fine words." Rather, he has in mind a "language fann'd by the breath of Nature, which leaps overhead, cares mostly for impetus and effects, and for what it plants and invigorates to grow." This is a language that "tallies life and character, and seldomer tells a thing than suggests or necessitates it." Whitman's cryptic comments on language are broad enough in scope to embrace all the poets examined here, from Eliot's terse speech rhythms in *The Waste Land* to Berryman's minstrel-dream speech invented for Henry in the *Dream Songs*. Indeed, whatever the theories of poetry spun by them, all these poets forged an individual language for their poems. It is all but impossible to encounter their language and not recognize their individual and personal voices within. And no one would claim that theirs is the language of correctness and propriety. Pound seemed to pride himself in adopting common "'murikan" speech in *The Cantos*, and Eliot included language from the music hall in *The Waste Land*. Williams made the quest of *Paterson* a quest for language, while Crane twisted and bent common language to the shapes deep within his (and sometimes his reader's) unconscious. Olson's open-parenthesis style forced the reader to complete the thought and close the parenthesis by intuitive leaps himself. What Whitman once said of *Leaves of Grass*—that sometimes he thought it was "only a language experiment"[20]—could equally have been said by Berryman of *The Dream Songs*, whose minstrel or drunken language seems at times indeed to "leap overhead." And Ginsberg's pride was in dragging the language of poetry out of the classroom into the street—and even sometimes into the alley.

These random remarks on the language of modern American poets must remain only fragmentary and suggestive, until that language attracts its own historian and analyst. But surely the beginning point for that history, when it is written, will be Whitman and *Leaves of Grass*. Whitman's theory that the process of reading will be not a "half-sleep" but a "gymnast's struggle," a process in which the reader himself will "construct indeed the poems," represents an insight that is relevant to the whole of "modern"—that is to say, difficult, hard, obscure—poetry. But this theory is suggestive, too, of some of the "new" critical movements represented by such disparate critics as Stanley Fish (in *Self-Consuming Artifacts*, 1972)[21] and Roland Barthes (in *S / Z*, 1970, tr. 1974),[22] in which reader-response (rather than literary text) becomes the focus of critical attention. Whatever Whitman might have intended by his concept of reading as a "gymnast's struggle," it represents an advance over an earlier view of the reader set forth in the 1855 Preface to *Leaves of Grass*: "The proof of a poet is that his country absorbs him as affectionately as he has absorbed it." (*CPSP*, p. 427) By the time Whitman wrote *Democratic Vistas*, he knew that America had not absorbed him as "affectionately" as he had absorbed it, and he was prepared to place a greater responsibility on readers. Not mere absorption was involved, but a "gymnast's struggle," expending intellectual and imaginative energy.

Whitman's concern for an audience has been a concern also of most modern poets. At the same time that they alienated readers by their difficulty, they placed the blame not on their own obscurity but on their readers' laziness. And they clearly yearned for larger audiences. Pound has never won readers in the numbers that his position in the history of modern poetry might seem to have earned him, and it does not seem likely that he will ever go through a period of popularity. Eliot, of course, ultimately earned a wide readership, especially in classrooms, as the New Criticism taught readers how to read his poems. Other poets have passed through periods of high critical esteem—Wallace Stevens, and later, William Carlos Williams. Like Pound, Hart Crane and Charles Olson seem destined to have a small, however passionately dedicated, readership. John Berryman's reputation seems gradually to be increasing, especially as his *Dream Songs* have become more familiar. And Allen Ginsberg, who might be said to have had a popular audience, has never achieved the kind of critical acceptance attained by poets like Eliot or even Williams. These questions are questions of popularity and reputation, and not necessarily of merit. Each reader would want to rank these poets after his own notions of excellence. And although clearly some rank above, some below others, it seems premature at this time to label some major, some minor poets. I would maintain that whatever the merit of these individual poets as determined by history, they are all worthy of serious attention by contemporary readers.

Moreover, it seems unlikely that the imaginative and creative energies flowing from Whitman have spent their force. The impulse to write the American epic and to create the country's Supreme Fiction runs deep and remains vital. Some sense of this impulse is conveyed in a poem published in 1975 by Lawrence Ferlinghetti, entitled "Popular Manifesto: For Poets, With Love." It is a poem with a ringing call for poets to come out of their closets, to open their windows, open their doors:

> Secret words & chants won't do any longer.
> The hour of *om*ing is over,
> the time of keening come,

> a time for keening & rejoicing
> over the coming end
> of industrial civilization
> which is bad for earth & Man.

In the process of cataloging the poetic drought and needs of America, Ferlinghetti had no doubt of the model the emerging poets should follow. He asked:

> Where are Whitman's wild children,
> where the great voices speaking out
> with a sense of sweetness & sublimity,
> where the great new vision,
> the great world-view,
> the high prophetic song
> of the immense earth
> and all that sings in it
> and our relation to it—
> Poets, descend
> to the street of the world once more
> And open your minds & eyes
> with the old visual delight,
> Clear your throat and speak up,
> Poetry is dead, long live poetry
> with terrible eyes and buffalo strength.[23]

Ferlinghetti's poem is a ringing call for America to continue the quest for its "new vision," a "great world-view," a "high prophetic song"—for, in short, a Great Idea or Supreme Fiction. Perhaps the secret of the continuation is that the vision and view lie not in a static achievement but in the quest itself, the movement on in restless search of a new vista, a pursuit of ever-receding vistas. As Wallace Stevens said of the Supreme Fiction, "It Must Change": "If ever the search for a tranquil belief should end, / The future might stop emerging out of the past."[24] Whitman indicated as much when he addressed the "Poets to Come":

> I myself but write one or two indicative words for the fu-
>   ture,
> I but advance a moment to wheel and hurry back in the
>   darkness
>
> I am a man who, sauntering along without fully stopping,
>   turns a casual look upon you and then averts his face,
> Leaving it to you to prove and define it,
> Expecting the main things from you.
>
> (CPSP, p. 13)

A final word:
from
"A Common Ground"

Denise Levertov

not illusion but what Whitman called
'the path
between reality and the soul,'
a language
excelling itself to be itself[25]

Notes

Preface

1. John Berryman, " 'Song of Myself': Intention and Substance," *The Freedom of the Poet* (New York: Farrar, Straus & Giroux, 1976), pp. 227–41.
2. Robert Duncan, "A Poem Beginning with a Line by Pindar," *Contemporary American Poetry*, ed. Donald Hall (Baltimore: Penguin Books, 1974), p. 62.
3. Louis Simpson, "Walt Whitman at Bear Mountain," ibid., p. 119.
4. Theodore Roethke, "The Abyss," *Collected Poems* (Garden City: Doubleday & Co., 1966), p. 220.
5. John Berryman, *Love & Fame* (New York: Farrar, Straus & Giroux, 1972), p. 65.
6. Walt Whitman, *Complete Poetry and Selected Prose*, ed. James E. Miller, Jr. (Boston: Houghton Mifflin Co., 1959), p. 349.
7. Pablo Neruda, "Ode to Walt Whitman," *Homage to Walt Whitman*, tr. Didier Tisdel Jaén (University, Ala.: University of Alabama Press, 1969), p. 43.
8. William Carlos Williams, "America, Whitman, and the Art of Poetry," *Poetry Journal*, Nov. 1917, p. 31.
9. Robert Creeley, Introduction to *Whitman*, poems selected by Robert Creeley (Baltimore: Penguin Books, 1973), p. 7.
10. Oscar Wilde, *The Artist as Critic: Critical Writings of Oscar Wilde*, ed. Richard Ellman (New York: Random House, 1969), p. 121.
11. Whitman, *Complete Poetry and Selected Prose*, p. 444.
12. Ibid., p. 454.

Chapter One

1. Robert Lowell, "On 'Skunk Hour,' " *Robert Lowell*, ed. Thomas Parkinson (Englewood Cliffs, N.J.: Prentice-Hall, 1968), pp. 132–33.

2. Ibid., pp. 19, 20–21.

3. Robert Lowell, "William Carlos Williams," *William Carlos Williams*, ed. J. Hillis Miller (Englewood Cliffs, N.J.: Prentice-Hall, 1966), pp. 157, 158.

4. M. L. Rosenthal, "Robert Lowell and the Poetry of Confession," *Robert Lowell*, pp. 117, 122.

5. T. S. Eliot, "Tradition and the Individual Talent," *Selected Essays* (New York: Harcourt, Brace & Co., 1950), p. 7.

6. Walt Whitman, "A Backward Glance o'er Travel'd Roads," *Complete Poetry and Selected Prose*, ed. James E. Miller, Jr. (Boston: Houghton Mifflin Co., 1959), p. 444.

7. Robert Lowell, *Notebook* (New York: Farrar, Straus & Giroux, 1970; rpt. Noonday Press, 1971), pp. 262, 265.

8. Robert Lowell, *History* (New York: Farrar, Straus & Giroux, 1973), p. 7.

9. See Allen Williamson, *Pity the Monster* (New Haven: Yale University Press, 1974), pp. 153–57. Williamson considers *Notebook* a continuation of *Near the Ocean* (1967), both in the tradition of the personal epic. Williamson sees Lowell's poem as not allied so much with the " 'open' tradition" of Pound's *Cantos*, Williams's *Paterson*, or Berryman's *Dream Songs* ("The author's presentation of himself is expansive and many-sided; his intelligence and observation, as well as his imagination, contribute to his authority") as with "another tradition" of Eliot's *Waste Land*, Crane's *Bridge*, and Berryman's *Homage to Mistress Bradstreet* ("These poems tend to start from intense inward experience, to base their authority on the poet's imagination and symbol-making power rather than his secular self, and to incorporate the larger, public realm by epiphany rather than direct narrative"). The two traditions Williamson defines might both be said to have their roots in Walt Whitman: the first in the whole of *Leaves of Grass*, and the second in the book's longest poem of "intense inward experience"—"Song of Myself."

10. Note in Lowell's last book published the year of his death, *Day by Day* (New York: Farrar, Straus & Giroux, 1977) his continuing experimentation with the form of the "personal epic."

11. Donald Davie, Review of John Berryman, *The Freedom of the Poet, New York Times Book Review*, 25 Apr. 1976, p. 4.

12. John Berryman, Interview with Joseph Haas, "Who killed Henry Pussy-cat? I did, says John Berryman, with love, & a poem, & for freedom O," *Panorama, Chicago Daily News* (6–7 Feb. 1971), p. 5.

13. The Whitman quotation appears in "A Backward Glance o'er Travel'd Road," *Complete Poetry and Selected Prose*, p. 454.

14. John Berryman, " 'Song of Myself': Intention and Substance," *The Freedom of the Poet* (New York: Farrar, Straus & Giroux, 1976), pp. 230, 232.

15. Ibid., p. 227.

16. Ibid., p. 232.

17. James E. Miller, Jr., " 'Song of Myself' as Inverted Mystical Experience," *PMLA*, Sept. 1955; included as chapter 1 in *A Critical Guide to Leaves of Grass* (Chicago: University of Chicago Press, 1957).

18. Lowell, *Day by Day*, p. 28.

Chapter Two

1. See the radical reassessment of Williams in J. Hillis Miller, ed., *William Carlos Williams* (Englewood Cliffs, N.J.: Prentice-Hall, 1966). For an account of Williams's views on *The Waste Land*, see chap. 7 below.

2. See chaps. 1 and 10.

3. Roy Harvey Pearce, *The Continuity of American Poetry* (Princeton: Princeton University Press, 1961), pp. 59–136.

4. Walt Whitman, "1855 Preface," *Complete Poetry and Selected Prose*, ed. James E. Miller, Jr. (Boston: Houghton Mifflin Co., 1959), p. 413.

5. John Berryman, *The Dream Songs* (New York: Farrar, Straus & Giroux, 1969), p. 376.

6. A. R. Ammons, *Sphere: The Form of a Motion* (New York: W. W. Norton & Co., 1974), p. 72.

7. Berryman, *Dream Songs*, p. 39.

8. Michael Wigglesworth, "Day of Doom," *Seventeenth Century American Poetry* (New York: New York University Press, 1968), p. 56.

9. Edward Taylor, "Preparatory Meditations," *The Poems of Edward Taylor* (New Haven: Yale University Press, 1960), p. 18.

10. Albert Gelpi, *The Tenth Muse* (Cambridge: Harvard University Press, 1975), p. 32.

11. See the facsimile reprint of the 1785 edition of Timothy Dwight's *The Conquest of Canaan* in *The Major Poems of Timothy Dwight (1752–1817)*, ed. William J. McTaggart and William K. Bottorf (Gainesville, Fla.: Scholars' Facsimiles and Reprints, 1969).

12. William Cullen Bryant, "Essay on American Poetry," *The American Literary Revolution, 1783–1837*, ed. Robert E. Spiller (New York: New York University Press, 1967), p. 201.

13. See the facsimile reprint of the 1825 edition of Joel Barlow's *The Columbiad* in *The Works of Joel Barlow*, ed. William K. Bottorf and Arthur L. Ford (Gainesville, Fla.: Scholars' Facsimiles and Reprints, 1970), vol. 2. The quoted passage appears on p. 747 of the volume (or p. 329 of the facsimile).

14. Daniel Bryan, "The Adventures of Daniel Boone," *The Mountain Muse* (Harrisonburg: Davidson & Bourne, 1813), p. 111.

15. Mike Weaver, *William Carlos Williams: The American Background* (Cambridge: Cambridge University Press, 1971), pp. 165–200.

16. Henry Wadsworth Longfellow, *Song of Hiawatha* (Boston: Ticknor & Fields, 1855), pp. 49–50.

17. See chapter 10 ("The Fascicles") and Appendix I ("The Fascicle Numbering") of Ruth Miller's *The Poetry of Emily Dickinson* (Middletown, Conn.: Wesleyan University Press, 1968).

18. Edward Arlington Robinson, *Tilbury Town: Selected Poems of Edward Arlington Robinson*, ed. Lawrance Thompson (New York: Macmillan Co., 1953).

19. Edgar Lee Masters, "The Spooniad," *Spoon River Anthology* (New York: Collier Books, 1962), pp. 281–91.

20. Wallace Stevens, *The Collected Poems* (New York: Alfred A. Knopf, 1965), pp. 380–408.

21. Wallace Stevens, *Letters* (New York: Alfred A. Knopf, 1966), pp. 863–64.

22. See Tim Hunt, Afterword to *The Women at Point Sur* by Robinson Jeffers (New York: Liveright, 1977) for a comparison of *The Women at Point Sur* with

Whitman's "Song of Myself" (pp. 198–200).

23. See Brother Antoninus, *Robinson Jeffers: Fragments of an Older Fury* (Berkeley: Oyez, 1968), p. 3.

24. H. D., *Trilogy* (New York: New Directions, 1973), p. 43.

25. In a review of *"A" 22 & 23* (presumably the last of Zukofsky's poem; *"A"* 24 was published previously), Hugh Kenner called *"A"* the "most hermetic poem in English" and predicted that "they" will "still be elucidating [it] in the 22nd century" (*New York Times Book Review,* 14 Mar. 1976, p. 7).

26. A. R. Ammons, *Tape for the Turn of the Year* (Ithaca: Cornell University Press, 1965; rpt. W. W. Norton & Co., 1972), p. 1.

27. Solyman Brown, "Essay on American Poetry," *American Literary Revolution, 1783–1837,* pp. 187–92.

28. William Cullen Bryant, "Essay on American Poetry," ibid., pp. 195–96.

29. Henry Wadsworth Longfellow, "Our Native Writers," ibid., pp. 387–88, 389.

30. Ralph Waldo Emerson, "The American Scholar," ibid., p. 453.

31. Ralph Waldo Emerson, "The Poet," *Selections from Ralph Waldo Emerson,* ed. Stephen E. Whicher (Boston: Houghton Mifflin Co., 1957), p. 238.

32. Ralph Waldo Emerson, "To Walt Whitman," ibid., p. 362.

33. Walt Whitman, "Beginners," *Complete Poetry and Selected Prose,* p. 10.

34. Hyatt H. Waggoner, *American Poets from the Puritans to the Present* (Boston: Houghton Mifflin Co., 1968), chaps. 5 and 6; Harold Bloom, *A Map of Misreading* (New York: Oxford University Press, 1975), chaps. 9 and 10.

35. Quoted in Gay Wilson Allen, *The New Walt Whitman Handbook* (New York: New York University Press, 1975), p. 19.

36. Alexis de Tocqueville, *Democracy in America,* ed. Richard D. Heffner (New York: New American Library, 1956), pp. 177, 181, 183.

37. Whitman, "1855 Preface," *Complete Poetry and Selected Prose,* p. 413.

38. Louis Simpson, *At the End of the Open Road* (Middletown: Wesleyan University Press, 1963), p. 55.

Chapter Three

1. Page numbers in parentheses after the Whitman quotations refer to Walt Whitman, *Complete Poetry and Selected Prose,* ed. James E. Miller, Jr. (Boston: Houghton Mifflin Co., 1959). Where lines can easily be located by title, no page reference appears.

2. Wallace Stevens, "Like Decorations in a Nigger Cemetery," *The Collected Poems* (New York: Alfred A. Knopf, 1965), pp. 150–51.

3. Alexis de Tocqueville, *Democracy in America,* ed. Richard D. Heffner (New York: New American Library, 1956), p. 183.

4. Wallace Stevens, "Notes toward a Supreme Fiction," *Collected Poems,* p. 389.

5. Thomas A. Vogler, in *Preludes to Vision: The Epic Venture in Blake, Wordsworth, Keats, and Hart Crane* (Berkeley: University of California Press, 1971), takes a somewhat different approach to the modern epic, emphasizing what he calls "preludes to vision," and, in bringing together both British and American examples, deemphasizes the national distinctions. In his valuable opening chapter, "In Search of the Epic," he writes: "I have my own set of intuitive criteria [for the epic] which has led me to exclude such long poems as

Southey's 'epics,' Tennyson's *Idylls of the King*, Browning's *Ring and the Book*, Morris's *Island*, and Hardy's *Dynasts*, while including Blake's *Four Zoas, Milton*, and *Jerusalem*, Wordsworth's *Prelude* (but not *The Excursion*), Shelley's *Prometheus Unbound* and *Triumph of Life*, Keats's *Fall of Hyperion* (but not *Hyperion*), Byron's *Don Juan*, Browning's *Sordello*, Tennyson's *In Memoriam*, Whitman's *Leaves of Grass*, Stevens' *Comedian as the Letter C*, Williams' *Paterson*, Pound's *Cantos*, and Hart Crane's *Bridge*." The latter Vogler calls "epics of consciousness": "the subject of the epic story becomes the history of the poet's attempts to find a vision" (pp. 12–13).

For a valuable survey of recent views of the traditional epic form, see Anthony C. Yu, *Parnassus Revisited: Modern Critical Essays on the Epic Tradition* (Chicago: American Library Association, 1973).

6. Tocqueville, *Democracy in America*, p. 180.

7. Ralph Waldo Emerson, "The Poet," *Selections from Ralph Waldo Emerson* (Boston: Houghton Mifflin Co., 1957), p. 238.

8. Jorge Luis Borges, Foreword to *Homage to Walt Whitman*, ed. Didier Tisdel Jaén (University, Ala.: University of Alabama Press, 1969), pp. xiv–xv.

9. Ezra Pound, "What I Feel about Walt Whitman," *Selected Prose, 1909–1965*, ed. William Cookson (New York: New Directions, 1973), pp. 145–46.

10. Walt Whitman, "Slang in America," *Prose Works, 1892: The Collected Writings of Walt Whitman*, ed. Floyd Stovall (New York: New York University Press, 1964), 2:572–73.

11. Roy Harvey Pearce, Introduction to *Leaves of Grass by Walt Whitman: Facsimile Edition of the 1860 Text* (Ithaca: Cornell University Press, 1961), p. xiii.

12. Malcolm Cowley, Introduction to *Leaves of Grass: The First (1855) Edition* (New York: Viking Press, 1959), pp. x, xi.

13. See discussion in chap. 5.

14. Walt Whitman, "To Emerson," *The Poetry and Prose of Walt Whitman*, ed. Louis Untermeyer (New York: Simon & Schuster, 1949), p. 526.

15. Louis Simpson, *At the End of the Open Road* (Middletown: Wesleyan University Press, 1963), p. 69.

Chapter Four

1. It was only after writing this passage that I came across Harold Bloom's related notion of past poets becoming "indebted" to their successors; see "*Apophrades* or The Return of the Dead," *The Anxiety of Influence* (New York: Oxford University Press, 1973), pp. 139–55.

2. Wallace Stevens, *The Necessary Angel* (New York: Alfred A. Knopf, 1951), p. 46.

3. Page numbers following *CP* after lines of Wallace Stevens's poetry refer to *The Collected Poems* (New York: Alfred A. Knopf, 1965). Lines that are sufficiently identified—especially in "Notes toward a Supreme Fiction"—are not further identified.

4. Joseph Riddell, "The Contours of Stevens Criticism," *The Act of the Mind: Essays on the Poetry of Wallace Stevens* (Baltimore: Johns Hopkins Press, 1965), p. 274.

5. Harold Bloom, *Wallace Stevens: The Poems of Our Climate* (Ithaca: Cornell University Press, 1977), p. 171. Diane Wood Middlebrook has also linked "Notes toward a Supreme Fiction" with "Song of Myself" (both poets "as-

pired to the same achievement: to give the myth of Man a credible contemporary poetic form") in *Walt Whitman and Wallace Stevens* (Ithaca: Cornell University Press, 1974), p. 179.

6. Quotations from Stevens's letters are identified in the text by *L* and page number, referring to *Letters of Wallace Stevens*, ed. Holly Stevens (New York: Alfred A. Knopf, 1966).

7. Whitman quotations are identified in the text by page numbers, referring to *Complete Poetry and Selected Prose*, ed. James E. Miller, Jr. (Boston: Houghton Mifflin Co., 1959). In cases where the poem title is sufficient identification, no page numbers are given.

8. Wallace Stevens, *The Necessary Angel*, p. 23.

9. R. W. Emerson, *Selections*, ed. Stephen E. Whicher (Boston: Houghton Mifflin Co., 1957), p. 21.

Chapter Five

1. Interview with Ezra Pound, *Writers at Work: The Paris Review Interviews, Second Series* (New York: Viking Press, 1963), p. 38.

2. See Hugh Kenner, *The Pound Era* (Berkeley: University of California Press, 1971), pp. 354–56.

3. T. S. Eliot, "Introduction to *Ezra Pound: Selected Poems* (1928)," *Ezra Pound: A Critical Anthology*, ed. J. P. Sullivan (Baltimore: Penguin Books, 1970), p. 102.

4. Ezra Pound, "What I Feel about Walt Whitman," *Selected Prose, 1909–1965* (New York: New Directions, 1973), pp. 145–46. The essay first appeared in *American Literature*, March 1955.

5. Walt Whitman, *Complete Poetry and Selected Prose*, ed. James E. Miller, Jr. (Boston: Houghton Mifflin Co., 1959), p. 375. Hereafter cited as *CPSP*.

6. Ezra Pound, "Dante," *The Spirit of Romance* (New York: New Directions, 1968), p. 155.

7. Ibid., pp. 168–69.

8. Pound, "Patria mia," *Selected Prose, 1909–1965*, pp. 123–24.

9. Albert Gelpi, *The Tenth Muse* (Boston: Harvard University Press, 1975), p. 32.

10. Ezra Pound, *Personae* (New York: New Directions, 1971), p. 89.

11. Ezra Pound and Marcella Spann, eds., *Confucius to Cummings* (New York: New Directions, 1964), p. 270.

12. Interview with Ezra Pound, *Writers at Work*, p. 58.

13. Robert Graves, "These Be Your Gods," *Ezra Pound: A Critical Anthology*, p. 225.

14. George Dekker, *The Cantos of Ezra Pound: A Critical Study* (New York: Barnes & Noble, 1963), pp. xiv, 202, 188.

15. Donald Davie, *Ezra Pound: Poet as Sculptor* (New York: Oxford University Press, 1964), pp. 204–29.

16. Noel Stock, *Reading the Cantos*, as quoted in *Ezra Pound: A Critical Anthology*, p. 346.

17. Kenner, *The Pound Era*, pp. 427–28.

18. John H. Edwards and William Vasse, *Annotated Index to the Cantos of Ezra Pound* (Berkeley and Los Angeles: University of California Press, 1957).

19. Whitman, *CPSP*, pp. 24, 63.

20. Page numbers after quotations in the text refer to Ezra Pound, *The Cantos* (New York: New Directions, 1972).

21. Whitman, *CPSP*, p. 444.

22. Ezra Pound, *Selected Cantos* (New York: New Directions, 1970), p. 1.

23. Allen Ginsberg, *Allen Verbatim: Lectures on Poetry, Politics, Consciousness,* ed. Gordon Ball (New York: McGraw-Hill Book Co., 1974), pp. 180–81.

24. Hugh Kenner, *The Poetry of Ezra Pound* (Norfolk, Conn.: New Directions, 1951), p. 300.

25. Kenner, *The Pound Era*, p. 532.

26. Daniel D. Pearlman, *The Barb of Time: On the Unity of Ezra Pound's Cantos* (New York: Oxford University Press, 1969), pp. 40, 29–30.

27. Interview with Ezra Pound, *Writers at Work*, p. 58.

28. For an excellent study of the post–Pisan Cantos, see James J. Wilhelm, *The Later Cantos of Ezra Pound* (New York: Walker & Co., 1977).

29. Ezra Pound, *ABC of Reading* (London: Faber & Faber, 1951; rpt. paperback, 1961), p. 26.

30. Pearlman, *The Barb of Time*, p. 4.

31. Pound, "What I Feel about Walt Whitman," *Selected Prose, 1909–1965*, p. 185.

32. Whitman, *CPSP*, pp. 411, 288.

33. Stephen Spender, *Love-Hate Relations: English and American Sensibilities* (New York: Random House, 1974; rpt. Vintage Books, 1975), pp. 149–50.

34. Wyndham Lewis, untitled, *Ezra Pound: A Critical Anthology*, p. 216.

35. Pound, "Patria mia," *Selected Prose, 1909–1965*, p. 124.

36. Interview with Ezra Pound, *Writers at Work*, p. 59.

37. Pound, *Selected Prose, 1909–1965*, p. 3.

38. Whitman, *CPSP*, pp. 422–23.

39. Dekker, *The Cantos of Ezra Pound*, pp. 3–107.

40. Remy de Gourmont, *The Natural Philosophy of Love*, tr. Ezra Pound (New York: Boni & Liveright, 1922; rpt. Collier Books, 1961).

41. Whitman, *CPSP*, pp. 84–85, 73.

42. Ezra Pound, *Guide to Kulchur* (New York: New Directions, 1938; rpt. paperback, 1968), p. 194.

43. Whitman, *CPSP*, pp. 293, 238.

44. Ibid., pp. 180, 181.

45. For extended and useful commentary on this Canto, see Roy Harvey Pearce, *The Continuity of American Poetry* (Princeton: Princeton University Press, 1961), pp. 85–88.

46. Whitman, *CPSP*, p. 375.

47. Irving Layton, "Walt's Reply," *Chicago Review*, Winter 1972, p. 126.

Chapter Six

1. Robert E. Knoll, Introduction to *Storm over "The Waste Land"* (Chicago: Scott, Foresman & Co., 1964), p. i.

2. I. A. Richards, *Principles of Literary Criticism* (New York: Harcourt, Brace & Co., 1948), pp. 290–91.

3. T. S. Eliot, "Tradition and the Individual Talent," *Selected Essays* (New York: Harcourt, Brace & Co., 1950), p. 7.

4. M. L. Rosenthal, "*The Waste Land* as an Open Structure," *Mosaic*, Fall

1972, pp. 181–82. This essay was incorporated in Rosenthal's *Sailing into the Unknown: Yeats, Pound, and Eliot* (New York: Oxford University Press, 1978); in this work Rosenthal maintains that the "main artistic contribution" of Yeats, Pound, and Eliot is "the modulation toward a poetry of open process, largely presentative, which tends toward a balancing of volatile emotional states.... We are talking about a significant evolutionary change of which the practitioners are only incompletely conscious (and the theorists almost completely unconscious, so that the main developments occur by a sort of instinctive collusion among the most highly sensitized poets at any given moment)" (p. 205).

5. Rosenthal, "*The Waste Land* as an Open Structure," pp. 188–89.

6. See this position sustained at length in James E. Miller, Jr., *T. S. Eliot's Personal Waste Land: Exorcism of the Demons* (College Park: Pennsylvania State University Press, 1977).

7. Sydney Musgrove, *T. S. Eliot and Walt Whitman* (Wellington: New Zealand University Press, 1952).

8. T. S. Eliot, Introduction to Ezra Pound's *Selected Poems* (London: Faber & Gwyer, 1928), pp. viii–ix.

9. T. S. Eliot, "Ezra Pound: His Metric and Poetry," *To Criticize the Critic* (New York: Farrar, Straus & Giroux, 1965), p. 177.

10. Donald Davie, *Ezra Pound: Poet as Sculptor* (New York: Oxford University Press, 1964), p. 82.

11. T. S. Eliot, Introduction to *Ezra Pound: Selected Poems*, pp. ix, xi.

12. T. S. Eliot, "Whitman and Tennyson," *Walt Whitman: A Critical Anthology*, ed. Francis Murphy, (Baltimore: Penguin Books, 1969), p. 207.

13. T. S. Eliot, "American Literature and the American Language," *To Criticize the Critic*, p. 53.

14. But see Sydney Musgrove's *T. S. Eliot and Walt Whitman* (n. 7 above), and James E. Miller, Jr., "Whitman and Eliot: The Poetry of Mysticism," *Quests Surd and Absurd* (Chicago: University of Chicago Press, 1967), p. 112–36.

15. T. S. Eliot, "Ode," *Ara Vos Prec* (London: Ovid Press, 1920), p. 30.

16. Page numbers after quotations from T. S. Eliot's *The Waste Land* or its manuscript version refer to pages in *The Waste Land: A Facsimile and Transcription of the Original Drafts*, ed. Valerie Eliot (New York: Harcourt Brace Jovanovich, 1971). This volume contains, in addition to the manuscripts, important informative footnotes and a reprint of *The Waste Land* as published in 1922 (and *its* footnotes).

17. Walt Whitman, *Complete Poetry and Selected Prose*, ed. James E. Miller, Jr. (Boston: Houghton Mifflin Co., 1959), pp. 237, 239.

18. Ibid., p. 444.

19. T. S. Eliot, "In Memoriam," *Selected Essays* (New York: Harcourt, Brace & Co., 1950), p. 291.

20. For examination of Eliot's various statements claiming *The Waste Land* as in some sense personal, see Miller, *T. S. Eliot's Personal Waste Land*, pp. 8–11.

21. Ezra Pound, *The Letters* (New York: Harcourt, Brace & World, 1950), pp. 169, 171.

22. Ibid., p. 180.

23. See Miller, *T. S. Eliot's Personal Waste Land*, pp. 66–67, 77.

24. The *Brihadaranyaka Upanishad*, tr. Swami Madhavananda (Calcutta: Advaita Ashrama, 1965), pp. 813, 17.

25. See Miller, *T. S. Eliot's Personal Waste Land*, p. 129.

26. Ibid., p. 77.

27. Ibid., pp. 7–16. See also John Peter, "A New Interpretation of *The Waste Land*," *Essays in Criticism* 2 (July 1952): 245; and "Postscript," *Essays in Criticism* 19 (April 1969): 165–75.

28. See Miller, *T. S. Eliot's Personal Waste Land*, pp. 17–18.

29. T. S. Eliot, "A Commentary," *Criterion* 13 (April 1934): 452.

30. See George Watson, "Quest for a Frenchman," *Sewanee Review* 84 (Summer 1976): 466–75; Miller, *T. S. Eliot's Personal Waste Land*, pp. 20–21.

31. See Miller, *T. S. Eliot's Personal Waste Land*, pp. 25–26.

32. Ibid., pp. 24–27.

33. Eliot, "Whitman and Tennyson," *Walt Whitman*.

34. For a fascinating experiment in the reading of Eliot's *Waste Land* and other poems for what they reveal in and of themselves (without benefit of any biographical data) of Eliot's psychic states, see Leon Edel, *Literary Biography* (Bloomington: Indiana University Press, 1973), pp. 70–88. Edel re-creates an Eliot purely out of the literary data who is quite similar emotionally and psychically to the Eliot we have attempted to delineate through speculation about the biographical data.

35. T. S. Eliot, *The Use of Poetry and the Use of Criticism* (New York: Barnes & Noble, 1933), p. 130.

36. Hart Crane, *The Letters*, ed. Brom Weber (Berkeley: University of California Press, 1965), pp. 127, 105.

37. William Carlos Williams, *The Autobiography* (New York: New Directions, 1951), pp. 146, 174.

38. Randall Jarrell, "Fifty Years of American Poetry," *The Third Book of Criticism* (New York: Farrar, Straus & Giroux, 1969), pp. 314–15.

Chapter Seven

1. Williams quotations are cited in the text, using the following abbreviations:

    A: *Autobiography* (New York: Random House, 1951; rpt. New Directions, 1967)

  CEP: *The Collected Early Poems* (New York: New Directions, 1951)

  CLP: *The Collected Later Poems* (New York: New Directions, 1963)

    I: *Imaginations* (containing *Kora in Hell, Spring and All, The Great American Novel, The Descent of Winter, A Novelette and Other Prose*) (New York: New Directions, 1970)

  IAG: *In the American Grain* (New York: New Directions, 1956)

    P: *Paterson* (New York: New Directions, 1963)

   SE: *Selected Essays* (New York: New Directions, 1969)

   SL: *Selected Letters*, ed. John C. Thirlwall (New York: McDowell, Oblensky, 1957)

2. William Carlos Williams, "America, Whitman, and the Art of Poetry," *Poetry Journal* 8 (Nov. 1917): 27, 31.

3. William Carlos Williams, "An Essay on *Leaves of Grass*," *Leaves of Grass One Hundred Years After*, ed. Milton Hindus (Stanford: Stanford University Press, 1955), p. 22.

4. William Carlos Williams, "The American Idiom," *New Directions 17* (New York: New Directions, 1961), pp. 250–51.

5. Louis Simpson, *Three on the Tower: The Lives and Works of Ezra Pound, T. S. Eliot, and William Carlos Williams* (New York: William Morrow & Co., 1975). This work is most valuable in interweaving and relating the lives and works of the three poets.

6. Quoted in Mike Weaver, *William Carlos Williams: The American Background* (Cambridge: Cambridge University Press, 1971), p. 120.

7. Ibid., p. 201.

8. Quoted in John C. Thirlwall, "William Carlos Williams' *Paterson*," *New Directions 17*, p. 263.

9. Ibid., p. 254.

10. Ibid., pp. 263–64.

11. Ibid., p. 281.

12. Walt Whitman, *Complete Poetry and Selected Prose* (Boston: Houghton Mifflin Co., 1959), pp. 424–25. Hereafter cited as *CPSP*.

13. Ibid., p. 349.

14. Quoted in Thirlwall, "William Carlos Williams' *Paterson*," p. 264.

15. Whitman, *CPSP*, p. 47.

16. Quoted in Joel Conarroe, *William Carlos Williams' Paterson* (Philadelphia: University of Pennsylvania Press, 1970), p. 55.

17. Quoted in John C. Thirlwall, "William Carlos Williams' *Paterson*," pp. 276–77.

18. Herman Melville, *Moby-Dick*, ed. Harrison Hayford and Hershel Parker (New York: W. W. Norton & Co., 1967), p. 169.

19. Ezra Pound, *The Cantos* (New York: New Directions, 1972), pp. 520–21.

20. Whitman, *CPSP*, pp. 52, 56.

21. Robert Lowell, "William Carlos Williams," *William Carlos Williams: A Collection of Critical Essays*, ed. J. Hillis Miller (Englewood Cliffs, N.J.: Prentice-Hall, 1966), p. 158.

22. John Berryman, *The Dream Songs* (New York: Farrar, Straus & Giroux, 1969), p. 346.

Chapter Eight

1. Quotations from Hart Crane's works are cited in the text using the following abbreviations; when lines are sufficiently located, by title of short poems or sections of poems, no citation appears:

L: *The Letters of Hart Crane, 1916–1932*, ed. Brom Weber (Berkeley and Los Angeles: University of California Press, 1965)

CP: *The Complete Poems and Selected Letters and Prose*, ed. Brom Weber (Garden City: Doubleday & Co., Anchor Books, 1966)

2. See John Unterecker, *Voyager: A Life of Hart Crane* (London: Anthony Blond, 1970), pp. 277–79, 465.

3. Ibid., p. 464.

4. Ibid., p. 479.

5. For a good account of the relationship of Crane and Frank, see Robert L.

Perry, *The Shared Vision of Waldo Frank and Hart Crane* (Lincoln: University of Nebraska Press, 1966).

6. Unterecker, *Voyager*, p. 247. See also P. D. Ouspensky, *Tertium Organum* (New York: Random House, Vintage Books, 1970), especially pp. 278–302.

7. Quoted in Brom Weber, *Hart Crane* (New York: Budley Press, 1948), p. 261.

8. Yvor Winters, "The Progress of Hart Crane," *Poetry* 36, no. 3 (June 1930): 153–65. See Unterecker, *Voyager*, pp. 620–23, for Crane's reaction to Winters's review.

9. Yvor Winters, *In Defense of Reason* (Denver: Alan Swallow, 1947), pp. 577–603.

10. R. W. B. Lewis, *The Poetry of Hart Crane: A Critical Study* (Princeton: Princeton University Press, 1967), pp. 237, 326.

11. Quoted in Unterecker, *Voyager*, p. 621.

12. Allen Tate, "A Distinguished Poet," *Hound and Horn* 3 no. 4 (July–Sept. 1930): 584–85.

13. Quoted in Unterecker, *Voyager*, p. 590.

14. Critics have tended to either deplore or ignore the extensive Whitman presence in *The Bridge*. A notable exception is Sherman Paul, whose *Hart's Bridge* (Urbana: University of Illinois Press, 1972) reverses this tendency. See his valuable discussion of *The Bridge*, pp. 166–283, 298–303.

15. Quoted in Weber, *Hart Crane*, p. 261.

16. Whitman quotations are taken from *Complete Poetry and Selected Prose* (*CPSP*), ed. James E. Miller, Jr. (Boston: Houghton Mifflin Co., 1959).

17. William Carlos Williams, *In the American Grain* (New York: New Directions Paperbook, 1956), p. 26.

18. Ibid., pp. 75–80.

19. Bradley Smith, *Mexico: A History in Art* (New York: Harper & Row, A Gemini-Smith Book, 1968), p. 51.

20. Irene Nicholson, *Mexican and Central American Mythology* (London: Paul Hamlyn, 1967), p. 38.

21. Quoted in Unterecker, *Voyager*, p. 605.

22. See ibid., p. 594.

23. Robert Lowell, "Words for Hart Crane," *Life Studies* (New York: Random House, Vintage Books, 1959), p. 53.

Chapter Nine

1. The unpublished essay "History," in the Charles Olson Archives of the University of Connecticut Library.

2. Quotations from Olson's works other than the Maximus Poems (see n. 10 below) are cited in the text using the following abbreviations:

AM: *Archaeologist of Morning* (New York: Grossman Publishers, 1971). Pagination supplied.

LO: *Letters for Origin* (London and New York: Cape Goliard Press in Association with Grossman Publishers, 1970).

SW: *Selected Writings*, ed. Robert Creeley (New York: New Directions, 1966); contains among other works "Human Universe," "Mayan Letters," and "Projective Verse."

3. Charles Boer, *Charles in Connecticut* (Chicago: Swallow Press, 1975), pp. 61–62.

4. See Egbert Faas, "Charles Olson and D. H. Lawrence: Aesthetics of the Primitive Abstract," *boundary 2* (Fall '73/Winter '74), special issue ("Charles Olson: Essays, Reminiscences, Reviews"), ed. Matthew Corrigan, 2, nos. 1 & 2: 113–26.

5. The Whitman-Lawrence relationship is explored in James E. Miller, Jr., Karl Shapiro, and Bernice Slote, *Start with the Sun* (Lincoln: University of Nebraska Press, 1960).

6. *The New American Poetry*, ed. Donald M. Allen (New York: Evergreen Press, 1960).

7. *The Poetics of the New American Poetry*, ed. Donald M. Allen and Warren Tallman (New York: Evergreen Press, 1973), p. ix.

8. Whitman quotations cited in the text by *CPSP* are from Walt Whitman, *Complete Poetry and Selected Prose*, ed. James E. Miller, Jr. (Boston: Houghton Mifflin Co., 1959).

9. D. H. Lawrence, "Preface to the American Edition of *New Poems*," *The Poetics of the New American Poetry*, pp. 70, 71–72.

10. Lines from the Maximus Poems are identified in the text by volume and page number: vol. 1: *The Maximus Poems* (New York: Jargon / Corinth Books, 1960); vol. 2: *Maximus Poems IV, V, VI* (London and New York: Cape Goliard Press in Association with Grossman Publishers, 1968), pagination supplied; vol. 3: *The Maximus Poems: Volume Three* (New York: Grossman Publishers, 1975).

11. *Oxford Classical Dictionary*, 2d ed. (1970), p. 658.

12. For exploration of the relevance of Maximus of Tyre, see Frank Davey, "Six Readings of Olson's *Maximus*," *boundary 2*, pp. 291–321. An earlier version appears as *Five Readings of Olson's Maximus* (n.p.: Beaver Kosmos Folio No. 2, 1970).

13. See Steve Ballew's discussion of the Maximus Poems' characters of opposed values in "History as Animated Metaphor in *The Maximus Poems*," *New England Quarterly* 47 (Mar. 1974): 51–65.

14. See Frank Davey's excellent discussion of Merry in "Six Readings of Olson's *Maximus*," pp. 317–20.

15. See Ballew, "History as Animated Metaphor...," pp. 52–60.

16. See *The Post Office: A Memoir of His Father* (Bolinas, Cal.: Grey Fox Press, 1975).

17. Robert von Hallberg has explored Alfred North Whitehead's influence on Olson in "Olson, Whitehead, and the Objectivists," *boundary 2* 2: 85–111. See also von Hallberg's excellent introductory book, *Charles Olson—the Scholar's Art* (Cambridge: Harvard University Press, 1978).

18. Olson's vision in this poem appears close to, but not so extreme as, that in any number of poems by Robinson Jeffers; and Olson's rejection of traditional humanism may well be related to Jeffers's cultivation of "inhumanism" (as in "The Inhumanist," *The Double Axe* [1948; rpt. New York: Liveright Publishing Corp., 1977]).

19. Robert Creeley, "Le Fou," *For Love: Poems 1950–1960* (New York: Charles Scribner's Sons, 1962), p. 17.

Chapter Ten

1. Most references to Berryman's *Dream Songs* cite the Song number, and thus are easily located. In other cases, citations in the text to Berryman's works use the following abbreviations:

DS: *The Dream Songs* (New York: Farrar, Straus & Giroux, 1969)
FP: *The Freedom of the Poet* (New York: Farrar, Straus, & Giroux, 1976)

2. Whitman quotations in the text are from Walt Whitman, *Complete Poetry and Selected Prose* (*CPSP*), ed. James E. Miller, Jr. (Boston: Houghton Mifflin Co., 1959).

3. John Berryman, Interview (with Joseph Haas) in *Panorama, Chicago Daily News* (6 Feb. 1971), p. 5.

4. John Berryman, Interview (with Peter A. Stitt) in *Paris Review* 14, no. 53 (Winter 1972): 190–91.

5. Ibid., p. 192.

6. John Berryman, "An Interview with John Berryman," *Harvard Advocate* 103, no. 1 (Spring 1969): 5–6.

7. Berryman, Interview in *Paris Review*, pp. 193, 195.

8. Ibid., pp. 194–95, 199.

9. Berryman, Interview in *Harvard Advocate*, pp. 5–6.

10. Berryman, Interview in *Paris Review*, p. 191.

11. Berryman, Interview in *Harvard Advocate*, p. 6.

12. Ibid.

13. Berryman, Interview in *Paris Review*, p. 191.

14. Berryman, Interview in *Harvard Advocate*, p. 5.

15. Allen Ginsberg, *Writers at Work: The Paris Review Interviews, Third Series* (New York: Viking Press, 1967), p. 309.

16. Berryman, Interview in *Paris Review*, p. 191.

17. Ibid., pp. 204, 207.

18. Berryman, Interview in *Harvard Advocate*, pp. 7–8.

19. See Erwin A. Glikes and Paul Schwaber, eds., *Of Poetry and Power: Poems Occasioned by the Presidency and by the Death of John F. Kennedy* (New York: Basic Books, 1964), pp. 44–47.

20. Berryman, Interview in *Paris Review*, p. 192.

21. Robert Lowell, "For John Berryman 2 (January, after his Death)," *History* (New York: Farrar, Straus & Giroux, 1973), p. 203.

Chapter Eleven

1. Quotations from Whitman in the text are from Walt Whitman, *Complete Poetry and Selected Prose* (*CPSP*), ed. James E. Miller, Jr. (Boston: Houghton Mifflin Co., 1959).

2. Quotations from Ginsberg's poems, when not identified sufficiently by title and volume, are cited in the text by the following abbreviations:

FA: *The Fall of America: Poems of These States, 1965–1971* (San Francisco: City Lights Books, 1972)
H: *Howl and Other Poems* (San Francisco: City Lights Books, 1956)
IH: *Iron Horse* (San Francisco: City Lights Books, 1974)
K: *Kaddish and Other Poems* (San Francisco: City Lights Books, 1961)

PN: *Planet News* (San Francisco: City Lights Books, 1968)
RS: *Reality Sandwiches* (San Francisco: City Lights Books, 1963)

3. Allen Ginsberg, Interview (with Thomas Clark), *Writers at Work: The Paris Review Interviews, Third Series* (New York: Viking Press, 1967), p. 289.

4. Jane Kramer, *Allen Ginsberg in America* (New York: Random House, Vintage Books, 1970), p. 174.

5. *Writers at Work: The Paris Review Interviews, Third Series*, pp. 301–3.

6. Ibid., pp. 308–9.

7. Kramer, *Ginsberg in America*, pp. 170–71.

8. Allen Ginsberg, "Notes Written on Finally Recording 'Howl,'" *A Casebook on the Beats*, ed. Thomas Parkinson (New York: Thomas Y. Crowell Co., 1961), p. 28.

9. Ezra Pound, *The Cantos* (New York: New Directions, 1972), p. 518.

10. Ezra Pound, "What I Feel about Walt Whitman," *Selected Prose, 1909–1965* (New York: New Directions, 1973), p. 145.

11. William Carlos Williams, "The American Idiom," *New Directions 17* (New York: New Directions, 1961), p. 251.

12. Charles Olson, "Projective Verse," *Selected Writings*, ed. Robert Creeley (New York: New Directions, 1966), pp. 19–21.

13. *Writers at Work: The Paris Review Interviews, Third Series*, p. 296.

14. Hart Crane, *The Complete Poems and Selected Letters and Prose* (Garden City: Doubleday & Co., Anchor Books, 1966), pp. 217, 235.

15. Allen Ginsberg, *Indian Journal: March 1962–May 1963* (San Francisco: Dave Haselwood Books and City Lights Books, 1970), pp. 53, 93–94.

16. *Writers at Work: The Paris Review Interviews, Third Series*, pp. 312, 314, 316.

17. Allen Ginsberg, *Allen Verbatim: Lectures on Poetry, Politics, Consciousness*, ed. Gordon Ball (New York: McGraw Hill Book Co., 1974), p. 18.

18. *Writers at Work: The Paris Review Interviews, Third Series*, p. 319.

19. *Allen Verbatim*, pp. 28, 32.

20. *Writers at Work: The Paris Review Interviews, Third Series*, pp. 317–18.

21. Ezra Pound, *Selected Cantos* (New York: New Directions, 1970), p. 1.

22. *Allen Verbatim*, p. 181.

23. Hart Crane, "The Bridge," *Complete Poems and Selected Letters and Prose*, p. 95.

24. *Writers at Work: The Paris Review Interviews, Third Series*, p. 315.

25. Pound, *The Cantos*, p. 520.

26. Thomas Wolfe, *Look Homeward, Angel!* (New York: Charles Scribner's Sons, 1929; rpt. Modern Library, n.d.), p. 2.

27. James Magner, "Lyric for Ginsberg," *The Dark is Closest to the Moon* (Cleveland: Ryder Press, 1973), p. 52.

Chapter Twelve

1. Quotations from Whitman in the text are from Walt Whitman, *Complete Poetry and Selected Prose* (*CPSP*), ed. James E. Miller, Jr. (Boston: Houghton Mifflin Co., 1959).

2. A. R. Ammons, *Sphere: The Form of a Motion* (New York: W. W. Norton, 1974), pp. 66–67.

3. Ezra Pound, *The Cantos* (New York: New Directions, 1972), p. 526.

4. T. S. Eliot, *The Waste Land: A Facsimile and Transcription of the Original Drafts*, ed. Valerie Eliot (New York: Harcourt Brace Jovanovich, 1971), p. 144.

5. William Carlos Williams, *Autobiography* (New York: New Directions, 1951), p. 392.

6. Hart Crane, *The Complete Poems and Selected Letters and Prose* (Garden City: Doubleday & Co., Anchor Books, 1966), p. 95.

7. Charles Olson, *The Maximus Poems* (New York: Jargon / Corinth Books, 1960), p. 15.

8. John Berryman, *The Dream Songs* (New York: Farrar, Straus, & Giroux, 1969), pp. 93, 301.

9. Allen Ginsberg, *The Fall of America* (San Francisco: City Lights Books, 1972), pp. i, 190.

10. Ezra Pound, *Selected Prose, 1909–1965* (New York: New Directions, 1973), p. 145.

11. Roy Harvey Pearce, *The Continuity of American Poetry* (Princeton: Princeton University Press, 1961), p. 57.

12. Ronald Hayman, *Arguing with Walt Whitman* (London: Covent Garden Press, 1971), p. 2.

13. William Carlos Williams, "America, Whitman, and the Art of Poetry," *Poetry Journal*, Nov. 1917, p. 31.

14. Harold Bloom, *Wallace Stevens: The Poems of Our Climate* (Ithaca: Cornell University Press, 1977), p. 10.

15. Harold Bloom, *The Anxiety of Influence* (New York: Oxford University Press, 1973), p. 71.

16. Robert Duncan, "Changing Perspectives in Reading Whitman," *The Artistic Legacy of Walt Whitman*, ed. Edwin Haviland Miller (New York: New York University Press, 1970), p. 89.

17. Walt Whitman, "Notes and Fragments," *The Complete Writings of Walt Whitman* (New York: G. P. Putnam's Sons, 1902), 9:5–6.

18. Duncan, "Changing Perspectives in Reading Whitman," p. 100.

19. M. L. Rosenthal, "Dynamics of Form and Motive in Some Representative Twentieth-Century Lyric Poems," *English Literary History* 37, no. 1 (Mar. 1970): 136–51. See also his *Sailing into the Unknown: Yeats, Pound, & Eliot* (New York: Oxford University Press, 1978).

20. Quoted in F. O. Matthiessen, *American Renaissance* (New York: Oxford University Press, 1941), p. 517.

21. Stanley Fish, *Self-Consuming Artifacts* (Berkeley: University of California Press, 1972). See especially the Appendix, "Literature in the Reader," pp. 383–427.

22. Roland Barthes, *S/Z: An Essay*, tr. Richard Miller (New York: Hill & Wang, 1974).

23. Lawrence Ferlinghetti, "Popular Manifesto: For Poets, With Love," *New York Times*, 5 July 1975, p. 17. See also Lawrence Ferlinghetti, *Who Are We Now?* (New York: New Directions, 1976), pp. 61–64.

24. Wallace Stevens, "Like Decorations in a Nigger Cemetery," *The Collected Poems* (New York: Alfred A. Knopf, 1965), p. 151.

25. Denise Levertov, *Jacob's Ladder* (New York: New Directions, 1961), p. 3.

Index

Adams, John, 82, 91
Allen, Donald M., ed.: *The New American Poetry*, 206–7; (with Warren Tallman), *The Poetics of the New American Poetry*, 206–7, 211
Allen, Gay Wilson, *The New Walt Whitman Handbook*, 336n
Ammons, A. R.: *Sphere: The Form of a Motion*, 16, 23, 320–21; *Tape for the Turn of the Year*, 23
Anderson, Sherwood, 171
Annotated Index to the Cantos of Ezra Pound, by John Hamilton Edwards and William W. Vasse, 78
Ashberry, John: *The Skaters*, 23; *Three Poems*, 23
Auden, W. H., 9

Ball, Gordon. *See* Ginsberg, *Allen Verbatim*

Ballew, Steve, "History as Animated Metaphor in *The Maximus Poems*," 344n
Barlow, Joel, 13; *The Columbiad*, 16, 18, 179, 335n; *The Vision of Columbus*, 16
Barthes, Roland, *S/Z*, 329
Baudelaire, Charles-Pierre, 104
Benét, Stephen Vincent, *John Brown's Body*, 22
Berryman, John, x, xii, 3–12 passim, 13, 330
  Dream Songs, ix, 7, 8, 12, 14, 16 17–24, 114, 124, 237–75 passim, 322–23, 324, 329
  77 Dream Songs (Books I–III), 246, 247–48, 248–52, 255
  His Toy, His Dream, His Rest (Books IV–VII), 235, 246, 248, 252–60
  Book I, 248–49
  Book II, 249–50

349